DATE DUE

Yale Series in the Philosophy
and Theory of Art

Engaging the Moving Image

Noël Carroll

Yale University Press

New Haven & London

Published with assistance from the foundation established in memory of Philip
Hamilton McMillan of the Class of 1894, Yale College.

Set in Adobe Garamond and Stone Sans type by The Composing Room
of Michigan, Inc.

Printed in the United States of America by Sheridan Books, Inc.

Library of Congress Cataloging-in-Publication Data

Carroll, Noël (Noël E.)
    Engaging the moving image / Noël Carroll.
        p. cm. — (Yale series in the philosophy and theory of art)
    Includes bibliographical references and index.
    ISBN 0-300-09195-8 (alk. paper)
    1. Motion pictures—Philosophy. 2. Motion pictures. I. Title. II. Series.

PN1995.C3557   2003
791.43'01—dc21

                                                        2003049678

A catalogue record for this book is available from the British Library.

The paper in this book meets the guidelines for permanence and durability of the
Committee on Production Guidelines for Book Longevity of the Council on Library
Resources.

10 9 8 7 6 5 4 3 2 1

Once again and as always
dedicated
to my beloved wife,
Sally Banes,
who returned to me from the dead.

Contents

Foreword

[The following exchange occurs after the screening of Sullivan's new movie.]
Mr. Hadrian: It died in Pittsburgh.
Mr. LeBrand: Like a dog.
Mr. Sullivan (contemptuously): What do they know in Pittsburgh?
Mr. LeBrand (mildly): They know what they like.
Mr. Sullivan (sneeringly): If they knew what they liked, they wouldn't live in Pittsburgh.
Preston Sturges, *Sullivan's Travels*

I suppose that Noël Carroll is best known within film studies as the unremitting arch nemesis of Big Theory, and certainly his 1988 book *Mystifying Movies* is a devastating systematic attack on the sweeping pretensions of the film theory that dominated the 1970s and 1980s. Potentially enhancing his grim reputation is the fact that Carroll introduced the philosophy of horror as a systematic topic in contemporary aesthetics. Anyone who knows Carroll personally, however, will have trouble sustaining an image of him derived from Dr. Mabuse or the Creeper or some other monster of mayhem and subversion. Car-

their disagreements, and begin to refine their conflicting initial judgments in the course of an extended dialogue. Whether Carroll is right to take this as a paradigm of evaluative argument, the choice of this model strikes me as characteristic of him and characteristic of his open, wide-ranging, undogmatic approach to theory, philosophy, and interpretation. The writing in this volume is ambitious in what it seeks to achieve, but its manner is unpretentious. The prose style is relaxed, and the address to the reader is good natured and helpful throughout. Each chapter exhibits the conversational virtues of forthright expression, honesty, wit, and intellectual resourcefulness. Equally they express Carroll's appetite for movies and his love of theoretical debate. As I read through *Engaging the Moving Image,* I was reminded by its tone and phrasing that its author is the friend who helped create the Pittsburgh Philosophy Department Film Club all those years ago. In reading these essays, I could almost hear him as he was back then, voicing enthusiasm for the evening's movie and introducing new arguments for his own interpretation of it. Sometimes, it seemed, I could almost *see* him again, lighting another cigarette, struggling into a winter coat and muffler, and toting his projector down the badly lit stairs.

George M. Wilson

NOTES

1. *Film as Film* (New York: Da Capo Press, 1993), pp. 133 and 131.
2. Karel Reisz, *The Technique of Film Editing* (New York: Hastings House Publishers, 1968), pp. 213–61; Lindgren quote on p. 213.
3. Quoted in Reisz on p. 213.
4. "Through Carroll's Looking Glass of Criticism," foreword to Noël Carroll, *Interpreting the Moving Image* (Cambridge: Cambridge University Press, 1998), pp. xii–xiii.

Introduction

This volume is a collection of my essays, written in the second half of the 1990s, on the topic of the *moving image*—the label that I prefer to use for the category comprising film, video, broadcast television, moving computer-generated imagery, and, in short, any mass-produced moving image technologically within our reach now and in times to come.[1] My reasons for speaking of the moving image rather than of film, video, or computer-generated images (CGI) revolve around the fact that those ways of speaking are too wedded to reference to particular media, whereas the moving image, as it has come to be a dominant form of expression and communication, is a transmedia phenomenon. Familiar strategies of articulation—such as parallel editing, point-of-view editing, zooming-in, and panning—can be implemented effectively across media, whether on celluloid or videotape. What the moving image is made of, in other words, is of less importance than its characteristic devices, strategies, and functions. Although film was the medium through which the moving image, as a means of expression, came to the fore in the twentieth century, the ensembles of techniques and traditions of visual expression it birthed will be carried forward into the future by different, additional media, many of which await conception.

That is, in future times—indeed, even at present—there is no reason to suppose that the destiny of the moving image is or will remain bound up with film. For already the characteristic modes of articulation introduced and refined by film are available in the domains of video and CGI. And one imagines other alternatives are yet to come. Who knows, perhaps there could even be a moving image artform based on sonograms. What is of primary importance aesthetically, in my opinion, is, in other words, that the image can move and not that of which the image consists. That is why I speak of the "moving image" rather than "film" in my title, even though most of the essays in this volume are keyed to film. And yet, as well, most of what I say of film—of film style, film documentaries, film evaluation, and so on—in this book can be generalized to the moving image and its multiple media.

Undoubtedly I make more reference to film in this volume than to other moving image media because, as a matter of autobiographical fact, I am more a child of the film age than of the television age, let alone of the computer age. Nevertheless, despite my provenance in a vanishing time, or maybe because of it, I see film, video, broadcast television, and now computer imaging as part and parcel of a continuous history of devices, strategies, concerns, and functions—a history that begins with Edison and Lumière, reaches through Hollywood to the BBC, MTV, and Direct-TV, to *Attack of the Clones,* CD-ROM, and is headed to the deeper reaches of who knows what.

I suspect that few ordinary viewers would refrain from calling something a movie because it was shot and/or distributed on videotape rather than film. Likewise I predict that spectacles developed by means of computer cameras and delivered by satellite feeds—with no celluloid intermediaries—will still be called movies by most of us; even if no *film* is involved. And, I submit, this terminology will be right, because, in the long run, the moving image is an artform rather than a medium. Just as painting is not reducible to the medium of oil, so the moving image is not reducible to film.

This anti-mediumistic approach to the moving image underlies a number of the more polemical essays in this volume, including "Forget the Medium!," "Kracauer's *Theory of Film,*" and "The Essence of Cinema?" In "TV and Film: A Philosophical Perspective," in particular, I attempt to undermine the prospects for a categorical distinction between film and television. In this essay I mean to challenge more traditional ways of theorizing moving image media, which ways attempt to isolate the essence of a medium, like film or television, and then use their conclusions like a philosopher's stone to unravel everything one wants to know about the form in question, including how it is best to use and not to use the medium at hand.

Moreover, I think that in times like these it is best to be on guard against such mediumistic essentialism, because it becomes a most attractive maneuver when technologies are being transformed into artforms. Film theorists opted for this kind of essentialism when they claimed the status of art for film. A similar gambit may thus tempt those who wish to promote CGI as an autonomous artform.

By opposing what I have just called mediumistic essentialism, I am signaling my opposition to one kind of foundational film theory—the sort that attempts to deduce the potentials and deficits of every element of film in light of a putative identification and assessment of the essential medium of cinema. I deny that cinema has an essence of this sort—one that comes replete with such implications about the ways in which film may and may not be deployed. But I also deny that cinema has other absolutely foundational functions, such as the propagation of ideologies which explain everything we want to know about the moving image (see, for example, "Prospects for Film Theory: A Personal Assessment"). Rather, I maintain that at this point in our researches concerning the moving image we are not yet (if we will ever be) in a position to develop a foundational theory either of film or of the moving image based either on the notion of an essence and/or a basic function of the moving image such that every aspect of our object of inquiry could be understood by reference to whatever we identified the nature of that foundation to be.

Consequently, the kind of theorizing that I presently advocate as appropriate to the moving image at this stage in our knowledge is piecemeal, i.e., theorizing limited to answering, albeit by means of generalizations, specific questions about this or that aspect of the moving image rather than presenting an overarching, unified theory of the moving image that answers every question about the moving image by means of reference to a handful of foundational premises concerning either the essence of the moving image *qua* medium or its putative basic function. Thus, it is primarily piecemeal theories devoted to certain aspects of the moving image that you find in this book.

For example, in "Film, Attention and Communication" and "Film, Emotion, and Genre," I attempt to evolve a series of hypotheses about some of the ways film addresses its audiences cognitively, perceptually, and emotionally, as well as noting how these dimensions of address often overlap and reinforce each other. Because most of the cognitive, perceptual, and emotive variables I emphasize in these essays are not cinema-specific, many of the observations in these essays can be extended to moving-image media other than film. Moreover, I do not claim that directing attention or eliciting emotion is the foundational function of all films or all moving images—so there is no categorical stylistic imperative implied here against moving images that disperse attention or freeze emotions. My theories apply only conditionally; they are relevant descriptively rather than prescriptively to moving-image works with certain commitments (although it should be conceded that there are many, many such works). Likewise, these theories are piecemeal because they do not pretend to tell the whole story of filmic address but only portions (albeit important portions) thereof.

The discussion of emotion in film leads to a consideration of certain moral questions, because emotions are often bound up with morality. In "Ethnicity, Race, and Monstrosity: The Rhetorics of Horror and Humor," I speculate about the ways that certain forms of emotional address, notably horror and comic amusement, can be mobilized in the service of noxious political purposes. The question of morality also arises in the essay "Is the Medium a (Moral) Message?" where I attempt to defend television against the charge that its very form of address has morally pernicious effects built into it. Given my anti-mediumistic bias, it should come as no surprise that I argue that a medium, such as television, has no essential moral valence by dint of its structure. Rather, as the essay on horror and humor indicates, the moral significance of the relevant structures depends on their use.

This book contains not only substantive theorizing about various forms of moving-image address, but also meta-critical reflections about how we conceptualize and talk about our experience of the moving image. In "Film Form: An Argument for a Functional Theory of Style in the Individual Film," I advance an analytic framework for identifying and explaining the operation of style in single films. Although I believe this account of style to be the most defensible one on offer, I should also admit, in the spirit of full disclosure, that it is the approach I presume in my own film analyses.[2] In addition to the theory of film analysis, there is also a contribution to the theory of film evaluation in this volume. Entitled "Introducing Film Evaluation," it is an initial attempt to show that to a large extent film evaluation can be objective. This essay does not show that every type of film evaluation is objective, but, then again, it is only an introduction to the topic.

If these meta-critical essays apply broadly across the range of moving-image works, there are other articles in this volume that pertain to issues of certain genres, narrowly defined. Three essays are about what are often called "documentaries." In "Fiction, Nonfiction, and the Film of Presumptive Assertion," I offer a conceptual analysis of what in common parlance is roughly alluded to by the term "documentary." Although the word "film" figures in my title, that which I finally call the film of presumptive assertion could also be called the moving image of presumptive assertion, because a video could fill the bill here just as easily as a film. The brief essay "Photographic Traces and Documentary Film" is effectively an attempt by me to reject an alternative theory of the so-called documentary to my own. And "Nonfiction Film and Postmodernist Skepticism" takes up a long-standing issue that arises perennially in the discussion of documentaries: whether they can be objective. I argue that they can be, despite recent theorizing to the contrary.

Another genre that I theorize in this volume is what in past days might have been called dance films or ciné-dances. I attempt to cancel the mediumistic bias in that nomenclature and instead offer a transmedia conception of this very lively, although often neglected, field of moving-image innovation.

Although most of the essays in this volume are theoretical and/or philosophical, three of them are exercises in criticism: "Cinematic Nation Building," written with my beloved wife, Sally Banes, is a discussion of Eisenstein's film *The Old and the New.* Among other things, this essay is an attempt to show how stylistic design can serve political purposes. Although it is also concerned with ideology, "The Professional Western: South of the Border" focuses more on traditional content analysis than on stylistic analysis. Along with "Cinematic Nation Building," however, it is included in this volume in order to substantiate the claim that I make in "Prospects for Film Theory" that I am not a formalist if that means someone who is methodologically oblivious to political content. "Moving and Moving: From Minimalism to *Lives of Performers*" is an examination of Yvonne Rainer's move from choreography to cinema.

Even though I had not planned it this way, I am particularly pleased that the three critical essays in this volume attend to three different registers of ambition: the popular cinema (the Westerns), the art cinema (Eisenstein), and the avant-garde (Rainer). For following Stanley Cavell, I too believe that one does not love film—or, for that matter, the moving image—unless one loves every kind of it.

NOTES

1. For a definition and defense of my notion of the moving image, see Noël Carroll, "Defining the Moving Image," in my *Theorizing the Moving Image* (New York: Cambridge University Press, 1996), pp. 49–74.
2. See my *Interpreting the Moving Image* (New York: Cambridge University Press, 1998).

Engaging the Moving Image

force. Names like Charlie Chaplin, Douglas Fairbanks, Sr., and Mary Pickford were known around the world. At the same time, film technique was refined—especially in terms of its capacity to narrate—to the extent that it not only entranced mass audiences, but also inspired intellectuals, from John Dos Passos and James Joyce to the Soviet Constructivists. A number of the techniques developed during this period—including the use of the close-up, parallel editing, cross-cutting, the master-shot discipline, point-of-view editing, and so on—became fundamental to narrative film practice, and remain so into our own day.

The name D. W. Griffith is often associated with many of these innovations, and, while it may be controversial to attribute the discovery of all these devices to him, he did do a great deal to popularize their acceptance. His 1915 epic, *The Birth of a Nation,* though undeniably racist, is, in effect, a demonstration of the essential emerging ensemble of devices that constitute what is now often referred to as the *classical cinema.* This cinema is in evidence daily not only in movie houses worldwide, but on our television screens as well.

During the silent period of filmmaking, which ended roughly in the late nineteen-twenties with the popularization of talking pictures, cinema became an international artform. Films were a means of visual storytelling; indeed, some of its proponents thought of it as a kind of visual Esperanto. It could cross national boundaries with ease; it was a form of international communication. The introduction of sound-dialogue, of course, presented a problem in this respect, but it was one that could be solved by subtitles and dubbing (where dubbing is an especially attractive technique for addressing large, sometimes illiterate audiences). Of course, many contemporary films, especially action films like *Waterworld,* use dialogue only sparingly, thus making themselves easy to follow even if one is not familiar with the language of the characters.[2] Someone who does not speak Chinese will not have much trouble understanding a John Woo film from Hong Kong.

American culture was an inevitable beneficiary of the international reach of film, since, given its possession of a major movie industry—what we call Hollywood—American culture was exported around the world. This raised complaints from other countries, like Britain, as early as the nineteen-twenties. Critics realized that the movies exported the American way of life and, in consequence, nurtured a taste for American products. Those worries continue in the present and can be heard issuing from Paris as well as the Third World.

Needless to say, there have been many formal and technical innovations in film technique since the twenties, including mastery of the deep-focus long

contemporary film theorists, though they might agree with some of my arguments so far, still find the notion of film language—understood in a way that is putatively more sophisticated than Pudovkin's version of it—viable. The theorists I have in mind are film semiologists.

Semiologists do not think of film as strictly equivalent in form to a natural language. They agree that shots are not words. But they do regard film as language-like, insofar as they believe that film communication is dependent, in the main, on conventional codes. For example, what I would call editing strategies—like the point-of-view format—they call editing codes. Indeed, some contemporary film theorists maintain that single-shot images—for example, a view of the Empire State building—are best understood as conventional signs. Commenting on a shot from Fritz Lang's *M,* Umberto Eco says: "on the basis of some conventions the addressee [the viewer] understands that those traces upon the screen send us back to the content 'a girl holding a balloon.'"[9]

For Eco, "understanding images must be learned."[10] What must be learned are conventions that link the image, or "traces on the screen," to its referent. Film is language-like insofar as it is an affair of conventions. Comprehending a shot is a matter of decoding it. And a condition for comprehending what a shot stands for is knowledge of a certain set of codes or conventions. Likewise, understanding an array of edited shots involves mastery of further conventions or codes. Moreover, these codes and conventions are culturally specific; they could have been otherwise. Thus, semiologists regard them as arbitrary.

On this sort of view, which is extremely popular among both film semiologists and poststructuralists, film comprehension is akin to reading. Films are decoded by audiences who have learned the conventions of cinema, including conventions for interpreting or deciphering what is presented in a single shot. Thus, for the semiologist, if film is an international mode of communication, then this can be explained by the dissemination and inculcation of certain codes and conventions worldwide. Moreover, where the film theorist is politically minded, the spread of these codes and conventions—their global diffusion—is explained as part and parcel of some larger process, such as Western imperialism or the expansion of capitalism.

But let us put the political issue to one side and concentrate upon the question of whether or not it is plausible to hypothesize that film comprehension is really exclusively or even predominantly a matter of learned codes and conventions. Is film a language in the sense that it fundamentally trades in codes and conventions? I want to argue that it is not and that we cannot explain the success of film as an international mode of communication on the model of codes and conventions. Moreover, I think that in showing what is wrong with the semiotic model of film as a language composed primarily of codes and conventions, we will open the way to seeing what is the real basis of film as an international medium of communication.

Consider the notion that the single shot is "read"—that it is deciphered or decoded by means of conventions. The single shot is typically a representation—more specifically, it is a *pictorial* representation. The semiotician's view that the cinematic shot is conventional is of a piece with the semiotician's conviction that pictures are conventional. Different cultures picture things differently; they possess different pictorial conventions. To understand the pictures of a different culture, we must, so it is presumed, learn its conventions, just as in order to understand a foreign language, one must learn its semantics and syntax. Film has built Western pictorial conventions into the very structure of the cinematographic camera. People from other cultures have learned to understand it, just as they have learned to understand our representational paintings and our language.

But this story is too hasty. Central to the claim that a shot is a matter of convention is the presupposition that one must learn to decipher its codes just as one learns a language. Yet there is important evidence to support the contrary view—the view that picture comprehension, including motion picture comprehension, requires no special process of learning or instruction.

For example, the psychologists Julian Hochberg and Virginia Brooks raised one of their children in an environment virtually devoid of pictures of any sort. He had no picture books or television; the labels with visual graphics were removed from commercial household products.[11] Moreover, "the child was never instructed in associations between words and pictures, never told that pictures represented anything, and was never read a story with illustrations in attendance."[12] Yet once the child's vocabulary was sufficiently large, at around the age of two, he was shown a selection of line drawings and black and white photographs and was asked to identify them. And he was able to identify most of them correctly.

In this case, there can be no question of the child's learning or being instructed in codes or conventions for decoding or reading pictorial images. The child was able to recognize what the pictures were pictures of simply by looking. The semiotic or conventionalist hypothesis fares badly with a case like this. A better hypothesis is that comprehending what a picture is a picture *of* relies upon a natural recognitional capacity that arises in tandem with the capacity to recognize objects. No special training is required to understand what a picture is a picture of, if one is already familiar with the kind of object being depicted by the picture in question. That is, one can identify a standard picture of x by looking, if one can identify x in "real life."

This is not to say that there are no such things as pictorial conventions. To know that a figure is the Anti-Christ in a painting by Bosch requires knowledge of iconographic conventions. But to understand that the figure depicts a man does not require special knowledge of conventions, or instructions.

Learning a language is a protracted process. It takes a great deal of instruction, involving trial, error, and correction. But the subject in Hochberg's and Brooks's experiment manifested the capacity for pictorial recognition in, so to say, "one shot." A child does not master the meaning of a word, let alone a series of words, like that. Thus, it is unlikely that anything akin to learning linguistic conventions is operative in picture comprehension. Rather, the more attractive hypothesis, given the data, is that humans acquire the capacity to recognize pictures naturally, rather than conventionally, at the same time that they acquire the capacity to recognize the objects that pictures represent. Picture recognition is not a skill that needs to be trained. It is a natural recognitional capacity that comes with object recognition.

Moreover, this recognitional capacity may not only be present in humans. Pigeons can recognize trucks in photographs.[13] And jumping spiders of the Salticidae family, when exposed to pictures of their usual prey, have attacked it in successive trials.[14] This at least suggests—though it does not prove—the hypothesis that the spiders recognized what the picture was a picture of. And if this hypothesis were to be further confirmed, it would challenge the conventionalist view dramatically, since it is unlikely that a spider (or a pigeon) could be trained in any alleged pictorial codes, Western or otherwise.

Of course, the human response to pictures is quite different than that of those jumping spiders. For if these spiders took the picture for their prey, the same cannot be said of humans. We do not confuse pictures with their referents, for even though we look "into" a picture, the muscles of our eyes register the difference between the location of the picture as the surface of an object that inhabits the physical space in which we are situated, versus the virtual space portrayed in the picture. The phenomenologically felt difference between the two, among other things, stops us from confusing the picture with its referent.[15] That is, unlike the spider, we have innate or hardwired capacities to recognize not only what the picture is a picture of, but also *that* it is a picture, a unique object in its own right, physically locatable in the real space before us.

The hypothesis that pictorial representations are those whose referents are recognized by untutored spectators—spectators who have not been trained in some special process of reading, decoding or inferring—simply by looking also fits nicely with what is known of the reception of pictures across cultures. The Japanese taught themselves the Western perspective system by comparing their own illustrations to the ones that they encountered in Dutch scientific texts and this, in turn, gave rise to the popular Japanese genre of Uki-e or "relief" pictures. The Japanese, in other words, were able to understand the European pictures simply by looking, even though conventions with which they were unfamiliar were in use. On the other hand, they could not understand European languages simply by listening. That required training and instruction.

And, of course, the same story can be told about our own Western encounters with the pictorial systems of other cultures. One can catch onto what is represented by a picture in the Egyptian "frontal eye" style of representation by looking at one picture and then go on to identify what is being depicted in virtually any other picture in that style. But we cannot perform a comparable feat with respect to the Egyptian language—that is, we cannot learn the meaning of one word and then go on to understand anything else said in ancient Egyptian. The fast pick up that we evince with respect to alternative pictorial styles, like the fast pick up the Japanese evinced with Western perspective pictures, is radically unlike anything we encounter when it comes to language acquisition. And this gives us a strong reason to think that our comprehension of pictures is very different from our comprehension of language.

Needless to say, when we are confronted with an Egyptian picture of Osiris, we may not be able to specify what god is being portrayed, unless we are familiar with Egyptian iconography. Convention is operative to that extent. However, that we are able to identify man-like figures and even the animal heads on those figures is not typically a matter of training. Likewise, though I may not initially be able to identify a Chinese representation of a lion as a lion or a Balinese representation of a monkey as a monkey without some background training, I can recognize sans instruction that both representations are depicting animals. That is, at the level of depiction, pictorial recognition does not require mastery of learned codes and conventions.

Undoubtedly, the preceding claims sound as though they contradict certain anecdotes, repeated endlessly in anthropology classes, about the incomprehension with which tribal peoples greet Western pictures. However, the first thing to stress in this regard is that the systematic evidence about the responses of pictorially inexperienced tribal peoples to pictures is overwhelmingly on the side of the hypothesis that they do, without instruction, recognize what the pictures with which they are presented depict.[16]

Furthermore, in those cases where subjects manifest some trouble in identifying the referents of the foreign pictures, it seems likely that their initial difficulties have more to do with misunderstanding what they were being asked to do, rather than with an inability to recognize the referents of the relevant pictures. For example, when Jan Deregowski presented pictures to members of the Me'en tribe of Ethiopia, they sniffed them rather than looking at them, because the pictures reminded them of a kind of cloth material with which they were familiar. They did not look at the pictures at all. However, when their attention was directed to the identificatory task at hand, the vast majority of the respondents had no problem comprehending the pictures. That is, their putative inability to understand the pictures had to do with their lack of familiarity with picturing things and not with an inability to recognize pictures, since once the practice of picturing was indicated to them, they had scant problems with identification.

Like the responses of the Japanese with respect to Western pictures and those of Westerners to the pictures of other cultures, the responses of the Me'en support the hypothesis that pictorial recognition is, most probably, innate. Or, minimally, the innateness hypothesis does a much better job with the data than the conventionalist story, since pictorial recognition, at least at the level of depiction, seems to require no instruction. Nor is the speed of comprehending alternative pictorial styles that is involved here as protracted as learning a code, such as a language.

Against the code/conventionalist account of picture comprehension, then, we must emphasize such facts as children's capacity to recognize pictures without training, the easy diffusion of pictures across cultures, and even the capacity manifested by some animals to recognize the referents of pictures. In none of these cases does the evidence seem to support the proposition that picture comprehension has been learned after the fashion of a language or a code. Indeed, in none of these cases does it seem reasonable to suppose that the subjects were trained in any conventions of comprehension, especially ones as arcane as Eco's suggestion that spectators move from "traces" to propositions. How could animals, like spiders, do that?

Recognition, rather than convention, is the key to pictorial comprehension. To recognize something, of course, requires that what is presented to us is something, or, at least, a type of something, with which we are already familiar. It is a matter of re-cognizing. So, pictorial recognition is a matter of realizing the referent of a picture where it is something—or an instance of a type of something—that is already known to us simply by looking rather than by reading or decoding.

Of course, this discussion of picture comprehension has direct relevance to film, since the type of single-shot image that we are considering is a picture. And if the argument so far is persuasive, then the film images that we are most familiar with are such that their referents are recognized by untutored spectators simply by looking (by means of certain natural recognitional capacities that I will leave to psychologists to specify with more precision). That is, spectators do not comprehend the reference of single shots by means of reading, or decoding, or inferring from traces to meanings, as the proponents of semiotic models of language-like codes and conventions maintain. The process proceeds by triggering recognitional capacities that are hardwired.[17]

Moreover, this debate between naturalists, like myself, and the conventionalists of the film as language persuasion over the reception of the single shot is not merely a matter of academic point scoring, since if the naturalistic position is correct it provides us with a significant inroad to answering the question of why film is so suited to play the role of an international mode of communication.

Though I have not stressed this point previously, it should be obvious that the single shot is the basic unit of filmic communication in the sense that without the single shot, other notable levers of cinematic communication, like film editing, must remain mute. Without single-shot units, there would be no editing. The single shot is, so to speak, the *sine qua non* of film communication. Or, to state it differently, if there were no single shots to be comprehended, there would be nothing for editing to do—nothing for it to organize. So, the single shot is the basic element of film communication.

But the single shot is standardly a picture, and, as we have seen, a picture is a very special sort of symbol. It is a symbol whose depiction is grasped by means of natural recognitional capacities. That these capacities are natural, of course, implies that they are comprehensible at the level of what they depict to most human beings, virtually automatically. Humans around the world can recognize what a picture—including a motion picture image—is a picture of, simply by looking. And this entails that motion picture images are accessible to nearly every human being without special training in any particular code or convention.

Thus, one crucial aspect of the way in which film is capable of performing the function of an international mode of communication is that the basic symbol in film—the single-shot image—is accessible to nearly everyone. The basic symbol of the motion picture is legible and accessible worldwide. No specialized form of literacy is required to comprehend what a single-shot, motion picture image depicts. Therefore, every potential spectator can enter and engage the basic level of filmic communication, irrespective of his or her nationality, racial or ethnic identity, level of literacy, class standing, gender, political affiliations, religious beliefs, or linguistic abilities. Single shots that rely on pictorial representation are transnationally and transculturally intelligible, at least at the level of depiction. And this explains, to an important extent, why films that are structured pictorially can function so effectively as an international mode of communication.

Linguistic models or semiotic models of the comprehension of the single shot face a major problem in accounting for the worldwide diffusion of film. If understanding an image really relies on mastering a convention that enables viewers to move from traces on the surface of the film to propositions, rather as words are correlated with their referents, then it would be difficult to explain how film is so readily exported across national, linguistic, ethnic, and racial boundaries. Wouldn't non-Western peoples have to master the so-called conventions in question in the manner that they master Western languages? But, as I have argued, there is no evidence that anything like this sort of language-like learning occurs. At the very least, the pick-up time required to comprehend motion pictures cross-culturally bodes badly for the linguistic, semiotic, or conventionalist models.

But in addition, such models also strike one as unlikely insofar as no one has any idea of what these codes or conventions might be. If it is by means of a code or a convention that I, while watching *M*, infer from some traces on the surface of the screen that "a girl is holding a balloon," what could the relevant code or convention comprise? To my knowledge, no one has even proposed a single model of this putative correlational pattern. How, then, is it possible that people are being taught such conventions if no one has a glimmering of what the supposed conventions even look like? How is it possible that film is disseminated cross-culturally by means of codes, if this involves the training of codes that no one knows?

The hypothesis that motion picture images are understood by means of natural recognitional capacities acquired in tandem with the development of our object recognition capacities does not face comparable embarassments. It solves the diffusion problem quite economically. Film images, the pictorial ones at least, are understood because of the way in which they engage the natural cognitive and perceptual capacities of virtually every human who does not suffer relevant cognitive and/or perceptual disabilities, like blindness. Filmic communication can be international, in part, because its basic strata of symbolism—the single shot—engages basic features of the human cognitive and perceptual constitution. Film shots, we might say, address human nature.

There is an important caveat in the preceding paragraph. I said that film images, *the pictorial ones at least,* engage natural recognitional capacities. But not all film images are pictorial. Some film images, especially those found in many avant-garde films, are emphatically not pictorial. They may be what are referred to as abstract, or nonobjective, or nonrepresentational images. Viking Eggeling's *Symphony Diagonale* and many of Stan Brakhage's films are examples of nonpictorial cinema. These experimental works number among some of the greatest achievements of the cinema, and I have no desire to demean them.

However, I think it is fair to say that abstract films are not what we have in mind when we talk about film as an international mode of communication. Abstraction is not what one typically finds at the local cinema, on TV, or at the neighborhood video store. Perhaps that is because the appreciation of such experiments requires a very specialized form of background education—at least in the world as we know it (and as opposed to the world to which utopian, avant-garde artists might aspire). Thus, I have excluded such exercises in abstraction from my purview, since my aim is to elucidate film as an international medium of communication, and avant-garde film cannot claim such a status. It is the motion *picture* image that is the cornerstone of that communicative practice, and it is the appeal of motion pictures to our natural recognitional capacities that explains their suitability to the task of facilitating communication globally.

Of course, the accessibility of the single shot to spectators around the world does not tell the whole story of why film can function as an international means of communication. It is only a contribution to an explanation of that phenomenon, since comprehending a film involves much more than recognizing what each of the individual film images stands for. A film is more than the sum of its individual shots, and so an explanation of how shots are individually accessible is only the beginning of an account of film as an international mode of communication. Film communication involves many more dimensions of articulation. And it will be the burden of the rest of this essay to discuss a number of the rest of these processes of articulation in such a way that their contribution to filmic communication is elucidated.

Nevertheless, the preceding examination of the debate between the friends of the linguistic, or semiotic, or conventionalist models versus naturalists (such as myself) with respect to the analysis of the single shot suggests a useful way in which to develop further hypotheses about filmic communication. So far, I have stressed the importance of the way in which film communicates, to a large extent, by engaging our natural cognitive and perceptual capacities. This view contrasts vividly with the inclination of semioticians and poststructuralists to presuppose that cinematic communication is a matter of codes and conventions, as they say, "all the way down." I have defended the contrary view, namely, that to a significant degree filmic communication engages with natural cognitive and perceptual capacities. In what follows, I will try to push this line of inquiry a little further; I will try to show that not only can the effectiveness of the single shot be explained naturalistically (rather than conventionally), but many other features of filmic communication, including certain aspects of film editing and camera movement, can be explained that way as well.

FILM AND ATTENTION

For nearly three decades, various forms of semiological theories have dominated the study of film. Where these theories do not speak of film as a language outright, they nevertheless favor explanations of filmic phenomena in the idiom of codes and conventions. As I have already indicated, I think that this overlooks the fact that a great deal of communication in film relies upon activating our natural cognitive and perceptual processes, and I further contend that an appreciation of this fact places us in a stronger position than film semiology does in explaining how film is capable of functioning as an international means of communication.

Nevertheless, before engaging this debate—what I call the debate between the conventionalists and the naturalists—I should be clear about what I hope to demonstrate. I do not intend to argue that everything that has to do with filmic communication can be explained naturalistically. Undoubtedly, there are many film conventions which are learned. Many of these conventions, for example, concern our responses to film genres. When a character wanders into an old dark house in a horror film and and starts heading for the attic (or the basement), we anticipate that he or she is apt to be attacked by some unearthly being. Here our expectations are not primed by hardwired responses to attics, but by our knowledge of the horror genre (along with the narrative context). Thus, not all filmic comprehension is reducible to explication in terms of our naturally endowed cognitive and perceptual abilities.

My contention is only that a great deal—but not all—is. Moreover, my hypothesis only possesses whatever originality it does because it is being advanced in a theoretical context where most other researchers think that nature, as opposed to culture, has little to tell us about the way in which film communicates. My position is simply that film communication has a lot more to do with engaging natural cognitive and perceptual capacities than contemporary film theorists suppose, and, *pari passu,* that codes and conventions explain a lot less than they assume. But I do not believe that at the end of the day either conventionalism or naturalism exclusively will succeed in explaining everything about film communication. To do that, we will have to advert to both nature and convention. The best theories will mix appeals to both our natural cognitive and perceptual responses to film, and to conventions, filmic and otherwise. However, in this essay, I will dwell primarily on the naturalistic contribution to this compromise.

Let us begin with what I hope is an uncontroversial premise: that film communication is, at the very least, concerned with attention. In order for film communication to proceed, the filmmaker must hold the spectator's attention and guide or shape it. In his *Principles of Psychology,* William James writes, "Every one knows what attention is. It is the taking possession by the mind, in clear and vivid form, of one out of what seems several simultaneously possible objects or trains of thought. Focalization, concentration of consciousness are of its essence. It implies withdrawal from some things in order to deal effectively with others."[18] For the filmmaker to communicate, he or she must, in James's colorful way of putting it, take possession of the spectator's mind—must concentrate the spectator's consciousness on the film. And, if the film is a narrative fiction, the filmmaker must also direct audience awareness to—must prompt us to focalize on—certain details of the fictional array (or "world") rather than others. In short, filmic communication, to a large extent, depends upon the filmmaker's control of the audience's attention.

For convenience, we can break down what is involved in controlling the film audience's attention into two parts: holding or fixing the audience's attention to the audio-visual array, and guiding it in such a way that the spectator attends to exactly those elements in the array of which the filmmaker intends her to take note. In order to understand how film communication operates, we need to review the ways in which film affords the possibilities for discharging both of these tasks: arresting attention, on the one hand, and guiding it to the appropriate objects in the fiction, on the other hand.

Holding attention. In order for film communication to take place, the audience's attention must be directed to what is on the screen. This is a necessary condition for film communication; if the audience is not looking at the screen, then there is no film communication. Needless to say, some of the factors that facilitate this are quite obvious. Characteristically, film theaters are darkened in such a way that there is little else to see except the screen, which, in contrast, is brightly illuminated. Of course, people go to movie theaters to watch the screen, so the projection arrangement is not the only thing that keeps them watching the screen. But, at the same time, the arrangement facilitates this vector of attention. It makes it harder for one's attention to wander or to shift to something else, since there is, effectively, little else for the audience to see. Perhaps one of the reasons that our attention to TV is often less concentrated than it is to the silver screen is that we often watch TV in well-lit surroundings.

Of course, one might say that it is only a convention that we typically watch films in darkened circumstances. But it is not a convention if what we mean by that is that it is arbitrary that theater owners turn the lights off in their movie theaters. It certainly is not an arbitrary choice that theater owners darken their auditoriums. Rather, it is a choice, predicated upon what is known about human perception, that they elect in order to enhance audience attention to the screen. It is a matter of exploiting natural human perceptual tendencies to keep the audience looking at the screen.

Needless to say, similar strategies for holding audience attention can also be found in modern theater. But film, in contrast to theater, employs scale, in addition to the contrast of darkness and illumination, to fill the audience's mind with its spectacles. If theater is standardly life-size—i.e., the actors are no larger than the spectator—then film is larger than life. That's why we call it the "Big Screen"; a close-up of Laurence Olivier's head can reach as high as thirty feet or more. The scale of film images arrests our attention. On the other hand, TV, as we know it, is smaller than life; Larry King's image is generally much smaller than we are. And, as is well known, filmmakers in the fifties, when they felt threatened by the rise of television, developed a number of larger-screen formats, like cinemascope, in order to sharpen their edge in the competition with the small screen.

Of course, one of the most important levers for securing the audience's attention to the screen was the very raison d'etre for the invention of cinema, viz., movement. As I have already noted, early film audiences went to the movies to see movement. That is what initially captivated them. Nor is this attentional lever irrelevant to contemporary moviemaking. John Dean, who worked as a consultant on Oliver Stone's recent film *Nixon,* complained to Stone that the former president never got up from behind his desk during meetings, whereas Stone directed the actor playing Nixon—Anthony Hopkins—to pace around the room furiously. Dean reports that in response Stone told him that if Hopkins stayed authentically planted in his chair, the audience would not be able to stand it.[19] Stone intuitively understood that in order to hold the spectator's attention, movement was an indispensable cue.

Of course, the evolutionary reasons for this are almost painfully evident. Human organisms are highly attuned to movement, activity, and change in their environment, as are animals in general. Movement, change, and activity draw attention to potential predators and prey. Sensitivity to movement is an indisputable survival advantage. Movement rivets attention. This is a hard-wired or innate perceptual tendency, one that is exploited constantly by filmmakers. Indeed, one might adopt the role of an armchair sociobiologist in conjecturing that part of the attraction of the action genre for filmmakers throughout the history of the cinema has been the capacity of such films to hold the attention of the audience almost automatically, due to our adaptive sensitivities to movement, activity, and change in the environment.

Noting that movement in itself is an important lever of attention in film does not do much to say what differentiates film from theater, since theater directors—like film directors—understand that it is important to keep the actors in motion. However, film, in addition to the movement of actors, has an arsenal of techniques to keep the spectacle alive with fluctuation, change, and motion. These include devices like editing and camera movement which keep the screen palpitating with visual activity and grab the audience's attention.

Compare stage versions of John Guare's *Six Degrees of Separation* with Fred Schepsi's film of the same play. Onstage, the play opens with a framing device. The Kittredges, Flan and his wife, Ouisa, are in a high state of consternation. They have just been gulled by Paul, a young African American confidence man, who had been impersonating a college friend of their children. He introduced himself to them as the son of the actor Sidney Poitier. Gradually, the Kittredges calm down and they address the audience directly, telling (or rather enacting) their misadventure in what we understand to be a flashback. Though punctuated with a few asides to the audience, the encounter with Paul dramatically unfolds predominantly in linear time. There are no breaks in location and, apart from the asides, few breaks in temporality.

In the film version, however, the story of Paul's night with the Kittredges is broken up into several different spatial and temporal units among which the filmmakers cross-cut frequently—including the Kittredges telling their story at various parties, flashbacks to their evening with Paul, and even more remote flashbacks to Paul working up his impersonations. As a result, there is a great deal more visual activity on the screen—most obviously due to the rapid scene changing afforded by film editing—than there is in the stage presentation. Moreover, I want to contend that this facilitates holding the audience's attention on the action to a greater degree than the same scene enacted on the stage does.

All things being equal, film rivets the spectator to the screen more effectively than do staged dramas. Why should this be? Perhaps Helmholtz suggests a clue. He maintains:

> An equilibrium of the attention, persistent for any length of time, is under no circumstances attainable. The natural tendency of attention when left to itself is to wander to ever new things; and so soon as the interest of its object is over, so soon as nothing new is to be noticed there, it passes, in spite of our will, to something else. If we wish to keep it upon one and the same object, we must seek constantly to find out something new about the latter, especially if other powerful impressions are attracting us away.[20]

William James reinforces this observation when he writes, "No one can possibly attend continuously to an object that does not change";[21] "what is called sustained voluntary attention is a repetition of successive efforts which bring back the topic to the mind";[22] and the "*conditio sine qua non* of sustained attention to a given topic of thought is that we should roll it over and over incessantly and consider different aspects and relations of it in turn."[23] Moreover, this natural tendency to shift attention has an evolutionary basis, since there are straightforward adaptive advantages for an organism in frequently updating its information by shifting its attention to other sectors of the environment where threats (in the form of predators) and opportunities (in terms of prey) may await.[24] That is, we are naturally disposed to shift our attention to other sectors of the environment, unless some change, such as a movement, keeps us focused on the object of our present attention.

Theatergoers, I submit, are often very aware of this pressure to shift their attention and to let their eyes wander away from the center of the drama, perusing aspects of the set and even the audience. It frequently requires some effort in the theater to keep one's eyes, at all times where, in the director's opinion, they should be. Of course, where the drama itself is compelling, the dialogue stirring, or the acting electric, our attention stays fixed. But, at the same time, I think that most theatergoers are aware that their attention can flag or can be deflected by wayward stimuli. Likewise, they are aware that, all things being equal, attending to a play requires more discipline than attending to a typical motion picture. Part of what is involved in being a practiced theatergoer is the ability to sustain attention on an often nearly static array and this, in turn, requires resources of energy and determination, built-up and reinforced by continual theater-going.[25]

Film viewing requires less effort than theater spectatorship, and, *ex hypothesi,* one of the reasons for that might be that in virtue of its continually changing views—secured by means of such devices as editing, camera movement, zooms, and the like—the filmmaker has the capacity to rejuvenate audience attention by introducing visual changes—cinematic activity and cinematic movement—into scenes. James says that in order to hold attention, one must roll one's attention over the object and consider different aspects of it and the different relations it bears to other objects. Changing camera positions visually does this automatically for us. Helmholtz says that sustained attention involves finding out something new about the object of attention. Again, at the level of visual stimulation, this is exactly what editing and camera movement make available.

Sustained attention demands effort, unless fluctuating stimuli abet it. Film supplies the relevant fluctuating stimuli by introducing cinematic devices. In the film *Six Degrees of Separation,* in addition to the cutting and camera movement in the opening scenes, there are also at least three different locations over which the dialogue of the play is distributed. The cinematic movement from one locale to another functions constantly to rekindle our attention.

The importance of cinematic activity for sustaining attention to the screen—especially in terms of film editing—has long been understood by filmmakers. When one looks at D. W. Griffith's films in the 1910s, one often finds cuts that do not seem to be completely motivated by dramatic concerns. Instead, one hypothesizes that Griffith introduced them in order to provide the kind of visual variety that would hold the audience's attention captive.

The early film theorist Lev Kuleshov was struck by the fact that Soviet audiences consistently preferred American films to Russian ones. When he studied the differences between these alternative styles of filmmaking, he was struck primarily by the degree to which American films relied upon editing, while the Russian films employed theatrical tableau formats. As a result, he hypothesized that editing was central to capturing the attention of the spectator, and he pioneered the style of montage filmmaking that is the distinctive contribution of the "Golden Age" of Soviet film to world cinema.[26]

Attention is biological; it is built into our neurological hardware.[27] It is a matter of our awareness being occupied by an object or an event. Movement, activity, and change draw our attention. Though we can consciously resist incoming stimuli of this sort, their typical effect on perception is involuntary. Filmmakers for the silver screen and for the television screen exploit this natural propensity in order to keep our eyes glued to their products, not only by presenting eventful scenes, but by articulating those scenes by means of all sorts of cinematic events—cuts, camera movements, pans, zooms, superimpositions, fades, wipes, rolls, flipped images, dissolves, rack-focusing, and so on—that constantly change the visual array in ways that renew our attention to it. Moreover, we do not respond in this way because we understand that these cinematic articulations are conventions that tell us where to look; we respond to these cinematic articulations as a result of the biology of attention.

The power of these attentional levers is no more apparent than on commercial TV. Many of us admit that the material may be banal, but we constantly find ourselves, nevertheless, lured into watching. What is it that holds our attention? One possible hypothesis is that on average, there are eight to ten cinematic events for every sixty-second period in commercial television programs; one rarely goes for more than twenty seconds without one cinematic event during a TV episode; and, of course, in the advertisements on TV, there are at least twice as many cinematic events as there are during the programs that we ostensibly tune in for.[28]

Undoubtedly, the way in which adolescents around the world are hypnotized by music videos owes a great deal to the fact that the cutting ratio of these de facto advertisements for popular music averages 19.94 shots per minute—and this statistic does not even take into account all the other cinematic events—swish-pans, camera movements, and the like—that music videos deploy with abandon.[29] These are machines for keeping the eye on the screen. As soon as the spectator loses interest in one image, his attention is recaptured by the introduction of another.

Moreover, if further evidence is required for the effectiveness of cinematic events in securing attention, consider the well-known habit of "channel surfing." We often find ourselves sitting in front of the television, clicking the remote control from one channel to another. On a moment-to-moment basis, we feel we should get up, but instead we find ourselves switching to a few more channels. What is going on here? My hypothesis is that because we are bored, we turn to another channel, and the introduction of a change in our visual environment holds our attention for a few more seconds.

In effect, we are auto-stimulating our own attentional responses. We have placed ourselves in a self-reinforcing cycle, one from which some effort of will may be required in order to extricate ourselves. To continue to channel surf is the line of least resistance, given the way in which changing visual arrays affect attention. And, of course, what we do to ourselves when we channel surf is what filmmakers and video makers do to us by punctuating their spectacles with a plethora of cinematic events. Channel surfing is a form of homemade editing that reveals how entrancing the editing on the screen can be for momentarily suppressing boredom by revivifying attention.

The rate of film editing proper has also been steadily increasing since the sixties.[30] By 1981, the average shot length was roughly six shots per minute.[31] There is some disagreement about the length of shots in the late eighties and nineties. Some commentators think that it has slowed down, while others suspect that it is getting closer to the rate in television. The average shot length for *Die Hard 2* is 3.1 seconds; for *The Fugitive,* it is 3.9 seconds; and for *The Crow,* it is 2.7 seconds. These, of course, are action films. But in *The Paper,* the rate was still as high as 4.8 seconds.[32] On the other hand, two cinematographers have estimated that there are roughly 1,200 shots in the average commercial film today, which at two hours a film, puts the average shot length at the 1981 rate.[33]

Moreover, a great many of these shots are close shots. Since most films are made with an eye to being shown on TV, perhaps the cutting rates and the proportion of close shots in recent films are a result of an attempt to bring them nearer to the TV standard. But, in any case, inasmuch as close shots tend to intensify audience attention, these strategies function to keep the spectator riveted to the screen.

Several commentators have also observed that over the last three decades scene transitions in commercial films have moved away from reliance on fades (which were popular in the twenties and thirties) and dissolves (which were popular in the forties and fifties) in favor of the straight cut.[34] From the perspective that I have been developing, one possible explanation for this stylistic evolution might be that insofar as an abrupt transition from one scene to another is apt to strike our attention more forcefully than a slow transition, the straight cut serves the desire of the contemporary filmmaker to control spectator attention more expeditiously than earlier techniques. Furthermore, one should not conceptualize the use of the straight cut in these transitions in terms of a learned convention, since first-time viewers, such as members of the Pokot tribe in Kenya, were able to comprehend this sort of transitional editing without training.[35]

In the preceding discussion, I have dwelt upon the way in which cinematic events, changes, and movement of a visual nature command audience attention. But, of course, it is not only through visual devices that the filmmaker holds our attention to the screen. Sound plays a crucial role as well. Perhaps the most dramatic example of this is the frequent use of loud noises in action films, science fiction films, suspense films, and the like. Massive explosions, the roar of a prehistoric creature, the pounding musical leitmotif of the shark in *Jaws,* or the screeching strokes on the violin in *Psycho* blare out, and we all but jump out of our seats. These are aggressive means for seizing the audience's attention.

Furthermore, it seems rather strained to regard these devices as conventional—at least in their attention-getting capacity. For our responses to loud noises are biologically determined responses—found even in infants—whose origin can be readily explained by natural selection. It is not a convention that we are startled by loud noises. Rather it is an adaptive reaction that primes us to either fight or flee. It is the kind of response that psychologists call "cognitively impenetrable," by which they mean that it bypasses higher-order cognitive processing—that is, it puts the organism on the alert, without thinking. And since no higher order cognitive processing is involved in the startle reaction, there can be no question of conventions and codes coming into the picture.

Like these sound cues, the visual devices that I have been discussing are also biologically endowed. They account, to an important degree, for those aspects of the film experience that Adorno and Horkheimer complain about when they describe it as semi-automatic and relentless.[36] These features of the film experience, in part, are a function of the way in which films proceed by triggering attention by activating the natural cognitive and perceptual dispositions of spectators. The devices in question are not conventions that must be learnt by the audience about where they should look. They are not like the convention, say, of Bunraku puppetry that direct the audience to look at the puppet rather than the puppeteer. One needs to be told to do that.

But no one needs to be told to quicken her attention when a filmmaker cuts in for a close shot. The psychological makeup of the spectator guarantees it. Indeed, the kind of attentional cues deployed by the cinema are engineered in such a way that they obviate the need for conventions and codes that must be learned. Primarily, it is our bodies, so to speak, that tell us where to look. Moreover, techniques designed like this are eminently suited for easy cross-cultural dissemination and, therefore, help explain why cinema can function as an international mode of communication.

Guiding attention. So far I have been examining film techniques simply in

terms of their ability to hold the audience's attention on the screen on a moment-to-moment basis. Yet though this is an indispensable function for film
communication, it is not the aim of the filmmaker merely to grab the attention
of the spectator. He or she also needs to shape and guide it—to assure that the
spectator is looking where she should be looking in order to follow the story in
the most appropriate way possible. The filmmaker must direct the audience's
attention. And here, once again, we find that the filmmaker, to a large extent,
relies upon engaging our natural perceptual capacities to secure this aim.

As we have already seen from our previous discussion, the flow of images in
a typical motion picture is fragmented—punctuated by editing and other cinematic events. The fragmentary nature of the image track might lead one to
predict that, as a result, film viewers would find it incoherent. But this is not the
case. Although films are fragmented, they are easy to follow. They are so readily
intelligible for the ordinary viewer that Adorno and Horkheimer describe the
cognitive response to films as semi-automatic.[37]

Despite the fact that the image track in film is fragmented, understanding
typical films, all things being equal, is not a challenge. Indeed, following a film
generally requires a lot less effort than following a comparable drama on the
stage. The standard play is presented in a continuous space. It demands effort
to track it. The spectator must search the dramatic array to find where and what
to attend. The spectator, of course, is aided in this respect by all sorts of theatrical devices, such as lighting, actor movement, and dialogue. But, as we have already noted, in theater there are a great many distracting stimuli to attract our
naturally endowed tendency to shift our attention. Especially in a large theater,
the spectator must exert some discipline in order to follow the spectacle appropriately.

But a similar problem does not characteristically arise with film. For the film
is possessed of a series of devices that assure that the spectator is almost always
looking at what, from the filmmaker's standpoint, she should be looking at.
Crucial, in this respect, is what we may call variable framing—the ability of the
filmmaker, by means of editing, camera movement, alternative lenses, zooms,
and the like—to present the action from different angles and from alternative
distances. It is this capacity that accounts for the fragmentary nature of the image flow, but rather than impeding the audience's reception of the narrative,
this makes its reception intelligible and virtually effortless.

Needless to say, film and theater possess many of the same techniques for
guiding the audience's attention. Some of these include: centrally positioning
the most significant characters and events; movement, especially against a sta-

tic background (e.g., freezing the gestures of all the characters, except for the intended focus of attention), and, perhaps less frequently, stasis in movement (e.g., everyone, save the intended focus of attention, is moving); characters' eyelines (all the other characters are looking at the intended focus); light colors on dark fields, or dark colors in light ones; sound, especially dialogue; variable illumination, including spotlighting; an economy of set details in order to minimize distraction; placement of major characters in arresting compositions, such as along diagonals; gesture, as a subcategory of both movement and dialogue; make-up, costuming, and so on. But in addition to these techniques, films have further techniques at their disposal than what one finds in theater, and, arguably, these devices are even more effective for directing the audience's attention than what is available onstage.

In both theater and film, lighting is an important device for guiding audience attention. But in film, the director has variable framing at her disposal as well. The filmmaker may not only enhance the illumination of the central character in order to draw our attention to him; the director can also show him in a close-up. Moreover, the hold of a close-up on the audience's attention, all things being equal, is more relentless than the use of lighting for the obvious reason that the close-up leaves the spectator with nothing else to see but that which the director mandates. Whereas in theater, our attention might be drawn from center stage to stage right, when it comes to a close-up, there *is* no stage right to divert our attention. It has been, so to say, deleted. By means of devices like the close-up, the film director can assure that the spectator is looking exactly where, from the perspective of the narrative, he should be, at precisely the moment that he should be looking there.

Comparable cinematic devices also include the use of soft focus, rack focus and the iris shot. Quite frequently in film, the foreground of a shot is in hard focus, while the background is blurry (or in "soft focus"). Thus, when the central character is speaking, our eyes stay on her because a natural tendency of the eye, exhibited in everyday perception, is to settle where the focus is sharpest. Placing the significant dramatic action in the most focused zone of the shot is not a convention; it is a design strategy, predicated on the way in which our eyes work, to prompt us to look where the director wants us to look.

Furthermore, the director can shift our attention from the foreground to the background by racking focus, i.e., by making the foreground blurry and the background sharp (or vice-versa) before our eyes. And, in this case, we will follow the vector of the altered focus. In a suspense film, for example, one frequently finds shots of the hero in the hard-focused foreground with a blur of movement in the background. Then the camera racks focus and we see the villain clearly, looming ominously in the background of the shot. Now we are apprised that the hero is in danger, and the director has controlled the rhythm or sequence of our awareness of this situation by the way in which she has modulated the focus of the shot in relation to the natural propensities of our perceptual apparatus.

Another example of this sort is the iris shot, which was particularly popular in the silent era. In this case, the director masks the shot in such a way that the pertinent character or detail is inscribed, often in a circle, in the center of the screen. This functions rather like a close-up. It compels the viewer to look where the director intends him to look by blocking out all other, potentially conflicting details.

Devices such as the close-up, variable focus, and the iris are more effective than the devices standardly found in theater, because they make it highly improbable and often all but impossible, at any given moment, that the spectator will be looking somewhere other than where the director intends him to look. Devices like these give the director immense control over the audience's attention, especially when compared to the resources of live theater. And insofar as such devices guide audience attention almost automatically, they make following a film less effortful than following a play onstage. Where in the theater, we need to search out the significant detail in a scene, albeit aided by many theatrical strategies, the film close-up delivers it to us, we might say, unavoidably. A theater is a big space in which we must find our way; the close-up is a big image which is nearly impossible to miss.

The close-up, of course, is not the whole story about how the film director controls our attention. It is an element of a larger system of articulation that I have already called variable framing. Variable framing is a matter of changing the dimensions, relative to the ongoing action, of the picture frame surrounding the characters, objects, and events that comprise the film. In a film, variable framing occurs when the camera is moved either closer or farther away from the action, or when the angle of the camera, relative to action, is altered by being raised or lowered. Editing and camera movement are the most frequent devices for changing the frame.

In the case of camera movement, we see the framing change before our very eyes. In Hitchcock's film *Young and Innocent,* we go from an overhead long-shot of a ballroom to a close-up of the eyes of the drummer in the band. In the context of this narrative, the heroine is searching for a man with a peculiar tic—a blink. The shot ends when, in an enormous close-up of his eyes, we see the drummer blink. The transition from the long-shot to the close-up is continuous; the framing alters literally in our view. With camera movement, reframing can occur either by moving the camera on the axis of its tripod—a process called panning—or the entire camera apparatus can be moved by some sort of vehicle to give rise to what is called a tracking shot or a traveling shot. A crane shot, as its name would suggest, occurs when the camera is raised or lowered by any device, like a crane, that changes the elevation of the frame. The shot of the celebrations in Babylon in D. W. Griffith's film *Intolerance* is one of the most majestic crane shots in film history.

In editing, on the other hand, the movement of the camera is, in a manner of speaking, excised. There is a long-shot; and then we cut to the close-shot. The process of moving the camera from one position to another is deleted. One might shoot a scene of two characters talking to each other by panning from one to the other. However, it is far more customary to cut from one to the other, showing first one talking head and then the other, with the transitional space between them (both the studio space and the fictional space) sublated from the array. Reframing by means of fades and dissolves can be considered as a subcategory of editing. And, in addition to camera movement and editing, variable framing can occur optically by means of zooming-in or zooming-out, or by changing lenses.

Editing, camera movement, and "lens movement" are the mechanical bases for variable framing. They, in turn, provide the filmmaker with three formal variables for influencing or directing the audience's attention. We may call these three variables indexing, bracketing, and scaling respectively. Indexing occurs automatically when the camera is moved toward its subject, whether by means of a camera movement, a cut, or a zoom. It functions like the gesture of pointing. One might think of it as a form of cinematic ostension. When the camera moves, that indicates that the spectator should be looking in the direction the camera is headed, if the camera's movement is being recorded, or in the direction that the camera is aimed, if the shot has been presented by means of a cut.

In *Casablanca,* there is a scene where Elsa visits Rick in order to plead with him to sell her a set of exit-visas. The relevant shot begins with Rick opening the door to his office screen right, and then the camera pans screen left to show us Elsa by the window. As the camera travels from left to right, our eyes follow it irresistibly. Its movement points us in the direction that we should be looking. Indexing is not an arbitrary convention for where we should look. It is a technique that guides our attention automatically.

In addition to indexing, the filmmaker also directs our attention by bracketing what we see. That is, as a camera is moved toward a character, an object, or an event, it effectively screens out everything beyond the perimeter of the frame. Moving a camera toward an object, by means of either editing or camera movement, indicates that what is important at this moment is what is on the screen. The frame acts as a bracket. Everything outside the frame has been bracketed from attention.

On the one hand, bracketing is exclusionary. What does not fall inside the cinematic bracket, in effect, should not concern the audience's attention, and, in the vast majority of cases, it literally cannot occupy the audience's attention. But bracketing is also inclusionary. The bracket indicates that what is important for the audience to attend to is what falls inside the bracket—what is visible in the frame. Again, that we look inside the bracket, rather than outside it, is hardly a convention. It does not need to be learned. For we have no other alternative, but to follow the placement of the bracket. Bracketing is not an arbitrary code. Rather, the technique is tailored virtually to compel viewers, endowed with the standard-issue perceptual apparatus, to attend to just what the director intends.

Most editing and camera movement function by employing the exclusionary and inclusionary dimensions of bracketing simultaneously—both to eliminate distracting detail and to focalize attention on the center of the bracket. Thus, bracketing both filters out irrelevancies and spotlights what is significant. However, in some cases (indeed, in enough cases that this option should be counted as a standard deviation), a filmmaker may deliberately place the bracket in such a way that what may be most significant for the narrative is left offscreen. This is often done for emotional effect. Thus, the murder is shown on screen, but the killer is "hidden" outside the bracket. This raises a certain *frisson* in the spectator and keeps us riveted to the screen in the expectation that sooner or later we will get to see the murderer.

Moving the camera forward not only indexes and brackets certain details rather than others. It also changes the scale of what the audience is looking at. In Hitchcock's film *Notorious,* there is a famous shot that begins on a second-floor landing and edges over behind a chandelier before it swoops down toward the character of Alicia Huberman, finally landing on her hand, where she has secreted the cellar key that she plans to give the American agent Devlin. As the camera approaches Alicia Huberman, it not only points to her and removes distracting detail from the key element of the shot, but it also makes it larger. That is, the key literally occupies more screen space at the end of the shot than at earlier moments. As it becomes visible, it "grows" in scale, taking up more screen space and more retinal space to boot. Moreover, the increase in scale alerts the audience to the importance of the key in the scene.

I suppose that someone might be tempted to say that this is a convention— that visual largeness should mark importance. However, is this really arbitrary? Would it be equally effective to make what is important in a scene small? But how then could a director be assured that the audience would take note of it? By means of scaling, the director fills the audience's awareness with whatever she deems appropriate. Likewise, scaling enables the director to make what is less significant to the narrative smaller and, therefore, a less likely object of audience attention. This is not merely a matter of marking an item as less important. It is a way of making it less probable that the audience will be looking at it, or that they will even be able to see it. Scaling may be a "conventional" device in the sense that it is frequently used in film; but it is not conventional in the sense of arbitrariness, since, given the human perceptual make-up, it is not arbitrary that we look at objects that dominate our visual field.

Scaling, bracketing, and indexing are three different ways at the director's disposal to make objects and events, characters, and actions salient to the audience. Through these means, the director guides the audience's attention to where it is more appropriate, given the purposes of the narrative, from moment to moment. Moreover, these devices help the filmmaker modulate the audience's attention over time. First the audience is shown a medium long-shot of a scene, and then the camera moves in, and by means of indexing, scaling, and bracketing, certain details are selected for special attention. Or, the scene may start with a close-shot, and then the shot is changed to a broader view, encouraging the audience to think of the detail presented in the close-shot in terms of its relevance to the larger gestalt encompassed by the altered bracket—for example, first we see the barrel of a gun, indexed, bracketed, and made large scale, and then we see the gestalt—a gunman and his prey—in a broader shot. Thus, constant reframing allows the director to control not only what we see, but *when* we see it, in terms of the sequence of views that is most advantageous for following the story.

Typically, scaling, bracketing, and indexing come into play whenever a camera is moved. However, they need not always occur coincidentally. One may change the bracket without changing scaling, for example, when a camera follows a character but maintains her screen dimensions. Or one may index a scene by moving the camera slightly forward without changing the scale or the bracket of the shot appreciably. Or one may emphasize the changing bracket in a shot, as in the famous trolley-car ride in *Sunrise,* without indexing anything in particular, or introducing notable scale changes. Nevertheless, scaling, bracketing, and indexing are generally employed in concert and when so employed, they afford a very powerful means through which the filmmaker controls the audience's attention.

In the typical motion picture, these means are placed in the service of the ongoing narrative. Bracketing, scaling, and indexing are generally deployed in such a way that, in addition to the attention-guiding devices that film shares with theater, they shape the audience's awareness, so that the first item or gestalt of items of which we take note in a shot will be the one that is most relevant to following the story. These devices make certain narrative details—characters, objects, and actions—salient; they make us cognizant of what it is (ideally) maximally significant for us to attend to in the story at the moment the shot appears. And then we are presented with new narrative information in the next shot, which has also been structured in terms of the principle that the first item or group of items that we see again be those that are most relevant to the progress of the narrative. Furthermore, as a consequence of this coordination of narrative purposes with visual structure, films are not only easy to follow, they seem perspicuous through and through.[38]

Of course, for various reasons, a filmmaker may deviate from the practice that the first item the audience is prompted to see be the one that is the most significant for the narrative. Frequently, a filmmaker, perhaps for expressive effect or emotional impact, may lead the audience's eye so that the most significant narrative detail is not evident immediately, but only after a second look. For example, first we might see a nervous-looking character and, only after first taking that in, are we prompted, visually, to notice that there is a man with a knife standing behind him. This kind of standard deviation itself, however, owes much of its forcefulness to the fact that the basic approach to visual narration in film is to show us the most narratively significant item in a shot first— that is, to coordinate all the visual strategies available to the filmmaker, including bracketing, scaling, and indexing, in such a way that the most important narrative item is the first thing our attention battens on in a shot.[39]

If we compare the stage drama to the film drama, we might say metaphorically that, in terms of attention, the narrative in film has been visually predigested for us. In theater, we must ultimately locate and select the object of our attention; we have to find the objects that are most relevant to the ongoing narrative. But in film, a great deal more of that work is done for us by variable framing than is done for us in the staging of the typical play, housed, as it usually is, under the proscenium arch.

The right standpoint on the action is delivered automatically to the viewer in film. That is why, I submit, film viewing seems to involve less effort than theater viewing. It is also why films may strike viewers with little experience of live theater as more readily intelligible than theater, inasmuch as each cinematic moment is such that it shows in bold relief what is necessary to see in order to follow the story.

In one of the earliest treatises on the cinema—*The Film: A Psychological Study*—Hugo Munsterberg, a distinguished philosopher/psychologist and colleague of William James at Harvard University, maintained that certain film techniques, like the close-up, performed the work with respect to cinematic narratives that mental processes like attention perform for us with respect to staged dramas. That is not quite right, since our attentional processes must still be activated in order to follow a film. But what is true, and remains central to film communication, is that relative to stage drama, cinematic devices like variable framing do *a great deal* of the kind of processing work that is left to our own efforts when we go to a play on Broadway.

Some of the most frequent metaphors for attention include the filter, the spotlight, the gate, and the zoom lens. As we have seen, these also describe the operation of bracketing, indexing, and scaling nicely. The bracketing operation visually filters out irrelevant narrative details, functioning as a gate, while, at the same time, what is included in the bracket is spotlighted. The metaphor of the zoom lens calls to mind both scaling and indexing, while the enlarging aspect of scaling brings filtering into play automatically. Compared to theater events, which are themselves already filtered in contrast to everyday experiences, film events, due to bracketing, indexing, and scaling, are even more prefiltered. Since some of the work of attention has already been supplied by the filmmaker, films give the appearance of being easier to follow and more intelligible.

One central function of attention is selection. Bracketing, scaling, and indexing enhance the process of selection for the viewer to a degree unprecedented in live theater. The filmmaker preselects the relevant features of the story for emphasis, and then the bracketing, scaling and indexing reinforce that by making it perceptually difficult and sometimes impossible for the spectator to select any other alternatives. Normal attention imbues its object with high clarity in the center and less at a distance from the center.[40] A typical film image is already structured like this, thereby meeting our natural attentional processes more than halfway (in a manner of speaking).

The cinematographer Vilmos Zsigmond says, "When a shot is only going to be on screen for three seconds, that composition and lighting has to be very good to allow the viewer's eye to see what you want them to. There's no time to decide what is important, so you have to direct their eye, *force* it. It pushes the cinematographer to light better, more three-dimensionally, graphically. So we worked to separate the foreground, background and middleground and used a desaturated color scheme to simplify the image. You can see things better that way."[41] By organizing the image in this way, the cinematographer is already doing some of the work that attentional processing would secure in our responses to comparable visual arrays in "real life."

Attention not only selects visual details and clarifies them. Attentional processing also involves perceptual preparation for the location of objects. Where we are already aware of the location of the next object of attention before it appears, we are able to process it more rapidly.[42] And, of course, in the cinema, we always know that the next target of attention will appear in front of us, on the screen. Thus, once again, we see that the design structure of the cinematic apparatus facilitates attention, in this case by virtually abetting the work of preparatory attention.

Through the devices discussed so far, the filmmaker (ideally) lays the relevant objects of attention before the audience in the order that is most appropriate for following the story. Of course, following the story involves more than seeing certain items in a certain order. The audience must put what it sees together, under the direction of the filmmaker. For example, consider the opening shot of *Notorious*. We begin with a close-shot that shows, in large scale, a camera with a flash-attachment of the sort used by professional cameramen; then the camera moves to the right, pausing to bracket a group of men with similar cameras; and then it moves upward, indexing a sign over an official-looking doorway, which says, "District Court of the United States." Here the indexing, bracketing, and scaling isolate the pertinent narrative elements, but it remains to the viewer to infer their significance, namely, that a newsworthy trial is going on behind those doors.

Undoubtedly, the sequence of the variable framing helps one reach this conclusion. First our attention is drawn to a certain kind of camera, and we look at it long enough to realize that it is not your everyday brownie. Then we see a group of men holding similar cameras, thus prompting us to ask ourselves what kind of people would be carrying professional apparatus of that sort. I think that the average viewer already has enough information to infer that they are likely to be newspaper cameramen, but if anyone is still entertaining the possibility that they represent a convention of professional photographers, the information that they are standing outside the District Court seems a bit incongruous. It is far more probable that the photographers are specifically newspapermen waiting to document the outcome of a court case.

Here we see that although the variable framing makes certain inferences likely, it still remains to the viewer to put it all together. Nevertheless, what is interesting about the way in which the viewer puts this information together is that it does not rely on special cinematic codes and conventions, but on the same sort of inferential and interpretational processes that we employ to negotiate situations in everyday life. Think about what goes on when one chances on a crime scene. First one begins to notice that there are a number of policemen milling about; then one takes in other details—barriers and the like. Gradually we colligate these details under the concept of a crime scene. Exactly the same mode of thinking comes into play in the opening scene of *Notorious*: we infer that there is a newsworthy trial by means of the same kind of reasoning that we employ to determine that we have just wandered onto a crime scene in everyday life.

This is not to deny that there is a great deal of artifice in the opening scene from *Notorious*. The shot has been blocked and structured in order to deliver the information we need to make the requisite inference in a very elegant and economical fashion. In everyday life, the ingredients required for our inference are not set out so neatly. Scenes have not been predigested for attention. And yet the way in which we put together these scenes that have been artificially prestructured for our attention is not different in kind from the way in which we interpret events in the world. That is, we do not read these events on the basis of some cinematic code. We recognize the elements of the events by looking and we come to surmise what is going on—e.g., that cameramen are awaiting an important moment in a newsworthy trial—by means of pretty much the same inferential resources we use in everyday life.

Here the qualification, "pretty much the same," is motivated by several considerations. First, there are certain movie conventions, especially with respect to genres, that we never employ in everyday life. When in a film a man with a heavily powdered and rouged face appears in a tuxedo and a cloak, we infer that he is a vampire, though we never make the same inference in life. And, furthermore, with film generally our inferences are contextually motivated and constrained to cohere with the ongoing narrative. That is, we do not infer what is going on in a scene simply on the basis of the visual information available in that scene, but rather we attempt to fit that information into our conception of the ongoing story.[43] This is unlike ordinary experience, inasmuch as we often lack such a well-developed scenario of what is happening around us, but it is not entirely unlike everyday experience, since we generally have some sense of the context in which the details we observe play a role.

Of course, it is quite interesting that the inferential processes engaged in making sense of the objects the filmmaker brings to our attention are of a piece with our ordinary computational processes. For it suggests that understanding films will, in great measure, involve many of the same capacities that we already possess in virtue of our capacity to get around the world. We do not need, for the most part, to master a special code or convention of reading in order to follow films. This is not to deny that there are film conventions, but only to deny that they are absolutely fundamental to the explanation of film comprehension. Rather, we comprehend what is going on in a film in much the same way that we figure out that those are news agents over there and that they are congregating because they probably expect that something newsworthy is about to happen.

Perhaps someone will argue that it is by means of a code that Hitchcock in this scene from *Notorious* marks newspapermen by correlating them with professional flash cameras. But it is not a code, if by code one means an arbitrary correlation. It is not arbitrary that professional cameramen carry professional camera equipment, nor could their status have been as effectively marked by having them carry parasols. As I have already argued at length, we recognize the referents of images by looking, where we are familiar with what the images are of in "real life." We do not use a code book to decipher film images. Rather, we recognize images of professional, thirty-five millimeter cameras with flash attachments, where we are already familiar with such equipment, and we also bring to narrative contexts in which such images figure the information that such cameras are used by certain types of people rather than others.

That much of the reasoning that we mobilize while following a film is continuous with ordinary, everyday reasoning—within the context of an ongoing narrative—of course helps to explain how film can function as an international means of communication. No special code is necessary to decipher film; to a great degree, films can be followed by using ordinary practical reasoning, including folk psychological understandings of human motivation. This is not to dispute that many films may require special background information and that there are genre conventions which the viewer must grasp if certain films are to be intelligible. My claim is only that much of what you need to follow a film is what you already know in terms of cognitive skills you already possess, and that this fact is clearly a decided advantage for the purposes of international communication. Understanding film does not require the acquisition of a special skill called cinematic literacy; it relies in large measure upon engaging the in-ferential and interpretational skills that we deploy in everyday life.[44]

Needless to say, a lot of what some people come to know, they come to know as the result of film. Perhaps one only knows that those flash cameras in *Notorious* are professional cameras because one saw cameras just like them in *King Kong,* or some other film. Perhaps you never saw one in "real life." Or perhaps the rural tribesman only knows of the practice of hailing taxis from watching movies. In these cases, which are legion, are we entitled to speak of filmic codes, since the correlations have been learnt by viewing films? My own inclination is to say no, because the learning, though via film, involves ordinary observation and contextualization rather than the memorization of a symbol.

Films are made to hold and guide attention without resort, for the most part, to codes and conventions. Film does not require from readers a special mode of reading, but generally only the sorts of practical and motivational inferences required by everyday life. Film can function as an international means of communication to a great extent because it is designed in such a way that it does not require knowledge of special codes and conventions. Instead, it engages cognition and perception in such a way that a filmmaker is able, in large measure, to signal her meaning intentions without the benefit of a cinematic semantics or syntax.

POINT-OF-VIEW EDITING

Thus far I have been advancing the naturalistic perspective by considering its pertinence to a wide-ranging series of cinematic phenomena. Now it may be instructive to focus our attention more narrowly and to concentrate upon showing the efficacy of naturalism with respect to a single cinematic structure.

Point-of-view editing is one of the most widely used film devices. It is an all but indispensable tool of film narration. Everyone is familiar with it. In the most typical case, there is a shot of a character looking offscreen. Then there is a shot of an object, event, or another character; and then this shot is sometimes followed by a return to the shot of the original character looking offscreen. When presented with such an array, audiences generally surmise that the second shot shows us what the character in the first shot sees—from roughly where the character in the first shot is standing.

One variation in this structure is to show us an object, event, or character first, and then to cut to a shot of another character looking offscreen. Once again, the typical audience response to this sort of editing is to suppose that what is shown in the first shot is what the character in the second shot is seeing. These structures enable the filmmaker to narrate through the point of view of the character. They provide a means for advancing the story line, as well as for informing the audience of the emotional responses of the characters to what they encounter. Whole films can be constructed on the basis of the point-of-view principle. Hitchcock's film *Rear Window* is probably the best known experiment of this sort.

Point-of-view editing is a widely used technique. One commentator claims that it amounts to as many as 97 percent of the cuts in contemporary sitcoms on TV.[45] This is undoubtedly a much higher rate of incidence than one would find in the majority of theatrically released films. However, few films forgo the use of this device entirely, and most films resort to it many times in the course of a narrative. The introduction and popularization of this device in the early decades of this century is always listed among the major stylistic breakthroughs in film style. By anyone's account, it is a central structure of the international mode of communication we call film. The question before us now is, how and why does point-of-view editing work?

Before beginning, however, a little terminological clarification is in order. By "point-of-view editing," I am referring to the structure that Edward Branigan has defined as minimally comprising two shots—the point/glance shot and the point/object shot.[46] The point/glance shot involves a character in the act of looking, generally offscreen. The point/object shot then follows, putatively showing us what the person in the point/glance shot sees. The elements in this structure can be iterated. Often in the early cinema, the structure as a whole was repeated several times, but nowadays it is customary to exhibit the pattern only once.

Moreover, the point/glance shot may precede the point/object shot, or the order can be reversed, giving rise to what Branigan calls the prospective and the retrospective structure respectively.[47] Through the point-of-view format, the filmmaker can narrate by showing us what a character is looking at and, thereby, indicating what is on her mind, as well as conveying to us what the character feels about what she is seeing—i.e., whether she is angered by it, horrified, disgusted, or amused.

Current scholarly thinking about the way that point-of-view editing functions regards it as a code. Indeed, a still influential article on the subject calls it the "tutor-code of classical cinema."[48] Naturalists like myself, however, regard point-of-view editing as an elaboration of our ordinary cognitive and perceptual experience. That is, we are able to understand it not because we learn it after the fashion of learning a grammatical rule, but because of the way in which it is related to our own characteristic perceptual behaviors.

In order to begin to see what I am getting at, consider a perennial childhood prank. A group of youngsters stand on a street corner and look upwards toward the top of a building. Passersby notice them and do likewise. The children think that this is immensely funny, because they are not really looking at anything; they merely want to trick the passersby into looking skyward. Now this practical joke is not very funny. But it is illuminating in what it reveals. It is predicated upon triggering a natural perceptual response from the passersby. Namely, when we see someone looking intently, it is natural for us to follow his glance to its target.

This perceptual response may be observed throughout the animal kingdom. It is an adaptive behavior of many mammals. It is a way in which one animal derives information about another animal. For the glance of a creature exhibits its interests and often its practical intents. In this respect, following the gaze of another creature possesses survival value. Moreover, this tendency is present in humans, as well as other higher primates. Human children, beginning at the age of two or three months, naturally follow their caregiver's gaze to its target objects.[49] This hardwired or innate response undoubtedly facilitates language learning. But as an adaptive response it also serves us well in navigating innumerable social situations in later life. We realize that our guests want to leave when we notice that they are looking at their watches, or that the dean wants to speak to the provost when she keeps looking in her direction.

By following a person's glance to its target, we learn about the human environment, since the human glance is an indicator of interest and a clue to intention. By looking where another is looking, we can often figure out or infer what he or she is thinking. We look at what they are looking at, we put ourselves in "their shoes," as the saying goes, and we ask ourselves why someone might be staring intently in that direction.

A preprogrammed, genetically endowed response of this sort surely helped our prehistoric ancestors in dealing with the environment—both the animal and the human environment. But this disposition also continues to be serviceable for us in detecting what our colleagues, loved ones, and foes are thinking about. And, in any case, even if the behavior were not still adaptive, it seems that our tendency to follow the glance of another to its target is virtually automatic.

Of course, there are cultures where people are trained to repress this natural response. But without such training, people are disposed to look at what other people are looking at as a natural means of information gathering. That is, it is a naturally inclined, perceptual behavior of humans, in the relevant circumstances, to follow the gaze of another person to its target object. This is a way of getting information about other persons and, indeed, about animals as well. Furthermore, this innate tendency is of such adaptive utility that it is probably a legacy of natural selection.

But what does this have to do with film? Let us proceed in steps. First, it should come as no surprise that this perceptual behavior—following the glance to its target—can be represented in film. In *Rear Window,* there is a shot of the murderer, played by Raymond Burr, looking downward intently; then the camera follows his line of vision, landing eventually on a small dog. This sets us to wondering about why he should be concerned with the dog, a question answered, somewhat gruesomely, later in the film.

Now in this case, the camera literally traces the trajectory from the murderer's gaze to the dog, thereby representing that natural tendency of the observer's eye to move from a glance to its target. To get from this sort of representation to point-of-view editing proper requires but a single modification, viz., subtract the camera movement from the murderer's glance to the dog, and, instead, cut directly from the murderer looking to a shot of the dog. That is, what happens in point-of-view editing—at least of the minimal, prospective variety—is that the camera movement between the gaze and the dog is deleted.

Where the camera movement between the murderer's glance and the dog is intact, we have no trouble recognizing it as a representation of typical perceptual behavior because of its striking similarity to it. However, even when the camera movement is deleted, we are still able to recognize the structure as a representation of the ordinary experience of tracking a glance to its target. Perhaps the reason that the deletion of the camera movement does not concern us is that in ordinary perceptual experience it is the endpoints of this activity, and not the space between, that command our attention. That is, we recognize that the point-of-view structure is meant to show us what the character sees because of the way in which it strikingly recapitulates the natural inclination to follow the glance to its target.

It is very difficult to see prospective point-of-view structures as not representing what the character in the point/glance shot sees. Even in contexts where the viewer knows that it is unlikely that the character in a point/glance shot could be seeing what is presented in the point/object shot, we are often tempted to see the cut as visually connecting a gaze to its target. In Vertov's *Man With a Movie Camera,* we often have the impression that people are "seeing" things that are not proximate to them geographically. Vertov counterfeits these "visions" for metaphoric effect. But what is interesting about them is that once the structural conditions for point-of-view editing are met, normal percipients are virtually compelled to regard such cuts as representations of looking. That is, so to speak, our default response to such cuts. It is almost as hard to regard these shots as perceptually disconnected as it would be to see a normal photograph of a horse as a photo of a lemon.

The ability to recognize a point-of-view editing structure as a representation of a person looking at an object does not appear to be learned in the way that one learns grammatical structures. First-time viewers, such as the members of the Pokot tribe of Kenya, have been able to comprehend edited arrays containing point-of-view editing without the benefit of any special training.[50] Point-of-view editing does not involve initiation into a specialized code. Rather, I hypothesize, it is recognized as a representation of the perceptual practice, familiar to every sighted person, of following a glance to its target. It does not resemble this perceptual experience in every phenomenological respect, since it deletes the space between the glance and its target. But it does resemble the disposition of the gaze to follow the glance of another to its target in enough salient phenomenological and functional respects that one is able to pick up the significance of this visual structure without training.

This is the naturalist's answer to the question of why point-of-view editing works. It works because of the way in which it engages our ordinary cognitive and perceptual makeup. Moreover, if this explanation is persuasive, it also indicates why point-of-view editing can function so well as an element in an international mode of mass communication. For, once again, we note that it is a communicative device that, inasmuch as it is keyed to innate capacities, will be legible and accessible transculturally.

I have just tried to explain why point-of-view editing can function so efficiently as a means of representing what a character sees. But this is not the only function of point-of-view editing. As already remarked, it is also a means for communicating what a character feels about what he or she is seeing. How, from a naturalistic perspective, can we explain that?

Since the twenties, some film theorists, influenced by Lev Kuleshov, have thought that the communication of information about character emotion by the point-of-view structure is primarily a function of the point/object shot. They are encouraged in this conclusion by reports of an experiment in which Kuleshov is said to have juxtaposed the same shot of an actor's face against a shot of a bowl of soup, and then against a shot of birds flying in a radiant sky.

The composure of the actor's face putatively remained the same in each juxta-position. Yet, when the face was juxtaposed to the bowl of soup, spectators said that the actor expressed hunger, while when the same shot was juxtaposed with a shot of the birds flying, the actor in it was said to express a yearning for free-dom.

Since the face did not change from one juxtaposition to the next, Kuleshov attributed the different reports about the actor's expression to the operation of the point/object shot. He maintained that viewers inferred what the character was feeling on the basis of what would be an appropriate feeling, given the point/object shot. The point/glance shot was a tabula rasa; the point/object shot invested it with emotional meaning.[51]

Whether or not the Kuleshov experiment ever occurred, it has influenced the way in which people think about the operation of point-of-view editing. However, this is unfortunate. For even if Kuleshov obtained the results he re-ported, his experiment is quite unlike what one normally finds in point-of-view editing. In Kuleshov's experiment, the actor's face was emotionally amorphous. He did not portray a specific emotion, and that may be what led viewers to rely so heavily on the point/object shot. But standardly, the actor's face is not inex-pressive in point-of-view editing. Generally, the actor's face does evince a very definite emotion in the point/glance shot, and this makes an important contri-bution to what the audience takes the character to be feeling.

For example, in a horror film, the point/glance shot of the character watch-ing a monster approach will generally register the disgust with which the char-acter regards the monster—his nose will wrinkle in the typical gesture of dis-gust, his upper lip will rise, his teeth will be clenched and his head and shoulders will start backward in a withdrawal response. Even before we see the monster in the point/object shot, the point/glance shot will already supply us with information about the character's emotional state. Thus, *pace* Kuleshov, the point/glance shot makes an important contribution to communication of emotion in the typical deployment of the point-of-view structure.

Of course, some commentators may be skeptical about the power of the point/glance shot to deliver information about the emotional state of the char-acter. They may believe that this is impossible without the sort of contextual-ization that the point/object shot supplies. However, there is a great deal of psy-chological data that support the hypothesis that, for certain *basic* ranges of emotional expression, humans, cross-culturally, are able to recognize and iden-tify emotional states on the basis of facial expression alone.[52] It is well known that humans have an innate capacity to recognize the faces of other humans as human; but it is also the case that the affect manifested by the face, to a certain extent, can be identified.

That is, when members of divergent cultural groups, including peoples unfamiliar with mass media representations, are shown pictures of facial expressions of emotion, they converge in their categorization of the emotions in the pictures at rates that preclude the possibility that the coincidence is random. People, indeed people from different cultures, are able to identify certain rudimentary ranges of affect—including: interest/excitement; enjoyment/joy; surprise/startle; distress/anguish; disgust/contempt; anger/rage; shame/humiliation; and fear/terror—on the basis of facial expression.

Thus, on the grounds of the empirical evidence, it seems reasonable to suppose not only that the point/glance shot is capable of conveying information about character emotion, but that it is able to do so, at least in part, by engaging the spectator's innate capacities to recognize the gross category into which a character's facial expression falls. In short, the point/glance shot is a device that is predicated upon activating our recognitional capacities in such a way that we identify the global emotional state of the relevant character in the point/glance shot.

This is not to deny that audiences may also determine the emotional state of the character in virtue of the narrative context. Rather, my point is simply that in addition to the narrative context, the facial expression of the character in the point/glance shot provides further information about the character's emotional state. And, of course, the point/glance shot can also supply that information by itself, where the narrative context has not prepared us for it.

If the followers of Kuleshov err by overestimating the importance of the point/object shot, I do not want to repeat their error by claiming that we can completely characterize the expressive power of point-of-view editing by reference to the point/glance shot. Both the point/glance shot and the point/object shot contribute to the expression of character emotion via point-of-view editing. The point/glance shot activates our recognition of the global emotional state of the character.

But the emotions expressed by films are often fine-grained. The fear on the character's face is not fear *simpliciter* but vertigo in the film of the same name. How do we get from recognition of the global emotion of fear, signaled in the point/glance shot, to the more specific realization that the fear in question is vertigo? It is here that the contribution of the point/object shot becomes especially relevant. For the point/object shot presents the audience with the object of the character's emotional state.

Emotions are marked by intentionality. That is, they are directed. One is not simply jealous. One is jealous *of* someone. One is not characteristically just afraid. One is afraid *of* something or someone. Thus, emotions have objects—the objects that they are directed toward: the person of whom I am jealous, or the thing of which I am afraid. In some cases, the object of my emotional state may also be its cause. Moreover, the way in which I perceive the object of my emotional state serves to identify the nature of the emotional state in which I find myself. If the object of my state is something that I regard to be harmful, then the emotional state I am in is fear; if the object of my state is someone who I think has wronged me or mine, then the state is anger. Thus, in supplying us with the object of the character's emotional state, the point/object shot helps define the emotional state of the character.

Though the human face can give us very broad, generally reliable information about the basic emotional states of others, that information can still be somewhat ambiguous. It may be hard for us to differentiate closely related emotions like fear and surprise, or to specify the emotion in a fine-grained way. Is this the face of a lover, a worshipper, or a patriot? In order to arrive at more fine-grained discriminations, we generally depend upon knowing the object or cause of the emotional state. And when it comes to point-of-view editing, the point/object shot generally affords us with this information.

That is, the function of the point/object shot is to supply the audience with the cause or object of the character's emotional state in order to define the emotional state of the character in a fine-grained way. In *Vertigo,* the character who is terrified of heights attempts to overcome his phobia by climbing up a short kitchen stepladder. Suddenly, his face, shown to us in a point/glance shot, manifests terror. Then the point/object shot shows us the object of his emotion. He is looking out the window at the street, several stories below. Once apprised of the object of his emotion, we are able to specify it. It is not merely fear; more specifically, it is the fear of heights. It is vertigo.

The relation of the point/glance shot to the point/object shot, where point-of-view editing is being deployed to portray character emotion, has a reciprocal structure. The point/glance shot sets forth a global range of emotions that we recognize as broadly characterizing the neighborhood of affective states that the character could be in. Then, the point/object shot shows us the object and/or cause of the emotion, thereby enabling us to focus upon the particular emotion—within the affective range set by the point/glance shot—that pertains to the character in question. The point/object shot focuses or selects the particular emotion being portrayed out of the spectrum of emotional timbres afforded by the point/glance shot.

In other words, the point/glance shot functions as a *range finder*, whereas the point/object shot functions as a *focuser*, specifying the relevant affect of the character as a particular emotional state within the range set out by the point/glance shot. Thus, both the point/glance shot and the point/object shot are key in the articulation of character emotion by means of point-of-view editing. Kuleshov was wrong to think that the point/object shot told the whole story.

Moreover, in addition to the preceding reciprocal relation between the point/glance and the point/object shot, there are further functional relationships within the point-of-view structure. For example, broadly speaking, the point/glance shot provides the viewer with a rough guide to what is emotionally salient about the point/object shot. The reason for this has to do with the fact that emotional states of a given sort are typically elicited by objects that share certain general characteristics or that meet certain criteria. The emotion of disgust, for instance, is elicited by objects that the emoter regards as noxious or impure. Thus, when a point/glance shot represents a character evincing the global state of disgust, that primes the viewer to expect that whatever is eliciting this state will meet the criterion of impurity. Consequently, when the point/object shot arrives on the screen, the viewer will survey it in terms of those features that correspond with impurity.

The point/glance shot provides a rough anticipation of what, emotionally speaking, should be salient in the point/object shot. So, if the point/glance shot presents us with a character transfixed by fear, then that indicates that we should attend to the lethal ax being wielded in the ensuing point/object shot and not to the killer's Armani shirt. In this way, the point/glance shot in the point-of-view structure functions as a means for managing the spectator's attention.

As in our account of how the spectator is able to comprehend point-of-view editing as a representation of looking, the naturalist account of how point-of-view editing conveys information about the emotional state of the character in the point/glance shot relies upon speculating about the way in which the device engages our constitutional makeup, including our cross-cultural capacity to recognize at least certain gross categories of emotions[53] along with the constitutive role that the object of the emotion plays in the identification of emotional states.

Alfred Hitchcock has stated: "I believe that we still have in our hands the most powerful instrument, cinema, that's been known. I know of no other medium where on a given night in Japan, Germany, in Paris, and in London and in New York, the different audiences of different nationalities can be shocked at the same moment at the same thing on that screen. . . . I enjoy the fact that we can cause, internationally, audiences to emote. And I think that this is our job."[54] Point-of-view editing has always been one of Hitchcock's major strategies for eliciting this effect. And if the naturalistic perspective is correct, the reason that point-of-view editing can function in this way internationally is that in addition to addressing our common cognitive and perceptual makeup, it activates our emotional constitution as well.

CONCLUSION

Film is now one hundred years old. And in the relatively short span of its existence, it has already become a major mode of international communication, not only in the sense that films are being shown everywhere, all of the time, but also in the sense that the ensemble of communicative techniques perfected in film provide the basis for visual communication in many other, worldwide media, including comic books, television, and CD-ROM.

It has been the burden of this article to explain how it is possible for film to be so effective on so large a scale. My recurring approach to this question has been to explore the ways in which the basic elements of film engage common features of human nature. For it has been my supposition that it is most plausible to explain the transcultural reach of the film in virtue of its capacity to touch something that is shared by its internationally diverse audiences. And, in this regard, features of our biologically endowed cognitive, perceptual, and even emotional capacities have seemed to be the most likely candidates.

Because my approach adverts to human nature, I have called it naturalism. It is meant to contrast to the approaches of semiologists and poststructuralists who attempt to discuss film in terms of language, codes, and conventions. One major problem with their position, which I have frequently stressed, is that it is ill-suited to explain the international dissemination of film and its expressive devices, since those devices are mastered so readily by people without the benefit of the sort of training that codes and language-like conventions would appear to require.

Indeed, many of the central devices of film—such as variable framing, point-of-view editing, and the single-shot pictorial image—seem to be attractive to filmmakers who aspire to address mass audiences because they bypass the necessity of learning codes or conventions. They are accessible to virtually everyone, and their fast pick up appears to be almost automatic. Surely, if someone set out intentionally to design a mode of international communication, it would be exactly devices such as these—devices that could be comprehended nearly on contact—toward which one would gravitate.

But what kind of devices can afford communication without resort to codes and conventions? The naturalist's response is devices that engage various innate cognitive and perceptual capacities. Of course, the naturalist should not claim that there are no film conventions. Obviously, there are many. Rather, the naturalist claims that much of our basic comprehension of film has less to do with convention and more to do with activating everyday cognitive and perceptual skills and capacities.

Moreover, filmmakers have had an obvious economic interest in discovering devices that address us in this way, since they aspire to command the largest audiences possible. Heavy reliance on codes that must be learned limits audiences, motivating filmmakers to find ways to forgo excessive dependence on codes. In effect, filmmakers throughout history have functioned as informal psychologists, experimenting with ways to communicate that are not, strictly speaking, linguistic. They have constructed a symbol system that can be virtually, universally accessible precisely because many of its central devices address elements of our common humanity.[55]

NOTES

1. For example, a reviewer of *Cutthroat Island* says that it stars Thailand and Malta. See Janet Maslin, "A Lot of Demolition with a Female Pirate," *New York Times,* 12/22/95, p. B1.

2. Indeed, there are some grounds to suspect that the popularity of many movies varies inversely with the proportion of language they contain. See: Terry Ilot, "Look who's talking (too much)." *Variety,* 9/9/91, p. 110. Moreover, American films also derive a special advantage as English is becoming the de facto international language—one person in seven speaks it. See: Susanna McBee, "English: Out to Conquer the World," *U.S. News & World Report,* 2/18/85.

3. Paul Farhi, "And the Oscar for Flop of the Year Goes to . . . ," *The Washington Post National Weekly Edition,* 1/8/96–1/14/96, p. 25.

4. Gladys D. Ganley and Oswald H. Ganley, *Global Political Fallout: The VCR's First Decade* (Cambridge, Mass.: Center for Information Policy Research—Harvard University, 1987).

5. V. I. Pudovkin, *Film Technique and Film Acting,* translated by I. Montague (New York: Evergreen Press, 1970), p. 100.

6. Gregory Currie, "The Long Goodbye: The Imaginary Language of Film," *British Journal of Aesthetics,* 33, 3, July 1993, pp. 207–218.

7. See, for example, Raymond Spottiswoode, *A Grammar of the Film: Basic Film Techniques* (London, 1935).

8. Noël Carroll, "Toward a Theory of Film Editing," *Millennium Film Journal,* no. 3, Winter/Spring 1979, pp. 79–99; Currie, pp. 217–218.

9. Umberto Eco, "On the Contribution of Film to Semiotics," in *Film Theory and Criticism,* edited by Gerald Mast and Marshall, second edition (New York: Oxford University Press, 1979), p. 232.

10. Ibid., p. 230.

11. Julian Hochberg and Virginia Brooks, "Pictorial Recognition as an Unlearned Ability," *American Journal of Psychology,* 75, 1962, pp. 624–628.

12. John M. Kennedy, *A Psychology of Picture Perception* (San Francisco: Jossey-Bass Publishers, 1974), p. 56.

13. Fred Dretske, *Explaining Behavior: Reasons in a World of Causes* (Cambridge, Mass.: MIT Press, 1988), p. 153.

14. Reported in E. H. Hess, "Ethology and Developmental Psychology," in *Carmichael's Manual of Child Psychology,* edited by P. Mussen (New York: Wiley, 1970).

15. Susan Feagin, "Paintings and their Places," *Australasian Journal of Philosophy,* vol. 73, no. 2 (June, 1995), p. 264.

16. See, for example: Jan B. Deregowski, *Illusions, Patterns and Pictures: A Cross-Cultural Perspective* (New York: Academic Press, 1980). Some of the key empirical evidence on this subject is nicely summarized by Paul Messaris in *Visual Literacy: Image, Mind & Reality* (Boulder, Colo.: Westview Press, 1994), pp. 60–64.

17. See Gregory Currie, *Image and Mind: Film, Philosophy and Cognitive Science* (New York: Cambridge University Press, 1995), p. 80. See also, Flint Schier, *Deeper Into Pictures* (New York: Cambridge University Press, 1986).

18. William James, *Principles of Psychology* (New York: Dover Editions, 1950), vol. 1, pp. 403–404. This book was originally published in 1890.

19. This anecdote was reported, via telephone, by John Dean on the CNN program *Talkback* on December 22, 1995.

20. Quoted by James, *Principles of Psychology,* on p. 422.

21. Ibid., p. 421.

22. Ibid., p. 420.

23. Ibid., p. 423.

24. David LaBerge, *Attentional Processing: The Brain's Art of Mindfulness* (Cambridge, Mass.: Harvard University Press, 1995), p. 38.

25. This generalization does not apply equally to all genres of theater. It probably does not apply to musicals, acrobatics, and vaudeville turns for reasons that are consistent with the arguments that I have advanced above.

26. Lev Kuleshov, *Kuleshov on Film,* translated and edited by Ron Levaco (Berkeley, Calif.: University of California Press, 1974), pp. 44–50.

27. LaBerge, p. 214.

28. These statistics come from Jerry Mander, *Four Arguments for the Elimination of Television* (New York: Quill, 1974).

29. Roy Anker, James Bratt, William Romanowski, Quentin Schultze, John Worst, and Lambert Zuidervaart, *Dancing in the Dark: Youth, Popular Culture and the Electronic Media* (Grand Rapids, Mich.: William B. Eerdmans Publishing Company, 1991), p. 206.

30. Barry Salt, *Film Style and Technology: An Analysis,* second edition (London: Starwood Press, 1992), p. 263.

31. Salt, p. 283.

32. The shot lengths for recent films were supplied to me by David Bordwell.

33. See John Hora, "Cinematographers Publicly Oppose HDTV Standard: The American Society of Cinematographers' Viewpoint," *Widescreen Review,* vol. 4, no. 6, (November/December 1995), p. 98; and Robert Primes, quoted in "ASC Message to Japan," *Widescreen Review,* 4, 6 (November/December 1995), p. 22.

34. John Carey, "Conventions and Meaning in Film," in *Film Culture: Explorations of Cinema in its Social Context,* edited by Shari Thomas (Metuchen, N.J.: Scarecrow Press, 1982), pp. 110–125; Mark Crispin Miller, "Hollywood: The Ad," *The Atlantic Monthly,* April, 1990, p. 50; and Paul Messaris, *Visual Literacy,* pp. 94–96.

35. Renee Hobbs and Richard Frost, "Comprehending Transitional Editing Conventions: No Experience Necessary," a paper presented at the Seventh International Conference on Culture and Communication, Philadelphia, October 7, 1989. This paper is discussed by Paul Messaris, *Visual Literacy,* pp. 95 and 96.

36. T. W. Adorno and Max Horkheimer, "The Culture Industry: Enlightenment as Mass Deception," from their *Dialectic of Enlightenment* (New York: Continuum, 1990), p. 127.

37. Adorno and Horkheimer, p. 127.

38. In this paper, I am only discussing certain visual devices that enable filmmakers to control audience attention. But clearly this is not a comprehensive account of the ways in which filmmakers direct audience attention, since it leaves out a consideration of the directional potentials of sound recording. I believe that a story like the one I have told about film's visual structures could also be told about film's aural structures; however, given space considerations, it is not feasible to begin it here.

39. Of course, avant-garde filmmakers often attempt to complicate our attention to the film by employing scaling, bracketing, and indexing in ways that do not forward the narrative neatly. They explicitly attempt to subvert our visual, as well as our narrative, expectations. Thus, in such films, visual structures and narrative structures are not coordinated in the simple way discussed above. Consequently, the preceding generalizations should be read as qualified; they do not pertain to all films, but to the kind of commercial narrative films that most exemplify "mainstream" cinema.

40. LaBerge, p. 27.

41. Quoted in David Williams, "Shooting to Kill," *American Cinematographer,* volume 76, number 11 (November, 1995), p. 56. Zsigmond is referring to his work on the film *Assassins.*

42. LaBerge, pp. 62–63.

43. David Bordwell calls this the principle of contextual primacy. See David Bordwell, *Narration in the Fiction Film* (Madison, Wisc.: University of Wisconsin Press, 1985), p. 128.

44. Messaris, Chapter 3.

45. Messaris, p. 85.

46. Edward Branigan, *Point of View in the Cinema* (Amsterdam: Mouton Publishers, 1984), p. 103.

47. Ibid., p. 111.

48. Daniel Dayan, "The Tutor-Code of Classical Cinema," *Film Quarterly,* vol. 28, no. 1 (1974), pp. 22–31.

49. George Butterworth and Lesley Grover, "Origins of Referential Communication in Human Infancy," in *Thought Without Language*, edited by Lawrence Weiskrantz (Oxford: Oxford University Press, 1988), pp. 5–24.

50. Renee Hobbs, Richard Frost, Arthur Davis, and John Stauffer, "How First-Time Viewers Comprehend Editing Conventions," *Journal of Communication*, 38, 4 (1988), pp. 50–60.

51. Kuleshov, pp. 53–54.

52. Paul Ekman, "Expression and the Nature of Emotion," in *Approaches to Emotion*, edited by Klaus Scherer and Paul Ekman (Hillsdale, N.J.: Lawrence Erlbaum, 1984), pp. 319–343.

53. This is not to say that all the emotions portrayed by means of point-of-view editing are cross-culturally recognizable. Sometimes, the emotions may be culture-specific, making it difficult for foreigners to understand. However, insofar as much film is designed to address an international audience, it tends to traffic in the sorts of basic emotions that the above model emphasizes. Needless to say, the above model cannot be advanced, without modification, to explain the communication of culturally specific emotions.

54. In "On Style: An Interview with *Cinema*," reprinted in *Hitchcock on Hitchcock: Selected Writings and Interviews*, edited by Sidney Gottlieb (Berkeley: University of California Press), p. 292.

55. The author would like to thank David Bordwell and Sally Banes for their special help in the composition of this essay.

Chapter 3 Film, Emotion, and Genre

FILM AND AFFECT

A nasty, largish beast rushes at the camera, backed by a pounding score and crushing sound effects, and the audience flinches. The villain abuses the innocent heroine and our jaws clench in anger; our longing for revenge keeps us pinned to the screen, awaiting the moment when the loutish brute is dealt his due. The young lovers are separated by the callous vagaries of fate, or the child dies long before his time, and we weep. Or perhaps the camera pans over a vernal landscape of rolling gentle greenery and a feeling of serenity wells up in us. These are very common movie events. They bear testimony to the hardly controversial observation that, in large measure, affect is the glue that holds the audience's attention to the screen on a moment-to-moment basis.

I have said "affect" here rather than "emotion," even though it might be acceptable in ordinary language to label all the preceding examples as instances of emotional response. My reason for this way of speaking is that the ordinary notion of *emotion* can be exceedingly broad and elastic, sometimes ranging so widely as to encompass hardwired reflex reactions (like the startle response), kinesthetic turbulence, moods, sexual arousal, pleasures and desires, as well as occurrent mental states like anger, fear and sorrow.

The everyday usage of *emotion* can be rather catch-all, referring to quite a lot of heterogeneous phenomena. It is not clear—indeed, it is very unlikely—that this conception of emotion, which can be found in everyday speech, captures a natural kind, like gold; therefore, using it in a discussion of film and something called "the emotions" is likely to be a barrier to the construction of precise, theoretical generalizations. As a result, in what follows I will use the notion of *affect* where everyday speech might talk of the emotions, reserving the term *emotion* to name a narrower subclass of affect, namely, what might be even more accurately called *cognitive emotions* (i.e., affects that include cognitive elements).

By subdividing the affective life—what might be called the "life of feeling"—in this way and putting to one side many of the phenomena that comprise it, I do not mean to privilege one sort of affect over others. I would not deny that many of the affects that I am ignoring are integral to the experience of film. Through the manipulation of sound and image, filmmakers often address audiences at a subcognitive, or cognitively impenetrable, level of response. Loud noises—either recorded effects or musical sounds—can elicit instinctual responses from spectators as can the appearance of sudden movement. The movie screen is a rich phenomenal field in terms of variables like size, altitude, and speed, which have the capacity to excite automatic reactions from viewers, while the display of certain phobic and sexual material may also call forth responses barely mediated by thought. Such transactions certainly need to be studied and analyzed.[1] By hiving these affects off from the category of the emotions, I do not mean that we can neglect the cognitively impenetrable affects. I only intend, for methodological purposes, to bracket consideration of them for the time being in order to focus upon the subclass of affect that I am calling the emotions.

Though I may be departing somewhat from certain ordinary usage in this matter, since I am not leaving everyday speech altogether behind me, I hesitate to say that I am *stipulating* what shall count as an emotion. For ordinary language has broader and narrower ideas of the emotions. I am certainly eschewing the broader usages in favor of the term *affect*. However, there are narrower senses of *emotion* in everyday speech and my account stays fairly close to those.

Certain phenomena, such as fear, anger, patriotism, horror, admiration, sorrow, indignation, pity, envy, jealousy, reverence, awe, hatred, love, anxiety, shame, embarrassment, humiliation, comic amusement, and so on, are paradigms of what counts as emotion in ordinary language, even if sometimes ordinary language also stretches farther afield.[2] These garden-variety emotions are the sorts of phenomena that I will regard as emotions proper in this essay. In this, I do not think that I am doing great violence to ordinary language.

Moreover, inasmuch as these garden-variety emotions are not only paradigmatic but also exhibit common structural features, I think that I am merely pushing ordinary language in a direction toward which it already inclines, rather than stipulating a brand-new concept of the emotions. That is, by treating certain states as paradigmatically emotional, ordinary usage perhaps already regards them as composing a core class of like phenomena. In this respect, my analysis may be regarded as a rational reconstruction of some already existing intuitions rather than as the invention of a new concept that, in fact, tracks a somewhat unified field of phenomena.

In this article, I attempt to develop some generalizations about film and what might be called "emotions proper" or "core emotions" or "garden-variety emotions." This requires that I provide a characterization of the emotions that I have in mind as well as suggesting their relevance to film analysis. In the concluding section, I discuss the applicability of my approach to film and the emotions to certain genres, including melodrama, horror, and suspense.

FILM AND THE EMOTIONS

Though I do not consider film in relation to every kind of affective state, it should be clear that the affective states I intend to look at—garden-variety emotions, like anger, fear, hatred, sorrow, and so on—are central constituents of the film experience as we know it. Often it is our hatred of certain characters, like the redneck boyfriend in *Sling Blade* (1996), that keeps us riveted to the screen. Our mounting anger at his treatment of his lover and her son, along with the way he continually insults and torments the gay store manager and the retarded giant, stoke our indignation and encourage us to anticipate hope fully and vindictively his downfall and even his death. A primitive feeling for retributive justice shapes the way that we attend to *Sling Blade*, along with so many other films. That is probably why most of the time astute filmmakers wait until near the end of the film to kill their villains off. If the characters that we love to hate die too soon, there may be little left onscreen to hold our interest.

It is surprising to what extent darker emotions like anger, hatred, and revenge provide the cement that holds our attention on the popular movies we consume. But more socially acceptable emotions can do the job as well. A certain *tristesse* pervades our experience of *Letter from an Unknown Woman* (1948). And, of course, most movies elicit a gamut of garden-variety emotions over the duration of the narrative. *God Is My Witness* (1992) engenders, among other emotions, both feelings of revenge toward figures like the bandit chief, and sadness for those other central characters who have been separated from their loved ones. The pleasure that attends the conclusion of the film is a function of the desires that subtend these different emotions being finally satisfied.

The garden-variety emotions underwrite our experience of most films, especially popular movies. Undoubtedly, the degree to which our experience of movies is emotional is so extensive that we may lose sight of it. Emotion supplies such a pervasive coloration to our movie experience that it may, so to speak, fly in under the radar screen. But a little apperceptive introspection quickly reveals that throughout our viewing of a film we are generally in some emotional state or other, typically one prompted and modulated by what is on screen.

Nor is it only the case that a great deal of our experience of films is saturated with emotion; it is also that our emotional engagement constitutes, in many instances, the most intense, vivid, and sought-after qualities available in the film experience. Perhaps that is why the Dutch film psychologist Ed S. Tan subtitles his recent important book *Film as an Emotion Machine.*[3]

Clearly, then, it is crucial for a theoretical understanding of film that we attempt to analyze its relation to the emotions. But in order to do that we first need a clearer sense of what constitutes an emotion proper.

If one reflects on the states that we paradigmatically think of as emotional, one is first struck by the fact that they involve feelings—sensations of bodily changes, like muscle contractions, often attended by phenomenological qualities, such as being "uptight." Such states are very apparent with respect to violent emotional states like fear, but they can also be detected in what Hume called the calm emotions. Thus, a first, albeit reductivist conception of the emotions is that they are nothing more than bodily feelings. Moreover, this position might be bolstered by noting that in English the term *emotion* is interchangeable with the term *feeling*.

In fact, a theory very close to this was quite popular in psychology for some time. William James claimed that an emotional state was just a perception of a bodily state.[4] For James, I notice myself crying and then label the state sadness. Since C. G. Lange proposed a similar theory at roughly the same time, the view is often called the James-Lange theory of the emotions.[5]

But neither of these views—the emotion-as-bodily-feeling view nor the emotion-as-bodily-feeling-plus-perception view (the James-Lange theory)—is adequate. The problem with the first view is that it excludes cognition from the emotional complex and the problem with the James-Lange view is that, in a manner of speaking, it puts the relevant cognitive states in the wrong place. In order to explain these objections, let's indulge in a little science fiction.[6]

First, if an emotion were simply a bodily feeling, marked by certain sensations, then if a person were presently in a bodily state that resembled exactly the bodily state she was in the last time she was angry, then we should be prepared to say that she is angry now. But that doesn't sound quite right. For imagine that we have enough pharmacology at our disposal that we can induce any bodily state along with any phenomenological quality in anyone we wish. The last time our subject was angry was when she discovered that her lover was cheating on her. We can provoke the same bodily state and the same phenomenological qualia in her now that she felt back then. Suppose we do it? Shall we say that she is angry?

I suspect not. Why not? Well, the last time that she experienced this bodily state and its attendant qualia, she was angry at her lover. But that was a while ago. She no longer has a lover, and if the truth be told, she's forgotten the old one. Thus, *ex hypothesi,* there is no one for her to be angry with now. But if there is no one for her to be angry with—if there is no object to her emotional state—can she really be said to be in an emotional state?

She is in a bodily state, probably an uncomfortable and even confusing bodily state. But is she angry? No—because there is no one or no thing with whom or with which she is angry. You can't be angry, unless there is someone or something that serves as the object of your anger. Emotional states are directed. You hate Marvin or you are afraid of the smog. This is what it means to say that emotions take objects.[7]

But sheer bodily states do not take objects; they are not directed. They are internal events with no external reference. Thus, the subject of our science fiction experiment is not in an emotional state. For her disturbed visceral state is not directed, nor does it have an object. Therefore, the view that emotions are simply bodily states cum some phenomenological qualia is wrong. Emotions may always involve bodily states and phenomenological qualia. However, something must be added to the mix if the state is to count as a full-fledged emotion.

What has to be added? Something that functions to connect the relevant bodily states and phenomenological qualia to some object. When I am angry at my lover for betraying me, I am racked by inner bodily turmoil. What is the bridge between that inner turmoil and my lover? Presumably, it is some cognition that I have about my lover. That is, I either believe or imagine that my lover has betrayed me. Of course, I can be mistaken in this. But in order to be angry with my lover in this case, I must believe or imagine that my lover has done me wrong *and* that cognitive state must be the cause of the inner consternation that buffets me. Together the cognitive state in causal conjunction with the bodily state and its phenomenological qualia comprise the emotional state of anger. This state can take objects and be directed—can have intentionality—because the cognitive states that are necessary constituents of the overall emotional states possess intentionality.

Emotions cannot simply be bodily feelings, since sheer bodily feelings lack intentionality. But if cognitions are necessary constituents of emotional states, this lacuna disappears. Thus, if adding cognition to bodily feeling is the right way to solve the preceding problem, then the reductivist theory that emotions are just bodily feelings is false, since emotions also require cognitive components (either beliefs or belief-like states such as thoughts and imaginings). This gets rid of the emotion-as-bodily-feeling view. But what about the James-Lange theory?

According to the James-Lange theory, emotions have a cognitive component. My brother is hit by a car; I choke up and I weep; I perceive these bodily changes and I interpret or cognize them as sadness. Here, the bodily state causes the relevant cognitive state. But the causal order seems backwards. The cognitive state appears epiphenomenal.

Undeniably, there are some occasions where a loud noise, say a firecracker, makes us frightened and where upon reflection we say, "I guess that really frightened me." But this is not paradigmatic of garden-variety emotional states. When I am jealous of a rival, that is *because* I believe that he is stealing affection that belongs to me; it is not because I observe myself overwhelmed by the phenomenology of the green-eyed monster and surmise that I must be jealous. To return to our science-fiction example once again, one can imagine pharmacologically counterfeiting the sensations of my last episode of jealous rage where it makes no sense to say that I am jealous now—perhaps because I have become a spiritual adept who has successfully renounced all earthly attachments.

Thus, our thought-experiment suggests that what we are calling emotions proper at least involve both cognitions and feeling states where the two are linked inasmuch as the former cause the latter.[8] In this account, certain affects—like the churning stomach sensations that viewers reported resulted from watching the car chases in *Bullitt*—are not examples of emotions proper.

Emotions proper require a cognitive component. Admittedly, not all of the affects that are important to the analysis of cinema fall into this category. What might be called cognitively impenetrable affects—like the startle response—don't. Nevertheless, a great many of the affects experienced in response to film are of the nature of emotions proper. To get a handle on them, we must now say a little more about the way in which the cognitive component in these emotions operates.

I am angry at Leslie because he is telling everyone that I failed my first driving test. I told this to Leslie in strictest confidence, but Leslie has broadcast this all around the neighborhood. When I learn and come to believe that Leslie has divulged my secret, my blood pressure skyrockets and I feel hot under the collar. My cognitive state, in other words, causes a spate of bodily disruption. How does this come about?

Notice that though in this case my anger is caused by Leslie's indiscretion, indiscretion is not the only thing that can function to elicit a comparable emotional response. If someone smashed my car or ruined my print of *The General,* I might also find myself in an angry state, if I believed that these things were done to me wantonly or inexcusably. That is, I will be angry where I subsume the events in question under the rubric of wrongs done to me or mine and where that formation of that belief functions in provoking some bodily disturbance in me. Cognitions, in other words, play not only a causal role in emotions in that they figure in the etiology of bodily alterations; they also play a role in identifying what emotional state we are in when we are in one. My response to Leslie is anger because I have subsumed or assessed Leslie's indiscretion under the category of a wrong done to me or mine, and forming that belief has caused the pertinent bodily upset.

What this example suggests is that emotional states, like anger, are governed cognitively by criteria of appropriateness. Where the cognitions in a given emotional state come about through the subsumption of a person or event under the category of wrongs done to me or mine, the emotional response is apt to be anger. Moreover, other emotional states are also like this. The harmful or the dangerous is the criterion (or the category appropriate to) fear; thus when I subsume the object of my state under the category of the harmful, I am, other things being equal, apt to undergo fear. That is to say, for example: I cognize the scorpion next to my hand under the harmful, that cognition causes my blood to freeze, and the overall state is fear.

Similarly, in order for me to feel pity for *x,* I must believe that *x* has suffered some misfortune; the criterion for pity, in other words, is misfortune, just as in order to envy y I must believe that y has something that I have not. If y cannot move and I know this, then I cannot envy y's athletic prowess. For in order to envy y I must be able to form the belief that y possesses some advantage that I lack, or some degree of advantage over and above what I take myself to command. Envying y signals that I have subsumed y under the category of someone who possesses more than I do.

Emotions require cognitions as causes and bodily states as effects. Moreover, among the cognitions that are essential for the formation of emotional states are those that subsume the objects of the state under certain relevant categories or conceive of said objects as meeting certain criteria. In fear, the object must meet the criterion of being harmful or, at least, of being perceived to be harmful. Anger requires that the object be perceived as meeting the criterion that it has wronged me or mine.

What "criterion" means above, functionally speaking, is that in order to be an appropriate object of the emotion in question, the relevant object must meet certain necessary conditions, or, alternatively, must be thought to be subsumable under certain essentially defined categories. For x to be the object of pity, x must be thought to meet the necessary criterion of having suffered some misfortune; for y to be the object of my envy, I must cognize y as at least meeting the necessary condition of possessing something I lack (indeed, generally something that I lack that I would prefer to have, if only upon learning that y has it).

Thus, when we speak of emotions as requiring cognitions, the cognitions that we have in mind—first and foremost—involve subsuming the objects of the emotion under certain categories or, alternatively, perceiving that the object meets certain criteria of appropriateness (harmfulness, for example, in the case of fear; wrongfulness in the case of anger).

Of course, this is not the whole story of what it is to be in an emotional state. Emotional states are temporal affairs; they endure over time intervals; they are episodes. When we detect the object of our emotional state and the relevant cognitions ensue, our perception becomes emotionally charged. It casts the cause or the object of our state in a special phenomenological light; it fixes our attention upon it and alerts us to its significance (e.g., x is dangerous).

The emotions gestalt or organize perception. They call our attention to those aspects of the situation that are pertinent by selectively guiding perception to the features of the stimulus that are subsumable under the criteria of the reigning emotional state.

There is also a feedback mechanism in operation here. Once in an emotional state, the prevailing state further structures our perception by drawing our attention to further elements in the array that are pertinent to sustaining the emotional state that we are in. Alerted by fear to the potential that there is someone or something prowling around our campsite, we scope out the scene in search of further signs of threat which, if found, reinforce both the state we are in and its related feedback processes. In this way, the emotions manage attention over time. The form that this perceptual management takes is to focus our attention upon those elements in a situation that are relevant to (that mesh with the criteria that govern) the presiding emotional state (e.g., dangers with respect to fear; slights with respect to anger).

The emotions can be analogized to searchlights. They direct attention, enabling us to organize the details before us into significant wholes or gestalts. Where the emotional state is one of fear, we scan it for details highlighted as dangerous; where the state is pity, it battens on elements subsumable under the category of misfortune. The emotions foreground such relevant details in what might be called a special phenomenological glow.

Furthermore, once we are in the grip of a given emotional state, we not only stay fixed upon the details it has selected out in the first instance; we scan the array for more details with a similar pertinence to our initial emotional assessment of the situation. The emotions manage our attention, guiding both what we look at and what we look for. Moreover, that process of attention management undergoes changes of adjustment. First our emotions alert us to certain gestalts (whose structure of inclusion and exclusion is governed by the criteria relevant to the ruling emotional state), and then the presiding emotion encourages further elaboration of our attention, prompting us to form expectations about the kinds of things that we should watch for as the situation evolves (where the pertinent kinds of things are those that fall into the categories that criterially determine our prevailing emotional state).

So far we have been talking about the emotions and their relation to perception in a pretty abstract way. How applicable is any of this to film viewing?[9] Can this abstract characterization of the emotions tell us anything about the relation of the garden-variety emotions to standard fictional films? I think it can, although in order to see how we must take note of one very large and obvious difference between the activation of emotional responses with respect to events in everyday life versus events in narrative film fictions.[10]

In life, in contrast to fiction, our emotions have to select out the relevant details from a massive array of largely unstructured stimuli. We are sitting in a room reading the newspaper. We hear sirens nearby, alerting us to potential danger. An incipient sense of fear prompts us to rise and to go to the window to search for indications of danger. We smell smoke. Warily, we look down to see if it is coming from our apartment building. If it is, we rush to the hallway in order to see if the flames of the fire have reached our floor. Our mounting sense of fear, in other words, shapes our perceptual itinerary. It organizes the situation for us in a way pertinent to action, which, in this case, all things considered, will probably eventuate in flight.

But with respect to fiction, things stand differently. The emotions are not called upon to organize situations de novo. To a much greater extent than in everyday life, situations in fiction films have already been structured for us by filmmakers. We do not usually rely upon the emotions to organize fictional film events for us as much as we rely upon the emotions to perform this task for us in ordinary life because, in the main, fiction film events have been emotionally predigested for us by filmmakers. That is, the filmmakers have already done much of the work of emotionally organizing scenes and sequences for us through the ways in which the filmmakers have foregrounded what features of the events in the film are salient. In contrast to the way that emotions focus attention for us in everyday life, when it comes to films the relevant events have already generally been prefocused emotively for us by the filmmakers. The filmmakers have selected out the details of the scene or sequence that they think are emotively significant and thrust them, so to speak, in our faces. The means that the filmmakers have to secure this end include camera position and composition, editing, lighting, the use of color, and, of course, acting and the very structure of the script or narrative.[11]

Very frequently in everyday life, when an acquaintance or colleague slights us—perhaps by a passing remark—we are not immediately angry, even if we are hurt, because we may wonder whether the insult was an intentional wrong rather than merely carelessness. But as such remarks recur, anger takes hold and we come to recognize a discernible pattern of nastiness directed at us. In typical fictional films, on the other hand, we rarely have to waver so long. So often, characters wear the meanness of their actions on their sleeve and, if that were not enough, we also have access to the disapproving judgments of the people around them. We not only have a pretty unmistakable gestalt of wrongness thrust in bold relief before us, but we also have the reaction of surrounding characters to reflect and to reinforce our assessments of the situation.

Thus, it is hard not to respond (initially) with anger to the father in *Shine* (1996) when he refuses to allow his son to accept various scholarships. Generally in fiction films, that is, the detection work that our emotions need to do for us is somewhat minimized because the scenes and characters in such films have very frequently already been made or designed from, so to speak, the point of view of anger to begin with; or, to say it differently, they have been emotively prefocused or predigested for us.[12]

But how is it possible for a character, a scene, or a sequence to be emotively prefocused? Here it is useful to advert to the general picture of the emotions that we developed previously. The emotions, we argued, are governed by criteria of appropriateness. To be angered, the object of our emotional state must be perceived as a wrong done to me or mine. I was angry with Leslie because I regarded his gossip as a wrong done to me. Likewise, if I am angry with a broker because I believe he has squandered my mother's savings, it is because I perceive it as a wrong done to mine (where mine can extend to friends, countrymen, and anyone else, including a fictional character, to whom I bear a pro attitude).

But just as emotions must meet certain criteria of appropriateness in everyday life, so must emotions in response to fictions be governed by criteria of appropriateness. Thus, a film text can be emotively prefocused by being *criterially prefocused*—that is, by being so structured that the descriptions and depictions of the object of our attention in the text will activate our subsumption of the relevant characters and events under the categories that are criterially apposite to the emotional state in question.

Once we recognize the object under the criterially relevant categories—like the harmful for fear or the wrongful for anger—the relevant emotion is apt (under certain conditions to be discussed shortly) to be raised in us. That is, as a result of entertaining the appropriate cognitions, we will be likely to undergo some physical changes: with comic amusement, ideally, we laugh; as we will see in the next section, with horror films our skin may crawl; with suspense films, we tense up; and with melodramas, we may shed a tear.

As well, our attention becomes emotively charged. Our emotional states fix our attention and illuminate it in a special phenomenological glow. Our attention is glued to those features of the object of the emotion that are appropriate to the emotional state we are in. Our emotional state prompts us to survey the event for further features that may support or sustain the presiding emotional state in which we find ourselves. And, protentively, our emotionally charged state shapes our anticipation of what is to come by priming us to be on the watch for the emergence of further details that are also subsumable under the categories of the dominant emotional state—our anger at a character in the first scene alerts us to be on the lookout for more churlishness from him in later scenes. Or, in summary, a criterially prefocused film text gives rise, in the right circumstances, to *emotive focus* in the audience, where by "emotive focus" I am referring both to the way in which the emotional state of the viewer fixes *and* then shapes her attention.

Central, then, to a theoretical understanding of the relation of the garden-variety emotions to film are the notions of the *criterially prefocused film text* in relation to the *emotive focus* of the audience. On our account so far, a criterially prefocused film text is a standard condition for securing emotive focus. However, it should be obvious that merely presenting viewers with criterially prefocused film texts, no matter how well designed, does not guarantee that spectators will respond emotionally. A criterially prefocused film can be viewed dispassionately. What makes for a passionate response? The notion of a criterially prefocused film text needs to be supplemented, if we hope to propose a theoretical model of the arousal of garden-variety emotions by narrative fiction films.

I hypothesize that what that supplement comes to is a concern or a pro attitude on the part of the viewer with respect to the way in which the depicted situation in the fiction is or is not going. That is, in addition to being criterially prefocused, the narrative must invest the viewer with certain concerns about the fictional characters and events (and their prospects) in the film. These concerns or pro attitudes function like the desires that are found in many everyday emotions, and when added to the mental content or conception of the object, derived from the criterially prefocused text, the combination, all things being equal, should elicit an emotional response (including emotive focus) from viewers in accordance with the criterial features of the film text that the filmmakers have made salient.

The structure of our emotional involvement with narrative fiction films, then, typically comprises a criterially prefocused film text plus certain concerns or pro attitudes, and together, in the standard case, these are apt to elicit broadly predictable responses (including emotive focus) in standard audiences (which, by stipulation, bars sociopaths). The criterially prefocused film text embodies a conception of a situation from an emotively relevant point of view. But a conception of a situation may not alone be sufficient to motivate an emotional response, if the audience is otherwise indifferent to what is going on. To prompt an emotional response and to secure emotive focus require that the audience be engaged by concerns—certain pro and con attitudes—about what is going on in the story.

This hypothesis presupposes that film narratives can enlist audiences in preferences about the way in which a story might go. This assumption should not be problematic. *Potemkin* (1925) enlists a pro attitude in the audience toward the crew of the battle cruiser which leads them to prefer that the fleet not destroy them. In *High Noon* (1952), the intended audience prefers that the sheriff survive. This is not to say that films always defer to the preferences that they engender in audiences. With *You Only Live Once* (1937), we may prefer that Eddie (Henry Fonda) escape, but he doesn't. Nevertheless, the special emotional *frisson* that attends the end of this film is a function of the fact that the filmmakers encouraged viewers to form a pro attitude toward another outcome.

Typically, narrative fiction films develop in such a way that spectators have a structured horizon of expectations about what might and what might not happen. And in addition to a sense of the possible outcomes of the ongoing courses of events, one also, generally under the guidance of the filmmakers, has convictions about what outcomes one would, in a certain sense, prefer to obtain in the world of the fiction versus those she would prefer not to obtain. In some cases, the preferred course of events correlates with the express goals and plans of the protagonists of the story; what they want to happen—say, delivering lifesaving medical supplies—is what the audience wants to happen. However, in a great many other cases, the film may proffer preferred outcomes independently of the express goals and plans of any of the characters. That is, the film may have its own agenda, as in the cases of all those fictional lovers who never wanted to fall in love in the first place.

But however motivated, audiences evolve concerns regarding the situations portrayed in films, and when those concerns are threatened, we tend to react with dysphoric (or discomforting) emotions, whereas when the concern in question is abetted by narrative developments, our emotions tend to be euphoric.[13] Which particular dysphoric or euphoric emotion is engaged, of course, depends upon the way that the film text is criterially prefocused. For example, considering some dysphoric emotions, if a character toward whom I bear a pro attitude is wronged—as when the character Zane, played by Charlie Sheen, in *The Arrival* (1996) is fired—in such a way that the injustice of the event is made criterially salient, then, all things being equal, I will feel anger; whereas if presented with the criterially prefocused misfortune of a group that has elicited my concern—say the victims in a disaster movie—then I am apt to feel pity for them.

Similarly, euphoric emotions of different sorts are also likely to evolve in accordance with the way in which the film text is criterially prefocused in those cases where our concerns or desires about the direction of the relevant courses of events are satisfied. When a character toward whom we bear a pro attitude overcomes obstacles, saliently posed in the film—as when the sheriff finally defeats the shark in *Jaws* (1975)—then we are likely to respond with admiration; whereas the manifestation of virtually limitless power by an agency of which we approve—for instance, nature or a god—will tend to evoke reverence.

My proposal, then, for analyzing our emotional response to fiction films is that a criterially prefocused film text is apt to elicit an emotional response from audiences where the audiences are encouraged to adopt pro attitudes to certain developments in the story. Where story developments mesh with those preferences, the response is likely to be euphoric; where they clash, the emotional response is apt to be dysphoric. Moreover, the emotional response involves engendering emotive focus in the audience and this emotive focus guides our reception of ongoing and anticipated screen events on a moment-to-moment basis.

Furthermore, if this hypothesis about our emotional involvement with fiction films is roughly correct, it suggests a certain direction for cinema research. To analyze the way in which a film arouses an emotional response from viewers, one needs to first determine the way in which the film or film segment is criterially prefocused. Here the critic, using herself as a detector, begins by noting the emotion the film has elicited in her. Perhaps she feels a global sense of pity. Next, using the criteria of the emotion in question as a hypothesis, she can review the way in which the filmic material is articulated in order to isolate the pertinent depictions or descriptions in the film that instantiate the concept or meet the criteria of the pertinent emotion.

Additionally, she will want to determine which features of the film are designed to engender pro attitudes in viewers, along with determining what those pro attitudes are. By following this procedure, one can pith the emotive structure of the film.

To "pith the emotive structure of the film" here means finding the aspects of the depictions or descriptions of the object of the emotion that satisfy the necessary criteria for being in whatever emotional state the audience is in. This is what explaining the emotional state of the audience generally amounts to (along with identifying the depictions or descriptions that give rise to the concerns and preferences the audience is meant to bear to developments in the narrative).

Of course, this order of research may not always be practicable. In some cases, the analyst may not be able to identify with precision his or her emotional response to a film or film segment. In that event, the analyst is better advised to take up the salient depictions or description in the text with an interest in seeing what they foreground. Then, after evolving some hypotheses or questions in this regard, the analyst can compare what the film has foregrounded with the criteria for the better-known emotional states. This may lead to a clarification of the emotional address of the film or film segment under examination.

Needless to say, the emotional address of some films may be designedly ambiguous, while other films may introduce novel emotional timbres. But even in these cases the methodology that I am recommending is still somewhat serviceable, since it will enable us systematically to get a rough sense of the general contours of the emotional ambiguities and novel emotional timbres of the films in question.

Undoubtedly, often when we are watching films that are remote from us in time and place, we will not be able to depend on our own emotional responses to the film because we do not have the appropriate cultural background. This is exactly where film history and the ethnographic study of film have an indispensable role to play. Film historians and ethnographers can supply us with the background necessary to make the emotive address of films from other cultures and other periods in our own culture emotionally accessible to us.

EMOTION AND GENRE

The framework for analyzing the relation of film and the emotions advanced above is general in the sense that it is supposed to be useful for analyzing responses to characters, sequences, scenes, and whole films. A great deal of our experience of film viewing is attended by garden-variety emotions in response to many different units of film articulation, ranging from single gestures and looks to the sorts of chase sequences that can last for half the length of a film. Attempting to illustrate the feasibility of the preceding method for every kind of case would require more detail than an essay allows. But perhaps empirical credibility for my theoretical proposals can be derived by illustrating what these hypotheses might facilitate with respect to the analysis of certain genres.

As I have said, emotion is engaged on a moment-to-moment basis throughout much (if not most) of our experiences of film. We track much of the unfolding action in films via what I have called emotive focus. My theory is intended to be instructive in analyzing virtually every instance of our emotional engagement and emotive tracking of cinema. However, there are certain dimensions of cinematic articulation, notably genre films of various sorts, where emotive address is particularly pronounced and obvious. Thus, at the very least, my theory should have something informative to contribute to the study of the relevant genres.

Some genres seem to traffic in certain specifiable emotions essentially. That is, certain genres appear to have as their abiding point the elicitation of specifiable emotional states in audiences. For example, Aristotle thought that the arousal of pity and fear was an essential feature of Greek tragedy.

Of course, all popular film genres engage emotions, generally a range of emotions. However, some genres appear dedicated to raising particular, predetermined emotional states in audiences just as Aristotle thought that Greek tragedy was predicated upon provoking pity and fear. That is, whereas all genres tend to evoke anger, joy, hatred, and the like, in addition to these emotions some genres also aim at arousing specific emotions in spectators as a condition of being an instance of the very genre in question. Or, to put it differently, raising various preordained emotions in spectators is the *sine qua non* of certain film genres. In these cases, the genres in question aim at the production of a particular emotion whose tincture colors the film as a whole.

Sometimes these genres are named by the very emotion it is their purpose to arouse. Suspense and horror are examples here. Moreover, other genres, like melodrama, though they are not named by the emotion whose point it would appear they are predicated upon provoking, nevertheless aim at arousing a roughly specifiable, preordained emotional response from spectators. This emotional response is dominant in the sense that it lends its aura to the film as a whole.

Suspense, horror, and melodrama, then, are three genres where films count as instances of the relevant genre only if they are dedicated to eliciting certain specifiable kinds of emotions from spectators. If my theory is to be even minimally convincing, it should have something to say about genres like these. Thus, for the remainder of this article, let me quickly review some of the applications of my theory to these genres.

Melodrama

The first step in applying our theoretical framework to a genre is to identify the dominating emotion that the genre aims to instill in audiences.[14] The term *melodrama* is perhaps an unwieldy one, and it may be difficult to isolate a single package of emotions that applies to everything that someone might be willing to classify under this notion. However, there is a relatively clear class of melodramas, often called "tearjerkers," that take as their subject matter what are loosely called "interpersonal relationships" and that appear to call forth certain massively recurring emotional responses. Three examples are *An Affair to Remember* (1957), *Back Street* (1932), and *Stella Dallas* (1937).

The fact that melodramas like these are often referred to as *tearjerkers* gives us an initial clue concerning their emotive domain. It should be something, all things being equal, that should warrant crying. Of course, crying can be elicited by many stimuli and can accompany many emotional states. Two such related states are sorrow and pity. Moreover, it should come as no surprise to the informed viewer that pity is the relevant tear-producing state that comes into play in the vast majority of melodramas.

Pity, of course, requires as a criterion of emotive appropriateness that its object be persons—we do not pity snowstorms—who have suffered misfortune. Thus, we expect from such melodramas that they be saliently comprised of misfortunes *suffered* by the protagonists.

I emphasize suffering here because the protagonists must feel the pain of their circumstances. Indeed, part of their misfortune is the pain that they feel as a result of their circumstances. Moreover, this misfortune—including the pain that, in part, comprises it—should not be seen as a matter of just desserts. We do not usually feel pity for villains who deserve to be annihilated. Melodramatic pity involves bad things happening to good people, or, at least, disproportionately bad things happening to people of mixed character.

It seems to me that the melodramatic emotion is not merely pity in the typical case of film melodrama. The standard film melodrama is not just a study in victimology. As already indicated, the ill-fortuned characters we weep for in many melodramas are of a certain sort. They are not victims pure and simple. They are people whom we admire; indeed, often we admire them for the way in which they negotiate their misfortune.

One important, recurring motif here is that the victim of melodramatic misfortune often accepts her suffering in order to benefit another, often at the expense of satisfying her own personal desires and interests. Sometimes, in fact, the character's misfortune is a result of the sacrifices she has made on behalf of others. For example, Stella Dallas's (Barbara Stanwyck) misfortune is the loss of her daughter, though she, in fact, has herself engineered this state of affairs on the basis of her belief that this will guarantee her daughter the best possible life.

Thus, we do not merely pity Stella Dallas. We admire her as well. The emotion that wells up in us as she watches her daughter's wedding from afar is not merely a result of pity, but is compounded of admiration as well. Often such emotions are called bittersweet. Perhaps the part that is pity is bitter (or dysphoric), but the part that we feel in response to Stella's noble self-sacrifice is sweet (or euphoric). To attempt to reduce our emotional states in cases like this to pity alone ignores the euphoric component in the response. We don't just feel bad about Stella, we feel good about her, too. That is because the dominating emotional response to the typical melodrama involves admiration—often motivated by a display of self-sacrifice—in addition to pity.

Were melodrama only a matter of pity—of witnessing horrible things happen to people—it might strike us as a particularly sadistic genre. It does not, I think, because typically the misfortunes in melodramas also provide the occasion for characters to exhibit noble virtues amid adversity, encouraging the spectator to leaven pity with admiration. A film of suffering unrelieved by virtue would be more likely an exercise in avant-garde realism than a melodrama. Melodramas are not all dark from the perspective of our emotional responses. Triumph is blended with tribulation so that pity comes in tandem with admiration.

In *An Affair to Remember* the female protagonist, Terry (Deborah Kerr), is struck down by a car on her way to a long-awaited rendezvous with her lover Nicky (Cary Grant). Their meeting, atop the Empire State Building, is supposed to symbolize their commitment to each other. Terry fails to make the appointment because of her accident. Terry's old boyfriend (Richard Denning) wants to tell Nicky what has happened, but Terry won't allow him. She feels that if Nicky learns that she has become disabled, his reaction will be pity, not love. Her silence is, in other words, principled. She does not want to take advantage of Nicky's sense of obligation. We may feel that Terry's course of action is ill-advised. But we admire her for her principles at the same time we pity her. Meanwhile, Nicky is becoming more and more embittered.

Perhaps the most emotionally wrought scene in the film comes at the end. Nicky still does not realize that Terry is disabled. He visits her apartment to deliver a shawl to her that his grandmother has bequeathed to Terry. He is still very hurt and angry. But just as he is about to leave, he realizes that Terry is disabled, that that's the reason why she missed their rendezvous, and, we presume, he also realizes that she didn't inform him because of a self-sacrificing desire to "protect him."

None of this is said. The audience infers that this is what is going on in Nicky's mind. Compactly, in a few seconds of screen time, this device encourages the audience to review the whole saga of Terry's adversity and nobility, jerking tears from man and woman alike. (I'm sniffling even as I write—and I don't have a cold.)

Similar scenes of recognition and acknowledgment are frequent in melodramas. The most moving scene in *Back Street* (1932), I think, occurs when the son learns of the sacrifices his father's mistress made in order to sustain their relationship, while in *What's Eating Gilbert Grape?* (1993) the "viking funeral" of Gilbert's mother stands as a commemoration to her ultimate maternal integrity, despite all her other limitations. As in the case of *An Affair to Remember,* recognition/acknowledgment scenes like these serve to remind the audience not only of the bad things that have befallen the protagonists, but of their virtues as well. Pity attaches to the misfortunes, while admiration attaches to the virtues.

Even the ending of *Letter from an Unknown Woman* concludes on a note of admiration. Once the pianist learns of the self-sacrificing love of the unknown woman, he no longer acts the cad; he rides off to a doomed duel, shedding his selfishness and recognizing that, since the best thing in his life has just passed away, the only appropriate action is to join her in death. We pity their demise, but admire their willingness to die for their love.

Melodrama, then, frequently is rooted in engendering a compound emotion, comprising pity and admiration. The depictions and descriptions in a film like *An Affair to Remember* are criterially prefocused by making, on the one hand, misfortune, and, on the other hand, character virtues—especially self-sacrifice—salient to the audience. This, in turn, prompts spectators to be moved to feel pity and admiration, at least in cases where the audience has a pro attitude toward the characters. In *An Affair to Remember,* this is secured by portraying Terry and Nicky not only as very attractive and desirable people, but by establishing them to be persons of superior wit and culture (this is done especially in the voyage section of the film).

Once this pro attitude is in place, misfortune strikes, encouraging us to pity them, especially Terry, while at the same time providing a dramatic forum for Terry to exhibit her self-sacrificing nobility (finally to be joined by Nicky's when his recognition of that nobility leads him to love her all the more).

Horror

Like melodramas of the tearjerking variety, horror films are also designed to elicit a compound emotion.[15] And also like the tearjerker, one of the constituents of this emotional response is pretty evident. If melodramatic tearjerkers can be said uncontroversially to be aimed at eliciting pity from spectators, little argument seems required to establish that horror films are designed to provoke fear. Harmfulness, of course, is the criterion for fear. Thus, the depictions and descriptions in horror films are criterially prefocused to make the prospects for harm salient in the world of the fiction. The relevant harms here take the form of threats—generally lethal threats—to the protagonists in the horror film, and the locus of these threats is standardly a monster, an entity of supernatural or sci-fi provenance whose very existence defies the bounds of contemporary scientific understanding.

These monsters possess powers or propensities that make them threatening to human life. Most often, they are also hostile to the human protagonists in the relevant films. Usually they are bent on destroying or enslaving the humans. Moreover, they have certain capacities or advantages—such as great strength, cunning, indomitable technologies, supernatural abilities, or even invisibility—that are not easily deterred. This makes them particularly dangerous and fearsome. Here the fear that the audience emotes with regard to the monster is not fear for its own survival. Our fear is engendered in behalf of the human characters in the pertinent films. We cringe when the Werewolf of London stalks his prey, not because we fear that he will trap us, but because we fear for some character in the film. When the outsized arachnid in *Earth vs. the Spider* (1958) awakens to the beat of rock 'n roll music, we fear for the teenagers, not for ourselves.

But though fear is a necessary condition for horror, it is not sufficient. Many films conjure up fear on the basis of scientific improbabilities without counting as horror films. Examples include time travel films where merciless fascists from the future are arriving in the here and now to gain a foothold, or *When Worlds Collide* (1951). Fear, in short, is not the whole of horror, just as pity is not the whole of melodrama.

Though fearful, our emotive response to the oncoming planet in *When Worlds Collide* is different from our reaction to the monster in *Species* (1995), *Xtro* (1983), or *The Relic* (1997). For we not only find those latter entities fearsome, they are also disgusting. Were a part of their anatomy to find its way into our mouth, like the tentacles of so many slimy aliens, we would want to gag and to spit it out.[16] The thought of ingesting a piece of such creatures invites nausea. If we touched one of them, we would try to scrub our hands clean at the soonest opportunity. Think of the zombies in *Night of the Living Dead* (1968), or the giant, dribbling snails in *The Monster that Challenged the World* (1957).

We find the monsters in horror films repulsive and abhorrent. They are not only fearsome, they are somehow unclean, reviling, and loathsome by their very nature. Vampires, for example, are frequently associated with vermin and disease.

Monsters generally fall into the category that the Bible calls abominations. Even if such monsters were not dangerous, their very being is such that we would wish to avoid them and to refrain from touching them. The very thought of them is repelling—enough to make our flesh crawl, our spine tingle, and our throat choke shut. The most suitable expletives for them are "Ugh" and "Yuck!"

Thus, the objects that comprise the objects of our emotional response in horror films elicit a compound reaction in terms of fear and disgust. The fear component of our response is grounded in the fact that in the world of the fiction these monsters constitute clear and present dangers. They are harmful. But they are also disgusting, and the emotive criterion for disgust is impurity. Thus, the depictions and descriptions in horror films are criterially prefocused in terms of foregrounding the harmfulness *and* the impurity of the monsters.

The harmfulness of the monsters is usually exhibited readily in their behavior. They are killing people, eating them, dismembering them, or taking possession of either their minds or their souls. But in addition to their evident harmfulness, horror-film monsters are also impure. Their impurity, in turn, can be manifested by means of several generally recurring strategies, usually involving the violation of standing cultural categories in various ways.

For example, horror-film monsters may be categorically hybrid, mixing different biological or ontological orders. The creature in *The Relic* blends various species, being part reptile, part human, and part (?) water buffalo. As the very title of the film signals, the zombies in *Night of the Living Dead* appear to be members of an ontologically self-contradictory set of things—creatures that are both living *and* dead at the same time. Many horror-film monsters violate defining characteristics of the categories they supposedly belong to. The giant spider alluded to earlier is at least a thousand times bigger than the largest possible spider.

Moreover, many horrific monsters are incomplete examples of their category—they are so often missing parts like arms, legs, eyes, and even heads. Or sometimes they are heads or just brains without bodies. And last, some horrific beings are altogether so formless that it would be hard to assign them to any category. The Blob is formless throughout the film of the same name. But, of course, many horrific creatures, like vampires, can assume formlessness at will or start out formless before they take over someone else's body.

The monster in *From Beyond* (1986) is designed in such a way that it exploits a number of these strategies for projecting horrific impurity. Edward Praetorius (Ted Sorel) has developed a machine whose sonic vibrations give him access to another dimension inhabited by noxious, ill-tempered creatures that resemble lampreys. During his first penetration of this alternative dimension, his head is bitten off. The police assume he is dead and they arrest his assistant as a suspect. Encouraged by a psychiatrist to work through his trauma, the assistant restages

Praetorius's experiment. As the alternative dimension becomes manifest, it turns out that Praetorius is not dead. He has gone over to live on the other side.

However, as is par for the course in mad-scientist movies, all is not well with Praetorius. His mind has melded with that of some other-dimensional being. He is evolving into a new kind of hybrid or composite entity. On Praetorius's second manifestation, much of his human body has disappeared into a mass of tissue. He is half a face attached to a gelatinous, decomposing mound of flesh. Not only is he mostly amorphous, but he can dissolve at will into oozing goo. Part of his horrific signature is his ability to go in and out of formlessness, formlessness of a sort that is all the more sickening for being sticky and saliva-like.

Praetorius cannot merely transform himself from bodily articulateness to formlessness, he can also take on parts of different genera. So the sucker of a giant leech can burst through his human forehead. Thus, in addition to exploiting the line between form and formlessness, Praetorius is also a categorically hybrid creature—sometimes displaying parts of several species simultaneously and sometimes changing from one kind of creature into another sequentially.

The categorical distinction between inside and outside is also contradicted and breached in Praetorius's biology; his extended pineal gland waves about externally like an antenna. Sometimes Praetorius has one arm, sometimes two. In addition to all his other problems, then, he is also at times categorically incomplete.

The creature Praetorius has been designed by the filmmakers of *From Beyond* as if in an attempt to touch all the bases when it comes to horrific impurity. There is something to disgust virtually everyone in Praetorius's makeup (both biological and dramaturgical).

And, perhaps needless to say, Praetorius is also quite dangerous. Like so many other mad scientists he, in concert with other-dimensional creatures who also inhabit his body, take it into his (their?) head(s?) to conquer the world. His great intelligence, amplified by his experience of other dimensions, poses a great threat to humanity as does his superhuman strength and telekinetic prowess. He represents the greatest potential harm humanity has ever known, so the film avows, and the portal he has opened to the other world must be closed.

Looking at a horror film like *From Beyond* from an analytic point of view requires dissecting, so to say, the way in which the monster has been designed to engender a horrified emotional response from audiences. One proceeds by noting how the monster has been composed and set into action in accordance to the criteria appropriate to the emotion of horror. In *From Beyond*, Praetorius's attributes rehearse the themes of impurity and danger in many dimensions. By saliently posing these criterially prefocused attributes, the filmmakers encourage the audience to subsume or to assess them under the categories of the impure and the harmful in a way that is apt to promote emotive focus of a horrific variety. Moreover, if my hypothesis is correct, once this sort of emotive focus takes control, the audience keeps surveying the image of Praetorius for further evidence of impurity and danger, thereby sustaining the operation of their ongoing emotional processes.

Suspense

Suspense is not exactly a genre unto itself, since suspense is an emotion that is often elicited in many other genres.[17] In *An Affair to Remember,* we feel suspense about whether or not Nicky will see that Terry never abandoned her love for him. And in so many horror films, suspense is engendered over the question of whether or not Earth can be saved from the onslaught of flying saucers, rampaging zombies, pod people, birds, or whatever. In *The Arrival,* which is a science-fiction horror film, suspense is generated over the question of whether the alien attempt to transform ("terraform") the atmosphere of earth can be unmasked. Suspense, it would appear, is a genre classification that cuts across other genre classifications.

Nevertheless, we do talk of suspense films. These, roughly speaking, are films, perhaps of almost any other genre, that either contain arresting or memorable suspense scenes as major parts of the narrative, or that conclude with a rousing suspense sequence, or, maybe most paradigmatically, films that are organized virtually in their entirety around resolving certain dominant, suspenseful questions, such as "can the assassination be averted?"

Suspense is a future-oriented emotion. In everyday life, we don't normally feel suspense about what happened in the past. I don't feel suspense about the outcome of World War II, since I already know it. Suspense is a posture that we typically adopt to what will happen, not to what has happened.

But suspense is not an emotion that takes possession of us with respect to just any future event. I do not feel suspense about whether or not I will go to work tomorrow because I think that it is highly probable that I will go and, moreover, I want to go. In everyday life, suspense takes over where the odds are against—or at least up in the air—concerning something that I want to happen, or, conversely, where something that I do not want to happen seems probable. If it looks like the candidate whom I oppose is either likely to win or has just as good a chance of winning as the candidate I support, then I feel suspense over the outcome of the election. But if the candidate I oppose cannot possibly win and the candidate I favor cannot possibly lose, then there is little room for me to feel suspense.

Suspense concerns probabilities. It is not simply a matter of uncertainty. I am uncertain about the outcome of many future events, but I do not feel suspense in regard to them. Suspense only takes hold where the probabilities seem to be running against some outcome that I prefer, or, to put it the other way around, where the probabilities are running in favor of some outcome that I would rather not obtain. Moving from everyday life to film fiction, for example, as the townspeople are savaged by the outlaws, we feel suspense, since what we want—the rescue of the villagers—is unlikely because the cavalry is still miles away.

The emotion of suspense takes as its object some future event whose desired outcome is improbable, or, at least, no more probable than the undesired outcome; indeed, with suspense, the undesired outcome is characteristically much more probable than the desired outcome. That is to say that the emotive criteria appropriate to regarding an event with suspense is such that the event promises that an undesired outcome appears likely, while the desired outcome seems unlikely. Thus, in constructing suspense episodes, filmmakers must criterially prefocus their depictions and descriptions in such a way that the audience's desires and the probabilities that attach to them come apart.

Perhaps the ways in which filmmakers structure events so that certain outcomes appear probable and others improbable requires little more explanation than the ways in which they make the plights of the characters in melodramas pitiable, or the monsters in horror films fearsome. The rescue of the heroine in the burning building is so unlikely because the flames are so high and the hero is so far away and anyway he is engaged in a losing battle with four implacable villains. Her life hangs on a slender thread, stretched to the breaking point. However, the answer to the question of how filmmakers dispose audiences to prefer certain outcomes over others may be less obvious.

In order to mobilize suspense in an audience, a fiction filmmaker has to get the audience to care about one of the outcomes of the course of affairs she is narrating. She has to engender the audience's concern in such a way that the audience desires the outcome that the narrative depicts as vastly improbable, or, at least, no more probable than the countervailing alternative. But is there any fairly reliable way for the filmmaker to do this? After all, the filmmaker is designing her movie for an audience most of whose members she does not know personally. She has no access to their private preferences and desires. How can she be fairly certain that by characterizing a situation one way rather than another, she will enlist the audience's concern in the way that she needs to in order to make the scene work in terms of suspense? This is a general problem that confronts all suspense filmmakers. Moreover, it has a straightforward solution that is in evidence in virtually every suspense film ever made.

In order to encourage the kind of concern that is requisite for suspense, the filmmaker has to locate some shared stratum of interests and preferences in diverse audiences about whom she has little or no personal knowledge. That is, she has to find some common interests or preferences in the audience such that they will support the suspense response. Here, morality turns out to be the card that almost every suspense film plays. Morality supplies a fairly common set of sentiments that are apt to be shared by most typical viewers. Thus we find in most suspense films that the object of the emotion is an event whose *evil* outcomes are probable and whose *righteous* outcomes are improbable, or, at least, no more probable than the evil ones.

When the train is no more than ten feet away from the heroine strapped to the tracks, the evil machinations of the villain seem inevitable. Likewise, in *Secret Agent* (1936) when "the General" is about to push the kindly old gentleman, misidentified as a spy, over the cliff, we find ourselves in the grip of suspense because averting the murder seems impossible (Ashenden [John Gielgud], the only person who could stop the event, is half a mile away in an observatory, watching the assassination, in anguish, through a telescope) at the same time that we regard the deed as immoral (in part because we share Ashenden's scruples and perhaps, in part, because we realize that the evidence that the old man is a spy is not only slim, but contradicted by his altogether generous, open demeanor). Similarly, in *Speed* (1994) suspense takes over for much of the film because there seems to be no way that the hurtling bus won't be blown to smithereens, killing all of the innocent passengers. In films like *Ransom* (1996), suspense seems to become most excruciating just when it appears that the villain is going to get away.

Of course, the sense of morality that operates in such films is not always the same as the morality that rules our everyday affairs. Often we feel inclined toward projects in films that we would never endorse in "real life." For example, caper films represent persons involved in perpetrating crimes that we do not usually condone. However, it is often the case that films shape our ethical responses to them in a way that diverges from our everyday moral judgments.

Perhaps the most important lever that filmmakers possess for influencing our assessment of the morality of scenes in suspense films involves character portrayal. That is, we tend to accept the projects of characters in suspense films who strike us as virtuous. With caper films, for example, we find that the protagonists in such fictions are standardly possessed of certain striking virtues; and in the absence of countervailing virtues in their opposite number, or possibly given the emphasis on the outright vice of their opponents, we tend to ally ourselves morally with the caper. The virtues in question here—strength, fortitude, ingenuity, bravery, competence, beauty, generosity, and so on—are more often than not Grecian, rather than Christian. But it is because the characters exhibit these virtues—it is because we perceive (and are led to perceive) these characters as virtuous—that we cast our moral allegiance with them.

If the protagonists are represented as possessed of some virtues and their opponents are less virtuous, altogether bereft of virtue, or downright vicious, suspense can take hold because the efforts of the protagonists are morally correct in accordance with the ethical system of the film. Of course, it is probably the case that generally the actions of the protagonists in typical films are morally correct in accordance with some prevailing ethical norms shared by the majority of the audience. However, in cases in which this consensus does not obtain, the protagonist's possession of saliently underlined virtues will project the moral valuations of the fiction and, indeed, incline the audience toward accepting that perspective as its own. Thus it turns out that sometimes even an antagonist can serve as the object of suspense, as long as he or she is presented as possessed of some virtues. In fact, at the limit, I suspect that even a vicious character and his plight can become the object of suspense when he is portrayed as an utterly helpless victim, since the audience's sense of rectitude recoils at the prospect of harming truly helpless victims.

Typically the criteria that an event in a fiction film will meet in order to serve as an appropriate object of suspense involve morality and probability. The depictions and descriptions in suspense films criterially prefocus the events they characterize in terms of outcomes in which the triumph of evil is likely while the prospects for righteousness are slight. Making these features of the courses of events in a fiction film salient is apt to elicit emotive focus in accordance with the criteria appropriate to suspense. Thus, spectators in the grip of suspense fix their attention on the details that contribute to the probability and morality rankings of the unfolding actions in the story. Moreover, once in the thrall of suspense, their emotive focus avidly tracks the fluctuating probabilities in the contest between moral good and evil on the screen.

Analyzing a suspense sequence or a suspense film, then, involves isolating the thematic and stylistic choices that play a role in the criterial prefocusing of the film text. With suspense, those will be the elements of depiction and description that lead the audience to make the relevant assessments concerning the probabilities and moral values of the alternative outcomes of the unfolding action.

Analyzing the ways in which horror films elicit the emotion after which the genre is named also involves attending to the way in which the film text is criterially prefocused. However, in this case, the relevant emotive criteria are not probability and morality, but harm and impurity, and the object of the emotion in question is a being, the monster, and not an event, as it is with respect to suspense. Thus, the horror analyst will attend to the way in which the monster is structured to bring properties in accordance with the criteria of harm and impurity to the fore, and to the way that the plot affords opportunities both to allow the monster to display these properties and to permit the human characters an occasion to talk about and to describe them.

With melodrama, criterial prefocusing is again crucial, though the criteria appropriate to what we might call the melodramatic emotion—a compound of pity and admiration—are misfortune and virtue (generally of an other-regarding and often of a self-sacrificing sort). Pithing the structure that gives rise to the melodramatic emotion involves attending to incidents that set forth the misfortunes and virtues of characters and to the ways in which these are emphasized dramatically, narratively, and cinematically.

CONCLUDING REMARKS

In this article I have proposed a sketch of a theoretical framework for analyzing the relation between film and what I have called the emotions proper (or, alternatively, the garden-variety emotions). I have also attempted to show the significance of this program for the analysis of various genres that are universally acknowledged to traffic in certain well-known emotional states.

Throughout, I have repeatedly stressed the importance of criterial prefocusing for eliciting emotive focus. My hypothesis has been that by criterially prefocusing the film text—where the criteria in question are the ones appropriate to certain emotions—filmmakers encourage spectators to assess or to subsume the events onscreen under certain categories, namely the categories pertinent to the excitation of the relevant emotional states.

Through criterial prefocusing we could say that the filmmaker leads the horse to water. But the circuit is not completed until the audience drinks. In order for that to occur, the audience must cognize the film text in the ways that the filmmaker has made salient through criterial prefocusing. That means subsuming the onscreen events under the intended criterially governed categories or, alternatively, assessing the onscreen events in light of the intended emotive criteria. But whichever way you prefer to put it, the audience's faculties of cognition and judgment are brought into play in the process of eliciting an emotional response to film. Thus we see that even when it comes to analyzing the relation of film to the emotions, a cognitively oriented approach to film theory has much to offer.

NOTES

1. By only alluding to cognitively impenetrable affects here, I do not want to suggest that other states—such as pleasure and desire—do not warrant study. I consider those to be topics for future research. I have even attempted some preliminary work on desire in my book *A Philosophy of Mass Art* (Oxford: Clarendon, 1998).

2. When I say that ordinary language treats these examples as paradigmatic, what I have in mind is that, when asked, competent language users will tend to offer phenomena like these—especially fear, anger, sadness and love—as central instances of emotional states.

3. Ed S. Tan, *Emotion and the Structure of Narrative Film: Film as an Emotion Machine,* trans. Barbara Fasting (Mahwah, N.J.: Erlbaum, 1996).

4. William James, "What Is an Emotion?" in *Mind* 9 (1884): 188–205.

5. Robert Solomon, "The Jamesian Theory of Emotion in Anthropology," in *Culture Theory: Essays on Mind, Self and Emotion,* ed. Richard A. Shweder and Robert A. LeVine (Cambridge: Cambridge University Press, 1984), 214.

6. Though the case that follows is made up, it is not entirely fanciful, since experiments like it have been run. A classic example in the literature is Stanley Schachter and Jerome E. Singer, "Cognitive, Social, and Physiological Determinants of State," excerpted in *What Is An Emotion?,* ed. Cheshire Calhoun and Robert C. Solomon (Oxford: Oxford University Press, 1984), 173–83.

7. Here is might be argued that there are some emotional states, like free-floating depression, that do not take objects. Rather than deny that there are such states, I prefer to take advantage of the distinction I drew earlier between affects broadly construed and paradigmatic emotional states. Perhaps free-floating depression is just not a core case of the emotions proper. Maybe it is an affective state brought about by chemical imbalances in the body.

8. Some garden-variety emotions may also include—in addition to cognitions and bodily feelings—desires as a typical or even a necessary component.

9. In this, I will restrict myself to the case of viewing narrative fiction films rather than to abstract and/or nonnarrative films. I have made this methodological decision not only because it makes the job easier, but because I think that we will be in a better position to understand the operation of the emotions in the latter when we understand it in relation to the former. Unfortunately, in this essay, I only have space to deal with the case of the fictional narrative.

I will also not be considering the role of music in engendering movie emotion in this paper. However, I have made a stab at that topic in Noël Carroll, "Notes on Movie Music," in my *Theorizing the Moving Image* (Cambridge: Cambridge University Press, 1996).

10. With respect to the arguments in this paper, see also Noël Carroll, "Art, Narrative and Emotion," in *The Emotions and Art,* ed. Mette Hjort and Sue Laver (Oxford: Oxford University Press, 1997); and my *Philosophy of Mass Art,* esp. chap. 4.

11. I address the use of point-of-view editing to prefocus audience attention emotively in my "Toward a Theory of Point-of-View Editing: Communication, Emotion and the Movies," in *Theorizing the Moving Image.*

12. I talk of what is "generally" or "very frequently" the case in fiction films here because sometimes a character or a scene in a film may be emotively marked in an initially ambiguous way. This is a *standard* deviation from the norm whose existence I would not wish to deny. However, above I am talking about the norm in order to illustrate what I mean by talking about the emotive prefocusing of scenes, sequences and characters. Moreover, even where the filmic phenomena are ambiguously marked, that too is generally (barring cases of ineptitude) a function of the filmmakers' design and prefocusing activity.

13. The notion of dysphoric and euphoric emotion here comes from Keith Oatley, *Best-Laid Schemes* (Cambridge: Cambridge University Press, 1992), 107−9, 174−77.

14. This section has been inspired by an important article by Flo Leibowitz. See her "Apt Feelings, or Why 'Women's Films' Aren't Trivial," in *Post-Theory: Reconstructing Film Studies,* ed. David Bordwell and Noël Carroll (Madison: University of Wisconsin Press, 1996).

15. The account of horror derives from Noël Carroll, *The Philosophy of Horror, or Paradoxes of the Heart* (New York: Routledge, 1990). See also Noël Carroll, "Horror and Humor," in my *Beyond Aesthetics* (New York: Cambridge University Press, 2001).

16. See David Pole, "Disgust and Other Forms of Aversion," in his *Aesthetics, Form and Emotion,* ed. George Roberts (New York: St. Martin's Press, 1983).

17. For further discussions of suspense, see Noël Carroll, "Toward a Theory of Film Suspense," in *Theorizing the Moving Image* (Cambridge: Cambridge University Press, 1996); and Noël Carroll, "The Paradox of Suspense," in *Suspense: Conceptualizations, Theoretical Analyses, and Empirical Explorations,* ed. Peter Vorderer, Hans J. Wulff, and Mike Friedrichsen (Hilldale, N.J.: Erlbaum, 1996).

Chapter 4 Ethnicity, Race, and Monstrosity: The Rhetorics of Horror and Humor

There are many conceptions of beauty. Some associate beauty with proportion and harmony; some with pleasure taken in the appearance of things; and some, more narrowly, with *disinterested* pleasure. Kant, of course, uses disinterested pleasure as the central mark of what he calls free beauty. However, Kant also speaks of dependent or accessory beauty, which pertains to the aesthetic judgments we make about things in relation to the determinate concepts under which the objects in question fall.[1] Human beauty, for Kant, is of this sort.[2] We call a human beautiful, he suggests, insofar as a person approaches being a perfect example of the category or concept of human being.

This approach to human beauty has a corollary. It implies what shall count as *nonbeauty*. If human beauty is, at the limit, the perfect realization of the concept of human being, then nonbeauty, the antithesis (or the family of antithes*es*) to beauty, is somehow an inadequate instantiation of the concept of human being. Moreover, these distinctions are relevant to our practices of representation: to represent a person or a group as beautiful, portray them as perfect or approximately perfect instances of the category human being (understanding that that category may be susceptible to cultural variation); to represent a person or a group as nonbeautiful, or as ugly (one of the most pertinent subcategories of nonbeauty), portray them as in some way or ways imperfect instances of the concept of the human.

In this essay, I am concerned with the representation of groups in popular culture. My interest has to do with the politics of representing people. The couplet beauty/nonbeauty (or, more specifically, beauty/ugliness) frequently figures importantly in the representation of groups, including most notably, for my purposes, ethnic and racial minorities. This couplet can be politically significant because beauty is often associated in our culture with moral goodness.[3] The beautiful exterior is taken as a sign of inward or moral goodness; the nonbeautiful or ugly exterior is often imagined to correlate with evil or depravity. Oscar Wilde's novel *The Picture of Dorian Gray* illustrates quite neatly this commonplace, which has had its philosophical defenders. For example, Francis Bacon maintained that "Virtue is nothing but inward beauty; beauty nothing but outward virtue."

Thus, beauty and nonbeauty can serve as a basis for political rhetoric. The moral credentials of a group—an ethnicity or a race—can be endorsed by means of an association with beauty, or it can be demeaned by being represented as nonbeautiful or ugly. To show, in a caricature, a representative of an opposing faction as an ogre is to call into question the moral worth of that faction. Similarly, Richard III's physical deformity is deployed to underscore his lurid politics.

I suppose that this much is fairly obvious and unobjectionable. But it raises the question of how exactly this rhetoric works, at least some of the time. Part of the answer to that question, I conjecture, can be obtained by focusing on the notion of human beauty which identifies it with the perfect realization of the concept of human being. This line of speculation suggests that the way to represent a human group as depraved is to portray it as nonbeautiful or ugly, that is, as an imperfect or defective instantiation of the category of human being. If one concept of human beauty (which is connected to ideas of goodness) sees beauty as the instantiation or near approximation of the concept human being, then the related idea of human ugliness (which is connected with ideas of moral degradation) is rooted in problematic exemplifications of the concept of the human. These "problematic exemplifications" can take many forms. The two that will preoccupy me in this essay are the imperfect exemplifications of the human found in the popular genres of horror and humor.

HORROR, HUMOR, AND CONCEPTS
OF THE HUMAN

One concept of beauty is applied to perfect or near-perfect examples of a kind. A perfect instance of an American Beauty Rose is called beautiful because it realizes the essential characteristics of its kind. This notion of beauty, which is fairly common in ordinary usage, is intimately connected with concepts. The beautiful object is one that at least accords maximally with the criteria for class membership for the category to which the item belongs. Often people refer to a picture as beautiful because it depicts a beautiful person, a person who is (or is thought to be) an exemplary specimen of the category of the human.

Finding a representation beautiful—or finding what is represented beautiful—is one kind of aesthetic response. There are others, such as finding a representation tragic or sublime. Of the variety of aesthetic responses we might undergo with respect to a representation, two that are especially interesting to consider in relation to finding an object beautiful are horror and comic amusement. These two responses are revealing when compared to the beauty response, because they too are intimately connected to concepts. However, while the beauty response is keyed to the perfect or exemplary realization of the relevant concept, horror and humor responses are connected to imperfect or defective instantiations of concepts. Horror and humor are, in this respect, antitheses of beauty, though antitheses that themselves diverge from each other as well in terms of their characteristic emotional timbres.

Perhaps the most straightforward way in which to substantiate this observation is to note that horror and humor both have as their natural terrain the ugly, even though they explore ugliness in different ways. The leading character in a horror movie, comic book, or the like is the monster, a creature most characteristically marked by ugliness so extreme that it is often capable of eliciting an aversive physical response.[4] Generally, the monster figure is explicitly aligned with the inhuman and its ugliness is a dramatic emblem for this.

Comedy, of course, has a more varied cast of characters. But one of particular interest is the clown type, who, like the monsters of the horror genre, is generally a subhuman being whose physical appearance deviates strikingly from the canons of human perfection: he or she is either too fat or too thin, or his or her parts (small heads, large torsos) combine disproportionately, and/or their features are vastly exaggerated—mouths, lips, and noses outsized; eyes minuscule. Clowns are designed to be ugly, though their ugliness is meant to be a source of mirth, whereas monsters are meant to horrify. Nevertheless, both monsters and clowns define themselves against the standards of humanity whose ideal approximation typically results in assessments of beauty (or, at least, dependent judgments of human beauty).[5]

Moreover, if we ask for an account of why horror and humor correlate regularly with ugliness, the answer would appear to be connected to the fact that horror and humor, like the kind of beauty we are considering, are also related to concepts. However, where beauty is connected with the perfect or near-perfect realization of concepts, horror and humor exploit intentionally pronounced deviations from concepts. Indeed, one might say that, albeit in different ways, horror and humor specialize in violating concepts.

Horror, at least in popular fictions, is a compound emotional response. It is made up of two components: fear and disgust. The horrific monster is fearsome. It kills people, maims them, possesses them, eats them. It is dangerous. But a horrific monster is not simply fearsome. It is also disgusting. Ideally, it makes our skin creep. It may make us gag. It is physically repulsive. Characteristically, we feel aversion for the monster in our body, where disgust, we might add, is a sensation that Kant himself singles out as a state that precludes the experience of beauty.[6]

But what is the basis of this feeling of revulsion? Speaking summarily, we can say that it is a reaction to the impurity of the monster. But why are monsters experienced as impure? Here it is useful to think in terms of categories and concepts. Horrific monsters violate our categories of things in various ways.

Many monsters are category errors; they contradict standing cultural concepts. They may be living and dead at the same time, like vampires and mummies, or they may be incongruous fusions of the animate and the inanimate, such as haunted houses possessed with wills of their own. Or, monsters may be interstitial figures, figures that blend, blur, or conjoin disparate categories: wolfmen, apemen, catwomen, and you-name-it-people that inhabit a conceptual space between recognized cultural categories. In addition, monsters may be incomplete realizations of standing cultural categories, like headless horsemen. That is why so many monsters are effectively amputees, like zombies without legs, missing vital parts that constitute our stereotypes for the kinds of beings in question. And, lastly, monsters may defy our standing categories and concepts by being altogether formless, shapeless, gelatinous masses of who-knows-what oozing their way to world conquest.

Where monsters are human-like, their impurity rests on their deviation from our norms of the human. They are violations of nature or, at least, of our conceptions of nature. Over the centuries, the creators of horror fictions have discovered an impressive variety of ways in which to violate our concept of the human, resulting in a bestiary of creatures that make our flesh crawl. In this respect, the popular genre of horror fiction stands outside what eighteenth-century French philosophers called the *beaux arts*. Of course, this is no accident. Horror is a genre predicated on exploring our fascination with the ugly, the anomalous, and the category violation.

Humor, too, is deeply involved with category violation. Consider, for example, the simple children's riddle: "Why did the moron stay up all night? He was studying for his blood test." Here the humor revolves around incorrectly subsuming a blood test under the category of a scholastic examination. Likewise, the humorous saying "Comedy is when you fall down and break your neck; tragedy is when I prick my finger" provokes laughter, in part, because it exploits the conceptual incongruity of assimilating a pinprick under the category of the tragic. Whether or not conceptual incongruity explains every instance of humor is the source of much theoretical debate. However, it is clear that conceptual incongruity plays an important role in a great deal of comedy.

Where comedy is aimed at the appearance of its human objects, the notion of conceptual incongruity is particularly informative. "Funny-looking people," such as the clown figures who are designed to elicit laughter, diverge strikingly from our paradigms of the concept of the human. As noted above, they are too short or too tall, too fat or too thin, or their limbs or facial features violate the ideal proportions associated with our concept of the human. Whereas beauty converges on our ideal of the human, comedy, or at least the comedy of human appearances, is a travesty of that ideal, instantiating the concept of the human in a way that violates its canons of perfection.

The comic and horrific, with respect to human appearance, are antitheses of beauty. The monster is a violation of the concept of the human predicated on engendering fear and disgust. Comedy also indulges in transgressing the concept of the human. Comic butts and buffoons are frequently subhuman in their intellectual abilities, but, in addition, where the humor trades in appearances, comic figures are generally misshapen to the point of being studied transgressions of our stereotypical conceptions of the human form.

Horror and humor, of course, differ from each other. The conceptual anomaly of the monster is presented in a fearful context, and the result is horror. In comedy, the incongruity is presented in a context bereft of fear, and the result is comic amusement.[7] Nevertheless, both horror and humor explore the terrain of concepts anomalously exemplified. When the concept in question is our category of the human, horror and humor are antitheses of beauty, the latter epitomizing the human form, the former instantiating it freakishly in order to provoke anxiety, on the one hand, or laughter, on the other.

ETHNICITY, RACE, AND RHETORIC

Inasmuch as there is an association between human beauty and goodness, this opens the possibility of using nonbeauty and ugliness as a sign of a demoted moral status. Horror and humor are genres that specialize in nonbeauty and ugliness. Thus, it should come as no surprise that horror and humor are serviceable and frequently exploited strategies for demeaning the ethical status of real or imagined political adversaries. This is readily borne out by the history of popular caricature, where it is common to rebuke pictorially the persons and factions the caricaturist suspects by rendering them either as monsters or as beings with comically exaggerated physiognomies, verging on and sometimes exceeding the clownish.

These strategies are often applied to individuals. But they can also be marshaled at the expense of entire groups—not only political parties and social classes, but ethnic and racial groups as well. In these cases, the rhetorics of horror and humor do double duty. For not only do they brand their objects as morally depraved, but they also figure their victims as subhuman and, therefore, as unworthy of the moral concern that befits a human person. That is, by portraying peoples of other ethnicities and races in terms of horrific and comic appearances, the notion that they are not quite human is literalized, while, at the same time, their distance from the canons of beauty, which symbolize our ideal concept of the human, measure their remoteness from the good.

Undoubtedly it is because horror and the humor of appearances are, like beauty, so intimately connected to our concept of the human—at the level of what we might call folk biology—that these genres provide such an employable set of rhetorical strategies for ethnic and racial scorn. By portraying their objects as antitheses of beauty, they not only associate them with evil, but render them not quite human—so far have they fallen short of our concept of humanity that they need not be treated morally. With the horror genre, the default is that we do not worry about the rights of monsters, while, with humor, the moral claims of comic butts can rarely be entertained without compromising the gag or the joke. Thus, in mobilizing the visual vocabularies of horror and humor, the ideologue not only puts the relevant ethnicities and races beyond the human pale but also deprives them of the moral consideration appropriate to members of the class of human beings.

Recurrent examples of the use of horrific and/or humorous imagery against ethnic minorities can be found in British pictorial treatments of the Irish throughout the nineteenth century. In the June 18, 1881, issue of *Punch,* John Tenniel produced an illustration entitled "The Irish Devil-Fish," which portrayed the Irish Land League as a composite figure, part octopus but with a grotesque human head where one might otherwise expect a tentacle.[8] The image is of the sort that one expects to find in a low-budget horror film. It is a literal fusion of the human with a mollusc, a violation of biological categories predicated on raising a sense of visceral disgust in the viewer—which disgust, of course, is designed to be transferred to the Irish in general.

This sort of composite figure is a staple of horror. Think how many horrific figures, like the Fly, are impossible hybridizations of discrete biological species. Fusions such as this raise a sense of impurity in us because they are category violations; they mix or blend biological features that we presume are, in the nature of things, separate. They are, for that reason, regarded as unnatural and monstrous, and when superimposed on an ethnic group that sense of impurity and monstrosity represents the relevant group as monstrous and impure in ways that are not only physically disturbing but that carry moral connotations as well.

In the case of "The Irish Devil-Fish," the pictorial logic works like a metaphor. The Irish are identified—through the rhetoric of the composite figure—with a non-human species, thereby taking on, by metaphorical transfer, salient features of octopi, like sliminess. At the same time, the Irish are represented literally as some sort of miscarriage of nature, absolutely alien to humanity and fit for suppression. Such images not only exploit culturally inculcated feelings of physical aversion toward the Irish and a sense of the impurity of the Other, but reinforce them as well.

The creation of visual category mistakes like this one is fundamental to the production of horror. A structurally comparable strategy for (mis)-characterizing and dehumanizing the Irish that appears again and again in British cartoons in simianization—the portrayal of the Irish as part human and part ape. Tenniel's "The Irish Frankenstein" appeared in *Punch* on May 20, 1882.[9] It portrays an Irish terrorist as the Frankenstein monster, already a horrific creature insofar as it is a contradictory being, both living and dead at the same time. What is additionally interesting about Tenniel's illustration here is that not only does he represent the Irish as Frankenstein's monster, but he depicts the monster in a decidedly ape-like way, hirsute and with a prognathous jaw.

The representation of the Irish as apes can also be seen in Tenniel's cartoon

"Two Forces" in *Punch* (October 29, 1881), which L. Perry Curtis notes "reveals the almost complete simianization of Paddy. Tenniel has given his villain such proverbially ape-like features as the simous nose, long, projecting upper lip, shallow lower jaw, and fang-like teeth."[10] An even more pronounced example of this visual equation of the Irish with apes is Matt Morgan's "The Irish Frankenstein," which appeared in *The Tomahawk* on December 18, 1869, and which depicts the head of a gorilla superimposed on a human body, with "Fenian" written across its chest.[11] Nor is this treatment of the Irish unique to the British; in Thomas Nast's "The Day We Celebrate: St. Patrick's Day, 1867," which appeared in *Harper's Weekly* on April 6, 1867, several of the Irish rioters are depicted as horrifying apemen.[12]

In these examples, the fusion of the Irish with the ape are all horrific. They are designed to frighten and disgust readers—to associate a reflex of physical recoil at the thought of the Irish. Where the imagery of beauty attracts, the projection of ugliness repels. But this sort of composite image—this sort of visual category error—can also be given a comic spin. In Frederick B. Opper's "The King of A-Shantee," from *Puck* (February 15, 1882), an Irishman with the head of a monkey and a chamber pot for a hat sits outside his broken down shack smoking a clay pipe and lazing about.[13] In this picture, unlike the previous examples, the Irish-ape is not portrayed as dangerous or threatening. Any sense of fear has been excluded from the picture. Thus, though the figure is as monstrous as the one in Tenniel's "Two Forces," it is not horrific but humorous, its incongruous fusion of the human and the ape engendering ridicule rather than terror. Indeed, the fusion suggested by this cartoon goes beyond an association between the Irish and the ape, since the title notes that the Irishman is sitting before *a shanty,* the verbal wordplay invoking the name of an African tribe, and thereby suggesting an identity between the Irish and blacks as both interstitial category mongrelizations, at best missing links.

As this example indicates, transgressions of the concept of the human can be used not only as vehicles of ethnic prejudice but of racial prejudice as well. During the Second World War, for instance, simianization was a recurring strategy in Allied representations of the Japanese. In 1943, an illustration accompanying an article in the *New York Times Magazine* asks "How Tough Are the Japanese?" and answers it by saying "They are not tougher than other soldiers, says a veteran observer, but brutality is part of their fighting equipment."[14] Pictured above these captions is the image of a colossal Japanese soldier holding a handful of cringing humans in his paw after the fashion of King Kong. The arms of the Japanese soldier are elongated and touch the ground like a gorilla's. His shoulders are hunched like an ape's, and his mouth protrudes and is enlarged with giant teeth, bared as though ready to chomp on his victims. The picture leaves little doubt about what kind of brutality the Japanese specialize in; it is as "inhuman" morally as its ape-like exterior insinuates.

The Japanese, like other Asians, were equated not only with apes, but with monkeys and chimpanzees as well. In "The Monkey Folk," published in *Punch* in mid-January 1942, the Japanese advance down the Malay Peninsula was portrayed as a pack of chimpanzees swinging through the trees with helmets on their heads and submachine guns slung over their shoulders.[15] Here the iconography seems satiric rather than horrific; perhaps it is an instance of a pictorial wish fulfillment fantasy—by representing the Japanese as less-than-dangerous simians, their threat might in some way be "magically" diminished.

Similarly, in David Low's cartoon "East or West," a monkey-like creature, labeled "Jap" and wearing spectacles, swings by its tail from a tree.[16] It has a wickedly shaped knife in its hand, and it hesitates as it decides whether to plunge the dagger into the back of a shirtless Anglo-Saxon sailor or a Russian soldier. In part, this cartoon is about the reputed duplicity of the Japanese, but equally important is the revulsion this species-crossed Japanese figure is intended to excite. There can be little doubt of the racial politics that underwrite this visual: in that the Japanese are at best incongruous instantiations of the category of the human, that they are impure, and, in this case, ridiculous, but also creepy, they are defective specimens of humanity. They are as morally deficient as they are grotesque; and, given that they are not quite human, they may be dealt with like animals. All this is etched in their ugliness, in their incongruous parody of the human form.

Not only Asians, but also blacks, have been recurrent targets of simianization. So frequent was this motif in the nineteenth century that upon seeing a lithograph that depicted a black public as dignified, Frederick Douglass was moved to write a congratulatory letter to the company that produced it—Prang's Chromo—because "we colored men so often see ourselves described and painted as monkeys."[17] The simianization of black people, as we have seen in our examples of the representation of the Irish and the Japanese, could take a comic form or a horrific one, but, in either case, the strategy relies upon superimposing the human with the animal in such a way that what results is a biological category error.

An example of the ostensibly humorous simianization of blacks can be found in a sketch by W. L. Sheppard for *Frank Leslie's Illustrated Newspaper* of April 27, 1872. Entitled "The Darwinian Theory Illustrated—A Case of Natural Selection," the street scene shows an organ grinder's monkey leaping onto the back of an onlooking black child, who flinches uncomfortably under the attack. What is intended to be the leading "joke" here, one surmises, is that the monkey has "naturally selected" to join someone like himself in the crowd. However, there also seems to be a second "humorous aside" in the picture; on its right hand corner, there is an adult black male, dressed in military attire, watching the fracas. His heavy, hairy muttonchops and the articulation of the bottom part of his face suggest, for satiric purposes, a simian visage, as if he and his kind have more in common with monkeys than with humans. The reference to Darwinism in this sketch also conjures up popular associations with the notion of a "missing link," where a missing link is by definition an imperfect realization of the category of the human.

Simianization can be orchestrated for horrific as well as comic effect. The drawings of George van Raemdonck for a Dutch comic book from 1927 bear the caption "a man-eater."[18] One of the pictures shows a naked black man walking on all fours, with his arms reaching the ground in the posture of an ape. Blood drips from his mouth, which is exaggerated and befanged, and he clutches a bone. An accompanying picture shows an enlarged black mouth— more of a maw—devouring two whites, clutched in each of the monster's hands, with their legs chewed off below the knees. Clearly this is an image meant to inspire horror in readers—meant to portray black Africans as thoroughly savage and inhuman, monstrous biologically and morally.

The association of the African with the simian, which recurs in popular culture, appears in the supposedly scientific writings of the West as well. Linnaeus described his *Homo Africanus* as having an "ape-like nose"; Darwin uncritically cited Robert Knox's description of the black face as akin to a baboon's; while Curvier alleged of blacks that "The projection of the lower parts of the face, and the thick lips, evidently approximate it to the monkey tribe."[19] If this "educated" correlation of blacks with simians did not cause the association of Africans and apes in popular culture, it surely reinforced it.

The association between blacks and simians, among other things, gave rise to the hypothesis that there was some transitional figure, some missing link, between humans and animals.[20] Edward Tyson proposed pygmies for that role; Bory St. Vincent suggested Hottentots.[21] Moreover, this transition between species was frequently "explained" by claiming that sexual intercourse between Africans and simians was not infrequent, the horror of racial mixing perhaps being projected onto a fantasy of sexual relations between apes and blacks.[22] Edward Long—planter, scholar, and administrator of Jamaica—wrote: "I do not think that an orang-outang husband would be any dishonor to an Hotten-tot female [*sic*]."[23]

This delirium of species impurity is exemplified by a 1795 illustration from Britain entitled "The Orang-Outang Carrying Off a Negro Girl."[24] The "Orang-Outang," with his captive in hand, is prominently displayed climbing to the top of a tree, while, in the background, three strange-looking figures, neither human nor simian but a mixture of both, loll about, suggesting, perhaps with satiric intent, what will be the unnatural issue of rapes such as this one.[25]

Almost 150 years later, we see similar iconography repeated in a wartime Italian cartoon depicting a black GI as a gorilla, carrying off the *Venus de Milo* as part of his loot.[26] Here the black man, slouched and with elongated, hairy arms, is contrasted with one of the icons of Western beauty in order to indicate the depths of American barbarity in contrast to an elevated Italian culture. But in its elision of barbarity with monstrosity—through the figure of the black apeman—the picture also reinforces the visual theme that African-Americans are at best defective people, interstitially blurring the categories of the ape and the human. Moreover, this picture is certainly intended to strike horror in the hearts of Italians at the prospect of an army of these black apemen, the very antithesis of Venus (the most beautiful of goddesses, according to Paris), invading and pillaging their cities.

The simianization of black people is also a feature of popular fiction. In Robert E. Howard's 1935 pulp fiction "Moon of Zambebwei," the first black character we encounter is described as apish in terms of his long arms and agility. This character is part of a black revolution, a revolution undertaken in the name of Zamba, who is described as "The *Black* God." It is hard not to interpret Zamba as a displacement for the allegedly apish blacks, such as the first one we meet, who follow Zamba. But what is Zamba? It is described thusly:

> a beast against nature—a beast that sought food strange to its natural species.
>
> The thing [Zamba] chained to the stake was an ape, but such an ape as the world at large never dreamed of, even in nightmares. Its shaggy grey hair was shot with silver that shone in the rising moon; it looked gigantic as it squatted ghoulishly on its haunches. Upright, on its bent gnarled legs, it would be as tall as a man, and much broader and thicker. But its prehensile fingers were armed with talons like those of a tiger—not the heavy blunt nails of the natural anthropoid, but the cruel scimitar-curved claws of the great carnivora. Its face was like that of a gorilla, low browed, flaring-nostriled, chinless; but when it snarled, its wide flat nose wrinkled like that of a great cat, and the cavernous mouth disclosed saber-like fangs, the fangs of a beast of prey. This was Zamba, the creature sacred to the people of the

land of Zambebwei—a monstrosity, a violation of an accepted law of nature—a carnivorous ape. . . .

The sight of the monstrosity filled McGrath [the hero] with revulsion; it was abysmal. . . . This thing was an affront to sanity.[27]

By calling Zamba the "black god," Howard plays on the ambiguity between "the god of the blacks" and "the god who is black," albeit in a symbolically exaggerated form. Given Howard's racist tendencies, evidenced in his other writings, I think that he intends us to think of Zamba as a figure for black people, and, in this regard, he not only characterizes the black race as an ape, but compounds that deliberate category error with a further one, since Zamba is also a violation of our concept of a gorilla, being a man-eater, indeed a man-eater who incongruously resembles a man in his upright position. Zamba also incarnates a black revolt, since he is the cause of the black uprising, and the nearly physical aversion his biologically anomalous status and horrific appearance are supposed to elicit in the reader is intended, in turn, to attach to the sort of revolution whose symbol he is.

I think that the simianization of black people may also explain one of the more peculiar features of the iconography in *Blacula* and *Scream, Blacula, Scream,* two Blaxploitation films of the 1970s. In both these films, but more evidently in the original, something occurs that I believe is unprecedented, though maybe only extremely rare, in vampire films. When the vampire, Blacula, otherwise a handsome, courtly black aristocrat, goes on the attack, he changes physically; what is particularly notable about this transformation is that he grows an abundance of facial hair as his sideburns spread across his cheeks.

I can think of no other example of this; it doesn't happen to white vampires in the genre. Nor is it that Blacula is a werewolf; his makeup doesn't resemble any of the standard strategies for portraying werewolves in movies, nor is anything said about his being a werewolf. So why is Blacula so hairy? I suggest that this involves, in part, tapping into the long-standing association of the black person with the simian and monstrosity. Blacula is not an apeman, but his makeup exploits a residue of that imagery for horrific purposes.[28]

Of course, the point of this makeup, first and foremost, is to produce a monster that is horrifying enough to engage horror fans. However, since the monster character is black, and since the makeup toys with the traditional rhetoric of simianization, the film has the perhaps unintended consequence of sustaining a dehumanizing stereotype, a charge it would not be liable to had Blacula remained as clean-shaven as Dracula.[29]

The horrific rhetoric of simianization works through appearances to pro-voke a gut response against blackness. It does this, in part, by representing blacks as category errors, as imperfect or incongruous realizations of the con-cept of the human. However, categorical incongruity can also be used for the purposes of a belittling variety of satirical humor. For example, Pat Turner has pointed out that in many nineteenth- and early-twentieth-century illustrations black children are depicted "like furry little animals," in order perhaps to mute the terrible things that happen to them, like being devoured by alligators, in the name of comic amusement.[30]

Nor is the simianization of the African-American for putatively comic pur-poses a thing of the past. It is thriving on the Internet on the Web site of Alpha, an organization that grew out of the United States of America Nationalist Party; their Web site is "dedicated to the countless Aryan men and women who have given their lives for our race."[31] The "humor" list on this Web site for Sep-tember 6–13, 1998, contained three verbal jokes identifying blacks with simians of various sorts, including a parodic "definition" that states outright that blacks are apes. In addition, the Web site includes a cartoon that shows a black man with wild hair all over his face and arms, a simian facial structure (most notably around his mouth), and his left hand bent backward like a monkey's.[32] The text that accompanies this caricature begins "Coon, coon/Black Baboon," leaving no doubt as to how we are to interpret the distortions sketched on the black body next to the "poem." This is clearly humor of the Hobbesian variety, invit-ing the vicious laughter of superiority.

Simianization is not the only rhetoric of incongruous category instantiation used against blacks. The classical horror figure most closely associated with blacks is the zombie, a creature reputedly brought into being by voodoo. The zombie is an interstitial thing, neither living nor dead. Though white people can be zombies, zombies are most characteristically black. They are virtual au-tomatons, moving mechanically with no will of their own, under the control of those responsible for casting them into this state.

Though zombies need not be ugly, black zombies in movies are typically made up to appear grotesque. In *I Walked with a Zombie*, released in 1943 and considered a classic film in the genre, the zombified white wife of the plantation owner, though stiff, still retains vestiges of her beauty, whereas the black zom-bie, who guards the precincts of the voodoo worshipers, is intended to violate our stereotypes of the human—he is painfully gaunt, and his huge, exaggerat-edly fixated white eyes pop out of the darkness preternaturally.[33]

The image of the zombie can be made to count doubly against blacks. There is the image of the zombie himself or herself, who can be made to function as an image of the black person as a mindless, subhuman slave. But there is also the priest or necromancer who has created the zombie by literally black arts, and where that priest is black, he serves as an icon of wickedness. In Wes Craven's film *The Serpent and the Rainbow,* the facially disfigured magician is also the chief of the secret police, projecting a fantasy of Caribbean politics as voodoo-like, unholy, unnatural, and altogether evil.

The zombie figure itself can be used to carry political rhetoric. In his 1936 short story "Black Canaan," Robert E. Howard returns to the theme of black revolt. A holy war is being raised in the name of Damballah. The troops are made up of black zombies. But these zombies are extra-anomalous conceptually. Not only are they neither living nor dead, but they live underwater, biologically on their way to becoming fish, and they rise up from beneath the swamp to take their victims unaware. When the hero grapples with one of these zombies and looks into its face, he notes "it was inhuman; as expressionless and soulless as that of a catfish; the face of a being no longer human, and no longer mindful of its human origin."[34]

Howard was a southerner who had inherited his culture's antebellum fear of black rebellion, reprisal, and revenge. The zombie serves as a symbol of his anxiety about the inhuman savagery that black vengeance would unleash. Blacks become the zombie menace, enabling him to portray the prospects of black vengeance with images predicated upon making the reader cringe viscerally. By dehumanizing blacks in this way, Howard rhetorically "justifies" not only keeping them down, but dealing with them brutally, a sentiment that the horrifically disgusted reader is invited to share.

That Howard chooses the zombie to exemplify black retribution is at least ironic, since one of the most salient features of zombies is that they are slaves. Thus, Howard's zombie revolutionaries bear the very mark of their history, their enslavement, which has brought them into opposition with whites. Moreover, insofar as Howard's story makes the master of these zombie slaves a black man, it is an exercise in pure projection.

In recent years, a new figure of black horror has emerged—The Candyman. Two films have been made in this series: *Candyman* and *Candyman: Farewell to the Flesh.* These films are based on Clive Barker's short story "The Forbidden." Oddly, the Candyman in Barker's original story is not black. He is not described as such, nor is anyone else so described. "The Forbidden" is set in London. But in the movie versions, both produced by Barker, the story has been transposed to America. In the first film, the Candyman haunts Chicago—his lair is in the black housing project Cabrini-Green—and, in the second film he stalks New Orleans.

Along with these geographic relocations, the Candyman, whose intentionally vague origins contributed to the horrific effect of the story, has become in the film series a nineteenth-century black artist, born in the slave quarters of a plantation in Louisiana. Hired to paint the portrait of the southern belle of the big house, he fell in love with his model and she with him. When their affair was discovered, a white mob descended upon him. They severed his painting hand and then smeared his body with cloying honey. A swarm of bees congregated on his body and flayed him alive. After death, the Candyman metamorphosed into a revenant who, like so many fictional ghosts, is bent on revenge.

The Candyman is an interstitial figure, ambiguously straddling the conceptual distinction between living and dead. He is also an incomplete instantiation of the stereotype of a man since he is missing a hand, which he has replaced with a particularly nasty-looking hook. In most of his apparitions he is handsome, save for his hook; he is tall, he is strong, and his face has classical proportions. However, when he reveals his true nature, that is another story. When he opens his massive cloak, we see that his bloody torso has had the flesh torn from it and that bees nest in his rib cage. This reinforces his status as an incomplete being. It also explains why when he is cut, bees crawl from the wound, promoting a rather revolting image. Moreover, his "true face" looks as though it is melting off his skull, making his head a gooey, gelatinous, formless mass, less a head than a we-know-not-what.

The figure of the Candyman exploits stark contrasts between beauty and ugliness, as well as between sweetness and disgust, for horrific effect. Understood as a combinatory image, he conjoins opposites in a way that is initially attractive but then repelling. His physical appearance, it would seem, mirrors his moral status. On the one hand, his existential commitment to retribution may encourage some measure of sympathy—it is hard to think of many who have been treated so unjustly. But in his rage, he has become morally monstrous as well as physically so, since he kills indiscriminately; indeed, in the first film, he kills mostly black people.

His revenge is cosmic; he is not an avenger involved in paying back the wrongs of slavery. He seeks retribution from humanity at large, attacking innocents and even kidnapping a black infant. Thus, in terms of the moral calculus of the story, he is ultimately evil and must be destroyed. Though the film elicits an appreciable measure of empathy for the Candyman's heinous persecution, when all the moral accounts are in, it is finally the Candyman's vengeance that is represented as the most horrifying and inhuman in the film.

In Howard's "Black Canaan," no thought is offered of motivating the black revolt in virtue of any claims of justice. Black retribution, personified by the zombies, is presented as unalloyed evil, which is associated graphically with and advanced by the iconography of ontological impurity. Through the zombies, the prospect of black reprisals is treated as horrifying—as both fearsome and disgusting. The *Candyman* films take black anger more seriously, but, in the last analysis, presuppose that humanity must oppose the Candyman and send him back to whence he came. His anger is exorbitant, monstrous in its proportions, and that moral monstrousness is symbolized by the horrific ugliness of his true appearance or essence, his transgression of the category of the human.

CONCLUSION

One leading concept of beauty associates beauty with the perfect realization of a concept; a beautiful Kentucky Walker is a perfect or approximately perfect example of its kind. When we say something is beautiful, in this light, we mean that it instantiates the conceptual category in this way. Human beauty has been characterized in this manner. At the same time, there is an enduring commonplace that beauty is connected to goodness: that the beautiful exterior reflects a righteous interior.

The link between beauty and goodness can yield a strategy of political rhetoric. In order to endorse a cause, portray it as beautiful. Thus, Liberty is pictured as a beautiful woman. But the couplet—the beautiful/the good—also suggests a further homology, viz., the beautiful/the good :: the ugly/the evil. And this homology affords an alternative political rhetoric. To portray something as evil, make it ugly.

Horror and humor are two genres that explore ugliness. Like beauty, horror and humor are essentially related to concepts including, notably, the concept of the human. Both create ugliness for their own unique purposes by violating, transgressing, blurring, contradicting, and/or otherwise jamming our concepts of the human. With horror, the results are monsters who are designed to frighten and disgust us. With humor, anomalous figures, like clowns, are designed to provoke laughter. Thus, where the iconography of beauty may be employed to advocate certain political persuasions, the imagery of horror and humor can be mobilized to stigmatize opposing political factions. Historically, the potentials of horror and humor to this end have been exploited frequently, often with reference to despised ethnic and racial groups, including the Irish, the Japanese, the African, and the African-American.[35]

As a rhetoric of hatred, horror and humor can be frighteningly effective. Like beauty, they do much of their work at the level of appearances, and they elicit a fast, visceral response from audiences. The almost immediate sense of aversion and disgust—along with fear—that arises in response to horrific monsters can be transferred smoothly from fictional apemen to what they stand for. Likewise, humor paints its assorted clowns and buffoons with bursts of ridicule that can attach to whole groups of people.

But in addition to their immediate effects, horror and humor can stab even more deeply. Insofar as they traffic in the transgression of the concept of the human, often at the level of folk biology, they suggest that their targets are not human, and, therefore, not appropriate objects of human concern, particularly moral concern. Monsters and clown types are beneath or outside ethics. At the same time, their ugliness suggests their moral defectiveness and sometimes their evil in ways that indicate that they deserve whatever harsh treatment and punishment they receive. If beauty—the perfect realization of the concept of the human—rhetorically implies goodness, ugliness and category violation encourage the suspicion of evil and moral defectiveness. Where beauty can be used to valorize, horror and humor can be used to dehumanize and to vilify and, for that reason, they are diabolically effective levers of ethnic and racial hatred—ones that operate pretty close to our nerve endings.[36]

NOTES

I would especially like to thank Eric Foner, John Szwed, Sally Banes, S. T. Ross, and David Bordwell for all their help in the preparation of this essay, though, of course, only I am responsible for the errors herein.

1. Immanuel Kant, *Critique of Judgment*, trans. Werner S. Pluhar (Indianapolis: Hackett, 1987), p. 76.

2. Ibid., p. 77.

3. Ibid., pp. 83–84.

4. This characterization of horror is defended in Noël Carroll, *The Philosophy of Horror* (New York: Routledge, 1990).

5. The relation of horror to comedy and of the clown to the monster is explored at length in Noël Carroll, "Horror and Humor," *Journal of Aesthetics and Art Criticism* 57, no. 2 (Spring 1999): 145–160.

6. Kant, *Critique of Judgment*, p. 180.

7. See Carroll, "Horror and Humor," for a defense of this contrast.

8. See L. Perry Curtis, *Apes and Angels: The Irishman in Victorian Caricature* (Washington, D.C.: Smithsonian Institution Press, 1971), p. 44.

9. Ibid., p. 43.

10. Ibid., p. 42.

11. Ibid., p. 49.

12. Ibid., p. 59.

13. Ibid., p. 63.

14. John Dower, *War without Mercy: Race and Power in the Pacific War* (New York: Pantheon, 1986), p. 187.

15. Ibid., p. 183.

16. Ibid., p. 182.

17. A letter from Frederick Douglass, dated June 14, 1870, reproduced in Katharine Morrison McClinton, *Chromolithographs of Louis Prang* (New York: Clarkson N. Potter, 1973), p. 37.

18. Jan Nederveen Pieterse, *White on Black: Images of Africa and Blacks in Western Popular Culture* (New Haven: Yale University Press, 1992), p. 116.

19. Ibid., pp. 40–43.

20. Talk of "missing links" fired the popular imagination. For example, in the Circus Museum in Baraboo, Wisconsin, there is a replica of a freak show tent. The statues represent a collection of some of the most popular "freaks" displayed by the Ringling Brothers and Barnum and Bailey Circus. Among the figures is a "missing link," a smallish black man called Zip. That the basis of the comic address of this figure rests on categorical incongruity is supported by the accompanying promotional material which asks of Zip "What is it?" One also wonders whether Zip's name isn't also connected to the name of one of the staple characters of the minstrel stage, Zip Coon who, though not a biological missing link, was a satirical representation of the black man as an imperfect realization of the concept of a cultured gentleman, a sort of cultural missing link.

21. Pieterse, *White on Black*, pp. 40–43.

22. Here, as in many horror fictions, one supposes that cross-species hybridization stands in for the terror of miscegenation. This sort of conflation, it seems to me, occurs often in horror literature. It is especially evident in the writings of H. P. Lovecraft, whose racist tendencies are widely acknowledged. See, for example, his story "The Shadow over Innsmouth," in which the monstrous citizens of the town are a result of inbreeding between South Sea Islanders, New England stock, and something else. Their children look simian and "what kind of foreign blood—if any—these beings had, it was impossible to tell." H. P. Lovecraft, "The Shadow over Innsmouth," in *The Lurking Fear and Other Stories* (New York: Del Rey, 1971), p. 134.

23. Pieterse, *White on Black*, p. 41.

24. Ibid., p. 38.

25. For a history of cross-species unions in cinema, see Rhona J. Berenstein, "White Skin, White Masks: Race, Gender and Monstrosity in Jungle Horror Cinema," in her *Attack of the Leading Ladies: Gender, Sexuality, and Spectatorship* (New York: Columbia University Press, 1996), pp. 160–197.

26. Pieterse, *White on Black*, pp. 85 and 228.

27. Robert E. Howard, "Moon of Zambebwei," *Trails in Darkness* (Riverdale, N.Y.: Baen Publishing Enterprises, 1996), pp. 203–204.

28. Similarly, in another film in the same cycle, the 1973 *Blackenstein,* vestiges of the simian-ization motif surface. Eddie, the amputee whom Dr. Stein is reconstructing, is adminis-tered the wrong drug, one with a tendency to induce atavistic or "throwback" reactions. When the effects of this drug begin to manifest themselves, Eddie's two initial symptoms recall simian imagery. First his brow thickens, becoming Neanderthalish or apish. Next, hair sprouts on the back of his hands. Admittedly, as Eddie evolves (or devolves) into a black Frankenstein monster, his makeup progressively imitates (though poorly) the ap-pearance of the Universal Studios horror films of the 1930s and 1940s. However, at least at first Eddie seems as though he is about to turn into an apeman.

29. Though I have been focusing on simianization, this is a subcategory of a wider strategy: the portrayal of the black man as beast. A discussion with examples of this figure can be found, among other places, in Marlon Riggs's TV documentary *Ethnic Notions* (KQED, 1987). See also Earl Ofari Hutchinson, "The Negro Beast or in the Image of God," in his *The Assassination of the Black Male* (Los Angeles: Middle Passage Press, 1994), pp. 7–17. Hutchinson argues that Rodney King was depicted in the vocabulary of the beast that was popularized in such texts as Charles Carroll's *The Negro a Beast, or, In the Image of God,* wherein it is alleged that "the black man was left out of human creation and was a sub-species of the animal world" (Hutchinson, "The Negro Beast," p. 8).

30. Pat Turner in *Ethnic Notions,* produced, written, and directed by Marlon Riggs.

31. See: www.alpha.org/jokes/jokes.html.

32. See: www.alpha.org/cartoons/cartoonsl.htm/.

33. Zombies can also be turned into amusing figures when their lumbering gait and deadpan stoic expressionlessness are contrasted with the excited, cowardly terror of a comic actor like Mantan Moreland in films like the 1943 *Revenge of the Zombies.* In effect, Moreland uses the zombie as a straight man.

34. This association of the black person with the aquatic also appears in Howard's "Moon of Zambebwei," where a black man is described: "His bullet-head was set squarely between those gigantic shoulders, like that of a frog." Howard, "Moon over Zambebwei," p. 177. I have also noted that there are several composite figures of blacks and aquatic figures fea-tured in *Ethnic Notions.* This leads me to wonder if there is a recurring motif that equates blacks with marine species. This is a topic for future research. However, if there were such an association, it might reveal a further source of the horror of cross-species misce-genation found in Lovecraft stories such as "The Shadow over Innsmouth," where the monsters are described as frog-like and fish-like as well as simian.

35. This is not to suggest that this rhetoric is only used against ethnic and racial groups. It is also employed against gays. For examples, see Harry M. Benshoff, *Monsters in the Closet: Homosexuality and the Horror Film* (Manchester: Manchester University Press, 1997) and Noël Carroll, *Philosophy of Mass Art* (Oxford: Clarendon Press, 1998), pp. 337–338.

36. Though I have stressed a recurring rhetorical association between horror and moral de-pravity in this essay, I should not be taken to be claiming that horrific ugliness always and necessarily connotes moral evil. There are standard deviations from this pattern. For ex-ample, there are many variations on the theme of beauty and the beast. Here the ugliness of the beast is to be taken initially as a sign of his moral depravity, but then the unfolding particularities of the story eventually reverse this valuation. So a horrific depiction need

not necessarily entail moral depravity. Its valuation can be redirected in the plot (though this is not always easy). All things being equal, horror will be a sign of moral defectiveness and beauty will be a sign of virtue. Those are our default assumptions. But sometimes all things are not equal, given the rest of the story. The comic book series *Spawn* is perhaps an example of this—an example where a black monster, as a result of the narrative, accrues a positive moral valuation.

That is, beauty, given the history of its association with moral goodness, is a *prima facie* cue for goodness; horrific imagery is a *prima facie* cue for moral depravity. These cues can either be reinforced or cancelled by the ensuing text (whether visual or verbal). Most frequently in popular culture, images of horror and ugliness will turn out to be evil, confirming our initial suspicion, based on the monster's ugliness. This initial suspicion can be reversed, but that takes extra work on the part of the artist. The homology—beauty/goodness :: ugliness/evil—provides the *initial* (or default) inference pattern that audiences generally use to decipher such imagery.

Chapter 5 Is the Medium
a (Moral) Message?

INTRODUCTION

The question to be addressed in this essay concerns the moral significance of the television medium. By 'medium' here I am not referring
to television as a business that churns out countless stories. Rather, I
am referring specifically to the historically standard image, especially
in regard to fiction, and to the ways in which it is typically elaborated
by structures like editing, camera movement, narrative forms, and the
like. Moreover, I will be concerned with the moral status of the television image as such, irrespective of what it is an image of.

Though the distinction between form and content may be historically outmoded and ultimately unsatisfactory, perhaps I can at least
provisionally demarcate my domain of interest by initially adopting
the distinction and by saying that this is an essay about the putative
moral significance of television from the viewpoint of some of its typical formal features—or, at least, from the viewpoint of a number of
its formal features that are alleged to be typical.

Furthermore, throughout this essay, I shall be primarily interested
with charges that, in some way or other, the relevant television forms

are morally suspect—that they have moral implications or consequences that should be ethically worrisome. I dwell on the negative perspective of the medium, rather than on perspectives that see it as positive or beneficial, since negative prognostications represent the dominant tradition; most commentators prefer to scorn television rather than praise it.

I suppose that there can be little debate about whether television has some moral consequences, though there is certainly a legitimate disagreement about how extensive these are. On the positive side, there is evidence indicating that people can learn about alternative lifestyles from television and that this can bring ethically significant changes in their everyday existence. People from Third World cultures can learn about ways of life in the First World and women can learn about male culture, and this exposure can encourage them to alter their lives. It is said that access through television to western ways of life contributed to the dissatisfaction and subsequent political resistance on the part of the citizens of the former Soviet empire. Likewise, a case can be made out that at least *sometimes* television befouls the moral atmosphere, perhaps by reinforcing oppressive social views. Obviously, certain programmes may traffic in outright propaganda and thereby stoke the flames of racism.

Such consequences as these, if and where they obtain, however, appear to be more a matter of the content of certain programming rather than the result of the historically typical forms of the medium. But the question before us is whether these historically typical forms of television—like the image—are morally significant. Specifically, are they inherently morally suspect?

Why would anyone think that they might be? Maybe one consideration has to do with the inordinate amount of time that the average viewer is said to spend watching the screen. These estimates seem to rise every year. One is often left with the impression that one's fellow citizens spend almost as much time watching television as they spend working and sleeping. Surely, the argument might go, it is reasonable to assume that if so much time is spent doing this, it must have some influence. Moreover, it also seems not implausible to assume—at least as a bit of armchair psychology—that part of that influence must be a result of the mode of presentation. For example, we often hear that the structure of programming has shrunk the audience's attention span, thus incurring a cognitive deficit. Analogously, one might conjecture that comparable moral deficits are also probable. Again, this hypothesis might be thought to be compelling just because television takes up such a large proportion of everyday life in the industrial world.

A second line of support for the view that the medium is morally significant might originate in the McLuhanite mantra that the medium is the message. That is, McLuhan urged a generation of researchers to look for the significance of television not at the level of its manifest content—its soaps and game shows—but at the level of its latent structure. McLuhan, himself, found a morally salutary message there: the prophecy of neo-tribalism and the global village. But since after half a century of television the world seems to many no better and perhaps worse, those who are convinced by McLuhan's mantra may begin to worry that the medium's message is far from wholesome. This is probably abetted by indulging the *post hoc, propter hoc* fallacy: since things have supposedly deteriorated morally to such a striking degree since the advent of television, it must be due, at least in part, to its emergence as a major medium of communication.

Of course, these suspicions are rather broad. The historically standard medium *might* have moral repercussions. Anything might. But before we become morally alarmed about these prospects, we want to be reassured that we are confronted by more than abstract possibilities; we want to have grounds for believing that some unsavoury moral possibilities are actually realised by existing television as we know it. This places a certain burden of proof on the critic. He or she must come up with some plausible compromising effect of the medium that is reasonably traceable to the traditional television formats (in the way that reduced attention spans at least *seem* to be a possible outcome of abbreviated televisual forms like advertisements, music videos and the rushed segmentation of game shows, headline news programmes, sit-coms and the like).

Another way to put this is that before we start being concerned that the medium carries untoward moral consequences, we will want to hear some concrete hypotheses about its likely immoral effects in conjunction with explanations of those features that are apt to bring these effects about. That is, we expect the critic to specify some mechanism that accords plausibly with an appropriate description of the medium and also seems of the kind likely to have unhappy consequences or implications for the moral life of viewers.

In this essay, I will consider three such hypotheses about such conjunctions of effects and mechanisms: what I call realism, escapism and hypnotism respectively. Though I believe that the tendency to resort to mechanisms like these is frequent in critical discourse about television, I also concede that my characterisations of them are ideal types. Television criticism is often quite fragmentary and elliptical, leaving many of its underlying premises unstated and unarticulated. What I will attempt to do is to give theoretical body to many of the intuitions that appear to be presupposed in some of the more frequently recurring diatribes against the medium. Thus, what follows is a rational reconstruction in theoretical form of what I take to be several of the leading anxieties about television's moral status.

However, since I intend to question each of these arguments against television, it might be objected that by 'rationally reconstructing' these viewpoints in order to confute them, what I am really doing is rigging the game from the start, assembling straw men for the purposes of igniting them. Against this, I would not only respond that these straw men are composed of real straws, gathered from the existing literature, but also that if there are better arguments than the ones constructed by either previous critics or me, then the burden of putting them forward now falls to the aspiring moralist.

The arguments about the degraded moral status of television that I am about to review—realism, escapism and hypnotism—are not peculiar to this medium. Some details derive from long-standing debates about popular art and media, especially visual media. Some elements in these arguments hark back to Plato and they have surfaced again and again in attacks on movies, comics, pulp literature, music and so on. In many cases, the recurring arguments against television seem to be a matter of far from new wine in very old bottles. This, of course, is to be expected, given the incremental evolution of culture, its tendency to accommodate the present by grafting it to elements of the past. But, if anything, this should lend more credence to my reconstructions of the arguments against television, since the gaps in those arguments can be so readily filled, in as much as they rely heavily on beliefs already abroad in the ongoing discussion of popular entertainment in culture.

REALISM

The standard television image is pictorial—a close-up of Johnny Carson's face or a long shot of Deep Space-Nine. Pictures, moreover, are processed by the same visual capacities that we use in everyday life. Arguably we use pretty much the same perceptual processes to recognise typical pictures that we use to recognise their referents in, so to speak, 'nature'. Picture recognition may, in fact, be a hardwired perceptual capacity. This, in turn, may provide part of the explanation of how television can be so accessible to such wide numbers of people, since the basic images in its system of communication are things that nearly everyone has access to in virtue of their innate perceptual capacities.

Of course, even if we prefer to speak of codes or conventions of perception rather than of hardwired recognitional capacities, we may still agree that the so-called perceptual codes used with respect to pictures, on the one hand, and with respect to the world, on the other hand, are pretty closely related. It is in this regard that the television image (as standardly used) is realistic: the visual codes or recognitional capacities that we use to navigate its images are the same or pretty much the same as the ones that we use to navigate everyday life.

It didn't have to be this way. The early technologies that gave rise to television were developed in order to broadcast words and sentences—such as financial news—over great distances, such as oceans. Had its evolution continued under that programme, if it had become an art, then it would have been more in the tradition of the novel; it might have been a delivery system for novels rather than in the tradition of the theatre and film.

But that is not how things happened. And, as a result, the standard small-screen image is realistic in the sense that it is normally processed in much the same way that we view ordinary objects, as opposed, say, to the way that we read words. The medium trades in visual appearances and those visual appearances trigger perceptual processes akin to those triggered by their real-world referents.

The association of television as we know it with realism is also bolstered by its relation to camera technology. Television stands in the cultural lineage of photography and film; indeed much of its material is initially generated by means of cinematography. Moreover, such camera technologies are associated with recording—both historically, given some of the original purposes of photography, and formally, since whether made on film or video, television imagery is standardly a record of events in the world, even when the event is people acting out a drama or fiction. The relation of television to recording, then, supplies further grounds, though different grounds, for calling its image realistic, since it typically derives from reality, a reality that includes the acting out of scenes later to be taken as fictional.

According to Plato, picturing involves little more than holding up a mirror to nature. It deals in visual appearances (and, for Plato, for this very reason, picturing is epistemically defective when compared to the knowledge available from contemplating the Forms). Whether or not painters ever proceeded in such a mechanical manner, certain views of the television image are that it is little more than an affair of mirrors, mechanically or electronically recording, it might be said, the appearance of real things in such a way that our ordinary, low-level object-recognitional capacities are activated or triggered.

If we regard television realism in this way—as engaging ordinary, everyday perceptual capacities through processes that, in part, involve recording—the idea seems at least credible. However, critics believe that along with this variety of perceptual realism comes another effect, which we may call the naturalisation effect. Through realism of the previous sort—through verisimilitudinous appearances and recording—the image imbues whatever it presents with the aura of being natural, that is, of being a representation of the way things (really) are (and must be).

Realistic imagery in our previous sense, in other words, is said to carry a certain rhetorical force, namely it leaves the impression that what it depicts is the case. Perceptual realism tends to convince viewers, in some sense, of the veracity of what they are seeing. Thus, if television imagery presents racial stereotypes via perceptually realistic imagery, viewers, it is thought, will be disposed to accept those stereotypes as true representations, for example, of the behaviour of black people.

Images that proceed by means of perceptual realism, it is claimed, have a spillover effect that inclines viewers to greet them as, to speak loosely, representations of the way things are. Images of black men as confidence artists, lay-abouts and rascals, that is, are thought to confirm, by dint of their perceptual realism, that this is the way these kinds of people actually behave.

Furthermore, this spillover effect is supposed to be even stronger than I have thus far indicated. The thesis has a powerfully deterministic flavour, connoting not merely that what is depicted realistically is somehow the case, but also that it must be the case; that the relevant modality is not just actuality, but some kind of necessity. For example, repeated realistic representations of nuclear families in television sitcoms—from *The Dick Van Dyke Show* to *Roseanne*—not only are thought to imply that the nuclear family *is* the basic social unit, but that it *must* be—that this is a fact of human nature, that it is natural.

Hence the naturalisation effect ultimately is thought to engender in viewers convictions about the inevitability of existing social relations. This effect is particularly relevant for morality, since if it indeed obtains, then it would blinker the moral horizons of viewers. It would obstruct their recognition of alternatives to existing social arrangements. This causes especial alarm for moral reformers who, for example, oppose the notion that only heterosexual marriage is natural and so oppose any sort of representation that precludes the possibility of other sexual relationships. Thus, the putative naturalisation effect is of particular interest to reformers who worry that it is used in a way that inclines ordinary viewers toward complacency about existing immoral and unjust social relationships.

By means of perceptual realism, the television image is thought to lend credibility to various immoral and oppressive social relations. Ethnic, racial, sexist and heterosexist stereotypes are presented and naturalised as are all manner of other relations, such as: those between employer and employees; between the police, the criminal class, and law-abiding citizens; between doctors, nurses, and patients; lawyers, judges and clients; parents and children; and so on. Perceptual realism supposedly suggests to the audience that these relations are not only the way things are, but the way that things must be—that father indeed inevitably knows best (or, if not, mother does).

Moreover, if ought implies can, then the television world limits the viewer's conception of what is morally possible to whatever is endorsed by the putative rhetoric of perceptual realism. That is, if the spillover effects of perceptual realism suggest that things cannot be otherwise, then the image short-circuits moral reflection about the types of social and interpersonal relations it depicts.

Furthermore, if the hypothesis about the naturalisation effect is coupled with certain observations about recurring portrayals of social relations on television, then the medium as we know it presents a clear and present moral danger. For its 'world' is generally at great variance with the real world. There is far more violence there, more doctors, fewer poor people, a disproportionately large number of white males, and so on. Thus, the 'world' that television offers viewers in a perceptually realistic way is a distortion of society. Implicitly, it is a prescription masquerading—in the cloak of perceptual realism—as a description. Consequently, if some correlative, naturalising, spillover effect disposes audiences to view the 'television world' as the way that things must be, then the spectators' parameters for moral evaluation will be effectively undermined. Therefore, the television image as such comes to be regarded as morally problematic.

This hypothesis proposes both an effect—that the image inclines viewers to the conviction that things (especially social relations) cannot be otherwise—and a mechanism—naturalisation via perceptual realism. Both these postulations seem dubious. Let us look at the effect first.

Is it plausible to suppose that television disposes viewers to believe that things cannot be otherwise, specifically that they cannot be improved morally? This seems hardly likely as a generalisation about all television, since much of it is of a strongly reformist bent. Many movies made especially for it, for example, are 'problem films', presenting issues like racism, child abuse, wife-battering, AIDS and so on for the express purpose of convincing audiences that the relevant social ills can and should be remedied. I have little reason to disbelieve that these efforts are sometimes effective in moving some audiences morally. Therefore, it cannot be the case that by deploying perceptual realism, television cannot propose that things can be otherwise in morally significant ways.

Moreover, researchers in the area called cultural studies regard television as a site of resistance, by which they mean that viewers contest many of the implications of the programmes. For example, Native Americans may cheer when white settlers are massacred; they do not docilely accept the inevitability of white imperialism. Perhaps people in cultural studies exaggerate the amount of resistance that is abroad with respect to people's viewing. But they have established that there is some resistance and that is enough to call into question the hypothesis that the so-called naturalisation effect automatically reduces viewers to moral inertia.

Of course, one always wonders about the theoretical grounds for postulating the naturalisation effect. Supposedly perceptual realism gives rise to certain spillover effects: the impression that what is represented is how things are and, in consequence, how they must be. The first step in this deduction appears to ride on an equivocation.

Realism as a style, it might be said, implies a commitment to representing how things are; thus audiences take realistic representations that way. But *perceptual realism* is not realism in this sense. It is committed only to presenting things in such a way as to activate ordinary visual processes, specifically recognitional capacities. It carries no commitment to representing the world, especially the social world, accurately. This should be obvious, since it is, in principle, compatible with fiction. The audience realises that perceptual realism is not, in principle, committed to an accurate representation of the world. They know that Amos and Andy are not existing persons. So why suppose that viewers take perceptually realistic television images to show how things really are?

At this point, it might be said that it is not particulars that audiences take to be real, but rather certain social types and situation types. Audiences know that Andy and Amos do not exist, but perceptual realism convinces them that types, such as the ones portrayed by Amos and Andy, are accurate. But, even if we are not Platonists, the question remains as to why perceptual realism would have any special relation to shaping viewers' conceptions of types, since its domain is generally particulars: individual persons, actions, objects and events. What is the psychological mechanism that gets us from the appearance of particulars in whose existence we do not believe to types whose accuracy we accept?

If the connection between perceptual realism and the conviction that 'this is how things are' is doubtful, then the connection with the impression that 'this is how things must be' seems even more strained. Why should perceptual realism lend an aura of fatalistic determinism to what is represented? The application of our standing perceptual processes to events in the world does not come in concert with fatalism; when I see that my den is in a mess up, I do not surmise that it cannot be otherwise (or if I do, my wife doesn't). So why should the operation of our normal perceptual processes while watching television leave us convinced that things cannot be changed?

If the answer here is that it is not perceptual realism that secures this effect, but narrative structure, then we shall need to point out that television narratives often herald social change in morally beneficial directions. That is, many such narratives behave in a way opposite to that which proponents of the naturalisation effect predict.

Thus I conclude that anxieties about the moral status of the television image as such, which are based on the perceptual realism of the medium, are woefully ill-founded.

ESCAPISM

One of the most frequent charges against television in the name of morality is that it is escapist. This charge is problematic at first blush because so many things can be meant by it, not all of which are bad. For example, if 'to escape' merely means to change one activity for another activity, which other activity may be rewarding (say, listening intently to classical music), then no necessary opprobrium should attach to the term. However, when television is called 'escapist' critics have something pejorative in mind.

One thing that might be labelled 'escapist' in the pejorative sense could be a tendency to do one thing when one should be doing something else. Shirking one's responsibilities and watching television instead would be escapist in this sense. This notion of escapism would appear to be in play when one is chided for spending too much time in front of the screen rather than improving oneself or undertaking political activity. But here the wrongness would appear to attach to one's avoidance behaviour and not to the medium itself, since it would be equally escapist in this sense to start working when one was supposed to be visiting a sick relative whom, perhaps, one dislikes. Thus when the label 'escapist' is used the critic must be referring to something else.

Perhaps it is this: escapism in this context has to do with the tendency to indulge in fantasy. Television, then, it is alleged, has something to do with inducing fantasy, where fantasy itself is regarded as morally disreputable. If this is what critics are arguing, then we need to know both what might be disreputable about fantasy and how it is that television, in particular, encourages it.

But what could be wrong with fantasising itself, especially where it is not the case that we are fantasising when we should be doing something else? One idea might be that fantasy involves decoupling our emotional responses from action. When we fantasise events—when we daydream—we undergo various emotional states, but these are divorced from action. We savour our indignation over various injustices around us, but we need not act; daydreaming disconnects affect from responsibility. This might be thought to be fraught with potential moral dangers, including: that by emoting indignation in our imagination, we deceive ourselves into thinking we have met the demands of morality; that we come to prefer emoting for the fantasised objects over real-world ones (for imagined poor people rather than real ones); that we come to prefer emoting over acting (putting watching television over community service).

But even if these specific problems are merely abuses that *might* arise from fantasy, it may still be argued that the bottom line is that it is of the nature of the structure of fantasy—its contents notwithstanding—to disconnect emotion and action. And this, it might be thought, is always a perversion of the normal function of our psychological system. Just as masturbation is alleged to pervert the sexual function, fantasy might be said to be a perversion of the emotion–action system. Detaching affect from action endangers the smooth functioning of the system; perhaps it makes us more likely not to respond to certain real-world events, just because we have accustomed ourselves to emoting without acting in our fantasy life. Thus, in so far as fantasy erodes or is likely to erode the linkage between emotion and action, and the linkage between emotion and action is essential for moral behaviour, fantasy as such—no matter what its contents are—is ethically suspect because it tampers with the conditions for moral activity. It leaves us satisfied with feeling the emotion without acting on it.

Moreover, it may be alleged that television is especially conducive to fantasy. That is, it encourages fantasy in a non-accidental way. Just as narcotics abet pure affective reveries divorced from action, so too does television. This is not simply a matter of people in certain circumstances turning to television when they should be otherwise engaged. The point about fantasy-encouragement is that it is supposed to be common to all television viewing, whatever the circumstances. It is about the medium as such and its inherent escapist proclivities. Moreover, this argument can be made without reference to any particular fantasy contents, such as the alluring (perhaps compensatory) imagery of wealth, sex and power. For the charge is that the medium itself encourages fantasy and fantasy as such is morally dubious.

But what is it about the medium that makes it complicit with fantasy? Here it may be argued that its images are illusionistic. Their compelling perceptual realism causes us involuntarily to suspend our disbelief about the existence of a creature such as the 'primate worm' in the *X-Files* episode entitled 'The Host', and, as a result, we experience the thrill of fear without the impulse either to flee or to fight. Likewise we feel outrage at the treatment of the black men in a television movie such as *Miss Evers' Boys,* but we don't have to do anything about it. Moreover, this process is based on a deception: our acceptance of a false belief, i.e. that the illusion before us is a real, occurring event—thereby adding lying to the moral harm involved in this characterisation of escapism.

Illusion, then, is the mechanism that enables the television image to promote fantasy, where fantasy itself is an escapist tendency in the morally pejorative sense. Since Plato, there has been a disapproving correlation of the visual and the emotional, though in the present argument it is not the emotions themselves that are subject to moral criticism, but rather the condition of undergoing (and enjoying) emotions divorced from action and the responsibility to act. Television activates the emotions illusionistically, but in a way so as to function as a kind of electronic prosthetic fantasy—prosthetic in the sense that it does our imaging for us, but is still a fantasy, since it requires no action on our part.

Television, then, is escapist because it encourages fantasy—an escape from the burden of action by its very nature—and it encourages fantasy through its deceptive or illusionistic imagery. But this argument seems flawed on two counts: both in its suspicion of fantasy and in its conception of the image as illusionistic.

The suspicion of fantasy seems to be based upon too narrow a conception of the psychology of the emotions. The emotions are typically connected to action and the linkage between the emotions and action is crucial to moral behaviour. However, this does not entail that entertaining emotions without acting is a perversion of human nature. The human capacity to undergo emotional states without the necessity to act is highly adaptive and, indeed, can make for more effective future action.

That children can be frightened by descriptions of counterfactual circumstances of danger prepares them for future predicaments. That we can envision future activities and undergo emotional responses with respect to our imaginings gives us information of what it would be like to do such and such, and, thereby, helps in making practical, and moral, decisions. Our capacity to emote without acting also enables us to simulate conspecifics and, in consequence, to modulate our responses to them, morally as well as prudentially. In all these cases, and many others, the capacity to decouple emotions and actions is an advantage to human psychology overall, not a perversion, and it is often relevant to, rather than disruptive of, moral behaviour.

Thus, where 'escapist' is opposed to 'adaptive', the bare faculty of fantasy is not necessarily escapist, nor is it necessarily alien to the moral life, since the capacity to imagine emotively without acting is at least relevant to deliberating morally about our own future actions; to learning to size up the counterfactual situations, including morally significant ones, that may one day become factual; and for gathering information, including morally pertinent information, about others both in terms of what they are feeling and what they are likely to do. Thus there is nothing morally wrong with fantasy in principle, but only with specific fantasies.

Similarly, if there is any special connection between television and fantasy, there would be no problem then apart from the specific fantasies—abetted by specific programmes and their content—in question. And even if there is no special connection, but only a connection that television shares with other media, there is also no call to presuppose that everything it encourages us to imagine emotively is morally compromised. Indeed, if fantasy—imagining emotively—can be serviceable in moral living in general, then there are no grounds to think that television as prosthetic imagining can't be serviceable too. Perhaps responding emotionally to fictions depicting racism and sexism can prepare us to focus in emotionally appropriate ways on comparable real-world occurrences of racism and sexism.

Of course, there is also something wrong with the story rehearsed earlier about illusionism. Supposedly, the television image is an illusion which leads us to suspend our disbelief about whatever is represented. This makes it possible for us to respond emotionally, since it is supposed that an emotion requires belief, and the suspension of disbelief puts us in the requisite condition: it leaves us believing what we are seeing.

However, one wonders whether there aren't at least two steps too many in this scenario. For if emotions can be generated by imaginings—thoughts entertained in the mind but as unasserted with respect to truth—and if perceptual realism alone, without any supposition of illusion, can provide the grounds for imagining (for example, that Miss Evers' boys are being treated unjustly), then we can dispense with talk about both illusion and the suspension of disbelief in a stroke. And this would be all to the good anyway, since both ideas appear to suggest that viewers believe what they see before them, leaving it a mystery, then, why they don't match their emotions with actions.

Thus, the view that television is escapist because its illusionist image abets psychological perversity appears ill-advised, both because fantasy—emotive imagining decoupled from action—is not necessarily escapist in any morally pejorative sense and because the image in question is not illusionistic. The television image is typically perceptually realistic, but this does not involve one in taking on false beliefs, but only recognising what visual arrays represent. And though perceptual realism may support emotive imagining, the moral status of such imagining depends on its content, not upon the kind of mental state it is.

Here it might be argued that I have changed the terms of the argument by talking about imagining rather than fantasising. But if fantasising is just the name for naughty emotive imagining, then clearly once again it is the content of the state, not the category of the state that we are assessing. It is true that television supports emotive imagining (though not by morally disreputable illusions), but since there is nothing wrong *per se* with emotive imagining, the medium as such is not escapist in any morally problematic way.

HYPNOTISM

If the problem cited in the escapism argument is that, in one sense, the medium encourages too much space for imaginative activity (abusively called fantasy), then the problem at issue in the hypnotism argument is that television allows virtually no room for the imagination at all. The hypnotism argument begins by taking note of the unexceptionable fact that the point of television is to draw our attention to it. Producers want us to watch it. In this they are no different from film makers.

However, in various respects, the movie maker has certain advantages over the television producer when it comes to compelling our attention. The film image is standardly much larger than the television one; the film screen is usually bigger than we are, whereas typically we tower over our television sets. Moreover, the resolution of the television image is typically not as bright or lustrous as the film image. Thus, along certain dimensions, the power of the former image can be said to be weak, particularly when compared to film. Whereas in a darkened screening room, our eyes are drawn to the large, illuminated film image—in truth we have little else to look at—in our living room, the duller, low resolution television screen competes for attention with other objects. It is easy for our attention to drift away from it. Thus, a primary task for the producer, given the tendency of our attention to drift, is to keep our eyes riveted on the screen.

A major resource for the television producer in this regard is the organisation of the image track. Our perceptual system is calibrated to be especially sensitive to change and movement. The obvious adaptive advantage of this is straightforward: movement in the environment in the early days of humankind was often the signal of the arrival of either predators or prey—of either danger or food. Thus our eyes are drawn to movement and change by reflex. The producer can make use of this in order to keep our attention on the screen by organising the image track structurally so that it bristles with movement and change.

Some of the relevant devices available for this purpose include: editing, camera movement, zooming, superimpositions, fades and so on. These sorts of visual devices, of course, are also available in film. However, their incidence in television—especially certain kinds (such as advertisements and music videos)—is often higher than it is in film. If we call the use of these devices 'structural articulations', then some commentators estimate that there are usually as many as eight to ten structural articulations per sixty-second interval in a commercial television programme and as many as ten to fifteen structural articulations per thirty-second interval in the average advertisement. Of course, the ration of structural articulations in commercial action programmes like *Miami Vice* can be even higher than the average for commercial programming, and cutting in music videos is frequently as high as nearly twenty shots per minute.

Needless to say, television not only deploys technical or structural changes of this sort. Fast movement inside the frame also commands our attention. This is why television loves basketball and football more than it loves baseball. Moreover, it is no accident that situation comedy is typically structured around rapid-fire repartee—trading insults in fast-paced *badinage*—because the cascade of punch lines, accompanied by rapid switching of shots from one person to another, holds our attention in the absence of compelling plot developments. Likewise, headline news programmes are always changing the story briskly, and cutting to the next visual, never giving our attention an instant to flag. Indeed, I have seen news reports where the visual cuts are repeated twice, presumably in order to maximise the number of cuts in the segment.

One pretty obvious function of the plethora of structural articulations on the visual track is to compel our interest in what is going on in the image by triggering our innate tendencies to fixate on movement and change. By means of structural articulations like cutting, the producer introduces movement and change into the visual array, often at a fairly pronounced pace. This is attention-grabbing; the structural articulations, so to speak, renew or rejuvenate our attention on almost a moment-to-moment basis, and they work against the tendency of our attention to drift away from the screen. The structural articulations, it might be said, trap our attention; they lure us into the imagery. They rivet our attention and stimulate our natural expectation that something significant is about to happen, since that is what our movement detectors are adapted to expect. Thus the structural articulations keep us watching and draw us ahead, deeper into the programme. Our attention, it is suggested, is locked involuntarily on the image track, as if we were in a hypnotic trance. Perhaps it might be added that this is part of the reason that people watch such an enormous amount of television.

But why, if structural features of the medium do function this way, is this morally problematic? Here it may be alleged that the way in which television holds our attention has us, in a manner of speaking, 'chasing after the image'. We have to keep up with the image track as one structural articulation comes fast on the heels of the previous one. We are so busy trying to deal with the onslaught of structural articulations that we have little time for thought—little time, for example, to exercise our powers of imagination. The exercise of our attention in tracking the rush of structural articulations squeezes out the opportunity for any other kind of cognitive activity.

That is, because producers exploit certain possibilities of their medium in such a way that the image captures attention to an extent that precludes or crowds out the operation of other relevant cognitive powers, television in its standard form, with its emphasis on a high incidence of structural articulations, is morally problematic. This judgement, of course, is connected to the specific cognitive powers that the critic alleges are thrust in abeyance by the intensive preoccupation of attention to the changing image track.

These cognitive powers are at least two in number: our critical powers and our imagining powers. The imagery purportedly goes by so fast that we are so busy keeping up with it attentively that we do not have time to assess it from the point of view of moral criticism. But an even more worrisome possibility is that the way in which attention is swamped with stimuli closes off the operation of our imaginative powers.

Here, the hypnotism argument shares a premiss with the realism argument. The imagination is said to be an essential feature of moral thinking because it is the power to envision alternatives. Moral judgement presupposes the recognition that things could be otherwise. The rapid succession of structural articulations, like cutting, does not allow the spectator the time to imagine moral alternatives; one is so occupied in simply attending to the visual array that there is no space for the moral imagination to take root. Thus, by precluding the operation of the moral imagination with respect to fictional and documentary material that calls for moral judgement, the typical structuring of television imagery is morally suspect.

Both the realism argument and the hypnotism argument maintain that what is morally problematic about the television imagery is that it prevents the spectator from envisioning alternatives, from thinking that things could be otherwise than the way they are portrayed on the screen. However, the two arguments reach this conclusion by different routes. The realism argument alleges that this effect occurs through naturalisation—through imparting the impression that 'this is the way things are'. The hypnotism argument maintains that the imagination is stultified by overwhelming our attention with unrelenting sequences of structural articulations.

The hypnotism argument can also be connected to certain notions of escapism. If the concept of escapism that we have in mind is that behaviour is escapist when we are doing one thing when we should be doing another, then it may be alleged that television, organised breathlessly around the succession of structural articulations, contributes to escapism by, so to speak, holding our attention to the screen captive. It is not entirely our fault that we continue to watch when we should be doing other things—improving ourselves, engaging in political activities, and so on—because producers are, for their own purposes, manipulating features of our perceptual make-up in ways that reinforce inertia. In other words, it is not entirely a result of our own character failings that we are couch potatoes. We have been hypnotised by the way television is typically articulated, irrespective of the content of the imagery.

All those people who watch so much television are virtually trapped by televisual images. But not only are they held in thrall before the screen for hour after hour. While they sit there, their powers of imagination, notably their powers of moral imagination, are effectively anaesthetised. Their attention is so engaged negotiating the imagery that moral judgement goes on holiday. And this makes the typical television format morally problematic in its own right.

There is no question that the image track is structured so as to secure maximal attention from spectators. In this, the proponent of the hypnotism argument is on solid ground. However, the question is whether or not the hypnotism argument overestimates the effectiveness of the medium in this matter. In my view, the hypnotism argument vastly exaggerates the power of the image track to hold the audience spellbound. It may characteristically be designed as a solution to the problem of wavering attention, but it is hardly 100 per cent successful in this regard.

Much viewing occurs in a highly distracted way. As a successor to radio listening, television viewing is often pursued in concert with other activities, including household chores. As the family sits around the set, what is on the screen often takes a back seat to conversations. Some commentators characterise our typical way of looking at television as 'the glance' as opposed to 'the gaze'. The notion of the gaze refers to the intent looking that marks our attention to movie images in cinemas. The glance is a more casual mode of attention, such as that shown by students who look up from their homework and catch a glimpse of the programme before returning to their algebra. I would not wish to argue categorically that television viewing is always a matter of 'the glance' in contrast to movie viewing which is always a matter of the so-called gaze. Nevertheless, it does seem to me that the television image is not as hypnotic as critics argue. However much structural articulations incline us to continue watching, it is very easy to escape their grip, as should be clear from the fact that people often half-watch television while they are doing something else.

The fact that one can do this also raises doubt about the extent to which television really crowds out the possibility of other occurrent cognitive activities. Certainly it does not preclude imagining: one can easily indulge in a bit of daydreaming while following an episode of *Star Trek*. Indeed, it seems wildly wrong to suspect that television precludes imagining, since certain forms of imaginative activity are probably required or presupposed in order to understand what is going on in any given programme.

Television programmes are edited, often intensively edited, as we have already noted. But in order to assimilate the meaning of those edited arrays, the mind must be engaged in some form of constructive activity and this, presumably, involves the operation of the imagination. The structural articulations we have discussed cannot preclude the operation of the imagination entirely; we cannot merely be attending to the parade of structural articulations in a frenzy of cognitively impenetrable reflexes. Otherwise the array would appear meaningless. But since these arrays characteristically appear meaningful, we must suppose that some form of constructive, imaginative mental activity is in play.

Moreover, not only is it the case that the operation of our constructive powers of imagination are engaged by watching television. Our powers of moral imagination must be in gear as well. Typical programmes—both fictions and news programmes—constantly call upon their audiences to make moral judgements. This presupposes the activity of the moral imagination. If we are to recognise that a certain character is evil, we must be able to recognise that his behaviour can be otherwise. How could typical TV programmes elicit the moral uptake they require in order to be intelligible if they, at the same time, shunt the moral imagination to the sidelines? Clearly, the moral imagination could not be so neutralised, if the programme is intended to communicate to viewers in a way that requires moral judgement. And just as clearly, the imagery does not neutralise our powers of moral imagination, since it does so frequently elicit the requisite moral judgements from viewers. In order to follow the programme, viewers must be making certain moral judgements. That they do follow such programmes indicates that their powers of moral imagination are suitably engaged. Following the image track in terms of attention, then, does not preclude following it with an alert moral imagination.

Nevertheless, here it might be argued that the moral imagination is shackled or constrained by television. We make moral judgements all right, but only the moral judgements that the producers want us to make about the content of their programmes. Yet this is palpably false. How could it be true at the same time that critics, including ordinary citizens, rage about violence and sex on television? Producers certainly are not happy about those moral responses, and did not intend them. Nor were the exercises of the moral imagination that were called on to make those responses in any way stultified by the organisation of the image track. In this regard, there is no reason to suspect that television as such, in its style of representation, necessarily poses a threat to the operation of the moral imagination. The hypnotism argument is no more compelling than either the realism or the escapism argument.

Nor does it seem very likely that the hypnotism argument explains why people watch so much television. The way the sequence of images is organised may draw attention to the screen, but its holding power is extremely limited; it takes a minuscule amount of effort to elude its grasp. That this is obvious perhaps explains why we often feel a guilty conscience for having overindulged our television habit.

If we watch too much television that is probably a function of the fact that in our culture we do not spend much time training people how to use the medium: how to integrate it in a fulfilling life-plan. This, of course, may itself reflect an unwillingness in certain societies to include as part of basic education thinking about how one might lead one's life and the habits one needs to develop to pursue such lives. The problem of excessive television viewing, then, is a moral problem, if it is a moral problem, because of a larger cultural failing. It is not an ailment to be attributed to the medium as such, nor to its characteristic stylistic elaboration of the image. Neither the medium nor the image is inherently immoral, though our systematic failure to educate people about how to use it may be socially irresponsible.

Chapter 6 Film Form:

An Argument for a Functional

Theory of Style in the

Individual Film

As with other artforms, the initial problem of talking about style or form in film is complicated by the fact that the concept of style can be applied to so many different kinds of things and at so many different levels of generality.[1] One might use "style" to refer to whole periods of filmmaking, speaking, for example, of the German Expressionist style, or Hollywood studio style in the thirties. Or one might apply the concept of style to the work of a particular filmmaker's oeuvre, referring, for instance, to the style of Stanley Donen or Yvonne Rainer or Theo Angelopoulos. In these cases, the domain of the concept of style fluctuates. That is, what it refers to shifts in terms of the range of things to which it is applied. When investigating a period style, we look at a domain comprising all the relevant films made in a stipulated spatio-temporal region. When considering a directorial style, we look only to the films of the director in question, including, where relevant, films of different stylistic periods.

Moreover, the concept of style can be mobilized for different purposes and, therefore, can take different directions of analysis. When interrogating a period style, our purpose is to say how all or most of the relevant films are similar, and, therefore, we look for what all the filmmakers under examination have in common. But when analyzing a directorial style, we look to features that differentiate a given filmmaker from other filmmakers—we look for what makes the director appear distinctive. And these different projects, of course, can pull in different directions. In discussing the work of Fritz Lang as a German Expressionist director, we may point to certain features of his work he shares with other directors of the pertinent movement and period, but when speaking of Lang's directorial style, we may omit some of these features, since they do not differentiate Lang from other directors.

Because the domains, purposes and directions of stylistic or formal research often diverge, the possibility of confusion—of talking past each other—can easily arise when speaking of "film style." Thus, in order to avoid such confusion, it is useful to separate out some of the different usages of the concept of film style in order to be clear about that to which we intend to apply it. Though other, more fine-grained, distinctions can be made with respect to the concept of style, a provisional cartography of common usages includes what we can call general style, personal style, and the style or form of the individual film.[2] Both general style and personal style refer to groups of film; their domain is a body of work. The style or form of the individual film refers to a specific film, such as *Kundun*. General style refers to a group of films by more than one filmmaker as in the notion of the Classical Hollywood Cinema. Personal style refers to the films of a single filmmaker, such as Edward Yang.

The category of general style can be further divided into at least four subclasses: universal style, period style, genre style, and school or movement style.[3] If we call the balanced shot outside the planetarium in Nicholas Ray's *Rebel Without A Cause*[4] "classical," we are using the concept of style in a universal sense, since we will call any such symmetrically poised composition, *from any period in film history* (and, perhaps in any visual artform), "classical" in this sense. The domain of the concept of style when used universally is at least all film. When we refer, however, to the tableau style or to the "clothes-line" style of composition of primitive film, though we are talking about a general style (and not the style of a specific filmmaker), our reference is restricted, with the exception of explicit references to atavisms, to films of the first two decades of this century. The universal concept of style applies to all films, whereas the concept of a period style applies only to some subset thereof governed by temporal/historical criteria and often by regional (sometimes national) considerations.

Generally, a filmmaker possesses a period style tacitly. She does not decide to work in that style explicitly. It is a prevailing style of norms and practices. Vincent Sherman did not decide to adopt a thirties studio style when he came to make his first film, *The Return of Dr. X.* He found it, so to speak, ready-to-hand. School or movement style, in contrast, is more a matter of express policy. A structural filmmaker decides to work in that style, perhaps by expanding its strategies in new directions. Though both period style and school/movement style differ from universal style inasmuch as they obtain in a subset of films of specific provenance rather than potentially in any film whatsoever, school/movement style differs from period style insofar as it is more a matter of self-consciously adopting a project than of settling into things as they are. School/movement style, however, generally does have something in common with period style, since schools and movements most frequently flourish in discrete historical moments.

With reference to general styles, there is also genre style. Many films fall into certain categories with relatively fixed, though variable, purposes, whose implementation often involves certain reliable, recurring strategies for getting the job done. These stylistic strategies may evolve and mutate from period to period, so genre style overlaps at times with the notion of a period style. Thus we speak of a film in the style of a fifties musical. But as in the case of a school style, the filmmaker adopts a genre style rather self-consciously: she is at least fully aware, for instance, that she is making a mystery film. Moreover, in contrast to the universal concept of style, the concept of genre style can be applied only to certain films, not potentially to all films. For example, it only makes sense to apply literally the style or form descriptors "ratiocinative versus hard-boiled" to detection fictions, but not to landscape films.

Personal style can be distinguished from the several categories of general style, since it targets the work of a specific filmmaker. Though historically, the director has been the filmmaker of choice in analyses of personal style in film, there is no reason in principle why one must restrict one's attention to directors. One might explore the personal style of a scriptwriter, a cinematographer, a set designer and so on. The preoccupation with the personal style of directors is often called *auteurism.* Its influence since the 1950s has been enormous. As a result, perhaps the most recurrent form of stylistic analysis in film studies has been keyed to discriminating personal styles.

Nevertheless, there is yet another project of stylistic analysis: the analysis of style or form in the individual film. The style of an individual film does not collapse, without remainder, into the personal style of its director. The reason for this is simple. Even a film by a director with a highly distinctive personal style may employ stylistic strategies not uniquely his or her own. A pronounced visual stylist like Brian DePalma may fall back on certain tried and true structures, common throughout the genre, for instilling suspense in order to solve his narrative problems. His use of these structures is not incidental, but integral to his film.

Thus, where the auteurist critic may overlook such choices—on the grounds that they do not differentiate a given film by DePalma from a mass of routine thrillers—if we are concerned with the style or form of the individual film, said structures are apt to loom large in our account. Because the analysis of personal style is concerned with taxonomy (and connoisseurship), it battens on those stylistic features that isolate the film in question as one by DePalma. But that is likely to leave a large number of a given film's stylistic features unaccounted for, since very few films are absolutely the product of uniquely personal strategies through and through.

For similar reasons, the analysis of the style of an individual film cannot be reduced to the analysis of its period, movement, or school style. Even if those are major ingredients in a given film, few, if any, films are merely unalloyed exemplars of their period, movement, or school. Each film will confront its own problems in achieving its point and/or purpose, even if those points and purposes are fairly generic ones. Each film will have its idiosyncratic formal solutions. And, in any case, no film will be a perfect exemplar of its period, movement, or school style insofar as it is highly unlikely that any film will employ every strategy of the general class to which it belongs. Thus, a concept of style or form in the individual film is unavoidable. My purpose in this essay is to suggest a framework for thinking about style in the individual film.

PART II: APPROACHING FILM FORM

In film studies, the examination of the style or form of the individual film is usually subordinated to frameworks that conceptualize the style or form of the individual film as exemplary of something else, usually the personal style of a director, or a period style, or the style of an influential movement or school. Interest in a given director, period, or movement leads the analyst to focus on certain formal features rather than others—obviously on the features that best exemplify what, for instance, is particularly Hawksian, thirty-ish, or Dadaist about the film under examination. While there is nothing wrong in calibrating research in this way, approaching an individual film in this manner is no guarantee that one will penetrate the form of the individual film, rather than possibly merely isolating at best a fragment of that form.

Consider Bazin's brilliant analysis of *Citizen Kane*. Because he was primarily interested in charting the evolution of a period style, he placed special emphasis on the deep-focus (or apparently deep-focus) shots in the film. This, too, is what most film instructors underline when teaching the film. But these shots, though immensely vivid and important to film, comprise only a small part of its formal organization. Accounting for them hardly amounts to a formal analysis of the film. For example, it pays scant attention to the recurring, probing camera movements that embody the investigative theme of the film. Bazin, of course, selected the elements of the film he did for emphasis because his concern was with what was emerging as a period style. But it would be a mistake to presume that an analysis of the period-relative formal elements of *Citizen Kane* suffices as an analysis of the form or style of *Citizen Kane* as an individual work of art.

Similar points can be made about formal analyses of films relative to the movements or schools to which they belong. One can discuss *October* as an illustrative specimen of the Soviet Montage school of the twenties, highlighting certain exemplary sequences and shot juxtapositions as paradigmatic of the movement. But inasmuch as the film also exhibits many formal choices that are not especially distinctive of the montage style, much of the film goes unanalyzed formally when it is treated as a stereotypical montage film.

Perhaps treating the style of the film as an expression of the filmmaker has a better claim than previous examples for isolating the form of the individual film. The concept of style has deep associations with the notion of personality. It is sometimes said that style is the man [the person]. People have personal styles, ways of being in the world that express their personality. There is some deep connection between style and expression; style is often taken to be what manifests or expresses personality. Thus, if we approach the style or form of the individual film as that which is expressive of its filmmaker's personality, as an auteurist does, then, it might be thought, we will gain our best insight into the style of that film.

The theoretical strength of auteurism is that it connects style with personal style or expressiveness. The auteurist explains the significance of Renoir's deeply-staged, multiplanar compositions in *Rules of the Game* in terms of his encompassing, compassionate, egalitarian vision—his openhearted concern for all of his characters as well as his view of the world as bustling, full, complex, and alive.

However, in order to pinpoint the style that is the director, the auteurist's unit of analysis must be the director's oeuvre, or some significant subsegment of it. Otherwise the auteurist cannot be sure that the director hasn't merely donned a mask for a specific film and that what appears as personality isn't just a persona. Thus, the auteurist searches for formal features that recur in the filmmaker's oeuvre; indeed, the auteurist looks especially for those recurring features that differentiate the pertinent filmmaker from other filmmakers. Since what the auteurist hopes to identify is the unique personality of the film-maker, what the auteurist searches for are the recurring stylistic features or formal mannerisms that make possible the manifest expression of the filmmaker's distinctive mode of being in the world.

This approach, nevertheless, carries with it certain obvious limitations. Inasmuch as significant formal choices in a film are frequently made to implement purposes not germane to other films by the director in question, they may not recur in other works of the filmmaker. For example, in *Sunset Blvd.,* Billy Wilder opts for interior shots of Norma Desmond's mansion that emphasize not only that it is large, but empty, at least in the sense of being bereft of people. Its *emptiness,* of course, underscores that Norma is isolated, that she is alone, with almost no one around her. The world has passed Norma Desmond by.

Wilder's stylistic choice of this way of shooting the interior of the mansion, especially the downstairs environs, answers the problem of the way in which to reinforce a central theme of the film—that everyone has abandoned Norma Desmond—by means of a formal articulation that makes her desolation almost visceral. It is a major formal contribution to the film. But since this use of space does not recur in other films by Wilder, it is likely to be neglected by the auteurist. Furthermore, insofar as this use of space is not particularly distinctive of Wilder—other directors have used vast interior spaces to connote isolation and loneliness—the auteur critic has an additional inclination to overlook Wilder's use of space in *Sunset Blvd.* Instead, the auteurist will probably pay more attention to the structures of irony that Wilder employs in the film, since irony, especially of a cynical sort, is a recurring feature of Wilder's work.

Emphasizing Wilder's irony in *Sunset Blvd.,* of course, is not so much wrong as it is incomplete. But exclusively using what one knows of Wilder's enduring concerns across his career as the filter for selecting the pertinent stylistic structures in *Sunset Blvd.* will draw attention away from many of the formal choices Wilder made in order to convey what he intended about Norma Desmond, her plight, and Hollywood culture in general. The project of *Sunset Blvd.* presented Wilder with various local problems that other stories and other films did not. The solutions to those problems, while determining the formal structures of

Sunset Blvd., need not be part of the account of what makes Wilder Wilder. Still they are indispensable contributions to what makes *Sunset Blvd.* as effective a film as it is. So, if we expect a stylistic analysis of an individual film to help to explain how it works, then auteurism is not enough.

A leading aim of auteurism is to differentiate one body of films from others—to say what is unique about the work of a given filmmaker. In this way, auteurism is connected to connoisseurship. This is not to say that auteurism need lack an explanatory dimension; the auteurist may explain how certain recurring elements in a work—for instance, the recurrence of vistas in John Ford's westerns—are expressive of his point of view about American history. The auteurist project, however, in terms of its "bottom line," remains tied to differentiating one filmmaker's oeuvre from those of others. And this concern with differentiation skews the stylistic analyses that the auteurist is apt to render of individual films.

Differentiation is also an important motive behind analyses of period, genre, and school/movement style. In each case, we want to identify the stylistic features that set off one group of films from another. Undeniably, this identification is worthwhile. But when used as an optic for the style of an individual film, the categorizing impulse behind stylistic analyses in terms of period, genre, or school/movement will gerrymander the form of an individual film for the sake of situating it in a class. But what distinguishes a film as a member of a stylistic category may be less important to the formal choices in a film than the particular problems the filmmaker solves in achieving the point or purpose of the film at hand, since those not only may involve choices not widely shared in other films of the generic type under examination but also features that do not differentiate the film in question from films of other periods, genres, or schools/movements.

Stylistic analyses bent on revealing the personal style of the filmmaker, period style, genre style, and school/movement style are fundamentally taxonomic in nature. Analyses of these sorts may do other things. But they are ultimately committed to categorizing the film. Thus, they are category-relative in a way that guides selectivity. And they may miss the trees for the forest.

As methods, these strategies of stylistic analysis do not promise to account fully for the form of a particular film, given its specific aims and context. They enable us to place the film, and, though that is genuinely informative, they may not explain why the individual film *qua* individual film possesses the stylistic or formal attributes it does. For that we need a theoretical framework for discussing form in the individual film.

PART III: TWO ATTEMPTS AT CHARACTERIZING
FILM FORM

Analyzing the style or form of each individual film in terms of personal style, period style, genre style, and school/movement style in turn supplies the analyst with a powerful heuristic for approaching an individual film. These approaches function as filters; they alert the analyst about what to look for. By saying, as I have, that they are not fully adequate to pithing the form of the individual film, I put us in a hard place. How are we to understand the form of an individual film, if not by placing it in stylistic categories like these? What is form in the individual film? How are we to conceptualize it? In order to answer these questions, let us look at alternative ways of clarifying the notion of film form in the hope of finding an adequate framework for talking about it.

One of the most common ways of thinking about artistic form in general and film form in particular is to conceive of form as one half of a couplet—the distinction between form and content. Many try to clarify this contrast by turning it into the distinction between meaning and mode of presentation. If part of the meaning of *Metropolis* is that factories turn workers into automatons, then the regimented blocking of the shots of the workers entering the factory is a formal device, a mode of presenting the meaning of the film. But, logically, this approach makes the concept of form wholly dependent upon the film's possession of something that we would be willing to countenance as a meaning. Therefore, if there are films without meanings, properly so called, as there seem to be, then this way of conceptualizing form entails that such films lack form altogether.

But this conclusion is mistaken. There are "meaningless" films, films that are dedicated to affording various perceptual and sensuous effects, including pleasurable ones. There are films that "say" nothing, but are simply beautiful or fascinating to look at. Some Structural Films are like this. They are films that we are often disposed to say are all form and no content, where content is understood as a matter of meaning. But on the view that form is the mode of presentation of content, where, in turn "content = meaning," one would have to say such films have no form whatsoever. And that seems just wrong.

This sort of objection suggests that we should attempt to find an alternative way of stating the contrast between form and content, one that does not rely upon the notion of meaning. One way of doing this is to propose that content is whatever makes up the film, and form is the *way* that whatever makes up the film is organized. Content is the matter; form is the manner. Form operates on whatever comprises the content of the film. Again, this makes our conception of the form of the film dependent on our conception of the content of the film. That is, one cannot determine the manner of its organization, until one knows what is being organized.

But there is an enormous problem here. What we are willing to call the form of a film depends upon our conception of the content of the work. But the notion of content, as just stated, is extremely ambiguous, and this ambiguity is apt to infect whatever we say about film form in such a way that the border between form and content becomes exceedingly shaky.

If we consider "content" to be "whatever makes up the film," think of all the things that we could have in mind. Imagine a short, one-shot film of an underprivileged child—the sort of advertisement that might be produced by a charitable organization. What makes up this film? In one sense, it is made up of— it consists in—photographic imprints subjected to light. At another level of description, it is made up of lines, colors, and closed shapes. These components then give rise to representational figures that refer to certain subjects or referents, namely the child and perhaps her empty bowl, which, in turn, may also be expressive of the human quality of pathos. Furthermore, the film may take a point of view toward the child, regarding her as worthy of concern and advancing that point of view as an implicit thesis. Indeed, the film may also promote an injunction about the child: that viewers should help her and other children in her condition.

An imagined film like this may be made up of many things: photographic emulsions, light, lines, colors, shapes, representations (and their subjects), points of view, expressive properties, theses, and injunctions. Moreover, this list could be even longer if our descriptions of the various dimensions of the film were more finely drawn. Which of all these sorts of things that can be said to make up the content of the film is the content of the film? The problem is that, at various times and in various contexts, any of these things or combinations thereof can be and have been identified as the content of films. But that renders the distinction between form and content unstable.

If we identify the content of a film with its lines, colors, and closed shapes, then not only is that at odds with the way in which we typically identify these elements in film, but it also leaves little else for film form to be. If the lines, colors, and closed shapes of the film do not constitute the formal elements of the film, then what does? Is there a way of handling the lines, colors, and closed shapes that is separable from these features? If shape and color are content elements in a film, and it is a nonrepresentational film, what is the form of the film? One might say that the form of the film is some emergent property of the colors and shapes—an expressive property, for example—but, then, expressive properties are usually taken to be part of the content of the work, not part of its form.

So, on the one hand, if one tries to deal with "contentless" films, by identifying their colors and shapes as the relevant content—to say that these films are about colors and shapes—then the film has no form. On the other hand, if one identifies the colors and shapes of such a film as its form, that identification is paradoxical, since on the view under consideration, there is no form without content. This is certainly an unsatisfying dilemma.

In fact, another reason that it is impossible to distinguish film form from film content (on the supposition that content is whatever makes up the film) is that speaking this broadly, form is undeniably one of the things that make up a film. Some might, of course, embrace the notion that there is no difference between form and content at this juncture, as the philosopher Croce did, but that scarcely helps in distinguishing the nature of film form.

In order to forestall difficulties like this, one might try to revert to ordinary language. In everyday speech, we frequently restrict content terminology to what the film represents. The content of the film is what it represents—its subject (for example, the impoverished child) and whatever it says about its subject. In this vein, we might say that the shapes and colors of the film are the formal elements that are deployed in a certain manner to articulate the content of the film—to represent the child and/or to represent her in a certain light or for a certain purpose.

But it is far from clear that the invocation of representation here will draw a reliable distinction between form and content. Think of point of view as a feature of films. It is a representational element of a film—one, for example, that is often connected to the theme of a work (what it says about its subject). Hatred of racism, for instance, might describe the point of view of a film. Since it is a representational feature of the work, it seems as though, according to ordinary language, it should count as a feature of the content of the film. And yet isn't it a formal feature as well? Isn't it a result of the way in which the representational material is being handled? Moreover, if we adopt the popular analogy that form is to content as a container is to the contained, isn't the point of view of a film that in which all the representational elements of the film are contained? Thus, invoking the concept of representation won't determinately mark the boundary between form and content for us.

And, of course, a related problem, which we have already encountered in this context, is that many films have no representational content. On the face of it, this entails that they have no form, since form is understood as correlative to content—as that upon which form must operate. But there are many nonrepresentational films that have form, such as *Diagonalsymphonie*. Moreover, if it is stipulated that such a film, and films like it, have content—for example, lines and shapes—then again we are left with no way to speak of their form. Either such works have content or they do not; but on either supposition, they appear to lack form on the view under consideration. Thus, either way, the view is not helpful. That is, the alleged distinction between form and content does not provide us with a comprehensive way of conceptualizing form in the individual film.

So far the problem has lain in trying to characterize film form in tandem with content. This characterization requires a way of drawing a line between the two. This, however, we have seen, appears to be extremely difficult. Consequently, an alternative approach that naturally recommends itself to us is to attempt to define film form without reference to content. This, at least, will halve our perplexity.

If we reflect upon the way in which we describe film form, we note that often we refer to it as unified or complex.[5] These are two frequently recurring comments about film form. They also provide us with a clue to the nature of film form. In order to be unified or complex, a film must be composed of parts. If, for example, a film's parts are related in such a way they appear co-ordinated, or, if certain relations between a film's parts are iterated—as when an opening composition is echoed in its concluding shots—we call those unity-making features of the film. If there are many different kinds of relations between the parts of the film, as there are in *Zorns Lemma,* or, if the relations between the parts are variegated and diverse, as they are in *Man with a Movie Camera,* we refer to the film as complex. The common threads that run through these formal descriptions are *parts* and *relations*.

Parts and relations, then, are basic ingredients of film form. When we make statements about the form of a film, we are speaking of relations between parts of the film. When we say that the figures on one side of a shot balance off the figures on the other side of the shot, we are talking about parts of the film in relation to each other. It seems reasonable to conjecture that whenever we make statements about the form of an individual film, we are making statements about some relation or relations between its parts. Form-statements, *ex hypothesi,* are always ultimately translatable as instances of the statement "x bears such and such a relation to y." Even where x and y are not mentioned, genuine form-statements can always be cashed-in by reference to parts and their relations. To say that a film narrative is unified is often supported by reference to recurring motifs—parts of the narrative that resemble or echo each other.

Films have many elements, and these can be related in many ways. Sounds may repeat, functioning as leitmotifs. Characters may stand in adversarial relations to each other. This is dramatic conflict, which is a standard formal feature of narrative films. It is a relation between parts of the film—the characters—and what they represent (good versus evil, the Allies versus the Nazis, intellect versus might, and so on). Volumes in particular shots can be in equilibrium or disequilibrium. Scenes may alternate between being fast and slow paced. These too are formal relations. A film may be complex because it has a wealth of different and contrasting characters. The quantity of characters and their clashing qualities are also formal properties of an artwork on the account under consideration.

Film form, then, it may be suggested, consists of relations between parts of an individual film. Films may have different parts that are related in different ways. Some of these ways may be co-ordinated, such as the way in which characters are related to the plot in most narrative films. Or they may be relatively uncoordinated. The color elements of a studio set, though related to each other, may or may not have any relation to the dramatic conflict in the narrative. But regardless whether the sets of relations in a film are hierarchically organized, all the relations are formal relations. Thus, it may be hypothesized, when we speak of the form of an individual film, then, we may take that to refer to *all the webs of relations* that obtain between the elements of the work.

This is a very democratic view of film form. Any relation between elements of an individual film counts as an instance of film form. This characterization of film form is very comprehensive. It obviously can apply to any film that has discriminable parts. They will all have form, though not necessarily commendable form. This conception of film form will count relations between representational elements of a film—such as the contrast between good and bad characters—as a contribution to the form of the film. But this is not an unfortunate result. Contrasting characters contribute both to the coherence and complexity of the films that have them.

We can call this approach to film form the *descriptive account.* According to the descriptive account, any instance of a relation among elements of an individual film is an instance of film form. On this view, in order to provide a full account of the form of a given film, one would list or summarize all the relations among the parts of the work. We label this approach the descriptive account because it classifies any relation among elements of a film as an instance of film form, irrespective of any principle of selection. On this conception of film form, the ideal analysis of the form of an individual film would be a long description of all the relations among the elements of a given film. Indeed, some proposed strategies for cinematic analysis, notably Raymond Bellour's notion of segmentation, have actually converged on the descriptive account.[6]

In favor of the descriptive account is its comprehensiveness. It doesn't appear to leave anything out. Arguably it can home-in on everything that one is likely to regard as an instance of film form. Nevertheless, the descriptive account does not seem to accord with what we usually are talking about when we discuss the form of an individual film. We rarely, if ever, encounter such exhaustive accounts of film form as one would expect if the descriptive account crystallized our ruling conception of film form. Nor is it clear that we even desire such descriptive accounts. The accounts of film form that mesh with our expectations are always more selective. Nor are they more selective simply because few would have the energy to read or to write up such exhaustive descriptions. They are more selective because typically we think of film form as comprised of only a subset of the relations among the elements of a film. But this raises the question "which ones?" If we can answer that question we may be on our way to clarifying the concept of form or style in the individual film.

PART IV: FILM FORM AND FUNCTION

The descriptive account of film form is very encompassing. It regards any relation among the elements of a film as an instance of its form. This is a plausible and coherent view of film form. But it does not seem to square with what we generally have in mind when we refer to the form of an individual film. In such situations, we only focus on some standard relations among the elements of a film, not all of them. The relations that concern us are the ones that contribute to the realization of the point of the film. On the descriptive account, a formal or stylistic element of a film is anything that stands in some relation to another element. But on our ordinary conception of film form, an element is a formal element if it contributes to the film's point or purpose.

That is, our ordinary conception of film form is *explanatory* rather than descriptive. It does not aim at listing every relation in the total web of relations discoverable in a film. Such a list, of course, could be indeterminately long. Rather, when we speak of film form we expect only a selection of just those elements and relations that promote the point or purpose of the film. The ordinary concept of film form seems to be functional. The form of the film is whatever functions to advance or to realize whatever the film is designed to bring about. The form of the individual film is what enables it to realize its point or purpose.

Louis Sullivan said "Form follows function." What he had in mind, for example, is that the form of the front doorway of a house—its dimensions—is a certain way in order to discharge its function (to permit people of average height and girth to pass through it with ease). The form of the doorway is related to what the doorway is intended to do. Similarly, the form of a film is ideally determined by what it is supposed to do—to achieve its point or purpose.

This approach, of course, assumes that films have purposes. But this assumption seems hardly controversial, once we realize how diverse such purposes may be. In some cases, the purpose of a film may be to propose a theme or a point of view, or the purpose may be to foreground an expressive property, or it may be to arouse feelings, including feelings of visual pleasure, in audiences. A film may be about communicating ideas—ideas about the world or ideas about the nature of film—or it may have no ideas or meanings, but simply be dedicated to engendering a certain sort of experience, such as repose, excitement, suspense or perceptual delight. Films may make points, or they may merely have points—to encourage viewers, for instance, to use their discriminatory faculties keenly and perceptively. It should not be difficult to concede that all or nearly all films have points or purposes—probably, in most cases, more than one—once we think of points and purposes in this broad way. The form of the individual film is that which enables it to realize its purposes. A formal element is an element that contributes to or serves as a means of securing the point or the purpose of the individual film. Film structure follows function.

One of the points or purposes of Wilder's *Sunset Blvd.* is to portray Norma Desmond as horrific. To this end, he makes a number of choices, including, among others, the use of the organ in Norma's mansion in a way that is reminiscent of horror films (like the *Phantom of the Opera*), the corpse of the dead monkey and its funeral, the iconography of the seemingly deserted old house (ruins "haunted" by Norma), Norma's attempted transformation of herself in preparation for her "new" film (which transformation cinematically resembles nothing so much as a mad scientist's experiment), the narration of the film through the voice of a dead man (a "ghost"), and Norma's final close-up, which is performed in a highly grotesque manner suggesting an unnatural, unearthly being slithering toward the camera (as if to devour it and her audience as well).

The point of these choices is to project the sense that Norma is monstrous, that she is "undead" (as a zombie film might put it), that her mode of being is analogous to that of a denizen of a horror film—that there is something horrible and not quite human about her, and that this monstrosity tells us something about the nature of stardom. Indeed, perhaps the metaphorical implication is that stardom creates monsters. The ensemble of choices enumerated above (along with others not enumerated) function to enable Wilder to realize one of the points of *Sunset Blvd.*—that stardom breeds monstrosity—in a way that hits home at the level of both the intellect and the emotions.

A film is designed to perform some purpose (or set of purposes, co-ordinated or otherwise) and/or to make some point. Formal choices are elements and relations in the film that are the intended means to secure those points and purposes, in the way that the aforementioned ensemble of choices enables Wilder to make his point both cognitively and emotively. A formal choice in a film is such that it has the design function to bring about or to facilitate a/the point or purpose of the film. A formal choice has the intended function to advance the point or purpose of the individual film under analysis.

The form of the individual film comprises the collection of formal choices that enable the realization of its points or purposes. Films, of course, may have more than one point and/or purpose, and these may be co-ordinated, as may be the subtending systems of formal articulations designed to realize them. But in other films, formal choices may not be interconnected or mutually reinforcing where they still nevertheless enable different purposes. Yet whether co-ordinated or not, formal choices are always functional contributions to the purposes of the film. And the form of the individual film is made up of all its formal choices—of all the formal articulations in the film that function to realize its purposes (its overall purposes, or the purposes of a particular part, such as a sequence of the film).

For obvious reasons, I call this the *functional account* of film form. According to the functional account of film form, *the form of an individual film is the ensemble of choices intended to realize the point or the purpose of the film.* This approach to film form is different from the descriptive account. The descriptive account says that the form of the film is the sum total of *all* the relations between the elements of the film. The functional account says that film form comprises *only* the elements and relations intended to serve as the means to the end of the film.

This account could include all the relations in a film, if they were all intended to serve the purposes of the film, but that occurs at most rarely, if ever, despite flowery critical language that sometimes commends films for being totalized organic wholes. Thus, almost all (if not all) of the time, analyses of the form of an individual film that accord with the functional account will be far less exhaustive than the ideal that the descriptive account of film form encourages. And this approach, of course, conforms better to the way in which we usually discuss film form than does the descriptive account. The descriptive account is much broader than the functional account, and the former, logically speaking, includes the latter. But the descriptive account is far too broad to provide a useful framework for discussing film form.

The functional account also differs from attempts to approach film form through the contrast between form and content. That way of speaking restricts film form solely to films with specifiable content. But by speaking of the point or purpose of the film, rather than solely in terms of content, the functional account is broader than the form/content account. Of course, where the point of a film is to advance something typically thought of as content (a theme, for example), the functional account will attend to the same formal features as does the form/content account. However, the functional account can also accommodate "contentless" films, which is one of the sticking points of the form/content approach.

That is, the functional account is a richer approach than the form/content approach, since it will be capable of tracking film form where there is a point to a film, but nothing that we standardly refer to as content. For example, films whose purpose is to provoke a perceptual state in the audience will still possess form according to the functional account—the form will involve whatever configurations promote the intended effect—while the form/content approach has no way of speaking of film form where the correlative category of content is inoperative. Thus, logically the functional account of film form accommodates everything that the form/content approach covers, while not being so restrictive. In this respect, the functional account lies conceptually somewhere between the descriptive account and the form/content account, being less inclusive than the former and less exclusive than the latter.

The functional account regards film form as generative. Film form is that which is designed to bring about the point or the purposes of the film. This account uses the notion of a function to explain why the individual film is the way it is. It enables us to say why the film has the shape and structure it has. The form serves a function. It is designed to serve a film's purpose (or purposes), a means to securing its point or points. It is that which makes manifest the point or purpose of the film. The functionalist account explains why the film is the way it appears by showing that a formal element has been selected because that element realizes the film's point and that the choice occurs in the work in order to realize its point.

In William Wyler's *Little Foxes,* for instance, there is a recurrence of arresting, sharply deep-focused, high and low angle shots of the main stairway. These shots cinematically reinforce and accentuate the film's abiding concern with power relationships. They make manifest the intensity of the power struggles in the film in a way that is visually accessible and emotionally forceful. According to the functionalist approach to film form, the film looks the way it does—has the form it does—in the relevant scenes because these angulated, strikingly aggressive deep-focus shots realize one of the purposes of the film (underlining the intense confrontations over power), and the choice of these shots occurs precisely for the purpose of realizing that point.

The formal elements of a film are referred to as *choices,* for when an artist contemplates the best way to articulate her point, she has an array of options before her. In *Little Foxes,* Wyler might have used a flatter style of image composition. He had to consider which of the compositional options available to him, given the norms, practices, technologies, and possibilities open to him, best suited his purposes. Creating a film involves electing the forms that the artist believes will function optimally to realize the point or purpose of the film. Forms are formal *choices* because they are elected from arrays of options.

Of course, in determining what options are historically available to a filmmaker, the analyst will have to consider the norms, practices, and technological possibilities open to the filmmaker in the pertinent situation. Moreover, in this respect, in order to appreciate the options that confronted the filmmaker, the analyst of a film's individual style will have to think about the period, genre, and school or movement to which the film may belong. But this does not reduce the analysis of the form of the individual film to one of these other categories of stylistic analysis, since its aim is not to classify the film or the techniques in question, but to clarify and explain the logic of the filmmaker's creative situation in terms of the formal resources available to him or her.

Forms are selected because they are *intended* or *designed* to perform certain functions. The notion of an intention is included in our characterization of film form in order to allow for the possibility of failure. Though its form may be defective, even a botched film still has form. A filmmaker may intend certain choices to have certain consequences, but those choices may not achieve their intended results. The point of a film may be to engender mystery, but it may fail to do so. A formal analysis of it will pick out the elements that were intended to inspire mystery and then go on to explain how they were compromised either by other elements in the work or by being put in place incorrectly. That is, the formal analysis of even a failed film will be functional.

In order to analyze the form of a film functionally, it is necessary to have some conception of the film's point. Often the point can be isolated rather easily in our experience of the film. But also quite frequently, the point may be elusive. This is why formal analysis of a film usually comes hand-in-hand with interpretations or explications of it. An interpretation identifies the theme as its point and uses the function of advancing the theme as a guide to the relevant formal choices. For example, if we interpret the divisiveness of the African-American community to be a major theme of Spike Lee's *School Daze,* then we remark upon all the devices in the film that accentuate the sense of division. These include the competition dances, the studied contrast in the juxtaposed scenes of the light black students versus the dark black students, and even the unusually abrupt scene transitions, marked sometimes by intertiles and sometimes by the salient horizontal wipes employing the Mission College pennant.

In this respect, explication is broader than interpretation. It may identify the point or the purpose in terms of some effect (rather than some thematic communication) that the film aims to bring about—for instance, raising a certain feeling, such as awe—and then explication goes on to isolate the elements of the film that conspire to bring about this result. In this regard, the functional account of film form is explanatory. Unraveling the form of a film explains how it is capable (or, in some cases, incapable) of making its intended points and actualizing its purposes. Undeniably knowledge of film history, including knowledge of the genre and/or the school of the film, and even knowledge of previous works by the filmmaker often contribute crucially to elucidating a film's point or purpose. But, again, history here serves the purposes of explaining the way in which the film works, not in categorizing it.

We have already granted that the descriptive account of film form is plausible and coherent. If there is nothing more to be said for the functional account than that it too is plausible and coherent, what reason is there to prefer the functional account over the descriptive account? Perhaps it is that the functional account is better suited to doing what we expect our concept of film form to do. Generally when we talk about film form or the formal analysis of a film, we expect that learning about the form of the film will contribute to our understanding of it. If we are mystified by a film, we think that concentrating on its form may illuminate it.

But this intuition seems to fit better with the functional account of film form than it does with the descriptive account. If the film as a whole is already confusing, our enumerating the undifferentiated totality of its internal relations will not leave us any better off. If, however, we approach the elements and the relations in the film by asking what they are designed to do, we are far more likely to grasp the rationale behind the work.

Similarly, when we speak of the *form* of a film, this has overtones of the systematic—of there being some formula(e), or rule(s), or guiding principle(s) in operation. This connotation of systematicity is entirely lost in the descriptive account of film form, for it deals in the totality of relations of the film with no principle of selection. The functional account, by contrast, does connect film form to underlying motivations. In that sense, it preserves the intuition of systematicity, especially in cases where forms are co-ordinated hierarchically to secure overarching purposes.

Earlier we noted that a strength of auteurism is that it acknowledges the deep association between style and expression. This acknowledgment is equally a strength of the functional account, since displaying expressive properties or expressive content is a widely recognized point or purpose of films. Thus, formal analysis is often dedicated to disclosing the choices that make the manifestation or communication of expression possible in the individual film. At the same time, however, since not all films make expression their point or purpose. the functional account, as outlined above, is more comprehensive in its reach than analytic frameworks that would make form and expression necessarily co-relative terms.

The functional account of film form is dynamic in that it ties form to the motive force—the points and purposes—that explain a film's constellations of choices. In this sense, the functional account contrasts with the descriptive account, which might also be called the structural account, of the individual film. Because such accounts provide no inkling of the impulse behind the form of the film, they are static. Admittedly, the functional account is teleological. But it is not strange to treat objects of human design teleologically. We assemble such objects in order to fulfill certain purposes. In film analysis, the functional approach is sensitive to this feature; it assumes from the outset that films are the way they are as the result of human design. But this, it seems to me, is not a problem. For there is no more reasonable nor powerful assumption with which to approach the question of the form of the individual film.[7]

NOTES

1. Throughout this essay, I will be using the idea of form in the individual film and style in the individual film interchangeably.
2. The categories on this list and what follows are not intended to be exhaustive, nor are they mutually exclusive; sometimes some of them may overlap in various ways.
3. The concepts of universal style, period style, school style, and personal style are derived from Richard Wollheim's extremely useful essay, "Pictorial Style: Two Views," in *The Concept of Style,* ed. Berel Lang (Ithaca: Cornell University Press, 1987), 183–202. I have added the concepts of genre style and style in the individual film to the list.
4. David Bordwell, *On the History of Film Style* (Cambridge: Harvard University Press, 1998), 244.
5. The alternative way of discussing film form, which is called the descriptive account in this portion of the essay, is extrapolated from Monroe Beardsley, *Aesthetics: Problems in the Philosophy of Criticism* (New York: Harcourt Brace & World, 1958), chapter 4.
6. It is important to note, however, that even Bellour's methodology is less strenuous than the descriptive account, as I have stated it, since he advocates primarily tracking repetitions, whereas a full-blooded proponent of the descriptive account would call for an enumeration of all the relations between the parts of the film, not just repetitions (and differences), but more fine-grained ones such as the relations of reinforcement, causation, and so on.
7. This article is an application to film of the theory of artistic form advanced in the chapter on form in Noël Carroll, *Philosophy of Art: A Contemporary Introduction* (London: Routledge, 1999).

Chapter 7 Introducing
Film Evaluation

When we first think of evaluating films, we think initially of film critics. These are people who are in the business of pronouncing on the value of films. There are so many films to see and so little time. Thus, almost all of us have to fall back on the recommendations of film critics in order to inform our choice of viewing fare.

There are several different ways in which the role of a film critic may be pursued. Some critics attempt to function as consumer reporters—trying to predict which films most of their readership will enjoy. For such readers, these critics serve as consumer guides. Other critics aim at being taste-makers—identifying which films are special, and in the best of cases, suggesting how the rest of us might go on to appreciate them. Readers who prefer their tastes confirmed will gravitate toward the consumer guides. Those who want their taste expanded are likely to admire the critics who are able to pick out singular cinematic achievements and to contextualize and explain them.

However, though the role of the film critic commands an important position in cultures awash with movies (both in movie theaters, and on television and video cassettes), it would be a mistake to think of film evaluation as exclusively a professional matter. For evaluating films is something that we all do all of the time.

Nor do I mean by this merely that we automatically form preferences for some of the films we see over others and rank some of them as better than the rest. As humans, we tend to do this with respect to most of our experiences. But with regard to film viewing, this is not something that simply happens to us automatically. It is something that we avidly pursue. Evaluating films is part of our everyday film culture. When we talk about films with others, most of our time is spent trading evaluations, comparing them, sometimes sharing them, and often arguing about them. Indeed, we frequently read critics after we have seen a film in order to enter imaginary conversations of this sort with them.

Film viewing is often portrayed as a solitary affair in which each spectator communes with a brightened screen in a dark room. But film viewing is more sociable than that. Film viewing is part of our social life. After we have seen a film, we want to talk about it with others. We want to tell them what we have seen, to exchange ideas with others who have seen the same films, and to discuss our reactions and theirs. Film viewing is a natural pretext for sociability. And film evaluating is at the crux of this very elemental form of social exchange and consolidation. It is through such encounters that we express and develop ourselves as cultural beings.

That is to put the matter very abstractly. But what I have in mind can be clarified by recalling a very common experience. You attend a film with some friends. Afterwards you go out for coffee, or sweets, or a drink. You talk about the film you have just seen, remarking on the parts you liked or disliked. But, of course, quite frequently the conversation does not just end with a summary of personal preferences. The discussion may often turn to whether or not the film is good or whether it worked. That is, there is an almost ineluctable tendency for the conversation to move from reports of subjective enjoyment or boredom to questions of objective evaluation.

Experiences like these are part of the typical life of film-going—which is to claim that evaluation is at the heart of this practice for most of us. It adds zest to the activity. It is something that ordinary film-goers care about deeply. It is something that they want to do. And yet it is this aspect of film-going to which recent film scholarship pays little attention. Where ordinary film viewers probably care more about evaluation, contemporary film scholars are more obsessed with interpretation. So, by way of balance, attention, in this chapter, will shift to certain selected issues concerning evaluation. Let us talk to the film-goer where she or he lives. Specifically, in what follows, I will discuss certain kinds of selected problems that arise inevitably in the course of film evaluation, the traditional way in which classical film theorists attempted to resolve those problems, and I will conclude with some programmatic remarks about alternatives to the classical solution.

SOME PROBLEMS OF FILM EVALUATION

I have suggested that film evaluation is something that we come to almost naturally. So in what sense could it be problematic? Well, recall the scenario I alluded to above. Suppose a group of us has just seen a film together—for example, *Speed* (1994). You like it; I do not. As often as not, the conversation will not stop there. You are apt to defend your liking of the film by saying that it is good. I may reply that I do not deny that you liked the film, but I add that that does not prove that it was good. It is perfectly consistent, I say, for you to like that film and for the film to be bad at the same time. Moreover, I add that *Speed* is a bad film.

At this point, notice that we have left off talking about our likes and our dislikes and we have entered the realm of objective evaluation. You are claiming that any reasonable and informed viewer should regard *Speed* as a good film, whereas I am denying that. In other words, we both accept each other's likes and dislikes. There is no more arguing about that than there is about our preferences in ice cream. But we are *arguing*—our discussion revolves around coming up with *reasons* that we believe should sway or even compel others to accept our viewpoint.[1]

A subjective report of a like or a dislike is a fact about us. It does not command the agreement of others. If you dislike spinach that is not a reason for me to dislike spinach, since reasons—as opposed to mere likings—are objective. Reasons are offered to others with an implicit claim on their assent. Thus, if you provide a reason for saying that *Speed* is a good film and if that reason is relevant and acceptable, you expect others to concur with your assessment. In our discussion of *Speed*, our behavior—our exchange of reasons—gives every appearance of being committed to objectivity. We do not pound the table and shout 'But I like it!' We try to find objective reasons that will convince others that our assessment is correct.

Here, in a nutshell, is the central problem of film evaluation (and, indeed, of all aesthetic evaluation). It emerges from a stubborn fact with which we are all familiar. That is the fact of disagreement. We disagree about our evaluations of film. Moreover, as I have already indicated, we do not act as though these disagreements are merely a matter of personal whims or preferences, since we argue about them, we advance reasons on their behalf, and we attempt to defend them.

When you say that *Speed* is good, you are advancing an objective claim, and your conversational behavior implies that you believe that your evaluation can be rationally adjudicated. But how is that possible? How can such disagreements be resolved rationally?[2] How can you hope to defend your assessment objectively?[3] Those are some of the central questions of film evaluation.

In order to get some sense of how such disagreements might be negotiated rationally, let us follow our imaginary dispute about *Speed* a little further. You say it is good; I say it is bad. What happens next? Very often we start mentioning other films. You might refer to other suspense films, such as *Die Hard* (1988) or *The Man Who Knew Too Much* (1934, 1956). Your purpose here might be to get me to agree that they are good films. For if I agree that they are good films, you will argue that consistency (a test for rational objectivity) demands that I agree *Speed* is also good, on the grounds that *Speed* shares essential features with the other suspense films that I have already conceded are good.

Here the conversation could go in several directions. I might deny that *Speed* is really analogous to the paradigms you have adduced, or I might deny that the other films you have mentioned are good. Let us explore the second option. Suppose that I deny that any of the three films are any good. At this point, you will begin to wonder what I think makes for a good film, and you may challenge me to produce an example of one. Say my example is *Riddles of the Sphinx* (1977), an avant-garde film that mixes disjunctive editing with dense, philosophical voiceover narration.

You agree that *Riddles of the Sphinx* is a good film, yet you cannot but feel that somehow I have missed the point. You say that that is not the kind of film that *Speed* is. *Speed* and *Riddles of the Sphinx* belong to different categories—they serve different purposes, and, in consequence, they have different standards of evaluation.

Perhaps one thing that this debate reveals so far is that when we evaluate films, part of that process involves placing the film in question in a certain category. This is a psychological fact about us. To evaluate, one categorizes.[4] The reason for this is that categories are generally connected to purposes and standards. When we categorize a piece of cutlery as a steak knife, we recognize that its purpose is to slice through thick pieces of beef and that, in consequence, a good-making feature of it is its sharpness. Sharpness, in other words, is a standard of goodness in steak knives because it is in virtue of its sharpness that a steak knife can discharge its purpose. In this way, categories, purposes, and standards form a matrix.

When we view a film, we also—as a matter of psychological fact—place it in a category, one that shapes our expectations and standards. Our dispute about *Speed* in the preceding example turns on the fact that we have situated *Speed* in different categories or comparison classes.

But, as I have said, this is only a psychological fact, not a logical one. We do not resolve the question of whether *Speed* is good by citing the different categories in which we regard *Speed*. That may clarify our differences, but it does not settle them. Our disagreement will not be adjudicated rationally until we are able to determine which of our competing categories is the *correct* one (or, at least, the more correct one).

Our dispute about the goodness or badness of *Speed,* then, has escalated, so to speak, into a disagreement about categories. Which category (or categories) is (are) appropriate or correct in this case? Our debate looks like it can be brought to a reasonable resolution only if we can determine which category is the correct one to bring to bear on the case of *Speed*. A great many problems about film evaluation could be resolved, if only we had a way to fix the correct category or categories for evaluating the film in question.[5] But how does one determine a correct category? That is the million dollar question. For without an answer to that question, it looks like our disagreement is just as rationally intractable as the question of whether or not *Speed* is good.

THE CLASSICAL SOLUTION

As we have just seen, one of the central problems of film evaluation is what we can call 'the problem of the correct category.' This is not a problem that has concerned recent film scholarship. However, there is a way of looking at classical film theory—film theory prior to the advent of semiotics and poststructuralism—such that the problem of the correct category turns out to be one of the central issues, if not sometimes *the* central issue, with which film theorists, such as Rudolf Arnheim and Siegfried Kracauer, were wrestling.[6]

Classical film theory is generally preoccupied with isolating the essence of film—what some people call the *cinematic*. The cinematic is what differentiates film from other artforms, such as theater and painting. Moreover, classical film theorists were not simply concerned with what in fact differentiated film from other artforms. The differentiae they sought were also often normative. That is, they were concerned with the way in which film *should* be different from other arts. Stated obscurely, they thought that films should be cinematic. Various classical theorists defined what constituted being cinematic in different ways. But for most of the classical theorists, they had a conception of what counted as cinematic. And for them, the failure of a film to be cinematic was a defect.

What does this notion of the cinematic have to do with the problem of the correct category? Well, effectively, for the classical film theorist, *all films*—or at least all the films that we would want to talk about from an aesthetic point of view—fell into one category which we might call *film as film*. Thus, debates about the goodness or badness of a given film could be referred back to the question of whether or not the film under discussion was cinematic, that is, whether it was a proper instance of the category of film as film. Consequently, if we want to determine whether *Speed* is a good film, then what we have to do is to show that it is cinematic.

One obvious advantage of a classical approach to the problem of the correct category is that it makes film evaluation a very unified practice. The notion of the cinematic, in the hands of a given classical theorist, provides a single scale on which all films can be weighed and compared. Whether or not a film is good (relative to the category of film as film) can be established by showing that it is cinematic, while how good it is can be gauged in light of how cinematic it is. Similarly, one can say that a film is bad if it fails to be cinematic, or that it is flawed to the degree that uncinematic elements intrude into its style. Moreover, films can be compared and even ranked as good, bad, better, and worse in accordance with a single measure—their degree of cinematicity.

This is a very tidy program. It would provide a way of rationally negotiating disagreements about evaluating films just in case one were able to characterize satisfactorily what counts as cinematic. But there is the fly in the ointment. For, as is well known, different classical film theorists tended to argue for different and often conflicting (or non-converging) conceptions of the cinematic.

Early film theorists, for instance, tended to locate the cinematic in terms of two contrasts—that which differentiated film from theater, on the one hand, and that which differentiated film from the slavish recording of reality, on the other hand. They emphasized the difference between film, properly so called, and mere recording, in order to establish the credentials of film as an artform—something that did not simply duplicate reality but that could reconstitute it expressively and creatively.

But they also differentiated film from theater. The point here was to demonstrate that film was a *unique* artform, an artistic category unto itself—film as film. Thus, these early film theorists, of whom Rudolf Arnheim[7] is a leading example, argued that film, properly so-called, was neither an imitation of nature, nor an imitation of any other artform, notably theater.

Whereas theater narration typically relies on words, cinematic narration, it was asserted, could and should emphasize movement, image, and action. If theater was primarily verbal, cinema, ideally, was primarily visual. Likewise, cinema had resources, particularly editing, that enabled filmmakers to manipulate spatial and temporal transitions with more fluidity than was customary in theater. Thus, editing, or montage, was generally celebrated as the most important, essential characteristic of cinema. On this view, film was essentially visual, its natural subject of representation was animated action, and its primary means of expression was editing or montage.

Other techniques were also regarded as cinematic—including close-ups, camera angulation, trick photography, visual devices such as fades, wipes, and superimposition, camera movement, and the like. As with editing, these techniques were prized because they both declared the difference between film and theater (inasmuch as the effects available through these devices were not easily achieved in theater) and departed from the 'straight' recording of reality. In other words, the use of these devices standardly indicated that film differed from theater and from what was thought of as 'normal perception'. They displayed film as a unique artistic category—film as film.

A feature of a film was cinematic, then, as long as it deployed techniques that underscored the putatively unique capacities of cinema. Stylistic features that failed to do this—such as the use of extended dialogue or stolid tableaux shots—were uncinematic. Excessive reliance on words at the expense of animated action, or the use of a single camera position to record the declamation of dialogue (rather than exploiting the powers of editing) was not only uncinematic, but downright theatrical. And to be theatrical or uncinematic flew in the face of the canonical standards of film as film. Theatrical or uncinematic films were bad films, inappropriate or defective examples of the category

A film such as *Speed* does very nicely on this conception of film. Dialogue here is in the service of action, of which there is quite a lot, which, in turn, is magnificently articulated through the editing. On the other hand, a film such as *Riddles of the Sphinx* would probably fare badly on this approach because of its extensive use of language. This approach to film evaluation could settle our earlier dispute in short order, if only its account of the essence of cinema were compelling.

But this conception of cinema is hardly incontestable. In fact, it was challenged by later film theorists in the classical tradition. These later classical theorists, of whom Siegfried Kracauer[8] is a noteworthy example, are often called realists because they thought that the essential feature of cinema is photography and that this feature committed cinema to meeting certain standards that emphasized the recording and disclosure of reality.

So whereas earlier classical theorists, such as Arnheim, thought that the capacity of film to diverge from the recording of reality implied that cinema should employ assertive devices such as editing to reconstitute reality, realist theorists, such as Kracauer, looked more favorably on cinema's provenance in photography and inferred that this argued for the realistic usage of film. Both Arnheim and Kracauer were classical film theorists—both believed in the cinematic. But they disagreed not only about what constituted the category but also about what standards, as a result, were suitable to bring to bear in evaluating films.

Indeed, their theories led them in opposite directions. Highly stylized films of the sort favored by Arnheim's theory were apt to be castigated by Kracauer's lights because of their disregard for the canons of realism. From Kracauer's view, for instance, a film such as *Speed* would be uncinematic because of the various ways in which it violates Kracauer's conception of the (normative) essence of cinema. Specifically, Kracauer thinks that cinematic realism requires a disposition toward the use of open-ended plot structures, whereas the narrative world of *Speed* is closed, and, by Kracauer's lights, unrealistically contrived.

In the debate over the cinematic, proponents of the earlier view—that film should reconstitute reality—and proponents of the later view—the realists— could both score points against each other. Each side could argue that the other side failed as a comprehensive theory of the nature of film, because each side was blind to certain kinds of cinematic achievement. The defender of realism could claim that theorists such as Arnheim ignored the accomplishments of films whose style gravitated more toward recording, such as the work of the Italian neo-realists (whose aspirations, of course, could be effectively explained from a realist point of view).

On the other hand, those who favored stylization and editing could explain many avant-garde experiments which were anything but realistic. Each side pretended to be a comprehensive theory of the nature of film, but opponents of either side could point out that the other side ignored or attempted to sublate or to subtract, in an *ad hoc* manner, massive amounts of the data of film history.

Furthermore, it did not appear possible to patch up this problem by simply combining these two schools of classical film theory because, in important respects, they contradicted one another. Adding the two lines of theory together would not lead to a more comprehensive theory, but only to an inconsistent one.

One explanation of how these two strands of classical film theory failed to deliver the goods is that, though each side presented itself as a comprehensive theory of all film, this was not, in actuality, what either of these theoretical approaches was about. Both were really characterizations of different stylistic tendencies that crystallized at different points in film history. Theorists such as Arnheim and Russian montagists, like V. I. Pudovkin,[9] were particularly sensitive to stylistic developments in the period of silent filmmaking, whereas realist theorists such as Kracauer and the French writer André Bazin[10] were especially attuned to stylistic developments of the sound film of the 1940s and early 1950s.

Both sides mistook certain period-specific developments in film history to reveal the essence of cinema. This is why their theories were suited to certain bodies of work, while being insensitive to achievements from other stylistic traditions. Whereas a theory of the nature of film should apply to films of all styles, these theorists inadvertently privileged certain styles over others to the extent that certain avenues of accomplishment were deprecated by them as uncinematic. Thus, their theories failed to be comprehensive because they were biased.

Undoubtedly, another—logically less flattering—way to put it was that these theorists proposed to demonstrate that certain options of film stylization were uncinematic by deducing the essence of cinema; but, in fact, what they did was to allow their stylistic preferences to shape their conception of the essence of cinema. Kracauer asserts that photography is the essential feature of cinema. But how does he know that photography rather than editing is the essential feature? The answer is because he already presumes that realist filmmaking demarcates the recognized body of achievement in the medium. But this, of course, begs a question.[11] And this fallacy is rampant throughout the corpus of classical film theorizing.[12]

One very ingenious attempt to reconcile the differences between the different schools of classical film theory can be found in Victor Perkins's excellent book *Film as film*.[13] This is an especially interesting text from our perspective because it is an explicit effort to provide a rational foundation for film evaluation. Though Perkins would probably bridle at this characterization, his book is an example of classical film theory, as his title—*Film as film*—indicates. Like other classical theorists, Perkins tries to develop a unified canon of evaluation for all films, irrespective of genre and period.

This canon is rooted in combining some of the insights of theorists such as Arnheim and realists such as Kracauer in a single, non-contradictory formula. From Perkins's view, in order to be good, a film must abide by certain realist standards of verisimilitude. This pays homage to the theoretical tradition of people such as Kracauer and Bazin.

But Perkins also pays his respects to the tradition of assertive stylization in classical film theory. For he maintains that the extra degrees of goodness that a film accrues (over and above the minimal accreditation as good that it receives for being realistic) are to be calibrated in terms of the extent to which the film is stylized—via editing, set design, camera angulation, camera movement, costume, and so on—just as long as that stylization is articulated within the bounds of realism. A film such as *Elmer Gantry* (1960), for example, can employ hyperactive montage metaphors just insofar as those metaphors are motivated realistically in the world of the film.

Here, realism and stylization do not contradict each other. Rather, realism constrains the legitimate compass of stylization. That is, realism and stylization are coordinated by a rule that says a good film contains both, but only to the extent that stylization stays within the bounds of realism. In *Elmer Gantry,* expressive cutting between a swelling fire and a religious frenzy is acceptable cinematically because the fire that comments on the frenzy is of a piece with the naturalist settings and narration of the fictional world. This use of editing contrasts to Eisensteinian montage, which sometimes resorted to similes that intruded upon the decoupage from outside the setting of the fiction.

By requiring that stylization be constrained by realism, Perkins proposes a principled way for films to exploit both of the tendencies advocated by the conflicting strands of classical film theory. It is a brilliant compromise solution between two opposing schools of thought. It seems to realize the dream of classical film theory—to solve the problem of the correct category by ascertaining a standard of evaluation applicable to all films.

However, if Perkins's approach represents one of the highest points in classical film theory, it is also unfortunately vulnerable to some of the same criticisms we brought against earlier forms of this sort of theory. We have already noted that a recurrent failing of classical film theorists involved their hypostatization of certain period-specific film styles—their tendency to mistake these styles for the very essence of cinema itself.

A similar problem is evident in Perkins's book. Perkins takes the exploration of stylization within the bounds of realism to be the quiddity of film as film. But why take this to be more representative of the essence of film than experiments in avant-garde irrealism? Why is Preminger more cinematic than Godard?

When one looks at the data base of Perkins's theory, the answer seems very apparent. Those examples come predominantly from Hollywood films of the 1950s and early 1960s. During that period, constraining stylization within the bounds of realism was, so to say, a rule of the practice. But in this respect, what Perkins has done, like Arnheim, Kracauer, and Bazin before him, has been to mistake an essential (or fundamental) feature of a specific practice for the essence of cinema as a whole. That is, Perkins's preference for a certain kind of filmmaking has biased his account of the nature of, as he himself calls it, film as film.

One of the greatest promises of classical film theory was that it would solve the problem of the correct category. For, if we could make a classical film theory work, we would have the one and only category for evaluating all films. By identifying an essence of film—one with normative implications—we would have a standard that could be brought to bear to resolve rationally most disagreements about the quality of given films. But the search for this kind of essence has proven chimerical.

In most cases, classical theorists have proceeded by begging the question. They have built in their stylistic preferences as premises in their deductions of stylistic imperatives and cinematic canons. This is rather like the magician who puts the rabbit in the hat and then draws it out. What is not really magic is not logic either.

Unfortunately, this sort of error recurs throughout the body of classical film theory, even in its most sophisticated representatives, such as Perkins. Thus, until this failing is repaired, the prospects for solving the problem of the correct category by means of the strategies of classical film theory appear foreclosed, and this suggests that another alternative needs to be explored.

AN ALTERNATIVE APPROACH

What we had hoped to inherit from classical film theory was a solution to the problem of the correct category. This problem is a pressing one for film evaluation, because if we are able to find a way to establish the correct category for evaluating a given film, then we are on our way to resolving many (though not all) of the disagreements that arise when we attempt to assess films. Unfortunately, we have seen that so far classical film theory has failed in this regard.

Undeniably, the failure of film theory is instructive. It shows something, but we need to be careful about what it reveals. It does not show that there cannot be correct categories for evaluating films. Rather, it only shows that it is unlikely that we can evolve a unitary theory of evaluation based on a *single* category such as film as film. That is, it only suggests that there is not a universal litmus test—such as the cinematic—for goodness in film. But the failure of classical theory does not show that categories as such are irrelevant to film evaluation.

The problems of classical film theory may incline us toward skepticism about whether there is a single evaluative category that subsumes all films. But this should not make us skeptical about whether films fall into various different categories, many of which come with perfectly respectable standards of evaluation. That film practices are too diverse to be all assimilated usefully under the sort of essential category that classical theorists hoped to discover hardly implies that films cannot be categorized.

Indeed, it is obvious that films can be categorized. We have lots of film categories, such as suspense films, horror films, structural films, trance films, neorealist films, art films, and so on. Nor is there any reason to think that regarding films under these categories rather than others is not often correct. Additionally, many of these categories come with subtending purposes and standards of accomplishment attached to them.

For example, some films are correctly categorized as melodramas. Part of the point of a melodrama is to move the audience to feel—at least for some segment of the duration of the film—sadness or pity for one of the protagonists. A correctly categorized melodrama that failed in this respect would be *prima facie* defective. A melodrama that succeeds in this regard would be *prima facie* a good melodrama. Likewise, a correctly classified classical detective film that fails to prompt speculation about whodunit (perhaps because the answer is too obvious) and a comedy whose gags are so disastrously timed that every laugh line falls flat are both presumptively failures. That is, if nothing can be said to justify the ways in which such films deviate from the standards of the categories by which they are fittingly described, then we can rationally ground negative assessments of these works.

Returning to the question of *Speed:* you said that it was good; I said that it was bad. However, in the course of our discussion, it became apparent that the likely basis for my negative assessment was that I evaluated *Speed* relative to an incorrect category. I compared it with *Riddles of the Sphinx*—a film in the category that is sometimes called the New Talkie—and clearly the aims and standards relevant to that category differ wildly from those appropriate to suspense films. New Talkies are designed to raise philosophical questions, and, though some suspense fictions may also do this, explicitly raising philosophical questions is not a standard expectation that we require every (or any) suspense film to fulfill. The failure to raise philosophical questions is not a basis for charging that a film correctly categorized as suspense is bad. Thus, if you can advance objectively creditable reasons for classifying *Speed* as a suspense film while also challenging my grounds for comparing it with a New Talkie, then you have a rational basis for dismissing my allegations. And if I cannot undermine your categorization with reasons, nor defend my own categorization, I should (rationally speaking) concede your point.

In this example, I have placed a great deal of emphasis on the role of reasons in supporting or dismissing categorizations. But this may strike the reader as obscure. What are these reasons and in what sense are they objective? In this regard, three kinds of reasons come into play most frequently.[14] The first kind of reason pertains to the structure of the work: if it possesses a large number of features that are typical of films existing in a certain category, then that is a strong reason to classify it as, for example, a suspense film. Conversely, the fewer features a film contains of the sort that are typical for a certain category, such as that of the New Talkie, the less likely it is that the film belongs to that category. The number of relevant features a film possesses or lacks may not always provide conclusive reasons in favor of one categorization over another, but statistics such as these generally provide evidence in the direction of one classification over another. Moreover, these reasons are objective inasmuch as it can be a matter of intersubjectively ascertainable fact that a film possesses or lacks a certain number of clearly defined features and that said features are typical of a certain category of film.

Another kind of reason that is relevant to the question of the categorization of a film concerns authorial intention. How a filmmaker or group of filmmakers intended a work to be categorized is quite often an intersubjectively ascertainable matter of fact, and, in a great many of the remaining cases, a highly plausible hypothesis about the intended categorization of a given film is available. Again, authorial intentions may not always provide conclusive reasons for categorization, though they may support a presumption in favor of one categorization over another. And when evidence of authorial intention can be wedded to structural evidence of the sort alluded to in the previous paragraph, the grounds for rationally preferring one categorization over another mounts appreciably.

Further reasons on behalf of the categorization of a film can be adduced from the historical and/or cultural context from which the film emerged. That is, if a certain category of filmmaking is alive and abroad in the historical and/or cultural context from which the film emerged (especially when competing categories are not), then that supplies rational grounds for film categorization. This too is a question of fact. That suspense films are common currency in the cultural enclave of Hollywood-type movie-making and that New Talkies and, for that matter, art films are not provides us with contextual reasons for arguing that *Speed* belongs to the comparison class of suspense films as opposed to many of the alternative categories against whose standards *Speed* might be discounted as defective.

Structural, intentional, and contextual considerations supply us with strong reasons for categorizing films one way rather than another. Where we have reasons of all three kinds, their combined force may sometimes be conclusive. Often these kinds of reasons dovetail, since contextual considerations frequently count as evidence of authorial intention—inasmuch as filmmakers generally have an interest in addressing audiences in terms of the categories with which they are familiar and since authors typically signal the category they have in mind by exhibiting well-entrenched structural features of the intended genre. Of course, in some cases, our categorization may not depend on all three kinds of reasons. Sometimes structural (or authorial or contextual) reasons alone will be sufficient, particularly where there are no persuasive, countervailing reasons available for competing categorizations.

Where does this leave us? First, it lends support to our conviction that there are objective grounds for categorizing films one way rather than another. Thus, if the objective evaluation of films depends upon our ability to categorize films correctly, then we have shown that this requirement can be met sometimes, if not often. Moreover, if we possess the wherewithal to categorize films correctly—and to defend certain categorizations over others—then we have the means to settle rationally some—indeed, I suspect many—disagreements concerning film evaluation. In order to defend our own evaluations of films against competing ones, we will often proceed by demonstrating that our evaluation rests upon a correct categorization of the film in question, while also arguing that rival evaluations depend on incorrect, unlikely, or, at least, less plausible ones. This will not resolve every disagreement about film evaluation, but it may dissolve a great many of them, thereby implying that, in large measure, film evaluation is a reasonable activity.

This approach to film evaluation is not as unified as the one proposed by classical film theory. Since classical film theory acknowledged only one category, it supplied a unitary metric according to which every film might be ranked. Every film could be compared for its cinematicity. The approach that I have been discussing is far more fragmentary, since I maintain that there are many different categories which we may call upon to evaluate different types of films.

This may dishearten some. They might complain that my approach makes the qualitative comparison of films of different categories impossible especially when contrasted to the capacity of the classical tradition to rank all films on a single grid. However, I find these objections exaggerated, on the one hand, and utopian, on the other. The worry that my approach makes all comparison between films of different categories impossible is hyperbolic because there is no reason to suppose that there are never shared, cross-categorical dimensions of evaluation, such as, for instance, narrative coherence.

At the same time, the wish to be able to compare all films with all other films has always seemed to me unrealistic. Why suppose that the best narrative film is strictly commensurable with *Last Year at Marienbad* (1961)? Sometimes it is a case of apples and oranges.

Another objection to my method is that it is formalist, since it primarily involves assessing films in virtue of things such as generic canons. But here the charge of formalism is misplaced if that means bracketing considerations of morality, politics and cognitive value, since many film categories themselves countenance such considerations. A social problem film that failed to portray injustice effectively would be a defective specimen of the category.

Perhaps a deeper concern is that my view makes a fundamental ontological mistake. It seems to suppose that there is one and only one category into which each film falls. And that is just false. But, of course, I readily agree that films may inhabit more than one category. However, that does not show that my approach is flawed. It only entails that evaluation may be more complicated than my examples have suggested so far. Films may be evaluated in light of several categories. Moreover, this may lead to mixed results. A film may turn out to be good in respect to one category to which it belongs, but bad in respect to another. But this should come as no surprise. Mixed results often figure in our assessments of films even when considering a film in light of only one category. That is, mixed results are just something—like gravity—that we have to learn to live with.

A related anxiety might be that my approach is too conservative. It appears to presume that categories are fixed. But film categories are also mutating. Some are disappearing, others are changing, and new ones are coming into existence. How can I handle films from categories that are in the process of evolution as well as films that herald the onset of new genres? Surely, I cannot deny the existence of such phenomena.

Nor would I want to. But film categories, like the films themselves, do not come from nowhere. New categories arise from earlier ones by well precedented processes of development—such as hybridization, amplification, repudiation, and other processes. Consequently, it is possible to track emerging categories along with their purposes and standards *in media res.* With respect to avant-garde cinema, this is even facilitated by the existence of manifestos and a lively film culture as well as frequently through the existence of related aspirations in adjacent art forms which suggest the rationale behind new developments. The category of the New Talkie, for instance, was comprehended virtually with the arrival of the first examples. Thus there is no reason to fear that talk of categories precludes receptivity to novel forms of filmmaking.

Finally, it may be said that, at best, this essay only gets us as far as evaluating films in terms of whether they are good, bad, better, or worse specimens of a kind or category. But we do not evaluate films only as good of a kind or genre. We may also wish to evaluate genres, arguing, for example, that some genres are better than others. This charge is fair but not decisive. Throughout I have said that my method resolves only *some* problems of film evaluation. One reason for that qualification is that I acknowledge that problems such as this one remain to be tackled.

At the same time, the question of ranking film genres and categories ultimately involves not only issues of film criticism and practice narrowly construed, but also general questions of axiology—such as whether the philosophizing of the New Talkie is more valuable than the emotional engagement of the suspense film. That is no reason to neglect this topic. But it may be a justification for breaking off an introductory chapter narrowly concerned with *film* evaluation at just this point and for holding off these larger issues for another time and place.

Nevertheless, though there is much work still to be done, one should not take that as a reason to dismiss the work done so far. We have traveled quite a distance since the beginning of this chapter. We started with the problem of disagreement, which from many viewpoints appears insuperable. However, we have argued that for a great many cases, disagreements can be resolved objectively and we have shown how this might be done. Indeed, I suspect that the considerations advanced in this chapter afford the tools to dismantle most of the disputes that arise in informal discussions about film. Of course, whether my arguments have been successful must be weighed carefully. But that too is something that can be done rationally.

NOTES

1. It is just this—our appeal to third parties and their standards of argument and evidence—that marks our discussion as objective (that is, as playing by intersubjective rules of rationality).

2. In this essay, I will try to show how at least *some* of these debates can be resolved rationally. I will not attempt to show that *all* evaluative disagreements can be so resolved. This essay should not be understood as claiming that, on the basis of its argumentation, all evaluative disputes are rationally decidable. But some may be, and that is all I want to establish in an introductory essay like this. An interesting question for students to pursue with respect to this chapter is to identify the kinds of disputes that the approach in this essay leaves unsolved. An even more interesting problem is for students to think about how some of these disputes might be rendered rationally tractable.

3. Some readers may feel that there is a short answer to questions such as these—namely, that these disagreements cannot be rationally resolved, nor can film evaluations ever be defended objectively. All these invocations of rationality and objectivity are really nothing but masks for something else—personal taste, the will to power, the play of class interests, gender biases, racial prejudices, and so on. Those are all positions represented in the literature. They are what are called 'debunking arguments'. However, for a debunking argument to get off the ground, it needs to be shown that there really is no prospect for rationality in this arena. Thus, students who want to dismiss the possibility of rational film evaluation need to show first that the procedures recommended in this essay are fallacious or fantastical before they go on to reveal them as exercises of an elitist will to domination.

4. There may be certain exceptions to this generalization. If Kant is correct, judgments of what he calls free beauty would defy it. See Immanuel Kant, *Critique of Judgment,* trans. Werner Pluhar (Indianapolis: Hackett, 1987). But this is not the place to discuss Kant's theory of aesthetic judgment. For heuristic purposes, I will pass over this complication except to say that the evaluations discussed in this essay are what Kant might have considered to be judgments of dependent beauty.

5. As this sentence indicates, though I think that figuring out the correct way to categorize a film solves a *great many* problems of film evaluation, I do not think that it settles them all. Even when one agrees on the correct category of a specific film, there will be many remaining questions, such as which standards are the ones appropriate to the category in question, whether or not the film under discussion truly meets those standards, and what is the worth of the relevant category relative to other categories of film. Thus, I do not suppose that all disagreement will disappear automatically with the determination of the correct category (or categories). My point in this short essay is only to suggest that many problems may be rationally resolved in this way. Showing that much is as ambitious as I am prepared to be in such an introductory discussion.

6. Rudolf Arnheim, *Film as Art* (Berkeley: University of California Press, 1957); Siegfried Kracauer, *Theory of Film* (Oxford: Oxford University Press, 1960). For a discussion of classical film theory, see Noël Carroll, *Philosophical Problems of Classical Film Theory* (Princeton: Princeton University Press, 1988).

7. Arnheim, *Film as Art.*

8. Kracauer, *Theory of Film.*

9. V. I. Pudovkin, *Film Technique and Film Acting* (New York: Grove Press, 1960).

10. André Bazin, *What Is Cinema?,* trans. Hugh Gray (Berkeley: University of California Press, 1968, 1971).

11. In order to see this argument worked out in detail, see Noël Carroll, "Kracauer's Theory of Film," in *Defining Cinema,* ed. P. Lehman (New Brunswick: Rutgers University Press, 1997), 111–31. This essay is also included in this volume.

12. This argument is developed in Noël Carroll, "Forget the Medium!," in *A Cinema of Ideas,* ed. M. Tjarks and F. Tillman (Honolulu: Hawaii Pacific University, 1996), 44–9. This essay is also included in this volume.

13. V. F. Perkins, *Film as film* (Baltimore: Penguin Books, 1972).

14. See Kendall Walton, "Categories of Art," *The Philosophical Review* 79 (1970): 334–67. Walton speaks of four categories, but I am only convinced of three of them.

Chapter 8 Nonfiction Film

and Postmodernist Skepticism

1

Perhaps no area of film theory invokes philosophy so quickly as does the discussion of nonfiction film. For inasmuch as a great many nonfiction films are meant to convey information about the world, film theorists are almost immediately disposed to reach for their favorite epistemological convictions in order to assess, and—nearly as often—to dispute the knowledge claims of nonfiction films.[1]

Among film theorists in times gone by, it was a popular sport to charge that insofar as nonfiction films unavoidably require selectivity—that is, cameras inevitably frame and focus; and editors must exclude and, just as importantly, *include*—then the pretensions of nonfiction filmmakers to deliver objective information about the world and to advance justifiable claims thereof are decisively vitiated.[2] For selectivity guarantees bias; and since motion picture technology is inherently and necessarily selective, it is necessarily biased. Bias, so to speak, is built into the apparatus itself. Therefore, any claims to objective knowledge on behalf of a documentary filmmaker are foreclosed a priori.

This argument contains two notions worth scotching: first, that there is something about nonfiction film, due to its inherent nature, that renders it, in contradistinction to other things (such as sociological treatises), uniquely incapable of objectivity; and second, that selectivity guarantees bias. Of course, the preceding argument connects these premises by means of a convenient essentialism: the film medium is by its very nature selective; therefore, it is by its very nature biased (incapable of objectivity).

But clearly, selectivity, even if it is an inevitable feature of film, is not a unique feature of film. Every mode of inquiry and its attendant channels of publicity—from physics through history to journalism—is selective. So nothing special is discovered by revealing the selectivity of the motion picture apparatus. Moreover, insofar as we do not regard physics or history as exiled from objectivity just because they select, then there should be no impulse to suspect the nonfiction film's credentials, on a priori grounds, merely because it is selective. We can't have chemistry or economics without selectivity. Indeed, it is their selectivity that makes them possible. Why should we expect things to stand differently with nonfiction films?

Needless to say, some film theorists may regard this response as too precipitous. They may argue that selectivity in any area of inquiry is suspicious. Thus, if I defend the possibility of objectivity in the nonfiction film by appealing to analogous practices of selectivity in physics, then, it might be argued, all that has been shown is that physics, along with any other mode of inquiry I choose for analogy, will also require reassessment. For selectivity implies bias and bias precludes objectivity.

Yet surely it is a mistake to presume that selectivity entails bias. It may in some cases be what makes bias possible; it may in some contexts even invite bias. But it does not *guarantee* bias. Furthermore, most (perhaps all) known practices of inquiry are alert to the possibility of bias. They possess established protocols of inquiry that, among other things, are designed to deter the operation of bias; and, moreover, if bias is detected as playing a role in the production of a certain body of research, then the burden of proof—that the findings are not thereby distorted—falls upon the researcher in question.

Modes of inquiry and their associated avenues of communication are governed by protocols that have been established in order to secure the objectivity of conclusions in the relevant area of discourse. Many of these protocols are concerned with filtering out or diminishing the epistemically baleful effects of bias. These protocols may not succeed in rooting out bias in every case; they do not make the operation of bias impossible. But there is no reason to suppose that they do not work some of the time or even much of the time.

That is, if selectivity makes bias possible or even invites bias, it is also possible to be aware of this and to design provisions against the influence of bias—both at the level of the individual researcher and at the level of the community of inquiry at large. Self-awareness can encourage self-regulation. Scientists, historians, journalists, and even nonfiction filmmakers can bring standards of objectivity to bear upon other inquirers in order to determine whether or not bias has distorted the claims they advance. And that we may criticize others for biases and correct them indicates that we can do the same in our own case.

Thus, selectivity can occur without bias; selectivity is compatible with objectivity; and there is no a priori argument from selectivity that shows that nonfiction filmmakers and physicists have no purchase on objectivity. For, among other things, the protocols of objectivity within an established community of discourse and inquiry provide a degree of insurance against bias which, though it may fail on occasion, is not predestined to fail always.

Undoubtedly, it would be misleading to talk as if there were simply one set of protocols or standards for nonfiction filmmakers. Nonfiction filmmakers abide by different, though not nonconverging, standards of objectivity relative to the type of inquiry in which they are engaged. For example, *Killer Whale,* directed by Jeff Foott and written by Malcolm Penny for the Time Warner series *Predators,* abides by the protocols of a certain type of popular-science writing, whereas *Truth or Dare* seems committed to respecting little more than the protocols of honest, eyewitness reporting—namely, that what is portrayed happened and, perhaps, that it be a fair sample of what happened.

Not all nonfiction films succeed in meeting the relevant standards of objectivity, just as not all scientific research is above reproach. However, there is no reason to suspect that all nonfiction film fails in this regard, just as a parallel judgment about physics would be unwarranted. Indeed, the very fact that we can say some nonfiction film fails to measure up to the relevant standards of objectivity suggests, if there is to be a meaningful contrast here, that some succeed, or, at least, could succeed. So, once again, the argument from selectivity appears philosophically harmless, since determining bias in a particular film is always an empirical matter and not the foregone conclusion of a piece of conceptual analysis.

Maybe as a result of its virtually transparent defects, the selectivity argument, as rehearsed above, is rarely mounted by film theorists nowadays. However, the obsolescence of the selectivity argument, at least in its simplest forms, does not signal any abatement in the skepticism with which film theorists regard the prospects for objectivity in the nonfiction film. For it appears that the selectivity argument has left the field only to be replaced by new arguments, derived from postmodernist dogma and preached with Post-Structuralist energy, which once again challenge the epistemic probity of nonfiction films on what are alleged to be generic, theoretical grounds. In the remainder of this essay, I will examine some of the leading postmodernist arguments of the moment concerning the nonfiction film for the purpose of refuting what I take to be overly facile skepticism about the possibility of making motion pictures that are genuinely in the service of knowledge.[3]

2

In the introduction to his anthology, *Theorizing Documentary*—a state-of-the-art compendium of received thinking about the documentary film—editor Michael Renov maintains that:

> In every case, elements of style, structure, and expositional strategy draw upon pre-existent constructs, or schemas, to establish meanings and effects for audiences. What I am arguing is that documentary shares the status of all discursive forms with regard to its tropic or figurative character and that it employs many of the methods and devices of its fictional counterpart.[4]

and that

> . . . all discursive forms—documentary included—are, if not fictional, at least *fictive,* this by virtue of their tropic character (their recourse to tropes or rhetorical figures). As Hayden White has so brilliantly described, "every mimesis can be shown to be distorted and can serve, therefore, as an occasion for yet another description of the same phenomenon." This is because "all discourse *constitutes* the objects which it pretends only to describe realistically and to analyze objectively."[5]

Both these quotations evince Renov's intention to deconstruct the distinction between nonfiction and fiction. Certainly, there is a strategic motive behind this; scholars specializing in the documentary film appear to feel their subject has always been eclipsed by the attention lavished on the far more popular fiction film. By claiming a parity with fiction, I suppose theorists like Renov hope to claim a larger piece of the pie, if not for themselves, then for their clients. Documentary filmmakers and documentary film theorists alike embrace an adversarial relationship to the larger institution of fictional film. Perhaps this deconstructive ploy expresses the desire to fight the fiction film by joining it (though in a way, I believe, that puts the integrity of the nonfiction film in jeopardy).

But, aside from the politics of the academic film world, a further point in deconstructing the distinction between nonfiction and fiction is to endorse "skepticism toward the traditional claims made for documentary's powers to see and to know. . . ."[6] The thinking seems to be this: If there is no principled difference between nonfiction film and fiction film, then the claims of the nonfiction film either to objectivity or to truth are no better than those of a fiction. The aforesaid documentary *Killer Whale* is in the same epistemic boat (or, to suit the case, *out* of the same epistemic boat), as the fictional movie *Free Willy.*

One reason that Renov introduces to call into question the distinction between nonfiction films and fiction films is that many of the devices that are used in nonfiction films—like flashbacks and crosscutting—are central narrative devices in fiction films. And, furthermore, techniques associated with nonfiction films, like jittery, handheld camera movements, can be appropriated by fiction filmmakers for heightened affect. This is all true. But it does not support the conclusion that Renov draws. For the distinction between nonfiction and fiction was never really based on differences in formal technique in the first place; so one cannot deconstruct the distinction by citing shared techniques in the second place.

This, of course, should have already been apparent to film theorists on the basis of literature. No one can tell by reading a passage whether it is nonfiction or fiction, for the simple reason that a writer of fiction can adopt any strategy associated with nonfiction writing for aesthetic effect, just as nonfiction writers can always try to approximate fictional techniques for their own purposes. Likewise, the distinction between nonfiction film and fiction film cannot be grounded in differences of formal technique, because, when it comes to technique, fiction and nonfiction filmmakers can and do imitate each other, just as fiction and nonfiction writers can and do. The distinction between nonfiction and fiction, therefore, does not collapse with the recognition of stylistic correlations, since the distinction never rested upon such formal or technical differentiae in the first place.

Standardly, when one attends a film, one does not have to guess—on the basis of how it looks and sounds—whether it is fiction or nonfiction. Nor does one typically guess whether a written narrative is a novel or a memoir. The film and the writing come labeled, or, as I say, *indexed,* one way or another, ahead of time.[7] When a film like *Killer Whale* is indexed as a nonfiction film that tells us something about its commitments, specifically that it is committed to certain standards of scientific accuracy and attendant protocols of objectivity. We, in turn, base our evaluations of such a film, to a large extent, on its achievement with respect to these standards and protocols in virtue of the film's commitment to a specific form of nonfiction exposition.

It is not a defect to present a killer whale who understands that petroleum is flammable in a science fiction film like *Orca,* but it would be problematic in a documentary such as *Killer Whale.* For in virtue of the kind of nonfiction that *Killer Whale* is, as signaled by the way in which it is indexed and circulated, *Killer Whale* must abide by certain canons of accuracy that a film like *Orca,* which is indexed and circulated as science fiction, need not respect. The distinction between nonfiction and fiction is a distinction between the commitments of the texts, not between the surface structures of the texts. Therefore, Renov's attempt to deconstruct the distinction between nonfiction and fiction on the basis of shared technique misses the point altogether.

But, of course, Renov's case for the allegedly fictive status of nonfiction film—the truth about nonfiction, as he puts it—is putatively based upon something deeper than shared narrative techniques between fictions and nonfictions. Following the postmodernist historiographer Hayden White,[8] Renov maintains that nonfiction film (like history à la White) is tropological and, therefore, fictive. What does this mean and why would anyone believe it?

According to Hayden White, historical writing is tropological. By this, he means to claim that historical writing, inasmuch as it is narrative, relies on certain recurring plot structures (such as Romance, Tragedy, Comedy, and Satire) which, in turn, are associated with certain rhetorical tropes or figures (such as metaphor, metonymy, synecdoche, and irony).[9] Historians use these narrative structures to organize the states of affairs and events that comprise their accounts into intelligible wholes, that is, into tidy packages comprehensible to readers.

However, although narrative structures organize the historian's accounts of sequences of states and affairs and events, the relations posited by said narratives have no basis in historical reality. Narratives, for example, have closure. But this is a feature of stories, not of the world. Likewise, one historian may narrate a series of events as a tragedy while another narrates the same series as a comedy, just as Shakespeare's recounting of those happenings in Denmark is tragic and Stoppard's hilarious. But in all these cases, comedy and tragedy are fictional; they belong solely to the order of telling, not being.

The states of affairs and events the historian alludes to do have a basis in historical reality, and the historian's claims about those states of affairs and events can be literally true or false. But the narratives in which those states of affairs and events figure are inventions, constructions, indeed, *fictions*. A romantic plot structure, qua representation, does not correspond to anything that has or will exist; subtract the events emplotted by the structure, and what remains— the plot—has no reference to reality.

The narrative structure in the historical recounting is not true or false; it is fictional. It is imposed on events by the historian and, as Renov's quotation indicates, it is thought to distort, presumably necessarily. Thus no historical narrative can pretend to accuracy or objectivity because in virtue of its possession of a narrative structure, it is both fictive and distortive. It merely *pretends* to refer objectively to the event-structures that plot structures appear to depict, because those event-structures are in fact the fabrications of narration—that is, "all discourse *constitutes* the objects which it pretends only to describe realistically and analyze objectively." Or, to put it differently, that which plot-structures seem to portray has no independent historical existence outside of narrative discourse.

Renov imports White's claims about historical writing to the case of the nonfiction film. By hypothesis, this is warranted by the fact that nonfiction films are often historical and even more often narrative, though it might also pay to note that frequently nonfiction films are neither historical nor narrative, just as historical writing itself is not always narrative. But, despite these flagrant problems, Renov somehow thinks that the matchings between White's subject and his own are significant enough to allow extrapolation of White's supposed findings about history to nonfiction film. Consequently, nonfiction films are said to be fictive in virtue of their tropological or narrative structures, which, it is thought, implies that they necessarily distort.

Moreover, the claims of nonfiction films to make objective reference to event-structures in the world must fail, for those event-structures belong to (indeed, are constituted by and in) discourse, and are not, therefore, ontologically independent from the order of telling. The nonfiction filmmaker is caught in a doxastic cocoon, precluding objectivity in any strong sense of the term. And this problem, added to the fictive and distortive nature of nonfiction narration, undermines any faith that one might entertain in the possibility that a documentary could deliver objective knowledge to audiences.

One of White's favorite slogans, derived from the late Louis Mink, is that lives are led, and stories are told.[10] By this, White means that narrative structure is an artifact of our talking about the past—an artifact of retrospection; it is not, in other words, an actual feature of past events, awaiting discovery. It is something we construct or invent and then impose on the past. Our life is not really a comedy until we reconsider it and construct it that way. This is putatively borne out by the fact that the same events can be satisfactorily reconfigured in different narratives with different structures. That is, one might, the idea goes, reconfigure one's life as either a romance or a farce.

Renov wants to mobilize a comparable slogan, especially in terms of the ethnographic film. He writes: "the very act of plucking and recontextualizing profilmic elements is a kind of violence, particularly when cultural specificity is at issue as it is with ethnographic texts. There the question of the adequacy of a representational system as a stand-in for lived experience arises most forcefully."[11] That is, once again, the nonfiction film does not represent the world objectively, but proffers a surrogate superaddition in place of something called "lived experience."

Though at present it is quite common to extend White's theory of history to other precincts of the humanities in exactly the manner Renov does, it is far from settled whether White's views have much to recommend them. The crux of White's position is that the narrative element or, if you will, the plot structure in historical accounts is a fictional imposition on a series of events which renders the telling of those events intelligible, but which has no basis in reality. Stories end; but reality just keeps moving on. Historians configure events as romances or comedies; the different plot structures are optional, for the plot structures refer to nothing.

But this doesn't seem plausible. A major ingredient in the stories that historians tell involves causal relationships. If causation is the cement of the universe, it is also the cement of narration. This is not to say, as some might,[12] that a historical narrative is fundamentally only a chain of causation. Nevertheless, causation is an important element in virtually all narrative structures. Moreover, there is no reason to think that the causal relationships that are hypothesized to obtain in a certain course of events are fictional. For though causation is an ingredient of narrative structure, it also possesses historical reality. Ex hypothesi, the causal relationships that integrate the details of a historical narrative correspond to actual causal relationships in the relevant courses of events.[13]

To consider an example pertinent to the discussion of nonfiction film, recall the episode on gliders from the TV documentary series *Wings of the Luftwaffe*. That installment ends by referring to the wide-bodied jet transports of contemporary warfare in such a way that the viewer comes to appreciate that the transport gliders developed by the Germans to storm England and those developed, partly in imitation of the Germans, by the Allies for the invasion of Europe on D-Day were, in fact, steps in the evolution of the giant jet aircraft that the United States relies upon for the rapid deployment of its troops today.

Now, if we suppose that the makers of *Wings of the Luftwaffe* are correct in identifying the significance of German glider research as a forerunner of, as well as a contribution to, the evolution of contemporary military aircraft, then the relation between the glider research and the present is hardly occult or fictional. German glider research and development, if the account in the film is true, was a causal element in the evolution of modern military transport aircraft. Putatively, this is a real causal relation in an actual course of events.

For example, the documentary asserts that the German gliders which were developed to deliver armor to the front line in the East bear a relation to our own contemporary rapid deployment cargo planes. This relation is neither fictional nor fictive. It is that of a contributory causal condition to an effect. Moreover, if the account presented in *Wings of the Luftwaffe* is accurate—and there is no reason to suppose that it *can't* be—then it would make no sense to refer to the narrative structure under discussion as an imposition. Rather the narrative structure, in this case, tracks actual relations between states of affairs and actions in real courses of events. Insofar as relations between causes and effects—and, for that matter, between reasons and actions—are part of the fabric of courses of events, narrative structures may be said to illuminate those courses of events rather than to impose upon them.

For the same reason, it is as incorrect to suppose that narrative is always a distortion as it is to suppose that it is a fiction. For a given narrative may in fact *discover* actual patterns of relations between causes and effects, reasonings and actions, influences and evolutions in real courses of events. Historical constructivists like White and Renov may believe that closure is simply an artifact of storytelling and that the narrative that leads to it is a purely fictional invention. However, World War I did end in 1918, and the Allied victory was a function of the entry of the United States into the conflict. The first person to realize that made a discovery, and the story that recounts those events tracks an actual course of events through its very sinews to its terminus.

So far I have argued that historical narratives and, by extension, nonfiction films (or, at least, those nonfiction films that are narratives) need not, in virtue of their narrative (or "tropological") structure be thought to be necessarily fictive, nor need they be thought of as impositions upon or distortions of historically occurring sequences of events. I think that this is obvious once one reflects upon the fact that basic elements of narrative structure—such as causation, influence, and rational action—correspond to actual elements of courses of events.

When Hayden White thinks of narrative structures, he has in mind generic structures, such as the romance, which supposedly correlate with certain tropes.[14] But perhaps this is just the wrong level of generality (or vagueness) to think about the structures of historical narration. Focusing at this level of abstraction results in overlooking and then fallaciously denying the straightforward way in which narrative structure is keyed—nondistortively—to the structure of courses of events.

Insofar as White and Renov are defending a universal claim about the nature of all nonfiction narration, it is enough for me to establish that there are some cases of nonfiction narration, like my example for *Wings of the Luftwaffe,* that defy their generalization. Of course, I do not wish to deny that *some* narratives may distort history and may impose preconceived ideas upon it. But that is something that must be determined on a case-by-case basis. There is no a priori argument for narrative distortion. However, needless to say, this is compatible with admitting that sometimes specific nonfiction narratives do distort.

According to White and Renov, historical narration and nonfiction film *constitute* their objects, pretending that these objects have some independent existence about which historians and nonfiction filmmakers imagine they hypothesize objectively. If *constitute* here means something like "bring into existence," then it is surely false that the makers of *Wings of the Luftwaffe* brought into existence the German air force, the Allied air force, contemporary jumbo jets, or the influence of the development of wide-bodied transport gliders on our own wide-bodied transport jets. All these things have an ontological status that is independent of the discourse of *Wings of the Luftwaffe.*

On the other hand, if *constitute* means something less dramatic—such as "find adequate conceptualizations for their objects"—then it is not clear that we need to accuse historians and nonfiction filmmakers of pretense. For even if the makers of *Wings of the Luftwaffe* had proposed a novel, unprecedented conceptualization of the relationship between gliders and jet transports, that conceptualization was in the service of a discovery of a causal relation that obtained, whether or not anyone ever recognized it.

Lastly, Renov seems to believe that we should be skeptical about the epistemic status of nonfiction films because there is some question about the adequacy of representational systems to "stand-in for lived experience." Now I suppose that, in some sense, we all agree with part of Renov's anxiety here; most of the time, we prefer to be with our lover rather than with a picture of our lover. We may even say things like "A photograph is a poor substitute for a loved one." But what in the world does this have to do with the knowledge claims of documentary filmmakers?

When I watch *Gates of Heaven,* I am not looking for a close personal encounter with the owners of some pet graveyards in California. Though I may be interested in observing them and in hearing what they have to say, I prefer a detached to a live experience of them. Nor do I screen *Not a Love Story* in order to simulate a visit to a strip show. I watch it in order to attend to an argument. That is, I do not typically expect a representation, especially a nonfiction film, to stand in for (to replace?) a lived experience. Nonfiction films serve many purposes, but I'm not convinced that they are supposed to serve that one very often, if ever. Thus, it is strange to hear Renov advance the failure[15] of nonfiction film to stand in for lived experience as a basis for questioning its adequacy in terms of, among other things, serving as a disseminator of knowledge claims. After all, we don't cite the incapacity of chain saws to stitch trousers as a reason to question their usefulness in clearing forests.

Renov's argument, in other words, is a red herring.

3

Representing Reality by Bill Nichols eschews those facile deconstructions of the boundary between fiction and nonfiction that conclude that nonfiction film is just like any other kind of fiction.[16] Rather, he argues, nonfiction film is fiction, but it is not exactly like other forms of fiction film. For in his view, nonfiction films are not merely narrative (and, à la White, fictional), but they are argumentative as well; so they are fictional, though they are not exactly like narrative fictions. However, whether this putative distinction will do the work that Nichols assigns to it—since some nonfiction films are exclusively narrative, while some fictional narratives are argumentative[17]—is less of interest to us than is Nichols's epistemological contention that objectivity is impossible in the documentary.

Nichols writes:

> . . . they [documentaries] share with fiction those very qualities that thoroughly compromise any rigorous objectivity, if they don't make it impossible. *This impossibility* is also evident in the more standardized and enforced objectivity of journalism.
>
> Objectivity has been under no less siege than realism and for many of the same reasons. It, too, is a way of representing the world that denies its own processes of construction and their own formative effect. Any given standard for objectivity will have embedded political assumptions.[18]

Undoubtedly, this quotation is initially perplexing, because many readers, if not most, will wonder what *political* assumptions underlie documentaries like

City of Coral (which was produced for the *Nova* series by Peace River Films in 1983). But Nichols believes that

> In documentary, these assumptions might also include belief in the self-evident na-
> ture of facts, in rhetorical persuasion as a necessary and appropriate part of represen-
> tation and in the capacity of the documentary text to affect its audience through its
> implicit or explicit claim of "This is so, isn't it?"[19]

So, summarizing Nichols thus far, objectivity in the documentary is impossible because documentaries deny their own processes of construction (and
their formative effects), and/or they make political assumptions, including
these: that facts are self-evident, that rhetoric is an appropriate part of representation, and that documentaries have the capacity to move audience members to accept what they've been shown as true. Do all documentaries fall afoul
of these accusations and, indeed, do all these accusations really amount to challenges to objectivity? My answer to both these questions is "no." In order to see
why, let us take up Nichols's accusations one at a time.

A typical documentary film like *City of Coral* does not, for the most part, call
attention to its own process of construction. I say "for the most part," in order
to accommodate the fact that it does have a credit sequence at the end of which,
of course, is something that Nichols will have to explain away if he wants to
make the charge that such films attempt to *deny* their own process of construction. For if they were serious in that attempt, why would they publicize those
credits?[20]

Nevertheless, I suppose that one would have to concede to Nichols the
premise that most nonfiction films spend little or almost no time revealing the
process of their construction to their viewers. But the question arises as to
whether *not calling attention to* such construction processes amounts to *denying*
the existence of those processes? In not exhibiting something about oneself, one
is not thereby automatically denying that feature of oneself. In many conversations, I do not call attention to my Irish-Catholic heritage, but that does not
entail that I have denied that feature of myself.

Denial, so to say, is its own speech act. In denying something, one generally
has to do something. It doesn't simply happen that I deny my heritage if I ask
someone to pass me the pepper without telling them I'm Irish. Similarly, *City
of Coral*, like so many documentaries and informational films, does not deny
anything about its process of construction (and certainly does not deny that it
was constructed) by not mentioning it.

Of course, the deeper question is: why should it matter, in terms of the issue of objectivity, whether a nonfiction film acknowledges or denies the process of its own construction? Why does Nichols make such heavy weather over it? Surely, everyone who sees a nonfiction film knows that it was, as Nichols put it, "constructed." It is nice to see *The Making of Brief History of Time* after seeing *Brief History of Time,* but I would have known that the latter was constructed even if I hadn't seen the former. Why does Nichols place such emphasis on reflexivity and what does this emphasis on reflexivity have to do with objectivity?

Nichols's concern with reflexivity can be explained, I think, by the fact that film scholars are primarily interested in one kind of documentary film, a kind which, by the way, is probably less statistically significant than documentary motion pictures or informational films like *City of Coral.* That type of nonfiction film is what might be called the art-documentary, examples of which include: *The Thin Blue Line, Tongues Untied, Roger and Me, Sherman's March,* and earlier films such as *Man with a Movie Camera, Le sang des bêtes, Las hurdes,* and *Chronique d'un été.*

These films, admittedly in often extremely different ways, display a concern with the themes of reflexivity and authorial subjectivity with which we are already familiar from modernist and postmodernist art. And in that context, calling attention reflexively to the nature of film, to filmic devices, to film history, to filmic rhetoric, to film stereotypes, to the construction, as it happens, of the film at hand, to the filmmaker himself or herself, and so on, are all artistically significant gestures.[21] What Nichols has done in requiring reflexivity for objectivity is to mistake a benchmark of what is interesting from the perspective of modernist aesthetics (and its derivatives) for a requirement for objectivity.

But this is clearly wrong. The fact that I have not confided in you whether I wrote this article sequentially or wrote the sections out of order, or whether I prepared the first draft with a quill or a word processor has no bearing whatsoever on whether this article is objective. Undoubtedly, this article is not a modernist masterpiece. But that does not compromise its objectivity.

Nichols further alleges that objectivity is impossible in the documentary because such films have political assumptions. On the face of it, given our ordinary understanding of what constitutes a political assumption, this seems false. One would be hard put to identify any garden-variety political assumptions in *City of Coral,* and I suspect that this is probably true of a great many typical informational films such as those concerned with how to go about trout fishing or canning fruit or break dancing or transmission repair.

Of course, we quickly see that Nichols has some rather expansive views of what counts as a political assumption. For him, political assumptions include:

the belief that facts are self-evident; that rhetorical persuasion is appropriate; and that documentary films claim of whatever they represent that "This is so, isn't it?" with the presumption that this will affect audiences. But is it true that documentaries that do not possess garden-variety political assumptions are likely to be guilty of these more recherché commitments?

If some nonfiction can be innocent of Nichols's allegations about political assumptions at the same time they do not *deny* their processes of construction, then Nichols's argument for the generalization about the impossibility of objectivity in the documentary will be undermined. Let us use *City of Coral* as a test case here, since we have already established that it is not in the state of Nicholsesque denial.

The film does not appear to be predicated on persuading us of anything, unless it be that the coral reef off St. Croix is interesting and the film, therefore, seems to make no assumptions about rhetoric.[22] Does the film assume that the facts are self-evident? Not really, since it is constantly preoccupied with explaining everything that we are seeing—that is, with enabling us to understand the nonobvious significance of whatever is in front of the camera, such as the adaptive relevance of various features of the flora and fauna. Indeed, if one had to identify an underlying presupposition of *City of Coral,* it might be that next to nothing about coral reefs is self-evident.

But maybe we are looking for the conviction of self-evident facts in the wrong place. Does the film assume that it is its own explanations, once offered, that are self-evident? I don't think so. In explaining the extremely thin girth of a gray angelfish, the narrator says that it *might* enable the fish to confuse predators by turning quickly and, thereby, virtually disappearing. And of the dorsal fin on the lancer dragonete, the narrator admits that it is mysterious, and he hazards three different hypotheses: that it might be used to frighten predators, to confuse predators, or to provide predators with a false target. That some of the narrator's hypotheses are tentative indicates that there is no presumption of self-evidence here.

It is true that the narrator speaks as though the film is committed to there being facts. We are told that pelican chicks grow down within a month after birth and that coral is part animal and part vegetable and leaves mineral deposits. But there is no indication that the filmmakers believe that these are self-evident facts, and if Nichols thinks that a belief in a fact is equivalent to a belief in a self-evident fact, then he is just confused.

But, in any case, one wonders why, even if the makers of *City of Coral* believe that there are some self-evident facts, that should count as a political assumption. Let me conjecture that the motivation revolves around the following error. Often it is argued that ideology proceeds by treating politically charged falsehoods as if they were self-evident truths. The belief that gay persons are unsuited for military service might be an example here. And, as a result of examples like this, one might become suspicious of claims of self-evident truths, especially concerning political matters.

However, it would be a mistake to infer from the fact that some claims of self-evident truth are politically motivated falsehoods that all claims that this or that is self-evident are politically suspicious. For, on the one hand, not every alleged self-evident fact concerns politics. On the other hand, not every alleged self-evident fact concerning politics need be an ideologically motivated falsehood. It may be prudent to inspect every alleged self-evident fact concerning politics scrupulously; but there is no reason to presume that none will pass inspection.

Of course, if Nichols thinks that the belief in facts is a political assumption, because there are no facts, then it is difficult to see how such a position would avoid self-refutation, since the claim that a belief in facts is a political assumption is presumably a fact.

Moreover, that politically pernicious propositions have sometimes been advanced as facts may warrant caution about factual claims, especially in political contexts, but it is no reason to deny that there are facts. For it is by means of facts that one unmasks politically oppressive falsehoods.

Nichols may, as a matter of philosophical conviction, believe that there are no self-evident facts. But even if there are no self-evident facts, it would not follow that those who assumed there are such facts are guilty of a political assumption. And if it is argued that it is a political assumption because the rhetoric of self-evidence is often employed for political purposes, that fails to show that claims about self-evidence are *always* a matter of political presumption. Even if it were false to say that it is self-evident that I am at least a thinking something, it is not a political presumption.

Not only is it the case that some documentary films do not assume that there are self-evident facts, but even supposing all nonfiction films did assume there were some self-evident facts, it would not necessarily be a political assumption. Consequently, insofar as Nichols worries that objectivity is impossible in nonfiction films due to their political assumptions about self-evident facts, he should worry no longer.

Nichols is also suspicious of the claims of nonfiction films to objectivity because such films, explicitly or implicitly, claim that what they show corresponds to the way things are and that this can influence audiences. This is somewhat baffling. For generally when people speak—save cases like irony and quotation—we take them to be making avowals about how they think matters stand. This is what makes lying possible.

If I say to you, "Here's an apple," I suppose you could say that that comes with an implicit claim that "This is so," along with my expectation that my assertion may affect listeners. But if such a claim is built into assertions in general, I find it hard to understand how that is particularly political, and, therefore, how it could possibly preclude objectivity. Consequently, on these grounds, if all the assertions in *City of Coral* are indeed accompanied with the "This is so" claim and the expectation of influence, I find that to be no barrier to regarding the film to be objective.

Nichols has an additional argument, not discussed so far, aiming to demonstrate that no nonfiction film can be objective. Basically he maintains that there is no viable notion of objectivity available to apply to nonfiction film. Nichols comes to this conclusion by examining and criticizing what he introduces as the three leading characterizations of objectivity that are relevant to the discussion of documentary film: (1) that the objective view is a third-person view; (2) that the objective view is one that allows each audience member to come to her own conclusion; and (3) that the objective view is disinterested.

Nichols contends that the identification of the objective view with the third-person view is not viable for nonfiction film because films that do not employ explicit first-person point-of-view devices may nevertheless be subjective. Moreover, I would hasten to add that grammatical personhood—and cinematic personhood, if there is such a thing—is not a test of objectivity, since a perfectly objective argument can be mounted in any grammatical person; if Eratosthenes had said "Given the evidence I have submitted about differences in shadow lengths, I hypothesize that the Earth is curved," that statement would nevertheless be objective, even though it is not in the third person.

Nichols rejects the notion that documentary films might be objective in the sense that they might present information in a way that leaves it up to the viewer to reach her conclusions on her own. Nichols's grounds here are his unshakable belief that rhetoric is necessarily inexpungible from any documentary. Nichols offers very little argument for this astounding surmise, save that Feyerabend and Kuhn say that rhetoric plays a role in securing scientific conversions.[23]

That rhetoric might have a role in conversions, is, of course, unsurprising, but how does that show that rhetoric is in operation in a film like Warhol's *Empire,* which is surely a documentary—indeed, perhaps the longest *actualité* in film history?[24] That is, some, if not, in fact, many nonfiction films are not in the business of persuasion, let alone conversion; so what grounds are there to suspect that they practice subliminal rhetoric?

However, even if Nichols is wrong in his reasons for rejecting the supposition that objectivity in the documentary amounts to inviting spectatorial freedom of choice, this position is surely irrelevant, on other grounds, to the question of whether a film is objective. A theorem whose steps are fully explicit and justified has a conclusion that is, from a logical point of view, not open to diverse opinions on the part of the readers, but it is nonetheless objective despite that. Similarly, many of Stephen Hawking's arguments in the film *Brief History of Time* are presented objectively, though they are not set out in a way that encourages the spectator to form alternative, differing hypotheses.

Structuring a film in a way that engages the spectators to think for themselves may be a virtue where one is committed to that form of liberalism which maintains that it is more important to develop a citizenry that autonomously arrives at its own opinions than it is for those opinions to be right. But this brand of political liberalism should not be mistaken for objectivity in the epistemic sense. For even if it is considered to be an important moral ideal, it is not a test for objectivity. It is an ethical standard, not an epistemic one.

The last notion of objectivity that Nichols rejects is that the objective view is disinterested. Nichols dismisses this on the grounds that disinterestedness is impossible. He claims that this

> definition—the absence of perceived bias—presupposes some englobing framework that can subsume personal bias and self-interest. This framework is, for individual filmmakers, the interpretive community of filmmakers that share a style, conventions, and a perspective, and—for journalists and reporters, along with anthropologists, sociologists, ethnographers, and other members of the scientific community—it is those institutional structures that regulate and control the shape of news and interpretation (networks, publishers, universities, and professional societies).
>
> What objectivity masks in this case is the specific point of view of institutional authority itself. Not only is there an inevitable concern with legitimation and self-perpetuation, other more historic and issue-specific forms of self-interest and partiality

may also prevail, often in the all-the-more-powerful form of unacknowledged predispositions and assumptions rather than stated interests.[25]

This is a strange argument against the notion of objectivity as disinterestedness. For one supposes that whoever uses disinterestedness as a test for objectivity would contend that views arrived at solely through considerations of institutional concerns with self-perpetuation, institutional legitimation, and other forms of self-interest are exactly the views whose objective status would be challenged and criticized under the disinterestedness conception of objectivity. That is, if claims to objective knowledge are found to be interested in the ways Nichols sketches, then according to the concept of objectivity under examination, the claims are open to dispute. Nichols's examples do not seem to be counterinstances to the view that objectivity is disinterested; rather the examples seem to constitute paradigmatic cases in which the conception would be used to show that the claims in question are not objective.

Moreover, oddly enough, Nichols seems to be in agreement with this; he appears to question the preceding claims to objectivity because he does not think that these examples are truly disinterested. But that view coincides precisely with the conception of objectivity as disinterestedness. Indeed, is Nichols himself using anything but that conception of objectivity to call into doubt the objectivity of examples of institutional bias? Yet, then, how can Nichols be challenging the conception of objectivity as disinterestedness by means of these examples, if these examples become compelling as breaches of objectivity just when one adopts the disinterestedness conception of objectivity? That is, Nichols appears to be undertaking the self-contradictory task of refuting the viability of a standard of objectivity as disinterestedness by employing that very standard in his own putative refutation of it. After all, he appears to deprecate institutional claims to objectivity on the grounds that the institutions are not genuinely disinterested.

Clearly, Nichols thinks that every institutional practice adopted by scientists, historians, journalists, nonfiction filmmakers, and so on, for the purpose of facilitating objective inquiry will *inevitably* fail to insure objectivity because every one of them will be interested.[26] Nichols appears to think that the presuppositions of institutions like physics amount to interests. But it is hard to see why the view that nothing travels faster than the speed of light should count as an interest.

Nichols has not really provided us with any argument to show that this conclusion concerning the inevitability of institutional interestedness is conceptually necessary. So his conclusion must be an empirical finding. But if it is an empirical finding, and no empirically discoverable mechanism has been introduced to show why institutional self-interest is built into the nature of things,[27] then the very most that Nichols could claim to command as evidence is that so far, in all known cases, there is no example of appropriately disinterested knowledge.

In response, the proponent of the disinterestedness view of objectivity will simply say that even if Nichols is right (which is unlikely), then the best Nichols can claim is that thus far we have no examples of objective knowledge. The concept of objectivity as disinterestedness is not overthrown. It is just uninstantiated. And if more claims to objectivity come before us, and they are as Nichols describes them, then we will merely deny their objectivity.

Furthermore, the proponent of the disinterestedness conception of objectivity will also want to ask Nichols about the status of his own generalization. Does the generalization about institutional self-interest apply to Nichols's own theory? That is, according to his own theory, Nichols himself should turn out to be an agent in the service of the self-perpetuation of the cinema studies institution. But if that is true, then we should certainly deny that Nichols's theory makes any viable claims to objective knowledge. Again, Nichols's attack on the disinterestedness conception of objectivity, unless qualified in appropriate ways, is curiously self-refuting.

Perhaps there is some way in which Nichols can, in a principled way, segregate his own generalizations from the charges he levels at the generalizations of other inquirers, thereby dodging charges of self-refutation. But that may not be so easy, and, in any case, the burden of proof here is with Nichols. Moreover, I believe that he, in particular, will find this a hard row to hoe just because he appears unbudgeably committed to the view that everything is politically partisan.

In addition, if one could show that the kind of methodological paranoia that Nichols practices is nothing but a strategy adopted by humanities departments to legitimatize themselves in their competition with the sciences, natural and social, then we would have almost as much reason to suspect Nichols's findings as we would to suspect them if they were shown to be solely the result of a bribe. I am not saying that Nichols might not be able to clear himself of such a charge. My point is only that however we adjudicate a case like this—whether for or against—notions of disinterestedness will come into play.

Undoubtedly, the concept of disinterestedness will have to be refined further than it has been so far. It will also have to be supplemented by other concepts before we have a fully adequate concept of objectivity. But, nevertheless, I do not think that Nichols has shown that the disinterestedness conception of objectivity is irrelevant to the discussion of inquiry in general or to nonfiction film in particular.

Nichols takes claims of objectivity to be forms of disguise. For the individual, "it helps defend him or her against mistakes and criticism."[28] For institutions, objectivity provides the camouflage behind which practices of inquiry self-interestedly perpetuate themselves. What is so bizarre about Nichols's indictments is that he reacts to the potential problems he discerns by condemning the notion of objectivity, rather than by regarding the infractions in question as abuses. Moreover, if one is concerned to criticize these abuses, as Nichols appears to be, then it is inadvisable to jettison the concept of objectivity. For the activities at issue seem only definable as abuses when one cleaves to standards of objectivity.

Against the disinterestedness standard of objectivity, Nichols inveighs as follows:

> The impression of disinterestedness is a powerful reassurance and a seductive ploy. What objectivity itself cannot tell us is the purpose it is meant to serve since this would undercut its own effectiveness (lest that purpose be one that adopts the shroud of objectivity itself as a final purpose: the pursuit of truth, the quest for knowledge, the performance of service for the community good).[29]

Close attention to this passage indicates that Nichols has no argument, but only an attitude. He asserts that all invocations of objectivity have ulterior motives. He challenges believers in objectivity to state their purposes. But if they respond, easily enough, by saying that the purposes of their protocols of inquiry are the pursuit of truth or the quest for knowledge, then Nichols scoffs, and dismisses these remarks as "shrouds." But no argument is given to show why one cannot embark upon an inquiry with the primary purpose and interest in obtaining knowledge—an interest, by the way, which is compatible with the disinterestedness relevant to the objectivity. Nichols certainly thinks that this view is contemptible; but perhaps this is one of his own unexamined predispositions. Does it belie an interest?

4

As indicated in the opening section of this essay, attacks on the objectivity of the nonfiction film by an earlier generation of film theorists proceeded as though this defect was a specific limitation of nonfiction film, due to the nature of the motion picture medium. Selectivity was of special interest to them, since this seems to be something that was built into the very cinematic apparatus itself.

Moreover, given this particular line of attack, it is quite easy to see how to deflect it. One has only to point to the fact that the feature in question is shared with some other forms of inquiry or information communication—like history, journalism, or science—where there are no doubts about the possibility of objectivity. Therefore, for example, if selectivity poses no problem for the prospects of objectivity in history and science, then there is no principled cause for alarm with respect to nonfiction film. Surely, we can all agree that objectivity might be difficult to secure; but it is still a possibility for nonfiction film if it is also a possibility for science or history.

This defense of objectivity in the nonfiction film is predicated upon confronting what might be called local skepticism about the documentary, that is, skepticism about the possibility of objectivity in nonfiction films, construed essentially, that raises no questions about the possibility of objectivity in other disciplines of inquiry and/or communication. But, as we have seen in the cases of both Renov and Nichols, the postmodernist attack on nonfiction film is not based on local skepticism about the documentary. In Renov's case, skepticism about the documentary comes in tandem with skepticism about history, whereas Nichols seems skeptical of just about any institution of inquiry and communication.[30] This postmodernist tendency toward suspicion of the nonfiction film on the grounds of global skepticism about the prospects for knowledge and rationality in general has been most blatantly advertised by Brian Winston.[31]

Noting the preceding strategy for defending the nonfiction film against attacks motivated by what I have just called local skepticism, Winston claims that the strategy is "easily attacked" when the opponent of objectivity in the nonfiction film opts for general skepticism, which Winston enthusiastically insinuates is irresistible under the postmodernist dispensation. Winston does not provide us with much by way of argument for his general skepticism, but, perhaps in the spirit of postmodernist pastiche, he lays on a series of quotations reassuring us that general skepticism is a foregone conclusion. One of the more over-the-top of these comes from Lorraine Nencel and Peter Pels and it goes like this: "It is no longer possible to salvage Western rationality or its totalizing potential from the clutches of context by ahistorical claims to a superior theoretical and methodological armament."[32] Whatever is meant by this is pretty obscure; nevertheless, Winston gleefully admonishes us that such postmodern skepticism applies even to the hard sciences.[33]

Winston's position seems to be that claims of objectivity in behalf of the nonfiction film cannot be sustained in the face of global postmodernist skepticism. For postmodern skepticism denies the possibility of objective standards of rationality in general; rather (or because) rationality is historically and contextually specific.

And yet, however schematic this argument is, it is still an argument. Reasons are being advanced to substantiate what is supposed to be a fact. And furthermore, the text gives every indication that Winston thinks that these reasons, which he believes to be rooted in facts, are in principle ascertainable by anyone and that they should be compelling in principle to anyone.

For instance, Winston offers these reasons dialectically in the course of a debate with people like myself who are more conservatively minded epistemologically than he and his colleagues are. I think that he expects us to recognize the logical force of mobilizing global postmodernist skepticism against local defenses of documentary objectivity, while recognizing the way in which the claims of history and context mitigate against faith in objective standards of rationality.

That is, Winston does not say that his argument is only an argument for fellow postmodernists or that it is an argument whose validity only takes hold in contexts of debate against local defenses of documentary objectivity. He does not say his reasons are good only for postmodernists and not for old fuddy-duddies like me. He expects his reasons to be generally convincing. But why? Mustn't he be presuming that there are some objective standards of rationality and that his reasons can be compelling in principle for anyone, including people with rival theories, in light of those objective standards?

Winston points out that local defenses of the objectivity of nonfiction film are outflanked by global postmodernist skepticism. Isn't that a logical point? Doesn't Winston write as though it should be conceded by friend and foe alike? But then Winston must presume that there are objective standards of rationality. And like Nichols's, Winston's position against the possibility of rational standards of objectivity teeters on the brink of incoherence, insofar as his argument *also* seems to presuppose objective standards of rationality.

Like other postmodernists, Winston enters the arena of public discussion and debate not only with other postmodernists but with unaligned readers and opponents like myself. In order for that conversation to proceed in a way that is intelligible, the participants must be able to recognize reasons when they see them—whether or not they welcome them—and be able to feel the force of good reasons when they are advanced, by whoever advances them.

Postmodernists cite facts, make arguments, and provide reasons. The conversation moves intelligibly. Epistemic conservatives like myself realize when postmodernists raise issues that require logical damage control, while postmodernists sometimes acknowledge some of the logical difficulties of their own position. However, none of this would be possible unless underlying the debate was the presupposition of objective standards of rationality. That is, objective standards of rationality are a precondition of the debate—a precondition of the possibility that the participants be able to recognize reasons and to find them compelling in certain instances and ill-founded in others.

But if objective standards of rationality are a precondition of the debate in which Winston and I find ourselves, then Winston's position is certainly paradoxical. For if he were right, the very conditions which make that possible could not obtain. But they must obtain, if his argument is to succeed. So if Winston were right, he would have to be wrong. That is, it is self-refuting to claim in the context of a debate like ours that there are no objective standards of rationality and yet proceed as if reasons could be recognized and be logically compelling.[34]

Winston is logically correct to point out that various defenses against local skepticism about documentary objectivity are useless against arguments based on global postmodernist skepticism. However, neither Winston nor any other contemporary film theorist with whom I am familiar has insulated global postmodernist skepticism from the sort of predictable charges of incoherence that I have leveled at Winston. Unless and until postmodernist film theorists address this problem, their position is effectively a nonstarter. For at this point in the dialectic, given the choice between believing that some nonfiction films can be objective and the alternative that there are no standards of objectivity in any aspect of human life whatsoever, it seems far more reasonable to me to think that nonfiction films can be objective. Hell, I even think I've seen some of them.

5

I began by taking note of the fact that scholars of the nonfiction film are prone to resort to philosophy quite frequently. For inasmuch as nonfiction films often (though not always) involve knowledge claims, questions of epistemology may seem relevant. Unfortunately, the philosophy that attracts nonfiction film scholars is either shallow or is superficially understood.

Too often the philosophy in question is uncritically accepted as a major premise in debunking arguments. Thus Winston supposes that something called Western rationality has been soundly refuted on the basis of some fashionable postmodernist fiat. But Winston fails to explore the possibility that this very pronouncement may be incoherent.

Surely it is ironical that debunkers like Winston buy into so much philosophy, embracing it as authoritative, without even thinking minimally about what might be wrong with it. Why are debunkers nowadays so often fervent believers when it comes to facile, postmodernist dicta? Skepticism, it appears, stops at home.

Theorists like Winston give one the impression that what are no more than presumptions are actually (as Nichols might put it) self-evident. They introduce these presumptions as givens, at least for everyone in the know. In effect, they substitute fashion reports for arguments. So-called Western rationality is as defunct as bell-bottom trousers because someone in the intellectual fashion industry says so.

But claims by such pundits about the state of the art of philosophy in terms of a consensus concerning, for example, conceptual relativism are vastly exaggerated, especially from a statistical point of view. The issues that Winston considers settled, in virtue of his authorities, are still very much in play in the arena of philosophy. One—particularly a debunker—should not blithely endorse pronouncements about what is philosophically established. Film theorists like Winston should become philosophers themselves and scrutinize claims about the refutation of rationality with the same debunking energy that they mobilize to challenge the knowledge claims of certain nonfiction films.

Perhaps in this regard, the flaws in contemporary nonfiction film theory show us something about one of the major problems in contemporary film theory in general. For there is a striking tendency for film theorists to repeat the errors of nonfiction film theorists insofar as they derive their preferred philosophical premises from second-hand sources. They do not evolve these premises themselves, but get them from authority figures, whom they paraphrase or have paraphrased for them by second and third-generation authority figures. Film academics typically do not subject these premises to criticism, but treat them as infallible axioms to be used deductively in film criticism and theory.

There is only one remedy for this sort of intellectual stagnation. Namely:

film theorists, especially nonfiction film theorists, must become philosophers themselves, or, at least, learn to think philosophically about their deepest presuppositions. Film theorists need to become interdisciplinary—not in the sense that they simply quote authorities from other fields—but in the sense that they become capable of thinking for themselves in terms of issues addressed by those other fields that are germane to film studies. Nonfiction film theorists need to learn to think philosophically—as well as historically, sociologically, and so on—if the field is to develop beyond its present state of arrogant sloganeering.

NOTES

1. Not all nonfiction films are in the business of making knowledge claims, which is why I limit my observation only to "a great many nonfiction films." That is also why nonfiction films cannot be characterized in terms of a commitment to providing objective information about the world. For further discussion, see Noël Carroll, "Reply to Carol Brownson and Jack Wolf," in *Philosophic Exchange: A Journal of SUNY College at Brockport* 14 (Winter 1983); and Carl Plantinga, "The Mirror Framed: A Case for Expression in the Documentary," in *Wide Angle* 13, 2 (Summer 1991): 40–53.

2. For further elaboration and documentation of the selectivity argument, see Noël Carroll, "From Real to Reel: Entangled in Nonfiction Film," in *Philosophic Exchange* 14 (Winter 1983).

3. I am indebted to Carl Plantinga for the idea that there is an emerging *postmodernist* approach to the nonfiction film. See Carl Plantinga, "Motion Pictures and the Rhetoric of Nonfiction Film: Two Approaches, *Post-Theory: Reconstructing Film Studies,* ed. David Bordwell and Noël Carroll (Madison: University of Wisconsin Press, 1996), pp. 307–324.

4. Michael Renov, "Introduction: The Truth about Non-Fiction," in *Theorizing Documentary,* ed. Michael Renov (New York: Routledge, 1993), p. 3.

5. Ibid., p. 7.

6. Ibid. In this quotation, Renov is speaking specifically about Trinh T. Minh-ha's skepticism with respect to the traditional documentary, but since he maintains that the same kind of skepticism echoes throughout his anthology (pp. 7–8), I take this to be a fair statement of Renov's attitude as well. Furthermore, in context, it is nearly impossible to read Renov's summation of Trinh T. Minh-ha's view as anything but an approving paraphrase of a position that he shares.

7. For a discussion of indexing, see Noël Carroll, "From Real to Reel," pp. 24–26.

8. For an elaboration and sustained criticism of Hayden White's philosophy of history, see Noël Carroll, "Interpretation, History and Narrative," *The Monist* 73, 2 (April 1990).

9. See Hayden White, *Tropics of Discourse: Essays in Cultural Criticism* (Baltimore: Johns Hopkins University Press, 1978), and Hayden White, *The Content of Form* (Baltimore: Johns Hopkins University Press, 1987).

10. White, *Tropics of Discourse,* pp. 90 and 111.

11. Renov, *Theorizing Documentary,* p. 7.

12. See Morton White, *Foundations of Historical Knowledge* (New York: Harper Collins, 1965), chapter 6; and Peter Munz, *The Shapes of Time* (Middletown, Conn.: Wesleyan University Press, 1977), p. 25.

13. There are at present certain debates in the philosophy of history about the status of historical causes. Are they only causally necessary conditions? Are they question-relative? And so on. Nevertheless, the existence of these debates does not compromise the preceding argument. For my argument only depends on the existence of processes of historical causation, however they are ultimately analysed. The debates about the status of these causes does not call into question the reality of processes of historical causation nor does it show that historians cannot track them. It addresses the issue of how we are to characterize them precisely. Moreover, the proposals available in this area of debate are all compatible with the claims that I make about the reality of causal conditions in the relevant courses of events.

14. There are numerous other problems with White's account of narrative structuration and its relation to the theory of tropes. For example, White's master narratives are so vaguely defined that he seems to be able to find them everywhere, whereas their relevance to historiography may be much less than he claims. For further criticism of White, see my essay, "Interpretation, History, and Narrative."

15. Can a nonfiction film be said to fail to stand in for lived experience if that is not its aim?

16. See Bill Nichols, *Representing Reality* (Bloomington: Indiana University Press, 1991), pp. 107–9.

17. Also, the distinction Nichols advances wouldn't differentiate documentary from historical accounts since they often mix narrative and argument as well. Thus, if you count history as fiction, for the reasons Hayden White advances, then documentary film would presumably be fiction in the same way history is. I am not, of course, endorsing White's view but simply pointing out that if you are drawn to it in the way that Nichols, like Renov, is, then it is not clear that one can agree, as a matter of logic, with Nichols that documentary is "a fiction (un)like any other."

18. Nichols, *Representing Reality*, p. 195 (emphasis added).

19. Ibid.

20. Also, most documentaries do not comment upon their formative effect on audiences for the obvious reason that before the film is screened the filmmakers don't really know what the formative effect of the film will be. Furthermore, the claim that Nichols makes about the *denial* by documentary filmmakers of the formative effects of their films on audiences can also be refuted by parallel arguments of the form that are used above to refute the claim that documentary filmmakers *deny* the processes of construction of their films.

21. In an interesting remark on contemporary documentary *art*-filmmakers, Paul Arthur calls attention to the way they fetishize their own failure, especially against backdrops of utopian epistemic expectations. Perhaps we might conjecture that documentary film theorists imitate their beloved nonfiction artists by incessantly replaying the drama of their failures with respect to utopian standards of objectivity, thereby ignoring the fact that lots of ordinary nonfiction, informational films are perfectly objective in straightforward ways all the time. For Paul Arthur's observation, see his "Jargons of Authenticity (Three American Moments)," in *Theorizing Documentary*, pp. 126–31.

22. This, of course, is not meant to suggest that there are not some information films that engage in persuasion. Carl Sagan's "The Shores of the Cosmic Ocean" for the TV series *Cosmos* is bent on coaxing viewers to sympathize with the view that there is life on other planets. However, this concedes nothing to Nichols's argument. For since he has advanced a generalization, the onus on us is to produce at least one counterexample. Of course, I think that there are far more nonfiction films than one which escape *all* of Nichols's defects vis-à-vis objectivity; but one is all that the counterargument really requires. Moreover, I should add that I am not convinced that the belief that rhetoric can be appropriate is necessarily an offense to objectivity. Rhetorical structures—such as rhetorical questions—often have a perfectly acceptable role to play in objective discourse.

23. Note that there is a presumption in Nichols's argument that rhetoric is always out of place and a defect with respect to objectivity. But unless one includes such defectiveness in one's definition of rhetoric, this is not immediately apparent. Is the presence of an enthymeme—which Aristotle claimed is the most effective rhetorical device—enough to compromise the objective standing of a sample of discourse?

24. Though it may prove to be a useful heuristic for film scholars like Nichols to always look for the possible operation of rhetoric in a nonfiction film, this serviceable heuristic should not be confused with a theoretical discovery. For even if the heuristic often works, one must also be prepared to find cases where it doesn't.

25. Nichols, *Representing Reality*, p. 197.

26. This raises the question of how we should regard whatever Nichols proposes to us as facts in support of his arguments. For shouldn't Nichols's own candidates for status of the facts, which are certainly implicated in institutional epistemic protocols, be assessed to fall short of objectivity, according to Nichols's own arguments? But if they fall short of standards of objectivity, then why should *we* believe them?

27. Perhaps Nichols feels he has suggested an argument like this: all institutional practices of inquiry have unacknowledged predispositions and assumptions which may involve even more powerful self-interests than the stated ones; therefore, all institutional practices are interested in a way that precludes objectivity. The problem here is that even if it is true that every practice of inquiry possesses some unacknowledged or unexamined assumption or predisposition, one must still demonstrate that these unacknowledged or unexamined assumptions or predispositions are institutionally interested in a way that compromises objectivity. That the assumptions are unacknowledged or unexamined does not pose a problem in and of itself; the problem only arises when what is unacknowledged is interested. And whether that can be shown, as far as I can see, depends on looking at one case at a time.

28. Nichols, *Representing Reality*, p. 195.

29. Ibid., p. 198.

30. Nevertheless, Nichols is altogether carefree about his own allegations of fact—which are material to his arguments—even though he is obviously the representative of a well-known institution.

31. See Brian Winston, "The Documentary Film as Scientific Inscription," in *Theorizing Documentary*, especially pp. 53–55.

32. Quoted in ibid., p. 54.
33. Ibid.
34. Perhaps it will be argued that I have misinterpreted Winston. Instead of regarding him as a postmodernist skeptic, as I do, it might be said that we should read him as only reporting that postmodernist skepticism is the unstoppable intellectual movement of the moment, though it is a movement about which Winston, himself, is agnostic. However, if Winston takes what he has said to be a historical *fact* with which, in principle, *anyone* who reflected upon the evidence should assent, then Winston himself believes in objective standards of rationality and he should not be agnostic, save on pain of self-refutation.

Chapter 9 Fiction, Nonfiction, and the Film of Presumptive Assertion: Conceptual Analyses

INTRODUCTION

In both film studies and the culture at large, there is an area of practice which is typically labelled 'the documentary', or perhaps less frequently, 'nonfiction film'. These labels are roughly serviceable for practical purposes, but they are not always as theoretically precise as they might be. Therefore, in this chapter, I will propose another label for the field—namely, 'films of presumptive assertion'—and I will attempt to define it.[1] In response to this statement of intent, some may worry that my new label and its accompanying definition are stipulative and revisionist. However, I will argue that they track the extension of films that film scholars want to talk about and refer to better than the alternative candidates do.

Current usage of the term 'documentary' to denominate the field in question appears to stem from John Grierson.[2] It was his preferred name for his own practice, and it has been extended by many to cover all work in what might be provisionally earmarked as the nonfiction film. However, when Grierson introduced the term, he had something rather specific in mind. He defined the documentary as 'the creative treatment of actuality'.[3] The notion of *creative treatment* in this formula had a very particular function. It was intended to distinguish the Griersonian documentary from things like the Lumière *actualité* and newsreels.[4]

In contrast to the *actualité* and the newsreel, the Griersonian documentary had a creative dimension by virtue of which it was explicitly conceived to be artistic. In this, Grierson's ambitions paralleled those of other filmmakers and theoreticians of the silent and early sound periods who wished to defeat the prejudice that film could merely function as the slavish and mechanical reproduction of whatever confronted the camera lens. They argued that film could be more than a record of the flow of reality. It could shape reality creatively and, therefore, it deserved to be taken seriously in virtue of its artistic dimension.[5]

One can certainly sympathize with Grierson's aims. However, once we see what is behind his definition of the documentary, I think it is pretty clear that the notion will not serve to demarcate the area of study that often bears its name today. For Grierson's concept is too narrow. It excludes such things as Lumière *actualités* and the videotape of the Rodney King beating—things that most of us, I conjecture, think belong legitimately in the curriculum of courses with titles such as *Introduction to the Documentary Film.*

Needless to say, this is not a criticism of Grierson. He meant to exclude candidates like these from the class of things he called 'documentaries'. And it is his privilege to call what he was doing whatever suits him. Rather, I mean to criticize those who carelessly try to stretch Grierson's notion to cover the whole field. For Grierson's notion of documentary picks out an extension of objects far more narrow than that referred to by most subsequent authors of books on the so-called documentary.

One might say 'so what?' Grierson meant one thing by 'documentary', and now we mean something else by it. But there is at least this problem. Whatever *we* might mean by it is obscure and perhaps equivocal. Thus, we find ourselves in a situation where we have, on the one hand, the relatively precise notion of the documentary that Grierson has bequeathed us, and, on the other hand, another more ambiguous idea. This at the very least courts confusion. I propose to relieve that confusion by granting Grierson his definition for what he was talking about and by introducing a new concept for what we wish to speak about.

Here it might be thought that we already have an alternative ready to hand in the concept of nonfiction. But if the Griersonian label of the documentary is too narrow for our purposes, the notion of nonfiction is too broad. Consider the way in which the couplet fiction/nonfiction divides up a bookshop. The novels, short stories, and perhaps plays will be found in the fiction section. Everything else is nonfiction, including children's drawing manuals. But when we consider what is discussed under the prevailing rubric of the documentary film, interactive lessons about the way to draw a flower are not what we have in mind.

Moreover, films like J. J. Murphy's *Print Generation*, Peter Kubelka's *Arnulf Rainer*, and Ernie Gehr's *Serene Velocity* are not fictions. They tell no imagined story. So, they are nonfiction. But, once again, they are not included in histories of, nor classes concerning, the so-called documentary. Thus, I take it that the suspicion that the category of nonfiction is too broad for our purposes is well motivated.

If I am right in supposing that our presiding labels and concepts are inadequate to our purposes, then the best solution, it seems to me, is to devise a new label, accompanied by a rigorous definition. This sounds very reformist. However, I think that my proposal in terms of films of presumptive assertion—which might more tendentiously be called 'films of putative fact'—does a better job of locating the body of work that concerns those who currently signal their domain of discourse by means of the idiom of the documentary or nonfiction film.

How might one substantiate this claim? One way is to argue that the notion of films of presumptive assertion makes more sense out of the debates that people have in this area of enquiry. For example, major debates over the so-called nonfiction film involve claims about the objectivity of the relevant films and about whether they can refer to reality. But if what we want to talk about includes films like *Arnulf Rainer*—a flicker film—then questions of objectivity and reference to reality fall by the wayside, since it makes no sense to ask of *Arnulf Rainer* whether it is objective or even subjective in its reference to reality. Its images are not fictional, but they are not referential either. It is a nonfiction film, but it stands outside the epistemic questions that obsess documentary film studies. On the other hand, the notion of films of presumptive assertion would not encompass works like *Arnulf Rainer* to begin with, but only films that play what we might call the assertion game, a game wherein epistemic questions of objectivity and truth are uncontroversially apposite.

I will pursue the analysis of films of presumptive assertion in stages. First, I will try to draw a distinction between fiction and nonfiction. Then, I will go on—exploiting what has been said about the fiction/nonfiction couplet—to propose an analysis of films of presumptive assertion (as a subcategory of the nonfiction film). Once I have worked out my analysis of films of presumptive assertion, I will then contemplate a series of problems or questions that my theory is likely to raise.

FICTION AND NONFICTION

The first step in defining the film of presumptive assertion is to draw a distinction between fiction and nonfiction, since the film of presumptive assertion, on my account, is a subcategory of nonfiction. However, many film scholars are likely to regard even this first step as quixotic. For they are persuaded that there is no viable distinction between fiction and nonfiction. They are convinced that it has been, as they say, 'deconstructed';[6] all films can be shown to be fictional.

Christian Metz, for example, has argued:

> At the theater Sarah Bernhardt may tell me she is Phèdre or if the play were from another period and rejected the figurative regime, she might say, as in a type of modern theater, that she is Sarah Bernhardt. But at any rate, I should see Sarah Bernhardt. At the cinema she could make two kinds of speeches too, but it would be her shadow that would be offering them to me (or she would be offering them in her own absence). Every film is a fiction film.[7]

Another reason why some film scholars suppose that the distinction between fiction and nonfiction is inoperable is that nonfiction and fiction films share many of the same structures—flashbacks, parallel editing, cross-cutting, point-of-view editing, and the like. And certain mannerisms found in nonfiction films, like grainy footage and unsteady camera movements, have been appropriated by fiction films in order to achieve certain effects—like the impression of realism or authenticity. Thus, on the grounds of formal differentiae, one cannot distinguish fiction films from nonfiction films.[8]

There is also another way to argue for the view that the distinction between fiction films and nonfiction films is unsupportable. Friends of this view, whom we will call 'deconstructionists' for convenience, might suggest the following intuition pump. Presented with a film, it is at least conceivable that an informed viewer—i.e. a viewer fully knowledgeable of film techniques and their histories—might not be able to identify it correctly as a fiction or nonfiction film. All the formal information in the world would not be conclusive. Perhaps the dissection segments of the notorious *Alien Autopsy* are a pertinent example in this respect.

But let us start with Metz's position first. Metz's argument seems to me to be clearly fallacious. In effect, it not only denies the distinction between fiction and nonfiction, but it undermines the distinction between representation and fiction as well. If the reason that a film of Sarah Bernhardt saying that she is Sarah Bernhardt is a fiction is because Sarah Bernhardt is not in the screening room, then an aerial photograph of a battlefield will count as a fiction. But clearly it is not a fiction. It does not represent an imaginary configuration of forces due to the fact that the enemy is not in the room as our General Staff examines said aerial photographs. Armies do not plan counter-attacks on the basis of novels. But that is tantamount to what they would be doing if the aerial photographs were fictions.

Perhaps the proponent of Metz will counter that, even though all representations are fictions, there are different kinds of fictions. The aerial photographs belong to one sort and *All that Heaven Allows* to another sort. But what then distinguishes these different sorts of fiction? Without further argument, it would appear that something like the fiction/nonfiction distinction needs to be reintroduced.

Perhaps it will be said that there are *fictional* nonfictions (the class to which the aerial photographs and *Hoop Dreams* belong) and *fictional* fictions (the class to which *Seven* belongs). But this seems to reinscribe the fiction/nonfiction distinction, rather than to dismiss it. And, furthermore, the aforesaid *fictional* prefixes to these alleged categories do no conceptual work—i.e. make no meaningful contrast conceptually—and, therefore, are theoretically dispensable.

But an even deeper criticism of Metz's argument is that it contradicts the logic of representation. Representations are not equivalent to whatever they represent. This is why we have representations. It is one of the reasons they are so useful. If a map had to be the very terrain it is a map of, it would be of no added pragmatic value when we are lost on the terrain in question. Representations standardly are not what they represent. But in requiring Sarah Bernhardt in the screening room for a film of her *not* to count as fiction, Metz is forgetting (and, indeed, contradicting) what a representation is, as well as conflating representation and fiction.

In response, one might say that what Metz has done is to discover that all representations are really fictions. But one wants to question the nature of this discovery. It certainly does not reflect the way in which we typically deploy these concepts. Maybe Metz is assuming some stipulative redefinition of these concepts. But can Metz defend his stipulative redefinition of these concepts on the grounds that it is useful to construe these concepts his way? I doubt it. Indeed, Metz's reconstrual of these concepts is more likely to cause more confusion than anything else. Imagine how counterproductive it would be to be told that the pictures on a wanted-poster are fictional?

Metz reminds us that when Bernhardt plays Phèdre, there is a person, Bernhardt, standing before us, whereas when we see a movie of the same event, Bernhardt is not present. Fair enough. But what Metz ignores is the fact that the actress, Bernhardt on-stage, is a representational vehicle, indeed a fictional representational vehicle. She represents Phèdre. And there *is* also, in fact, a representational vehicle present in the screening room with us, namely the cinematic apparatus projecting the film of Bernhardt/Phèdre. So far there is no significant theoretical difference between the stage case and the film case in terms of the presence of representational vehicles. Moreover, in neither case is what we literally see a fictional character. What we literally see is a representational vehicle which may present either a fiction or nonfiction. Therefore, the question of the presence or absence of a representational vehicle is irrelevant to deciding a difference in the fictional/nonfictional status of the two cases.

Furthermore, what Metz vaguely calls absence would appear to be an essential characteristic of representations, irrespective of whether the representations are fictional or nonfictional. Thus, Metz seems guilty of a conceptual confusion inasmuch as he conflates representation and fiction.

Let us now turn to the second line of dissolving the distinction between fiction and nonfiction. This 'deconstructionist' attack begins with a series of reasonable observations. Many of the structures of the fiction film are shared by the nonfiction film. It is certainly true that nonfiction filmmakers have imitated narrative devices that originated in the fiction film. And fiction filmmakers have imitated nonfiction stylistics. Nevertheless, the lesson that those who favour the view that every film is fictional draw from these observations is too quick. They surmise that these considerations indicate that there is no difference between fiction and nonfiction. But another conclusion, equally consistent with the relevant observations, is that the distinction between fiction and nonfiction *does not rest* on a principled difference between the stylistic properties of fictional and nonfictional films.

Consider the analogous case of literature. There are no textual features—linguistic structures, writing styles, or plots—that mark something as a fiction. You might suppose that there are certain structures that could appear only in fiction, such as internal monologues. But, in fact, you can find them in nonfictions such as *Armies of the Night*. Moreover, this problem is necessarily insurmountable, since any linguistic structure, writing style, plot device, or other textual feature that characteristically appears in a fiction can be imitated by the nonfiction writer for a wide range of aesthetic effects.

And, of course, there is the mirror-image problem regarding the fiction writer. He can imitate any of the textual features characteristically associated with nonfiction writing for a broad assortment of purposes, including that of imbuing his fiction with a sense of heightened verisimilitude. So, since nonfiction and fiction authors alike can appropriate any of the formulae or devices associated with fiction and nonfiction respectively, we are compelled to the unavoidable conclusion that fiction and nonfiction cannot be differentiated by pointing to some linguistic or textual features that belong to all and only fiction or nonfiction respectively.

Of course, this is a theoretical rather than a practical problem, since we rarely encounter texts not knowing their status as fiction or nonfiction. Generally, we know before we start reading a text whether it is fiction or nonfiction. We do not adopt the role of detectives, trying to determine whether the story we are reading is fictional or nonfictional. Typically the story comes to us labeled one way or the other. Thus, the issue is theoretical and not practical.

Admittedly, it might be a problem which, though rarely arising, nevertheless could arise. We might find a text from the distant past, about which we possess no contextual information. In such a case, we might look at stylistic and textual features for some evidence about whether the work is fictional or nonfictional. But though this is a way in which we might proceed, such speculation is neither the only evidence we would look for,[9] nor would it be conclusive. Such evidence is at best probable and contingent because of what has already been said—namely, that any nonfictional device can always be imitated by the fiction writer, and vice versa for the nonfiction writer. But the distinction between fiction and nonfiction is ultimately not a matter of probability; it is a conceptual matter.

Yet even the preceding case does not show that there is no distinction between fiction and nonfiction, but only that nothing is conclusively fiction or nonfiction writing on the basis of the textual or linguistic features that it possesses. A text does not, for example, have the status of a fiction by virtue of the textual features it has or has not got. The fictional status of a text is not constituted by its textual features, even if, to a limited extent, the textual features, in some circumstances, might provide us with *some* evidence or clues that we might use to hypothesize its status where it is otherwise unknown.

Another way to make the point is to say that the fictionality of a text is not constituted or determined by its *manifest* textual properties. That is, you cannot tell whether a text is a fiction simply by looking at its linguistic, stylistic, or other textual features. You cannot tell for sure whether a text is fictional by reading it in a decontextualized way, where the only permissible information involves the consideration of its linguistic and textual features. Whether or not a text is fictional depends on its non-manifest (relational) properties (which I will specify further anon). You cannot tell whether a text is fictional in virtue of its manifest properties, inspected in isolation. You have to consider the text in relation to something else—something else that is not manifest in the text; something else that cannot be read off the surface of the text.

As it is with literature, so it is with film. One does not conclusively identify something as either a fiction or a nonfiction film by looking at its manifest structural features. This is not what film-goers do. Like the readers of literature, film-goers generally know whether the film they are about to see has been labelled one way or the other. This information circulates in the film world before the work is seen—in the form of advertisements, distribution releases, reviews, word of mouth, and the like. This is why the previous intuition pump is so contrived and unilluminating. We do not go to films and attempt to guess whether they are fictions or nonfictions. In the largest number of cases, we know ahead of time how to categorize the films in question. Moreover, it is hard to see what motivation practitioners in the institution of film would have to replace the current system with guessing games.

Film scholars are correct in noting the overlapping stylistics of the fiction and nonfiction film. However, they are wrong to understand this as entailing that there is no distinction between fiction films and nonfiction films, and that all films are fictional. Their error is logical. For they presume that if there is no stylistic differentia between fiction and nonfiction films, then there is no differentia whatsoever. But this is baldly a non sequitur. For they have not foreclosed the possibility that there may be differentiae other than stylistic or formal considerations in virtue of which the distinction can be drawn.[10]

Of course, revealing the lacuna in the argument for the reduction of all film to fiction on the grounds that it has failed to preclude the possibility that it has not eliminated all the potential candidates for drawing the distinction, though logically correct, is unlikely to be persuasive, unless it is possible to come up with a plausible alternative candidate for distinguishing fiction from nonfiction. Thus, in order to carry my case across the finish line, it is incumbent upon me to show that there are eminently reasonable grounds for thinking that there is a viable way to make the distinction that the 'deconstructionists' have overlooked, and to defend it.

By denying that one can demarcate fiction from nonfiction on the basis of stylistics, the 'deconstructionist', in effect, is denying that one can determine whether a candidate film is a fiction, for example, on the basis of the intrinsic, manifest properties of the work. I agree. But this does not mean that the distinction cannot be crafted by considering certain non-manifest, relational properties of the works in question. This is the line of argument that I want to pursue. Specifically, I want to argue that we can draw a distinction between fiction and nonfiction on the basis of certain authorial intentions.[11] The authorial intentions I have in mind may, of course, not be manifest in the work, and, moreover, they are relational properties of the work—i.e. properties of the work in relation to the author, and, as we shall see, in relation to spectators as well.

Furthermore, if the analysis in terms of authorial intentions can be defended, then, from the perspective of logic, the burden of proof falls to the 'deconstructionists'. That is, if they still wish to maintain that there is no distinction between fiction and nonfiction, it falls to them to show the error in my proposal.

As I construe the problem, we begin with a presumption in favour of a distinction between fiction and nonfiction. There is a presumption in favour of it because it is deeply embedded in our practices and it is at the centre of our conceptual scheme. It is difficult to see how we can get along without it. But a presumption is not a proof. The presumption must be backed up by compelling reasons. Moreover, as we have seen, the presumption cannot be defended on stylistic grounds. We can imagine fiction films that are stylistically indiscernible from nonfiction films, and vice versa. We cannot 'eyeball' the distinction between the two. That is one indication that the problem before us is philosophical.[12]

Because we cannot 'eyeball' the distinction by looking at a given film, the distinction, if there is one, must rest upon some non-manifest, relational properties of fiction films and nonfiction films respectively. But what can that distinction be?

In order to answer that question, I shall take advantage of what might be called an intention-response model of communication. This approach is frequently employed nowadays by philosophers in order to develop theories of art as well as fiction.[13] The approach is broadly Gricean in its inspiration. Applied to art, it presupposes that an artist or an author, such as a filmmaker, communicates to an audience by way of indicating that the audience is intended to respond to his or her text (i.e. any structure of sense-bearing signs) in a certain way, where the reason that the audience has for mobilizing the response or the stance in question is the audience's recognition of the sender's intention that they do so.

This approach is social, at least in the sense that it depends upon certain relations, rooted in our communicative practices, between the senders and receivers of sense-bearing signs. Moreover, if this approach can be applied to the cases of fiction and nonfiction, it will propose a non-manifest, relational property of the texts in question as that which determines the status of the text as fictional or nonfictional. And that is just the sort of property that we are looking for in our endeavour to distinguish fiction and nonfiction films.

Since the Gricean-type intention-response model of communication has provided insights already to philosophers, psychologists, and linguists alike, it seems a reasonable theoretical option to try out, at least hypothetically, though, of course, the hypothesis must be defended subsequently. Thus, applying the intention-response model to the case of fiction, we may begin by hypothesizing that a structured set of sense-bearing signs, such as a novel or a film, is fictional only if presented by an author, filmmaker, or sender who intends the audience to respond to it with what we might call the fictive stance on the basis of recognizing the author's, filmmaker's, or sender's intention that the audience do this on the basis of recognizing what we might call the sender's fictive intention. A compact, jargonistic statement of the theory, then, is that a structure of sense-bearing signs is a fiction only if it is presented by a sender with the fictive intention that the audience respond to it by adopting the fictive stance on the basis of recognizing the sender's fictive intention that they do so.[14]

Of course, this definition is pretty obscure. It needs to be unpacked—more needs to be said about what is involved in a fictive stance and a fictive intention. What is a fictive intention? It is the intention of the author, filmmaker, or sender of a structure of sense-bearing signs that the audience imagine the content of the story in question on the basis of their recognition that this is what the sender intends them to do.

Suppose we are buying a can of lemonade from a vending machine. After we put our money in the machine, we then press one of the selection buttons. Why do we do this? Because we realize that this is what the designer of the machine intends us to do, presupposing that we wish to use the machine in the way it was designed to be used. Similarly, there is a design intention when it comes to fiction—namely, that we imagine the content of the story in question. Moreover, we adopt this attitude when consuming a fiction because we recognize that this is what the sender intends us to do, presupposing that we wish to use the story in the way in which it was designed to be used. So, when we read that Sherlock Holmes lives on Baker Street, we imagine that he lives on Baker Street. Moreover, our mental state or attitude here is one of imagining, rather than, say, one of believing, because we recognize that Conan Doyle intends us to imagine rather than to believe that Sherlock Holmes lives on Baker Street.

Undoubtedly, there may be epistemological questions about the way in which we come to recognize whether the sender's intention is fictive or non-fictive. But we can put them to one side for the moment and come back to them later. For our concern now is ontological, not epistemological, since what we are pursuing is the question of the nature of fiction. It is one thing to say that fiction is constituted by an authorial fictive intention, and another thing to say how we go about recognizing that intention.

In *Metaphor and Movement,* the dance historian Lincoln Kirstein intends us to believe that *The Sleeping Beauty* ballet was produced in 1890, when he presents us with propositions to that effect, whereas in the novel *The Moor's Last Sigh,* Salman Rushdie intends us to imagine that Aurora is a great Indian painter. Moreover, Rushdie does not intend us to adopt this mental state as the result of magic or drugs. He intends that we adopt this mental state on the basis of the recognition that this is what he, the designer of the text, intends us to do with the novel.

With respect to *The Moor's Last Sigh,* one of Rushdie's fictive intentions is that we imagine that Aurora is a great Indian painter. I say *one* of his intentions because he has others—for example, he also intends that we imagine that Aurora is married to Abraham. Furthermore, all these fictive intentions can be subsumed under one, overarching fictive intention—namely, that the reader imagine all the objects, persons, actions, and events that comprise the story of *The Moor's Last Sigh.* In publishing *The Moor's Last Sigh,* Rushdie intends that the reader shall imagine the persons, actions, objects, and events of the story.

Shall here is normative, not predictive. That is, Rushdie's fictive intention prescribes or mandates how we should take his story in order to use it as it was designed to be used. Someone might, of course, mistake it for a history book and come to believe, rather than to imagine, that Aurora was a great Indian painter. Yet that only shows that to prescribe certain behaviour is not to predict behaviour, a fact brought home to God more than once since the time he promulgated the Ten Commandments.

But, in addition, Rushdie's fictive intention does not simply involve a prescriptive component—that the reader shall imagine the content of the story. It also contains what we might call a reflexive, reason-giving component—that the reader imagine the content *for the reason* that he recognizes that this is what Rushdie intends him to do. Thus, Rushdie's fictive intention is that the reader imagine the propositional content of *The Moor's Last Sigh* for the reason that the reader recognizes that this is what he is intended to do.

We have already effectively described what is involved in the fictive stance in the preceding discussion of the fictive intention. The notion of the fictive intention looks at the matter from the author's side of the transaction; the notion of the fictive stance refers to the audience's part of the bargain. The author intends the audience to adopt a certain attitude toward the propositional content of the story. That attitude is the audience's stance.[15] Where the work is a fiction, the attitude or stance is one of imagining. The fictive stance, then, is a matter of the audience's imagining the propositional content of a structure of meaning-bearing signs whether they be of the nature of words, images, or something else.

So far, our analysis says that a structure of sense-bearing signs is a fiction only if it involves the audience's adoption of the fictive stance on the basis of its recognition of the author's fictive intention. However, the analysis contains at least one major obscurity. The fictive stance involves imagination. But what is meant by the notion of *imagining?* This problem is compounded by the fact that the histories of literature, psychology, and philosophy are littered with many different, often non-converging notions of the imagination. So how are we to understand that term in a formula such as: *x* is a fiction only if the sender intends the audience to imagine the propositional content of *x* for the reason that the audience recognizes that this is what the sender intends?

The way in which we conceive of imagining here is crucial to the attempt to defeat the 'deconstructionist'. For certain concepts of the imagination are likely to encourage 'deconstruction' rather than to thwart it. For example, one concept of the imagination, found in Descartes's *Meditations* and echoed by Kant in *The Critique of Pure Reason,* is that the imagination is the faculty that unifies perceptions. That is, I have the discrete perception of the front of a building, and another discrete perception of the back of the building. But my mind unifies them as parts of the same building. How is this done? By what we might call the imagination.

But if this is the concept of the imagination that we bring to the preceding analysis of fiction, the prospect of 'deconstruction' looms again, since both the historian and the novelist intend us to mobilize what can be called the *constructive* imagination. Indeed, if Kant is right, the constructive imagination is always in play so its operation cannot serve to distinguish anything involving cognition from anything else.[16]

Of course, there are other major notions of the imagination. One is that it is the capacity for mental imagery. But this will be of no use to us in defining fiction, since the audience's prescribed response to a fiction does not require mental imaging. I can imagine the proposition that Aurora is a great Indian painter, even if I do not have a mental image of her. And as well, it is possible for the reader of a history book to have mental images on the basis of the text.

The imagination has received a great deal less philosophical attention than mental states such as belief. As a result, the notion has often served as a catch-all category of last resort. Thus, we have inherited a mixed bag of faculties and mental functions under the rubric of the imagination. Consequently, if we intend to use the concept of the imagination in our formula for fiction, we must specify what exactly we take *the imagination* to refer to. We cannot have either the constructive imagination or the mental-imaging imagination in mind in our formula for the reasons already given. Instead, my claim is that the relevant sense of *imagination* for my formula is what I will call the *suppositional imagination.*[17]

Often in the course of a discussion, we may say something like, 'I'll grant you x for the purposes of the argument.' Or, in a mathematical proof, we may begin by saying, 'Suppose x.' These are examples of what I mean by the *suppositional imagination.* In such cases we are entertaining a certain thought or propositional content—namely, that x—without committing ourselves to it by way of belief. We hold x in our mind as, so to speak, a hypothesis, rather than as an assertion. Or we can say that we are entertaining that x as an unasserted thought. To believe x, on the other hand, is to entertain x as an asserted thought. The idea here is that we can entertain thoughts or propositional contents—such as that Aurora is a great Indian painter—as either asserted or unasserted. To entertain a thought or a propositional content as unasserted is to imagine it in the sense of the *suppositional imagination.* And it is suppositional imagining that is pertinent to the analysis of fiction advanced above.

Fictions, then, in this sense are communications that authors intend the audience to imagine on the grounds that the audience recognizes that this is what the author intends them to do. That is, in making fictions, authors are intentionally presenting audiences with situations (or situation-types) that we are meant to entertain in thought.[18] The author, in presenting a novel as a fiction, in effect signals to the reader 'I intend you to hold these propositions (p) before your mind unasserted'—that is, 'suppose p', or 'entertain p unasserted', or 'contemplate p as a supposition'.

Of course, it needs to be added that when an author invites you to imagine the propositional content of a story, he is not providing you with a *carte blanche* to imagine whatever you wish. He is inviting you to imagine *his* story—its propositional content, including what it presupposes and implies. The audience's suppositional imagination is to be controlled imagining, normatively speaking. That is, it is supposed or meant to be constrained by what the author mandates by way of presenting his text. The details of the text control what it is legitimate for the audience to imagine in response to the author's fictive intention.

With this conception of the imagination under our belt, we can say that a structure of sense-bearing signs *x* by sender *s* is fictional only if *s* presents *x* to an audience *a* with the intention that *a* suppositionally imagine the propositional content of *x* for the reason that *a* recognizes this as *s*'s intention. This is the core of our proposal of what it is for a text—filmic or otherwise—to be fictional. It constitutes a necessary condition for fictionality, though further conditions would have to be added to bring the formula to sufficiency.[19]

Moreover, once we have the crucial defining condition of fiction in our possession, the formula for nonfiction is also within our reach. We can generate it by negating the core defining feature of fiction. So, a structure of sense-bearing signs *x* is nonfictional only if sender *s* presents it to audience *a* with the intention that *a* not suppositionally imagine *x* as a result of *a*'s grasp of *s*'s intention. That is, a nonfiction *x* is such that it is presented by an author to audience with the intention that the audience recognize that it, the audience, is *not mandated* to entertain the propositional content of the relevant structure of sense-bearing signs as unasserted. This, of course, is only an essential, defining, necessary condition of nonfiction; the complete formula would have to be more complicated.[20]

Inasmuch as this account of nonfiction is simply a negation of the core defining feature of fiction, it encompasses a great many structures of sense-bearing signs, indeed it includes any structure of sense-bearing signs that is not a fiction. Any film, for example, that does not authorially prescribe that viewers entertain its propositional content as unasserted falls into this category. And that will incorporate not only films that mandate that their propositional content be entertained as asserted, but also films that lie outside the assertion game, like Kubelka's *Arnulf Rainer* or Gehr's *Serene Velocity.*

But *Serene Velocity,* I submit, does not tell us anything about how we are to entertain the shots of the hallway that comprise it. Are we to imagine there is such a hallway, or are we to believe it? It really makes no difference to the effect of the film one way or another.[21] It does not mandate that we entertain as unasserted the thought that there is such and such a hallway, since the filmmaker is neutral or perhaps indifferent to how the images of the hallway are to be entertained by us. Thus, it is nonfiction, since, for the reasons given, it does not mandate that we imagine that there is such a hallway. The shots of the hallway function purely as stimuli. So *Serene Velocity* is *not fiction*. But as I claimed earlier, *Serene Velocity* is not at the same time the sort of film that people in the field of the so-called documentary film have in mind. We need a more fine-grained concept than nonfiction in order to capture that narrower extension of films.

FILMS OF PRESUMPTIVE ASSERTION

Against 'deconstructionists', we have introduced a principled distinction between fiction and nonfiction. However, as we have seen, the concept of nonfiction that we have defined is broader than what we need for film studies. Nevertheless, I think that we can locate a category, suitable to the purposes of film studies, which is a subcategory of the preceding concept of nonfiction.

We derived our concept of nonfiction by negating the fictive stance component of our concept of fiction. In effect, we characterized nonfiction as the logical contradictory of fiction—that the audience *not* entertain as unasserted the propositional content of the structure of sense-bearing signs in question. That is, the non-fictive stance involves not imagining the propositional content of the text, or, summarily: nonfiction = not the fictive stance. So, we might generate a narrower concept than nonfiction by producing the logical contrary of the fictive stance.

The fictive stance involves entertaining as unasserted the propositional content of the text. An alternative, logically contrary stance, then, is that the audience entertain as asserted the propositional content of the text. In plain English, the mandated audience response to fiction is that the audience imagine the propositional content of the text. An alternative audience attitude is mandated when the author intends the audience to believe the content of the text.

Our concept of nonfiction was essentially negative. It was based on specifying what the author intended the audience to refrain from doing, namely, imagining the propositional content of the text. Our present suggestion is a positive characterization. It specifies what the author intends the audience to do with the propositional content of the pertinent structure of sense-bearing signs. To wit: we are to entertain the propositional content of the relevant structure as asserted thought. This characterization is key to defining the film of presumptive assertion.[22]

With the film of presumptive assertion the filmmaker intends that the audience entertain the propositional content of his film in thought as asserted. Thus, in the CBS *Twentieth Century* instalment entitled *Born to Kill*, the audience is not only mandated *not* to imagine that Jeffrey Dahmer and Ted Bundy were found guilty, but, in addition, the filmmakers prescribe that the audience should entertain this proposition in thought as asserted. We might say that in contrast to the case of fiction, the sender of a structure of sense-bearing signs of this sort possesses an assertoric intention which prescribes that the audience adopt an assertoric stance toward the propositional content of the text on the basis of their recognition that this is what the sender intends them to do.

This is a necessary condition for the species of cinema that I am calling films of presumptive assertion. I call them films of *presumptive* assertion not only because the audience presumes that it is to entertain the propositional content of such a film as asserted, but also because such films may lie. That is, they are presumed to involve assertion even in cases where the filmmaker is intentionally dissimulating at the same time that he is signalling an assertoric intention. Moreover, in light of this presumption, the films in question are assessed in terms of the standard conditions for non-defective assertion, including: that the filmmaker is committed to the truth (or plausibility, as the case may be) of the propositions the film expresses *and* that the propositions expressed in the film are beholden to the standards of evidence and reasoning appropriate to the truth (or plausibility) claims that the film advances.[23]

In the case of the film of presumptive fact, the filmmaker presents the film with an assertoric intention: with the intention that the viewer entertain the propositional content of the film as asserted. In order for the filmmaker's assertoric intention to be non-defective, the filmmaker is committed to the truth or plausibility of the propositional content of the film and to being responsible to the standards of evidence and reason required to ground the truth or plausibility of the propositional content the filmmaker presents.

Recognizing the filmmaker's assertoric intention, the audience entertains the propositional content of the film as asserted thought. This means that the audience regards the propositional content of the film as something that the author believes to be true, or, in certain circumstances, that the author believes is plausible, and as something that is committed to the relevant standards of evidence and reason for the type of subject-matter being communicated. If the audience believes that the filmmaker does not believe the propositional content of the film, despite the fact that the filmmaker signals an assertoric intention, they suspect that the filmmaker is lying. If the audience member thinks that the film is not committed to the relevant standards of evidence, he suspects that the film is apt to be mistaken, and, in any case, that it is objectively unjustified. Such audience expectations are part of what it is to take the assertoric stance—to entertain the propositional content of the film in thought as asserted.

Stated compactly, then, a crucial, defining condition of the film of presumptive assertion is that it involves an assertoric intention on the part of a filmmaker that the audience adopt an assertoric stance to the propositional content of the film, where the audience adopts this stance on the basis of its recognition of the filmmaker's assertoric intention. This gives us the core ingredients of the film of presumptive assertion. However, more is required to define the film of presumptive assertion completely. For not only does the audience have to discern and respond to the filmmaker's assertoric intentions. It must also grasp the meanings communicated by the film. That is, the maker of a film of presumptive assertion not only intends that the audience adopt the assertoric stance to his film, but he also intends that the audience understand his film. So a complete definition of the film of presumptive assertion involves not only an assertoric intention on the part of the filmmaker, but a meaning-intention as well.

In order to accommodate this requirement, let us adopt a Gricean account of what is involved when an utterer means something by x. Let us say that 'a sender means something by x' is roughly equivalent to 'the sender intends the presentation of x to produce some effect in an audience by means of this intention'.[24] Applying this pattern, then, to the film of presumptive assertion, I contend that:

> x is a film of presumptive assertion if and only if the filmmaker s presents x to an audience a with the intention (1) that a recognizes that x is intended by s to mean that p (some propositional content), (2) that a recognize that s intends them (a) to entertain p as an asserted thought (or as a set of asserted thoughts), (3) that a entertains p as asserted thought, and (4) that 2 is a reason for 3.[25]

Or to put the matter more succinctly, something is a film of presumptive assertion if and only if it involves a meaning intention on the part of the filmmaker which provides a basis for meaning pick-up on the part of the audience as well as an assertoric intention on the part of the filmmaker which provides the grounds for the adoption of the assertoric stance on the part of the audience.[26]

In order to appreciate what is involved in this theory of the film of presumptive assertion, it is instructive to compare it to an alternative theory of the way in which we might characterize the so-called 'documentary' film. Using the intention-response model, we might hypothesize a category which can be called 'the film of the presumptive trace'. On this account, the relevant structure of sense-bearing signs is such that the filmmaker intends that the audience regard the images in the films as historic traces as a consequence of the audience's recognition that that is what the filmmaker intends them to do. Regarding the images as historic traces, in turn, involves entertaining the thought as asserted that the images in the film have originated photographically from precisely the source from which the film claims or implies they originated. Nevertheless, these are called 'films of the *presumptive* trace', since, of course, the filmmaker may be dissimulating.

In a fiction film, we see an image of a house and we imagine that it is Tara, the home of Scarlet O'Hara. In the case of the film of the presumptive trace, when we see an image of a tree and we are told something about trees in the Amazon rainforest, we entertain as asserted—so the theory of the film of the presumptive trace goes—that the image of the tree we are seeing is the photographic trace of some tree in the Amazon rainforest. We do not regard the image as the historic trace of some tree in a botanical garden in Brooklyn. We regard it as the historic trace of some tree in the Amazon; nor do we use the image to imagine that there is such a tree. We take the image as having been produced by a camera aimed at a specific tree in the Amazon rainforest.

Moreover, we regard the image in this way because we recognize that the filmmaker intends us to regard the image of the tree as an authentic historic trace. In effect, we recognize that the filmmaker intends that we regard as asserted the proposition that this image of a tree was photographically produced by some actually existing tree which does or did luxuriate in the Amazon rainforest.

The concept of the film of the presumptive trace is different from that of the film of presumptive assertion. The film of presumptive assertion, for the most part, is broader, since it refers to works where the filmmaker possesses any sort of assertoric intention, whereas the film of the presumptive trace refers only to films where the makers have a very particular assertoric intention, namely, that the images be entertained in asserted thought as being historic traces. The notion of films of the presumptive trace captures the 'document' dimension that many associate with the so-called documentary film. One might even regard it as deriving inspiration from the *actualité*. Films of presumptive assertion, on the other hand, not only include *actualités*, but any film made with an assertoric intention, including an animated simulation of the trajectory of a satellite.

Given these two contrasting concepts, the question arises which one we should prefer. Both seem perfectly intelligible. Is one more attractive than the other? Needless to say, in order to answer this, we have to consider the use we wish the concept to serve. If we wish to define the *actualité,* the notion of the film of the presumptive trace does a better—more precise—job of tracking the phenomenon. However, if we want to capture what film scholars generally have in mind when they talk about documentaries or nonfiction films, I think that the notion of the film of presumptive assertion is superior. The reason for this is that scholars in this field have always talked about films where the audience was clearly not intended to regard every shot as the historic trace of its subject.

Consider, for example, the History Channel's film *Nautilus.* Quite clearly not all of the images are historic traces, nor are they intended to be taken as such. In the first part of the film, there is a discussion of nineteenth-century submarines. As the narrator discusses a progression of these early submersibles, we see outline drawings of them superimposed over water; we also see a model of Fulton's submarine, in living colour, likewise superimposed over water. These are not historic traces of antique submersibles, nor are they intended to be so taken. The audience realizes that they are merely illustrations of them. Audience members understand that they are being shown these images in order to gain a sense of what these contraptions looked like.

Similarly, when the narrator of *Nautilus* recounts the sinking of the cruiser HMS *Cressy* by a German U-boat in the First World War, we are shown a shot in colour—of palpably contemporary origin—of a sailor's cap floating to the bottom of Davy Jones's locker. Later, when we are told that a U-boat sank a merchant ship, we see another colour shot, this time of a life-preserver labelled *Falada,* the name of the doomed ship. But the audience does not take these shots as historical documents.

Nautilus is clearly what scholars, and film distributors, are prone to label a 'documentary', but its makers do not intend that the aforesaid shots be regarded as historic traces of the naval engagements in question. The audience understands that they are at best factually based illustrations of something that plausibly happened when, respectively, the *Cressy* and the *Falada* sunk. What the audience is intended to entertain in thought as asserted is simply that the *Cressy* and the *Falada* were torpedoed with lethal effect.

Throughout *Nautilus,* we are shown maps sketching the journeys of various submarines. The audience correctly regards these as informational, but nothing indicates that one is to take these shots as historic traces of actual submariners plotting their courses on authentic naval charts. Moreover, the film has some re-enactments, in colour footage, of what was involved in life in the close quarters of a U-boat. The audience understands that this is not actual archival footage, but only presumptively accurate visual information bringing home concretely to the viewers what the narrator means when he tells them how very cramped the space in a vintage submarine was.

I submit that *Nautilus* is a film that falls into the category that everyone in the field of the so-called documentary wants to talk about. But if we are employing the notion of the film of the presumptive trace to model that category, *Nautilus* would be excluded.[27] Of course, the issue is not simply whether *Nautilus* should be included. Rather, the point is that the techniques to which we have drawn attention in *Nautilus* are pretty common in the so-called documentary film. Thus, if we are trying to capture conceptually what people generally mean by 'documentary' today, then the film of the presumptive trace is too narrow a concept.

The concept of the film of presumptive assertion is a better idea. For it allows that the films in question can involve re-enactment, animation, the use of stock footage, and the like. In fact, a film of presumptive assertion could be comprised completely of animation or computer-generated imagery. For the notion of the film of presumptive assertion merely requires that the structure of sense-bearing be presented with the assertoric authorial intention that we entertain the propositional content of the film as asserted thought. It does not require that we regard the images as authentic historic traces. The notion of the film of presumptive assertion countenances a state of the art, computer-generated programme on the life of dinosaurs as falling under its rubric, whereas it seems to me that such a programme could not be contained in the class of things denominated as films of the presumptive trace.

Unlike Grierson's notion of the documentary, the concept of the film of presumptive assertion encompasses the *actualité*. But in contrast to the concept of the film of the presumptive trace, it also covers much more. It includes every sort of film of putative fact, irrespective of whether those facts are advanced by means of authentic archival footage or by other means. And in so far as it captures this wider domain, it better suits the purposes of film scholars, filmmakers, film distributors, and the general public than does the idea of the film of the presumptive trace.

SOME OBJECTIONS

In developing the concept of both the film of presumptive assertion and the film of the presumptive trace, I have taken advantage of the intention-response model of communication. Both concepts require that the audience recognize a certain intention of the filmmaker. However, many film scholars are apt to reject this type of theorizing, since, like their confrères in other humanities departments, they do not believe that we can have access to authorial intentions, and, therefore, they do not believe that theories of this sort are practicable.

Perhaps the very first thing to say in response to this objection is that it misses the point, since the theory of the film of presumptive assertion is an ontological theory—a characterization of the nature of a certain type of film—and not an epistemological theory about the way in which to identify such films. However, having said that, let me also add that I do not believe that the theory would be impracticable if used to distinguish different sorts of film. And so even though the objection misses the mark, I will attempt to show that the allegation of impracticability is also mistaken.

If film scholars think that the concept of the film of presumptive assertion is compromised because they presuppose that intentions are always unfathomable, then they need to be reminded that we constantly attribute intentions to others with an astoundingly high degree of success. When someone holds a door open, I take this as a signal of their intention that I walk through it. And most of the time when I make this inference, I am not mistaken. When someone at the dinner table hands me a plate of potatoes, I infer that they intend that it is my turn to take some potatoes. And again I am almost always correct in this. Likewise, when the notice comes from the electrical company, I always recognize that they intend me to pay my bill. And every time I pay my bill in response, it turns out that I was right. Or, at least, they never send my cheque back.

Social life could not flourish if we were not able to discern the intentions of others. We could not understand the behaviour or the words and deeds of others if we could not successfully attribute intentions to them. This is not to say that we never make mistaken attributions of intentions to others. But we are all more successful in this matter than we are unsuccessful.

Consequently, the film scholar who is sceptical of the practicability of the category of the film of presumptive assertion on the grounds that we are incapable of correctly attributing intentions to others, including filmmakers, is immensely unconvincing. We do not typically have any principled problems in discerning the intentions of others. The social fabric could not cohere, unless we were *generally* successful in attributing intentions to others. The social fabric does cohere because we are so adept at discerning the intentions of others, including even filmmakers. There are no grounds for thinking that, in principle, the intentions of others are unfathomable. For in fact, they are not.

Moreover, our ability to attribute intentions to others successfully is not restricted to living people. Historians scrutinize the words and deeds of the dead with an eye to determining their intentions. And there is no reason to suppose that they do not often do so successfully. Are historians wrong when they hypothesize that by early 1941 Hitler intended to invade the Soviet Union, or that in 1959 Kennedy intended to run for the presidency? Perhaps Hitler and JFK took some of their intentions to the grave with them. But some of their intentions are certainly accessible to historians. Not all the intentions of historical agents, including filmmakers, are ontologically obscure. Historians, including film historians, confront no unscalable barriers when it comes to surmising the intentions of past persons.

Scholars in film studies and the humanities in general distrust talk of authorial intentions because they believe that powerful arguments with names like the 'intentional fallacy' and 'the death of the author' have demonstrated that authorial intentions either are inaccessible or should be treated as such. These arguments are inconclusive, and I, and others, have attempted to show at length why they are mistaken.[28] However, rather than enter that debate once again, let me now point out that even if the preceding arguments were uncontroversial, they would still not provide grounds for scepticism with regard to the assertoric intentions required for films of presumptive assertion, since the intentional fallacy and the death of the author argument pertain to the interpretation of the meaning of texts,[29] not to their categorization. Thus these arguments, even if they were sound (which they are not) are irrelevant to the question at hand.

According to the intentional fallacy and the death of the author argument, invocation of authorial intention is either illicit, impossible, or impermissible when we are interpreting the meaning of a text. The meaning intentions of the author are, so to speak, out of bounds. But when presenting a work, meaning intentions are not the only intentions at issue. There are also what we might call *categorical intentions*—i.e. intentions about the category to which the relevant work belongs. And these are hardly inscrutable in the way that friends of the intentional fallacy and the death of the author allege the meaning intentions of the author to be. Can anyone doubt that Stanley Kubrick intended *A Space Odyssey* to be regarded as at least belonging to the category of the science fiction film or that John Ford intended *My Darling Clementine* as a western? What grounds are there to suppose that these attributions of intention are mistaken? Surely the reasons for scepticism about the attribution of meaning intentions do not cut against such attributions of categorical intentions.[30] We might argue about the intended meaning of the Star Child in *A Space Odyssey;* but we do not think that the attribution of categorical intentions raises the same kind of epistemological problems. It would take something like the postulation of a Cartesian demon to be seriously sceptical about the attribution of the preceding categorical intentions to Stanley Kubrick and John Ford.

The force of the intentional fallacy and the death of the author argument is that the reference to authorial meaning intentions is either irrelevant or prohibited when interpreting the meaning of a poem. But it is one thing to interpret a poem on the basis of a hypothesis of what an author intends to mean, and another thing to identify a poem on the basis of a hypothesis that poetry is the category in which the author intended to write. Indeed, it may be that in order to be agnostic about authorial meaning intentions even requires that an interpreter know (as he almost always does) that what he is dealing with is intended to be a poem and not a laundry list.

The relevance of this discussion of categorical intentions, I hope, is clear-cut. The assertoric intention of the maker of a film of presumptive assertion is a categorical intention. It is not, therefore, the kind of intention at which either the intentional fallacy or the death of the author argument is directed. Categorical intentions are at the very least more publicly determinable than meaning intentions are supposed to be according to proponents of the intentional fallacy and the death of the author argument. Personally, I do not believe that meaning intentions are as inaccessible as these fashionable arguments allege. But even if (*a big if*) meaning intentions were, that would provide no reason to be suspicious concerning the categorical assertoric intentions of the makers of films of presumptive fact.

Of course, this defence of the practicability of reference to the assertoric intentions of filmmakers is rather abstract. It provides a very theoretical reassurance that the assertoric intention is not, in principle, inaccessible. But the conscientious film theorist will want to know in some detail how we go about recognizing the filmmaker's assertoric intentions before he or she is willing to grant that my formula is feasible for identifying films of presumptive assertion. So how do we determine that the filmmaker has the assertoric intention that we adopt the assertoric stance when we see a film?

Actually, the answer to this question is so obvious that only a film theorist could miss it. Films come labelled, or indexed, as to the type of films they are, and where these labels index the films as 'documentaries' or 'nonfiction films' the audience has access to information about the assertoric intentions of the filmmaker.[31] The way in which a film is indexed is a perfectly public matter;

there is nothing occult or obscure about it. We have access to the filmmaker's assertoric intentions through many routes. There are press releases, advertisements, television interviews, film listings and TV listings, previews, critical reviews, and word of mouth. Moreover, information in the title cards of the film may also be relevant, as in the case of the *National Geographic Society Special— Rain Forest.*

Through many redundant, public channels of communication, the typical viewer knows the kind of film he is about to see. When one chooses to see a film, one generally knows that it is what is called a 'documentary' ahead of time because the film has been indexed and circulated that way. And knowing this much, the film viewer knows that he is intended by the filmmaker to adopt what I have called the assertoric stance.

Of course, it is possible that while channel surfing we come across a film whose indexing is not already known to us. Perhaps we ask ourselves, what kind of film is this supposed to be? But we can figure this out pretty quickly—by fairly reliable inference if it is on the Discovery Channel or the History Channel, or, more directly, by looking it up in a TV guide. And we can also wait for the end credits which will generally reiterate information pertinent to indexing the film. Needless to say, we may also use the content, the look, or the sound of the film as evidence about the category to which the film belongs. And this generally works, but, for reasons discussed earlier, a conclusive determination hinges on ascertaining the filmmaker's intention through indexing.

Another apparent problem case might be the situation of the film historian who discovers film footage in an archive and wonders what kind of film it is. He cannot be sure by just looking at the film. And let us suppose that the titles are missing. What is he to do? Well, probably what he will do is attempt to find some paper record of it. He will look at newspapers, film histories, memoirs, the records of distributors and filmmakers, and the like to find a description of something like the footage he has discovered. He will attempt to identify the footage by appealing to historical data. And in searching for the identity of the film, he will also be searching for its indexing.

Historians have to evaluate, identify, and authenticate documents all the time. Very often they are successful in their endeavours. There is no principled reason to think that a film historian searching for the indexing of a film need be any less successful than any other historian dealing with primary sources of uncertain origin.

Admittedly, it is logically possible that our film historian may never discover the way in which a given film was indexed. Thus, it may turn out that in such cases the assertoric intentions of the filmmaker are lost to us forever. What would be the consequences of such cases for the theory of films of presumptive assertion? Not much. First of all, it would not compromise the theory as a definition of films of presumptive assertion because that is an ontological theory. Our inability to determine whether or not the film in question was a film of presumptive assertion would not challenge our claim that the film falls in that category just in case its makers were possessed by an assertoric intention. That we are uncertain of the relevant intention is compatible with the fact that the maker had an assertoric intention, but that we do not know it. The film is or is not a film of presumptive assertion, whether or not we know it is.

Moreover, the practicability of our formula is not unhorsed by the fact that sometimes our formula will leave us with undecidable cases. For, given the phenomenon of indexing, our definition will give us a *generally reliable* way of sorting films of presumptive assertion from other types of film. If there are some cases where there are empirical obstacles to applying the theory, then that does not show the theory is not generally practicable. The theory does not guarantee that we can ascertain with every case whether a given film is a film of presumptive assertion or not. But, nevertheless, it gives us the wherewithal to tell most of the time, and, more importantly, there are not principled reasons to suppose that the formula is not generally reliable. The only problems that may arise are with possible isolated cases where the record of the indexing of the film has been completely obliterated. But this is not likely to occur very often.[32]

In general, then, by virtue of the way a film of presumptive assertion is indexed we recognize the maker's assertoric intention that we entertain the propositional content of the film as asserted thought on the basis of his intention. Thus, when I go into a Blockbuster video outlet and peruse a cassette of *Reptiles and Amphibians,* by Walon Green and Heinz Seilman, I recognize that it is intended to be a film of presumptive assertion, not only because it is in the section labelled 'documentary', but because the information on the sleeve of the cassette iterates this indexing. Moreover, when I put it in my VCR, the title cards indicate that it is a National Geographic Society presentation. As a result, I know that, *ceteris paribus,* the filmmakers intend that I entertain the propositional content of *Reptiles and Amphibians* as asserted thought.

Thus, when the film shows and/or tells me that the vine snake of southeast Asia lives in trees, that the Komodo dragon is really a monitor lizard and that it sometimes eats small goats, that the sea snake's venom is the most toxic, and that, before engaging in ritual mating combat, male tortoises bob their heads, I entertain these propositions as asserted thought, I presume that Walon Green and Heinz Seilman believe these things to be true, and that they are committed to the probity of these propositions in accordance with the canons of evidence and reason-giving appropriate to this type of information.

Were I to learn that Green and Seilman did not believe that these things were true, I would accuse them of lying, even if, unbeknownst to them, these things were actually true. Moreover, if the filmmakers were not committed to the appropriate canons of evidence and reason-giving—if they came up with all this stuff about reptiles and lizards by reading tea-leaves—I would have grounds for criticizing the film as a nature film of presumptive assertion. Likewise, the fact that *Roger and Me* knowingly plays fast and loose with the evidence is a bad-making feature of that film, just as if it knowingly advanced propositions that could not be supported by the relevant canons of evidence and reason-giving.

That films of presumptive assertion are beholden to the interpersonal canons of evidence and reason-giving appropriate to the kind of information they convey entails that such films are committed to objectivity. This, of course, does not mean that all, or even most, films of presumptive fact are objective, but only that they are committed to it, which, in turn, entails that their failure to respect the requirements of objectivity provides us with reasons to criticize them *qua* films of presumptive assertion. We may have further reasons to commend such a film—perhaps, its editing is bravura. Nevertheless, the failure to meet its commitment to objectivity, entailed by the assertoric intention that we take an assertoric stance toward it, is always *a* bad-making feature of a film of presumptive assertion, even if, in addition, the film possesses other good-making features. A film of presumptive assertion that fails to meet our expectations with respect to objectivity, which are based on our recognition of the filmmaker's assertoric intention that we adopt the assertoric stance, can never receive anything but a mixed critical verdict. If *Roger and Me* is acclaimed as effective anti-capitalist propaganda, outrageous street theatre, or comic high jinks, it should also at the same time be criticized for its failure to respect the evidentiary record.

Of course, in arguing that according to the theory of films of presumptive assertion such films are necessarily committed to objectivity, I am courting rebuke by film scholars. For they believe that it has been conclusively demonstrated that objectivity is impossible in the sort of films I am talking about. Thus, if I maintain that such films are necessarily committed to objectivity, they are likely to respond that, inasmuch as 'should implies can', there is something profoundly wrong with my theory. That is, I contend that makers of films of presumptive assertion, in virtue of their assertoric intention and what it entails, should abide by canons of objectivity. But film scholars are apt to counter that this must be wrong because it is well known that such films necessarily cannot be objective.

Of course, I disagree with this presupposition, and I have argued at great length against it elsewhere.[33] It is not true that such films necessarily always fall short of objectivity because they are selective—a popular argument among film theorists—since selectivity is an essential, non-controversial feature of all sorts of enterprises, such as sociology, physics, biology, history, and even journalistic reportage. Thus, if selectivity presents no special problem for the objectivity of these areas of enquiry, then it is not an a priori problem for makers of films of presumptive fact either. Filmmakers, like physicists and historians, may fail to meet their commitments to objectivity. But where that happens it is a matter of individual shortcomings and not of the very nature of things.

Moreover, postmodern theorists who contend that objectivity is impossible in the film of presumptive assertion because it is impossible to achieve in any form of enquiry or discourse champion a position that is inevitably self-refuting. For such theorists act as if they are presenting us with objective reasons that support the truth or the plausibility of their conjectures about knowledge claims in general. But how is that possible if the notion of objective reasons is to be regarded with suspicion? For if all reasons fail to be objective that includes their reasons. So why are they advancing them as objective reasons, and why should anyone believe them?

Likely grounds for rejecting the theory of films of presumptive assertion involve scepticism about the accessibility of authorial intentions and scepticism about the prospects for objectivity. In this section, I have tried to undermine both these anxieties. If my efforts in this regard have been successful, then the theory of films of presumptive assertion is provisionally creditable, and the burden of proof falls on the sceptics to show otherwise.

CONCLUSION

In this chapter I have advanced a theory of what I call films of presumptive assertion. It is my claim that this concept captures what people mean to talk about when they speak informally of 'documentaries' and 'nonfiction films'. Whether the theory is successful depends, in part, on how well it picks out the extension of films we have in mind when we use terms like 'documentary'. Undoubtedly, it is up to the reader to see how well my theory tracks usage.

I began developing this theory with the presumption that there is a real distinction in this neighbourhood. I tried to defend this presumption by (1) criticizing the plausibility of 'deconstructionist' arguments to the contrary, and (2) showing that we could develop persuasive theories of fiction, nonfiction, and films of presumptive assertion by employing the intention-response model of communication. In effect, my argument is transcendental in nature. I take it, after clearing away various sceptical arguments, that there are genuine distinctions here to be drawn and then I propose candidates for what I argue are the best ways of making those distinctions. Thus, at this point in the debate, it is up to others (such as the 'deconstructionists') to show either that my distinctions are flawed (logically, empirically, or pragmatically), or that there are better ways of drawing the distinction than mine. Until that time, I propose that what has heretofore been regarded as documentary film in common, contemporary parlance be reconceived in terms of films of presumptive assertion.

Of course, 'films of presumptive assertion' is quite a mouthful. And it does not have a nice ring to it. So, I am not suggesting that we attempt to make ordinary folk replace 'documentary' with this cumbersome locution. We would not succeed, even if we tried. Rather, I am suggesting that for technical or theoretical purposes, we understand that what is typically meant by saying that a film is a 'documentary' is really that it is 'a film of presumptive assertion', unless we have grounds for thinking that the speaker is using the term in the Griersonian sense. The reform I am suggesting is not primarily a linguistic reform, but a theoretical one. Moreover, if other film theorists think that this reform is ill advised, it is up to them to say why.

NOTES

1. Though I constantly refer to film in this chapter, this is really a *façon de parler*. For I also mean to be talking about TV, videotapes, and computer imaging. A more accurate way to talk about the extension of visual media I have in mind would be to speak of *moving images*. But that would not only be cumbersome and perhaps confusing. It would also add even more jargon to an essay that already uses quite enough. Nevertheless, when I refer to film in general in this chapter, it should be understood as referring to moving images of all sorts including TV, video, and CD-ROM. For an account of what I mean by *moving images*, see Noël Carroll, 'Defining the Moving Image', in *Theorizing the Moving Image* (New York: Cambridge University Press, 1996).

2. According to Chuck Wolfe, by way of Carl Plantinga, the term *documentaire* was widely used in France in the 1920s before Grierson used its English translation to refer to *Moana*.

3. Paul Rotha, *Documentary Film*, 2nd edn. (London: Faber, 1952), 70. This book was originally published in 1935.

4. Brian Winston, *Claiming the Real* (London: British Film Institute, 1995).

5. Showing just this was a pressing issue for early filmmakers and film theoreticians. For an

account of this ambition, see Noël Carroll, *Philosophical Problems of Classical Film Theory* (Princeton: Princeton University Press, 1988), ch. 1.

6. Throughout this chapter, I have placed terms like 'deconstructed' and 'deconstructionists' in scare quotation marks in order to signal my recognition that some may charge that what I refer to is not strictly Derridean deconstruction. I call the practitioners I have in mind 'deconstructionists' because they wish to erase the distinction between fiction and nonfiction. However, in dismissing this distinction in favour of calling everything 'fiction', these practitioners might be accused by Derrideans of *privileging* fiction.

7. Christian Metz, 'The Imaginary Signifier', *Screen*, 16: 2 (Summer 1975), 47.

8. Michael Renov suggests an argument like this one—among other arguments—in 'Introduction: The Truth about nonfiction', in his anthology *Theorizing Documentary* (New York: Routledge, 1993). For criticism of Renov's overall position, see Noël Carroll, 'Nonfiction Film and Postmodern Skepticism', in David Bordwell and Noël Carroll (eds.), *Post-Theory: Reconstructing Film Studies* (Madison: University of Wisconsin Press, 1996).

9. Other evidence that we would look for might include the search for mention of this work by historical commentators who might identify it one way or the other, or, at least, suggest the appropriate identification, given information about the context of the work (in terms of its production and/or reception).

10. It also pays to note that there is a second logical error in their argument. For even if it were demonstrated that there is no differentia between fiction and nonfiction films, it would not follow that all films are fictional.

11. Trevor Ponech explores a similar line of argumentation in *Film Theory and Philosophy*, ed. Richard Allen and Murray Smith (Oxford: Oxford University Press, 1977).

12. This view of the nature of philosophical problems is defended by Arthur Danto in his book *Connections to the World* (New York: Harper & Row, 1989).

13. Examples of the intention-response model with respect to art theory include: Monroe Beardsley, 'An Aesthetic Definition of Art', in Hugh Curtler (ed.), *What Is Art?* (New York: Haven, 1983), and Jerrold Levinson, 'Defining Art Historically', in his *Music, Art, and Metaphysics* (Ithaca, NY: Cornell University Press, 1990). Examples of the intention-response model with respect to fiction include: Gregory Currie, *The Nature of Fiction* (Cambridge: Cambridge University Press, 1990), and Peter Lamarque and Stein Haugom Olsen, *Truth, Fiction and Literature* (Oxford: Clarendon Press, 1994).

14. The notion of a 'fictive intention' derives from Currie's *The Nature of Fiction*. 'Fictive stance' is used both in Currie's book and by Lamarque and Olsen in *Truth, Fiction and Literature*.

15. I use the notion of propositional content in its technical sense. It does not refer narrowly to sentences. Propositional content is what is conveyed by a structure of sense-bearing signs, where the sense-bearing signs need not be restricted to sentences of natural or formal languages.

16. It seems to me that a move like this, which film 'deconstructionists' might attempt to emulate, is made by Paul Ricoeur in his 'The Interweaving of History and Fiction'. However, I think that this move is mistaken because Ricoeur is trading on the notion of what I call the 'constructive imagination', whereas I maintain that the relevant sense of the imagination for this argument should be what I call the 'suppositional imagination'.

See Paul Ricoeur, *Time and Narrative,* vol. iii (Chicago: University of Chicago Press, 1985), 180–92.

17. In this I disagree with Kendall Walton, who employs the notion of make-believe. Walton and I might appear to be in agreement, since we both think that fiction involves mandating that the audience imagine. But we have different concepts of imagination. Mine is the suppositional imagination, whereas Walton thinks of the relevant function of the imagination in terms of make-believe. For some of my objections to Walton's notion of make-believe, see Noël Carroll, 'The Paradox of Suspense', in P. Vorderer, M. Wulff, and M. Friedrichsen (eds.), *Suspense: Conceptualizations, Theoretical Analyses and Empirical Explorations* (Mahwah, NJ: Lawrence Erlbaum, 1996), 88; id., 'Critical Study: Kendall L. Walton, Mimesis as Make-Believe', *Philosophical Quarterly,* 45: 178 (Jan. 1995), 93–9; and id., 'On Kendall Walton's *Mimesis as Make-Believe*', *Philosophy and Phenomenological Research,* 51: 2 (June 1991), 383–7. Walton's view is stated most elaborately in his book *Mimesis as Make-Believe: On the Foundations of the Representational Arts* (Cambridge, Mass.: Harvard University Press, 1990).

18. Kendall Walton objects to the assimilation of the imagination to the notion of 'entertaining thoughts'. He contends that entertaining thoughts restricts us to occurrent imaginings, whereas in order to follow a narrative fiction the non-occurrent imagination must be employed as well in order to deal with such things as the presuppositions and implications of the fiction. But I worry that this is a matter of quibbling over words. For if I ask you to entertain the thought (unasserted) that Taras Bulba is a man, then, *ceteris paribus,* I am also asking you implicitly to entertain all the presuppositions and implications of that thought. I am asking you to entertain the propositions (unasserted) that he has a heart, a circulatory system, that he requires oxygen, and so on. *Pace* Walton, not everything that you are invited to suppose and that you implicitly suppose need be in the spotlight of the theatre of the mind.

19. One reason that this analysis requires more conditions is because, as stated, nothing has been said about the audience's understanding of the meaning of the structured, sense-bearing signs in question. Thus, a fuller account that takes heed of this would be:

A structure of sense-bearing signs *x* by sender *s* is fictional if and only if *s* presents *x* to audience *a* with the intention (1) that *a* recognize that *x* is intended by *s* to mean *p* (a certain propositional content), (2) that *a* recognize that *s* intends *a* to suppositionally imagine *p*, (3) that *a* suppositionally imagine that *p*, and (4) that 2 is the reason for 3.

Undoubtedly this analysis could be further refined. For example, see Currie's *Nature of Fiction,* 33. Though Currie and I disagree on some important points, the structure of my analysis was inspired by his.

20. The complications derive from the same considerations found in the preceding note. A more complete definition of nonfiction would look like this:

A structure of sense-bearing signs *x* is nonfictional if and only if *x* is presented by sender *s* to audience *a* where *s* intends (1) that *a* recognize that *x* is intended by *s* to mean *p*, (2) that *a* recognize that *s* intends them not to entertain the propositional content of *p* as unasserted, (3) that *a* does not entertain *p* as unasserted, (4) that *s* intends that 2 will be one of *a*'s reasons for 3.

21. I would not wish to deny that *Serene Velocity* might be involved in providing something like an object lesson concerning the impression of movement in film. But it is not material to that object lesson whether the images of the hallway be entertained by way of the suppositional imagination or belief. The object lesson will obtain either way. Thus, since Gehr does not prescribe that we entertain the propositional content of his shots— that here is a hallway—as unasserted, *Serene Velocity* is not a fiction; therefore, it is nonfiction.

22. Though from here on I talk about the film of presumptive assertion, it should be clear that the analysis could be applied more broadly to what we might call either 'texts of presumptive assertion'—like history books or newspaper articles—or what we might call, even more commodiously, 'structures of sense-bearing signs of presumptive assertion'.

23. For a discussion of assertion, see John Searle, *Expression and Meaning: Studies in the Theory of Speech Acts* (Cambridge: Cambridge University Press, 1979), 62.

24. This is the Gricean way of putting it, but, as Richard Allen points out, the relevant effects that the reader should have in mind here are what might be called 'meaning effects'.

25. I say *a* reason here because there may be other reasons as well having to do with the verisimilitude of the image.

26. This analysis shares a number of points with the one proposed by Carl Plantinga in his article 'Defining Documentary: Fiction, Non-fiction, and Projected Worlds', *Persistence of Vision*, 5 (Spring 1987), 44–54. I suspect that, despite the difference in language, our theories are compatible. Plantinga expands on his view in *Rhetoric and Representation in Non-fiction Film* (New York: Cambridge University Press, 1997).

27. Perhaps the defender of the notion of the film of the presumptive trace would deny this, claiming that the makers of the film intend the audience to regard all the footage in the film as historic, but that, in addition, they are lying. I, however, can find no grounds to suppose that the filmmakers are trying to mislead the audience about the provenance of the footage described above.

28. See Noël Carroll, 'Art, Intention, and Conversation', in Gary Iseminger (ed.), *Intention and Interpretation* (Philadelphia: Temple University Press, 1992); id., 'Anglo-American Aesthetics and Contemporary Criticism: Intention and the Hermeneutics of Suspicion', *Journal of Aesthetics and Art Criticism*, 51: 2 (Spring 1993).

29. Of course, the intentional fallacy also pertains to the evaluation of texts. But, once again, evaluation is not categorization.

30. Interestingly, Monroe Beardsley, one of the leading progenitors of the intentional fallacy, uses the intention-response model in order to present his theory of art. He, at least, thinks that reference to an artist's categorical intentions is not problematic, while also arguing that reference to an artist's meaning intentions falls foul of the intentional fallacy. He believes that being open to categorical intentions while rejecting meaning intentions is logically consistent, and this leads him to a mixed view—accepting the invocation of authorial intentions for the purpose of categorizing a work, but disallowing it in the interpretation of a work. See Beardsley, 'An Aesthetic Definition of Art'.

31. Indexing is discussed in Noël Carroll, 'From Real to Reel: Entangled in Nonfiction Film', in *Theorizing the Moving Image*.

32. The reader may wonder about a case where a filmmaker dissimulates by presenting

cooked-up footage, but indexes the film as a documentary. My view is that we regard it as presented with an assertoric intention, since the filmmaker has prescribed that the audience entertain its propositional content as asserted thought. It does not become a fiction film because the filmmaker has counterfeited the footage. It is still a film of presumptive assertion. But it is a *bad* film of presumptive assertion because the filmmaker has failed to live up to his commitments to the standards of evidence and reasoning appropriate to the subject-matter of the film.

33. See Carroll, 'From Real to Reel: Entangled in Nonfiction Film', and, 'Postmodern Skepticism and the Nonfiction Film'.

Chapter 10 Photographic Traces and Documentary Films: Comments for Gregory Currie

In his characteristically stimulating and carefully crafted article "Visible Traces: Documentary Film and the Contents of Photographs," Gregory Currie introduces a sophisticated theory of the documentary film.[1] For Currie, a documentary film is one comprised of a preponderance of photographic images that function in the context of the relevant film as traces of the objects and events that causally produced them. An image of Gregory Peck in a documentary film is a representation of Gregory Peck, a photographic trace of the actor at a certain time and place. And a documentary about Gregory Peck is constructed mostly of such images.

Whereas in a fictional film, like *To Kill a Mockingbird,* photographic images of Gregory Peck are used to represent the fictional character Atticus Finch, in a documentary film—such as a biography of Gregory Peck—traces represent the living actor. A documentary film is one in which the preponderance of images function representationally as traces. Moreover, when a documentary film is narrative in nature, the images support or contribute to the narrative in virtue (preponderantly) of their being photographic representations (or traces). So in a documentary film, the image of the battleship *Arizona* firing its sixteen-inch guns represents its photographic trace content: the battleship *Arizona* firing its sixteen-inch guns.

Currie's theory of documentary film places heavy emphasis on one way of producing cinematic images, albeit the most standard way prior to the advent of digital technology (and, in all likelihood, still the most standard way today). It is the use of photography to imprint the image of whatever stands before the camera. This is the capacity of the photograph to produce a *document,* one whose causal provenance gives it a certain evidentiary authority not shared by paintings and testimony.

In fiction films, these images are embedded in fictional contexts, where they function, "secondarily" in Currie's terminology, to provide information about characters like Atticus Finch. However, in documentary films, these images function as documents of the people, places, and things of which they are traces. Thus, we might call Currie's view a "documentation theory of documentary film."

Such an approach is not unknown to film theory. In the past, oftentimes film theorists have (confusedly to my way of thinking) challenged the possibility of objectivity in the documentary film by pointing out that many of the images in documentary films do not function as literal documents of what they represent—sometimes stock footage of the battleship *Arizona* is interpolated into representations of events from which the battleship *Arizona* was historically absent. But Currie, thankfully, does not enmesh himself in debates about the objectivity of the documentary film, spending his energy instead on defining such films. Though Currie may share, and, indeed, clarify, one of the premises of those who challenge the "documentary" status of what are called documentary films, he does not question the possibility of objectivity in such films.

For Currie, it would seem, the ideal documentary film (and documentary video), definitionally rather than aesthetically speaking, would be surveillance-camera footage. Such a documentary would be a causally produced, non-intentionally mediated record of the events that transpired before the camera. The story it told would be the trace of the events photographically imprinted. Such a view of the documentary film is logically coherent; it is not internally self-contradictory. However, if what we expect a definition of the documentary film to do is to capture our ordinary concept of the documentary, then Currie's theory is highly revisionist.

Admittedly, people's use of the notion of the documentary film is sometimes inconsistent and calls for some regimentation—for striking a reflective balance between our intuitions and our best theoretical hypotheses. Nevertheless, in my opinion, Currie's theory of the documentary so neglects ordinary usage and so violates everyday intuitions that it appears to be merely a stipulative redefinition of the documentary, rather than a conceptual reconstruction of our actual use of the category. Currie, at best, has offered us a concept of documentary that we might use (though he is vague on for what purpose); but it is not the one that we do use.

For Currie "documentaries are filmic narratives, the images of which support the narrative in virtue (mostly) of their being photographic representations [*qua* traces]" (Currie, p. 296). One problem here is that sometimes what are called documentaries are not narratives; sometimes they are arguments; sometimes they are just catalogues of views; and sometimes just single shots sans stories (e.g., Lumière *actualités*). But even if we repair Currie's theory with this in mind, it should be clear that many (most?) of what are called "documentary films" are not such that they are preponderantly composed of images that function as traces.

Many documentaries freely use stock footage. Images of naval artillery barrages from the Normandy invasion can be interpolated into documentaries about the Okinawa invasion. Shots of Hitler speaking produced on one occasion can be used to represent Hitler speaking at another point in his career. This is not an occasional practice. It happens all the time.

Many (most?) documentaries need to be filled out with footage from the archive that is not a literal trace of any of the events recounted by the film-as-a-whole. This standard practice is well known, especially among those who label films documentaries. Sometimes most of the images in a film will be of this sort. But it does not stop us from calling these films documentaries, most notably where the film-as-a-whole is dedicated to imparting factual information. Thus, it cannot be a necessary condition for the application of our ordinary concept of the documentary that such films contain a preponderance of images that are literal trace-representations of precisely the events that gave rise to them.

It seems uncontroversial that there are many documentaries about the future, such as Disney programs from the fifties about space travel. But as Currie correctly points out, you cannot have photographic traces from the future. Consequently, these documentaries supplemented existing footage of missile testing with animated representations of how the multi-staged rockets of the future would operate. If memory serves me, a preponderance of the images in these programs were animations, not traces. But we still called them documentaries (given their informational purposes). So, once again, it does not seem that Currie has supplied us with a necessary condition for what counts as a documentary.

Currie appears to be aware of anomalies like this, and others, that compromise his theory of the documentary. To deal with them, he introduces the notion of a B-relevant documentary (Currie, 294). Thus, for Currie, my Disney example is not a documentary of space travel proper, but a "space-travel-relevant documentary"—that is, something from which you could learn and perhaps are intended to learn facts about space travel. However, the very fact that Currie has to resort to a neologism to accommodate for this potentially impressively large body of counterevidence indicates that his "documentation theory" does not track our ordinary concept of the documentary.

If Currie's theory fails to supply a necessary condition for documentary, it also fails to yield a sufficient condition. Many films (and videos) contain a preponderance of images that function as representations of that of which they are a trace (in Currie's sense), but which are not documentaries. One place where there is an abundance of films of this sort is the historical avant-garde. Leger's classic *Ballet Mécanique* is composed preponderately of trace-representations of moving objects, but it is not classified as a documentary, but rather as a kind of ciné-poem. Moreover, there is an entire long-standing tradition of *ballets-mécaniques.* Though such films contain a preponderance of trace-representations, they are not, *pace* Currie's definition, typically classified as documentary films.

Likewise, Ernie Gehr's *Serene Velocity* is comprised of shots all of which are trace-representations of the same institutional hallway, but the film is not a documentary. The images are edited together at different cadences, not only to project interesting rhythms, but to reveal the perceptual conditions of the impression of movement. The result is a reflexive comment on the nature of cinema, not a document of the day in the life of a hallway. The imagery functions as stimuli, after the fashion of a psychological test, not as documentary footage. *Serene Velocity* belongs to the tradition of meta-cinema, not to the tradition of the documentary. It is not something we would find on the syllabus of a documentary film class. Thus, were we to employ Currie's criteria here, we would mistakenly classify *Serene Velocity.*

Nor need we look only to the avant-garde for counterexamples to Currie's theory. In the fiction film *Soylent Green,* the character Sol Roth goes to a facility that specializes in euthanasia. Once poisoned, he lies back and is surrounded by filmic trace-representations of restful nature scenes, cut to the music of the *Pastorale.* This film, of course, is fictional, since it is embedded in a larger science fantasy story. However, there are filmic trace-representations like it—mood-films, often accompanied by music—that are not parts of fictions, but which we do not classify as documentaries.[2] Film students make them every semester, and some music videos are also pertinent here. Trace-representations edited together, with or without music, for the purpose of promoting affective states are not documentaries, though it is difficult to see how Currie will avoid this conclusion.

Similarly, avant-garde experiments like Bruce Conner's *Mongoloid* and *America Is Waiting,* along with the recent feature film *Baraka,* contain images that are mostly trace-representations, but they do not seem to fit our ordinary category of documentary. Therefore, it appears that a preponderance of trace-representations is not a sufficient condition for the status of documentary film, at least as that concept is typically employed.

Maybe Currie will respond to counterexamples like these by saying that, since they are not narratives, they are not documentaries. But, as we have already noted, not all documentaries are narrative. Thus, invoking narrative as a necessary condition for documentary film in order to exclude these counterexamples can only be attempted at the cost of a different kind of error. And, in any case, even if, for the sake of argument, we allowed that narrative were a necessary condition for documentary status, there might still be troublesome counterexamples to Currie's theory.

Consider a thought experiment—a fictional film called *My Own Vietnam.* Imagine that every image in this film is a trace-representation of events from the Vietnam War. However, there is also a soundtrack on which a fictional character, a foot soldier of my own concoction, not only describes the battle scenes shown on the screen, but notes his psychological reactions to what is shown. Every image in the film is a trace-representation, and everything on the soundtrack is correlated to precisely the events whose literal traces are being shown on screen. When the fictional commentator says that on such-and-such a date Agent Orange was sprayed on such-and-such a location on the Mekong Delta and that it sickened him spiritually, we see a trace record of the spraying on the date and at the place where the spraying is reported to have occurred. Nor does the commentary on the soundtrack claim that the fictional character was present at the events depicted on the image track, but only observes his feelings about it. *My Own Vietnam* is not a documentary, but a fiction film. Therefore, a preponderance of trace-representations does not a documentary make.

Currie mentions one film—Chris Marker's *San Soleil*—which might seem like *My Own Vietnam.* He appears to argue that it is not a documentary by his lights, since its trace-representations of events do not contribute to the "asserted narrative" of those events (Currie, pp. 293, 297). I am not exactly sure what Currie means by an "asserted narrative"; it is unfortunately undefined in the text. I infer that he thinks that the asserted narrative in *San Soleil* concerns the correspondence, discussed on the soundtrack, between the fictional characters Sandor Krasna and Florence Delay, a narrative that no one could ever possibly glean from the image track alone.

But *My Own Vietnam* is not like that. It is an asserted narrative of the Vietnam War told chronologically. When the narrator says, "American troops invaded Cambodia," we see trace-representations of the requisite time and place of the invasion. All the trace-representations of the Vietnam War in *My Own Vietnam* do contribute to the asserted narrative of the Vietnam War. In fact, one could retrieve the relevant history of the war from the image track. But *My Own Vietnam* is still a fiction film. Therefore, unless what is meant by an "asserted narrative" can be explicitly and persuasively redefined to exclude cases like *My Own Vietnam,* a preponderance of images that are trace-representations is not a sufficient condition for documentary status.

Currie begins his essay by noting that his way of dividing the documentary/ nondocumentary boundary is not the only one, but that, given certain purposes, it is interesting. I have argued that it does not provide a fair approximation of the way in which the concept of the documentary is commonly applied. If Currie's proposal is interesting, then, it must serve certain purposes other than that of reconstructing our ordinary concept of documentary. Thus, I think that it is incumbent on Currie to be more forthcoming about what those purposes might be. If we understood Currie's purposes better, perhaps we might prefer his stipulative redefinition of the documentary to a reconstruction of existing usage.

Currie does make many valuable observations in his paper. He does an excellent job of explaining why photographic documentation has the evidentiary power it does. He, in effect, illuminates the salience that the documentation capacity of film has had for previous film theorists, most strikingly Bazin. And he provides an immensely useful discussion of the trace. However, even here I have one important reservation about Currie's findings. He claims that traces—in which category he includes not only photographs, but footprints and death masks—are more emotionally compelling than handmade pictures. But this seems to me to be a very unguarded generalization, since not only are many paintings more stirring than either photographic or cinematic traces of comparable events, but footprints and death masks are hardly ever moving.

APPENDIX

In his "Preserving the Traces," Gregory Currie has sketched several responses to my article "Photographic Traces and Documentary Film."[3] For me, the most striking is his continued commitment to narrative as a necessary condition of documentary film. It seems to me fairly obvious that, with respect to ordinary usage of the concept of documentary film, narrative is not a necessary prerequisite. The evidence for this is that the *actualités* of the Lumière brothers are paradigmatic documentaries, but some of them are not narrative.

In response to observations like these, Currie alludes to the Lumière short entitled *Workers Emerging from a Factory* and he argues that it is a narrative—or, at least, that it is easy to extract a narrative from it. Perhaps. However, whether narratives are retrievable from *some* Lumière *actualités* hardly indicates that *all* Lumière *actualités* can be recuperated by Currie in this manner. Many, I submit, are not susceptible to this maneuver.

For example, one Lumière *actualité* simply shows waves crashing against a barrier. Sometimes, as Jinhee Choi has pointed out, Lumière cameramen simply mounted their apparatus on a moving vehicle and recorded whatever the camera took in.[4] Thus we have *Skyscrapers of New York from North River* (1903) and *Georgetown Loop (Colorado)* (1903) as well as a moving camera shot taken from a barge as it floated down the Nile. These films "documented" distant sights for curious audiences.

These are all Lumière *actualités*. Nothing worth calling a narrative can be derived from them.[5] If they are what are called documentaries—as common parlance and the discourse of film historians suggest—then Currie's characterization of the documentary is false, since these cases imply that narrative is inessential to belonging in the category in question.

That then leaves us with Currie's requirement of a preponderance of trace-images. But this is not a sufficient condition for a documentary film. For example, consider the 1994 videotape *Kitty Safari*. It is composed of images of assorted birds, squirrels, rats, mice, and guppies cavorting before the camera. Every image is a trace-image of an actual animal. However, these trace-images are not intended to document anything. They were chosen in order to make your average household cat purr with pleasure. It is a mood movie for felines. It was produced for and marketed to cat lovers hoping to bring comfort to their domestic captives.

Nor is a preponderance of trace-images a necessary condition for documentary. The documentary *Supernova* contains a NASA computer animation of the eruption of a galaxy. This does not compromise its status as a documentary, since its implicit claims are factual. Were a film composed primarily of similarly fact-asserting computer-generated simulations I suspect that ordinary viewers and documentary film historians alike would be inclined to count them as documentaries. To the extent that Currie refuses this categorization, his theory is revisionist.

Currie also resists the thought experiment that I called *My Own Vietnam*. He says it might be like a Disney documentary in which Mickey Mouse is the "host," directing our attention here and then there. But this is not how I envisioned *My Own Vietnam*. My imagined narrator is not merely an expository or heuristic device. My imagined narrator is what the film is about. Of that possibility, Currie says that his theory will not count it as a documentary, as I allege he should, because, though it contains trace-images of every event mentioned, it contains no trace-image of the narrator, since this is impossible, given that the narrator is fictional and, therefore, nonexistent. However, I worry that there is an equivocation on the trace-image requirement here. In a comparable nonfiction film, trace-images of the narrator would not be required. Imagine a documentary film about Eisenhower—in which no image of him appears—showing certain events of World War II accompanied by a voice-over of his reactions to them as gleaned from his diaries. We would not discount this as a documentary about Eisenhower. Why should things stand differently with *My Own Vietnam?*

In "Preserving the Traces," Currie also goes on the offensive, challenging my notion of films of presumptive assertion. He cites the case of a lawsuit in which Carlton Television in Britain was fined two million pounds because it putatively presented footage of "actual male prostitutes" who turned out to be TV employees play-acting the relevant roles. Unfortunately, I have not seen this footage. But I think that I understand the point Currie intends to make: namely, viewers presumed that the footage was a trace-image of actual prostitutes, but it was not. Carlton Television was found to be guilty of some form of "documentary" malpractice. This finding only makes sense, Currie assumes, if something like his theory of documentary, rather than my theory of films of presumptive assertion, governs our use of the relevant concepts.

However, in principle, I see no reason why my conception of films of presumptive assertion cannot handle cases like these. In some instances, so-called documentaries will *claim* or strongly *implicate*—that is, *assert*—perhaps due to the subgenre to which they belong, that the images in question are trace-images of what they represent. When this happens and it is false, umbrage follows.

This is perfectly comprehensible within my theory of films or moving images of presumptive assertion. If an assertion is made or implicated that is false, the audience will complain that the audience-filmmaker contract has been broken. My theory of films of presumptive assertion can explain this; the presumption advanced by the film-maker has been violated in such a case.

I cannot—since I am unfamiliar with the documentary at issue—pinpoint what it was about the Carlton Television production that led viewers to believe that the images were trace-images. But there must have been something that led them to do so, since the expectation that all images in a documentary be trace-images is not a default assumption of viewers. For, as I argue in my article on films of presumptive assertion, there is too much evidence in the opposite direction, notably with respect to the use of stock footage and historical reenactments. Why people found the Carlton Television case to be misleading on this score, then, seems to me to be a question for documentary film criticism, not a cause for reconsidering my theory of the documentary, or, as I prefer to label the category, moving images of presumptive assertion.

NOTES

1. Gregory Currie, "Visible Traces: Documentary Film and the Contents of Photographs," *Journal of Aesthetics and Art Criticism,* vol. 57, no. 3 (1999). Henceforth page references to this article are embedded in the text of my article.

2. James Gleick notes "Some hospital television systems now feature a 'relaxation channel,' with hour after hour of surf, wind, leaves, and babbling brooks." But these are not documentaries. See: James Gleick, *Faster: The Acceleration of Just About Everything* (New York: Pantheon Books, 1999), p. 17.

3. Gregory Currie, "Preserving the Traces: An Answer to Noël Carroll," *Journal of Aesthetics and Art Criticism,* vol. 58, no. 3 (Summer 2000), pp. 36–308.

4. Jinhee Choi, "A Reply to Currie on Documentaries," *Journal of Aesthetics and Art Criticism,* vol. 59, no. 3 (Summer 2001), pp. 317–319.

5. On the criteria of narrative, see Noël Carroll, "On the Narrative Connection," in my *Beyond Aesthetics* (New York: Cambridge University Press, 2001).

Chapter 11 Toward a Definition of Moving-Picture Dance

Almost since the inception of moving pictures, those pictures have often featured dance. The obvious reason for this is that the natural subject of moving pictures is movement. And dances—along with hurtling locomotives, car chases, cattle stampedes, tennis matches, intergalactic dog-fights, and the like—move. Thus, a significant portion of the history of moving pictures involves dance movement. Many moving-picture makers have devoted admirable amounts of effort and imagination to portraying dance in or through media as diverse as film, video, and computer animation. The purpose of this essay is to attempt to offer a philosophical characterization of this field of activity; that is, I will try to define moving-picture dance.

Many readers, learning of my intention, are apt to groan "labeling again, how boring." To a certain extent I can sympathize with that sentiment. It is far more interesting to talk about work than it is to set about classifying it. The concrete achievements of the field are more important than abstractions about it. Nevertheless, despite my ready acknowledgment of this, I will persist for several reasons.

First, whenever festivals of this sort of work are held, it is very likely that at one time or another almost everyone present will be tempted to say of some work that it doesn't really belong on the program. Everyone complains about labeling, but sooner or later most people feel compelled to invoke some favorite definition of their own. For human beings, categorizations are unavoidable, even if we like to pretend indifference to them. And most of us can feign indifference only for so long; most of us have a breaking point. Thus, it seems to me a good idea to get this issue out in the open and to discuss it abstractly—to compare and contrast the various categorizations in play and to develop dialectically from them a comprehensive framework that makes sense of our practices and that resonates with our intuitions about its compass.

Second, though defining things can be a tedious affair, it is also a very powerful way to learn about the contours of a field. For when we attempt to define the strengths and weaknesses of alternative and even rival proposals, we come to recognize the complexity of the field, since different definitions will highlight certain tendencies in the work in question, even if they obscure others. Definitions, that is, even when they are unsuccessful, as I suspect mine might be, can be illuminating. For definitions do not merely demarcate the boundary of a field from other fields, but they can reveal the intricate landscape within a field as well.

Definitions, in short, have a heuristic or pragmatic use, often flushing out perspicuously data and complications heretofore neglected, ignored, overlooked, or unappreciated. This is true even where the definition turns out to be ultimately unsatisfactory. So even though my definitions may appear either too narrow or too broad, I offer them as a way of advancing the discussion.

Another reservation about definitions, popular in the humanities today, is the suspicion that all definitions are covert exercises of power, privileging some work and disenfranchising other work. I am skeptical of this general position about definitions and, in the concluding passages of this paper, I will try to show why my definitions of motion picture dance are not an ideological brief in favor of some stylistic practices rather than others. But I will not be in a position to defend that view until you have read my proposals and the arguments in their behalf.

However, even now, at the outset of this definitional exercise, let me at least register the plea that my intention here is not to create a definition that is stylistically exclusive; rather, I will attempt to craft a category that is as broad as possible, while at the same time being something we are willing to count as a genuine category.

Indeed, I am motivated to construct a broad category of moving-picture dance just because I think that existing ways of defining the field are too nar-row—too narrow especially in ways that cause friction, as creative artists at-tempt to exploit new technologies. For example, those who think of the field in question as ciné-dance wonder whether computer animations of dance should be at the same festival or on the same program or in the same historical overview as works by Maya Deren. Many ways of construing the field, that is, are wedded to certain moments in the development of moving-picture tech-nology—such as the heyday of film. But conceiving of the field only in terms of film stands athwart history—that is, it blocks the prospects, conceptually and sometimes practically, of an innovative engagement on the part of makers of dance images with new technologies.

It seems obvious that alternative technologies for the creation of motion pic-ture dance will continue to proliferate. In order to facilitate experimentation, we will need a broad conception of the field, one that will make the exploration of previously undreamt-of possibilities easier, rather than closing down op-tions. It is in that spirit that I have offered the present definition—to invite change and development, rather than to defend the status quo. In fact, I see my definition, in contrast to existing alternatives, as a means of emancipating cre-ativity, at least in terms of promoting an openness to the inevitability of tech-nological change, rather than as a strategy for canonizing entrenched stylistic practices. Perhaps someone will discover a way in which my proposals serve some hidden dance-world agenda. But one must spell that out in letter and verse. One cannot presume a priori that all definitions serve the interests of some vaguely defined establishment. Some may even liberate.[1] Whether mine does or not remains to be seen.

Undoubtedly, you will have already noticed that I have introduced a new name—"Moving-Picture Dance"—for the field under discussion. I have opted for this conceptualization rather than other, more familiar ones, such as: ciné-dance, film dance, video dance, camera dance, and even screen dance. One way to begin to approach the problem of defining the field is to articulate the reasons for preferring one mode of nomenclature rather than others.

Traditionally, the area has been called ciné-dance or film dance. Since ciné-dance is probably the most popular way of referring to the field, it is worthwhile to spend some time explaining its limitations. The problem with characterizing the field in terms of ciné-dance is that it is too narrow. Obviously, it is too medium specific. It restricts the phenomenon to work made in cinema or film. It is, so to speak, a celluloid-based conception. It also perhaps belies the mod-ernist bias behind much early work in this area.

That is, it seems to suppose that each artistic medium has its own peculiar limitations and/or potentialities, and that it is the duty of the artist to foreground those unique features of the medium in her work. Thus, many have thought that for a candidate truly to belong to the corpus of ciné-dance, it would have to exploit the unique features of cinema, where those are customarily understood in contrast to the possibilities and limitations of theater, including theater dance. Ciné-dance or film dance, under this construal, is always avant-garde, inasmuch as it is implicitly allied to modernist commitments to the purity of the medium.

For example, Ed Emshwiller claims:

> To me there are characteristics that distinguish ciné-dance from a straight dance film. When the dancer is used in filmic terms, rather than dance terms, space and time are flexible. The images projected on the screen may seem to move forward and backward in time, may be discontinuous, in fast motion, slow motion, frozen, repetitious, or simultaneous. The dancer can appear to shift instantaneously from one location to another, can be compressed, elongated, distorted or seen from widely varying perspectives. These manipulations are some of the means the filmmaker has to choreograph his work. By means of the camera and the editing table, he creates image movements, and relationships different from those of the dance choreographer.[2]

However, though this view was once extremely enabling, this conception of the phenomenon is at present clearly obsolete for two reasons. First, by now the work that we all agree belongs to the field in question includes all sorts of work in media other than cinema. Video is the most obvious exception. But also, work which no one would deny falls into the category that concerns us can be achieved through computer processing, such as the technique known as motion capture, which was used in the production of Bill T. Jones's *Ghostcatching* (1999).

If film was the medium in which endeavors of the kind that concern us first appeared, that can be regarded, in one sense, as an accident of history. For the visual culture established in the film medium has evolved and been refined by other media, and is likely to undergo even further development in media not yet imagined. This is why, rather than speaking of film studies or cinema studies, I prefer the concept of moving-image studies, which includes as its object not only film, TV, video, laser discs, and CD-ROM, but also whatever else is to come as future technologies abound and generate descendents of our current moving-image practices.[3] Similarly, this is why I think we should speak of moving-picture dance, rather than ciné-dance, film dance, and, for the same reason, video dance, since these categories, insofar as they are each medium specific, are too restrictive. The phenomenon at hand crosses media, and, therefore, calls for a label that reflects this fact.

A second reason to eschew medium-specific characterizations of the field is related to the implicit modernist prejudices concerning the purity of the medium that often come in tandem with this way of speaking. On the modernist conception, a ciné-dance should be uniquely cinematic, or uniquely videomatic—that is, something realizable only in film (or video), and not by means of some other medium of expression, notably theater. Thus, Talley Beatty's famous leap in Maya Deren's *A Study in Choreography for the Camera* (1945)—a legendary example of Doug Rosenberg's notion of recorporealization[4]—is regarded as a quintessential example of ciné-dance, for a grand jeté of that length would be humanly impossible on stage, but is rather an artifact of what some might call film-space and film-time.[5]

But this modernist bias is overly exclusive. On the one hand, what is called "film-space" and "film-time" are realizable in other media, including, if not theater, then at least video.[6] And, on the other hand, it is far from evident that whether or not something is realizable theatrically is the relevant criterion here. This approach, as we saw in the previous quotation from Emshwiller, seems to favor editing and special effects as the true tests for membership in the class of ciné-dances. But, as Roger Copeland has pointed out, we may wish to include in the relevant category dances, such as some numbers by Fred Astaire and Ginger Rogers, that, though made for the camera, are executed in long-take, deep-focused shots that capture movement in a continuous space.[7]

Do we wish to exclude these—what might be called "Bazinian ciné-dances"—from our perspective, just because it is conceivable that they could be staged in real time on the space of a theater stage?[8] Likewise, something like David Woodberry's *Invisible Dance* (1981)—a Tati-like exercise in discovering dance amidst the flow of everyday life—could be refashioned as an instance of street theater.[9] But still, the version of *Invisible Dance* that we possess on film, I think, is something that most of us would agree is a ciné-dance or, at least, whatever we wind up calling this category.

Indeed, the same point might be made with respect to Elliot Caplan and Merce Cunningham's *Beach Birds for Camera* (1993), since not only is it artistically impure, given its self-avowedly painterly ambitions, but also, arguably, with enough money, enough elaborate set machinery (including rotating stages), and an arsenal of lighting effects, something very like it could be realizable theatrically. And yet it belongs to the category that concerns us.

Of course, by arguing that this category should not be tied to a specific medium, I do not mean that the artist should ignore the medium in which she is working, but only that the medium and certain favored uses of the medium should not be the test of class membership here. The artist is well advised to understand the capabilities of her materials, including the lenses, film stocks, chromakeys, and the like which she intends to deploy. The point is simply that which of these media and their capabilities she chooses does not determine whether her work is an instance of what I call moving-picture dance.

My dismissal of the physical medium as criterial in this regard may strike some of you as too hasty. For the notion of a medium can refer not only to the materials from which an artwork is constructed, but also to the implement used in constructing it. Not only sounds, but musical instruments, like clarinets, can be referred to as musical media. And, in this sense, it may seem that everything in the category of moving-picture dance shares a medium—an instrument through whose agency they are all contrived. And that instrument is the camera. So why not call the category camera-dance or dance for the camera?

There are several problems with this proposal. The first is that there are so many different kinds of cameras that one hesitates to say that we've got hold of a single medium here. And, one can also imagine moving-picture dance imagery generated not by a camera but by means of sound—sonograms, after the fashion of radar. But, as well, in a less science-fiction vein, we may worry that thinking in terms of camera-dance is too restrictive. Aren't there animated dances, which, though they depend on cameras to be mass produced, are not primarily the result of photography, but of drawing? And would a dance composed exclusively in the realm of CD-ROM by computer animation and exhibited on computer monitors be discounted from a festival of work of the relevant sort, merely because it was not camera generated? This is another reason why I prefer the label moving-picture dance to the alternative label camera-dance.

The notion of screen dance, which I myself once found very promising, may seem to avoid the kinds of problems we've encountered so far. For it might be supposed that it is not medium specific; screens, it might be said, are shared by films, video, TV, and computer monitors. But, though this may seem perverse on my part, I think that this supposition is false, if we take the notion of a screen literally.

A screen, in the pertinent sense, is a support upon which we project an image. But, in this respect, a screen is not a necessary condition for showing even a film. As is well known, Edison originally had the idea that films would be shown at peep shows, on devices that we would now call movieolas. It remained for the Lumières to project films onto screens. Thus, early dance films like *Annabelle the Dancer* (1894–1895) and possibly *Crissie Sheridan* (1897) were not examples of screen dance. Moreover, the movieola/peepshow circuit did not end with the Lumières. From my adolescence I remember peepshows of exotic dancers and strippers, available on coin-operated movieolas in amusement parks and adult bookstores. Nor were these films only single-take documentations of prior theatrical performances; many were made for the camera and edited. Films do not need to be literally screened or even to be destined for screening in order to count as films, and, therefore, there can even be film dances that are not screen dances.

Another problem with the notion of screen dance is that the concept of a screen does not really apply to television, though certainly televised dance should not be automatically excluded from our catch area. Televisual images are not projected onto a screen. We look directly into them; we do not look at their reflections or projections on a screen. Standardly, film scholars attempt to distinguish between film viewing and TV viewing this way. Because of movieolas, I do not think that this distinction is as ironclad as they do. But still, they make a legitimate point about the typical TV viewing apparatus (rather than, say, cassette projectors): in the usual case, we look into the projection and not at a reflection of the projection. The same can be said about looking at moving images on computer monitors.

Denying that TV images of dance are literally cases of screen dance may strike you as outlandish. After all, we talk about TV screens all the time. But what does this mean? Is the TV screen the front glass on the monitor—the thing that people clean with Windex and sometimes call a screen? But this is not a screen properly so called. That is, it is an entirely different animal than a film screen. For first of all, the TV image is projected through this glass and not onto it. And second, this glass is not a necessary feature of the TV image. You can remove it and there will still be a moving image. Try it, if you don't believe me.

But perhaps what people have in mind when they talk about the TV screen is the phosphor screen in the cathode ray tube. This lies between the shadow mask and the front of the glass of the picture tube. It is coated with phosphor strips that glow when different colored beams of light hit it. But the phosphor screen is part of the picture tube—which is to say that it is part of the projection mechanism, i.e., once again, part of the picture tube. It is not a screen onto which the image is projected. It is a device for generating the image; it is a device for projecting the image. Typically, there is no screen onto which the projector beam throws the image. In television, we usually look directly into the projection mechanism rather than at a screen onto which something is projected. Thus, most televised dance, including, for example, Twyla Tharp's *Making Television Dance* (1977) with all its special effects, does not literally count as screen dance.

Here I can imagine some complaints. On the one hand, some of you might say that even if the television screen is not equivalent to a film screen, it is like another sort of screen, namely the wire mesh on a screen door. Yet, if this is how you understand the notion of screen in "television screen," then you must admit that the category of screen dance is much more heterogeneous than it sounds, since the way in which one applies the concept to film dances versus TV dances is radically different, and, in some respects, contrary. The locution "screen dance" thus blurs important distinctions and muddies the waters, rarely an admirable tendency when trying to craft a concept. In addition, the analogy with the wire mesh on screen doors may not be a felicitous one to adopt here, since I assume that we would not want to call a live, three-dimensional dance, executed by live bodies, that is staged on the opposite side of a screen door an example of screen dance in the relevant sense.

Another complaint that some of you may have with my rough treatment of the idea of screen dance may be that when composing a film dance, a video dance, or a computer dance, one must be attentive to the dimensions of the picture plane on which one works. If it is a square or a rectangle, if it is in cinemascope or Todd-AO, the image composer must be aware of this—if only to make sure that viewers get to see what the composer intends them to see. And, more than that, if one hopes to make a genuinely effective dance image, one should study the shape of the visual expanse upon which one is working.

This is all true. And yet it is, I think, to be really talking about the frame, rather than the screen, since it is the frame whose exact dimensions make certain compositions more efficacious than others. That is, for example, with film, we are not actually talking about the surface onto which the image is projected, but the shape of that surface. Likewise, with regard to TV, we are talking about image ratios and their relevance to placing figures saliently inside their borders. Though we may speak of sensitivity to the screen here, that is really just a shorthand way of referring to framing, whether what is framed appears in a phenomenologically deep space or a shallow one.

And finally, if you remain unmoved by any of the previous objections to the notion of screen dance, there is also the problem that the concept does not seem well prepared for the future. For we can readily imagine holographic dances and dances in virtual reality that we might wish to regard as part of our evolving tradition of moving-picture dance, but which will not require screens. And what of the developments that we cannot foresee? In the future there may be no screens, yet the practice of moving-picture dances (may and probably will) still be with us.

Given the problems with previous designations of the field, it seems useful to try a new tack. As already indicated, I propose to call the field moving-picture dance. This conceptualization has three components: "motion," "picture," and "dance." First, in order to belong to this category, an example must be a moving image. This requires that the work in question be made by a technology in which the possibility of movement is at least feasible. Most dances of this sort will contain either figures that are moving, or images that elicit the impression of movement by means of devices like fast editing or special effects. Though this covers a lot of ground, some of you may say it is not broad enough, since there are still dances, like Douglas Dunn's *101* (1974), and, therefore, we shall want to count as part of the field images thereof.[10] But if we make motion one of the criteria here, such efforts will be excluded.

This would be a problem if the requirement were that the image had to be moving; however, that is not how I've stated it. I've only required that it be made by means of a technology where movement is possible. So a film of a still dancer will nevertheless fall into the category, since movement is a possibility in film. It is not, on the other hand, a possibility with slide projections. So a slide of a still dance will not be counted in the category of motion-picture dance, though a comparable still film, even if it appears to be perceptually indiscernible from the slide, will so count.

Is this just arbitrary? I don't think so. For in the film case, since movement is a possibility, the fact that the image has no movement is a pertinent stylistic choice. In order to plumb the significance of what the artist has done, we need to ask why she has chosen to make a still image. We need not ask that question about a slide, since movement is necessarily impossible in a slide. If the image could move, it wouldn't be a slide. Movement is not a possible choice with respect to a slide—all slides must be still—so there is no point in asking why the slide is not moving. But if a film shows no movement, that is an unavoidable question, since in that case the artist eschews one of the fundamental possibilities of her technology.

Thus, because of its relevance to artistic choice, style, and significance, the choice of movement versus no movement is a defining feature of film, and other forms of moving images, whereas it is not a conceivable choice with respect to slides, or, for that matter, paintings and photographs of dance. That is why I state the motion condition so broadly in terms of the possibility of movement. Of course, most moving-picture dances move: either their figures move or the impression of movement is conveyed by devices like editing and special effects. This is what immediately differentiates them from other visual forms, such as paintings, sculptures, and photographs of dance.

The notion of moving-picture dance also requires that the moving images in question be pictures of dance. But this raises the question of what is meant by dance. Richard Lorber has attempted to define dance as "the sum of all non-functional movement behaviors."[11] This does not seem quite right, however, since the mattress-moving in Yvonne Rainer's *Room Service* (1963) should count as dance movement, but it is functional. Indeed, the exploration of ordinary movement by the early postmodern dancers at Judson Church might appear to render the concept of dance utterly undefinable, since if ordinary movement is dance, then it would appear that any kind of movement could be dance. That is, dance cannot be defined in terms of its internal movement properties, like expressivity or rhythm.

That sounds persuasive, but it does not mean that we lack the wherewithal to differentiate dance from other sorts of behavior. Specifically, we may be able to identify something as a dance historically, even if we are unable to define it essentially. That is, dance, like the concept of a biological species, may be a historical concept—a concept whose members we determine, as we determine membership in a biological species, by telling narratives or genealogies of their descent. So, something counts as a dance movement (or a dance stillness) if it is an example of a historically identifiable dance form or a recognizable descendent thereof. In order to establish that a candidate for membership in the category of dance is a recognizable descendent of a previous dance form or a combination of previous dance forms, we need to tell a plausible historical narrative of its evolution from bona fide origins, as we do when we explain how postmodern dance evolved dialectically from modern dance.

I will not deny that the notion of a historical concept deserves more attention than I have just given it.[12] However, even the little that has been said should give you an inkling of how I propose to tackle the problem of whether or not we are dealing with a specimen of dance. Of course, if you have a better way of identifying dance, you are welcome to use that for the explication of the idea of moving-picture dance which, at this point, I am defining as an image array composed of movement from a recognizable dance vocabulary, where a dance vocabulary is identified either historically or by whatever means you have discovered.

But this is not yet the complete definition, since I have called the field "moving-picture dance" rather than "moving-image dance." What, if anything, hangs on talking about pictures rather than images? Pictures are things whose referents we recognize simply by looking.[13] Pictures are of the kinds of things we find in the world—specific objects, events, persons, and actions. "Image" is a broader term of art, signifying any form that is visible. An image can be what is called nonfigurative, or nonobjective, or abstract. Jackson Pollock, Wassily Kandinsky, and Frank Stella are famous for their images, not for their pictures, since pictures are of recognizable things or, at least, recognizable kinds of things.

Thus, the term moving-picture dance narrows the field to visualizations of recognizable things, specifically to dances, which, it would seem, are necessarily composed literally of humans and human movement, or personifications thereof. So, at least according to me, when I claim that the concept of moving-picture dance describes our field of interest, I am saying that something belongs in our area if and only if it is a moving visual array of recognizably human movement or stillness (or a personification thereof) drawn from an identifiable existing dance vocabulary or a descendent therefrom. Or, more simply but less accurately: a moving-picture dance is a moving picture of dance movement.

Let me call this the central concept of moving-picture dance. As we shall see, it needs to be supplemented with another concept—what I will call the extended concept of moving-picture dance. But before we get there, allow me to say a few things about the central concept.

I'm sure that some of you have already formulated objections to this characterization of what I allege to be the central concept of the field. These objections may take at least two forms: that the notion of moving-picture dance so defined is, in certain ways, too narrow and, in other ways, it is too broad. For some of you, it will be too narrow because it excludes too much, since it excludes what are called ballet mécaniques like Fernand Léger's and Oscar Fischinger's, on the one hand, and abstractions, such as Doris Chase's *Circles I* (1971), *Rocker* (1976), or *Pelexi Radar* (1981), on the other hand. I hope to deal with these shortcomings when I introduce the extended concept of moving-picture dance.

At the same time, the category, as I've sketched it, may seem too broad, since it includes things like film-dance documentations, sans editing, taken from a fixed-camera position. And many of you will argue that that is just not the kind of thing with which we are concerned. Even the notion of ciné-dance gets closer than what I am calling the central concept of moving-picture dance to that.

This is a fair point, and it calls for immediate comment. From my perspective, the concept of moving-picture dance, as defined so far, only marks the genus of the things that concern us. Anything that centrally concerns us must fall into this genus as I've defined it. However, this genus includes several species, notably: moving-picture dance documentations, moving-picture dance reconstructions, and moving-picture dance constructions. As these labels perhaps already indicate, it is primarily moving-picture dance constructions that we generally gather to honor at festivals. So the preceding objection is an apt one to the definition of the genus of moving-picture dance, but the damage can be repaired when we categorize the subtending species in the genus and take note that one of them—moving-picture dance constructions—is the category that most interests us.

What exactly are these species? In order to get a handle on this, it pays to recall that moving-picture dance is a hybridization of two forms: motion pictures and dance. Thus, one way to differentiate these species is to examine the way in which each species relates these two constituents. One relation is that in which the dance is the predominant or lead element—where the motion picture subserves the dance element. That is moving-picture dance documentation. Another possibility is where the motion-picture component calls the tune. That is moving-picture dance construction. Between these two, there is the possibility where the motion-picture elements and the dance elements are co-equal determinants in the results; moving-picture dance reconstruction fills this category.[14]

In order to be a little less abstract, I will say something about each of these categories. Moving-picture dance documentations take advantage of technologies like cinema and video in order to imprint records of the past chemically, mechanically, and/or electronically in their medium. Documents of this sort are invaluable to dance historians and to choreographers involved in reconstituting the classics; they supply a temporal telescope into dance history. Traditionally, the preferred style of these documents is the frontal long-take single fixed-camera-position approach. Examples would include Virginia Brooks's 1983 video of the Dayton Contemporary Dance Company at the Riverside Dance Festival, Talley Beatty's 1948 *Bench Piece* from Jacob's Pillow, and the video documentation of the stage version of Li Chiao-Ping's *Yellow River* (1991).

Recently, moving-picture documentations have come in for a great deal of bad press, especially from dance notators. They argue that moving-picture documentations—or docudances—are not really very good records, especially of historic choreography, because they restrict themselves to single performances, with a single cast of dancers replete with their personal mannerisms, taken from a single angle which may not always be the best one from which to notice, understand, and appreciate the relevant movement qualities. That is, docudance is a poor instrument for telling the dancer from the dance.

In this regard, notators have a point, though it may not be precisely the point they have in mind. For the complaints they voice really only pertain to a certain style of docudance, albeit a very pervasive style, but not to docudance as such. That is, the limitations they point to belong to one style of docudance and can be remedied easily by moving-picture dance documentators through countervailing stylistic strategies.

Undoubtedly, there are a great many examples of docudances that are too selective, that are restricted to a single performance, or that favor medium-long shots from a single camera position, and which, thereby, lose important details and dance qualities. But it is certainly within the resources of the moving-picture dance documentator to transcend these difficulties.

Appearances to the contrary, the notator really has certain films and videos in mind when she chastises existing films and video records of dance. She has not really thought about the possibilities of docudance as such. For example, she has in mind films of a single performance where the camera holds back to a respectful long shot. And there are a great many examples of this. But there are no grounds to think that a moving-picture dance documentation needs to be restricted to a single performance. A film can show many different ballerinas performing the character of Giselle, as one finds in the film *A Portrait of Giselle* (1982). Or, if one does not wish to interrupt a performance, one can provide alternative versions of the scenes in the sorts of appendices that are becoming more and more popular in laser discs, or one can nest the alternatives in the hypertext of a CD-ROM, or one can place them on the alternative tracks of a DVD. Indeed, in the 1980 docudance of Doris Humphrey's *Two Ecstatic Themes* (1931), two soloists, Carla Maxwell and Nina Watt, perform the dance in full—one after the other—thereby enabling the viewer to begin to discriminate the personal from the choreographic (the dancer from the dance).

The problem of the medium long shot can be overcome by similar devices. If long shots obscure details, then take shots from many angles, including close shots, and locate them in appendices. This is not only a conceptual possibility.

Sally Banes and Robert Alexander do just this in their document of Yvonne Rainer's *Trio A* (1978). And, of course, there is no reason why a moving-picture dance documentation cannot show a dance more than once from different angles, or at different camera speeds. Babette Mangolte's film of Trisha Brown's *Water Motor* (1978) presents the dance first at twenty-four frames per second and then in slow motion, affording what Vertov calls a microscope in time that enables one to attend to the dance in fine detail.

Once we realize that it is only a stylistic choice that limits moving-picture dance documentation to showing us a continuous stretch of choreography— once we realize that either parts or the entire performance can be taken from different vantage points for different reasons—then a solution to the problem of selectivity is within our reach. The notator presents the documentarian with a dilemma: either select variable camera positioning and editing, thereby doctoring the record, or go for the problematic medium-long shot, thereby occluding significant detail. But this is a false dilemma. For the documentarian can do both. She can shoot the dance from end to end from a medium shot, thereby rendering it in all its integrity, and then show us alternative views from more suitable angles of details of the dance, and even alternative views of parts of the dance as performed by different principal dancers. These alternative views can be presented either sequentially—that is, in appendices following the dance proper—or as insets in medium-long shots via segmented or split screens, or again, they can be nested in the hypertext of a CD-ROM. In short, the notator's argument against moving-picture dance documents rests upon exaggerating the limited imaginations and stylistic approaches of past documentarians. The notators, I believe, mistake such examples as inherent limitations of moving-picture dance documentation as such. But dance documentators, as we have seen, can surpass those limitations effortlessly, at least if they have enough money.

This is not said in order to argue against the production of Labanotation scores of dance; in the best of all possible worlds, we should want such scores *and* moving-picture dance documentations.

If in the case of moving-picture dance documentations, the motion picture component is in the service of the dance, in the case of moving-picture dance reconstructions, the dance component and the motion picture component are more like co-contributors to the result.[15] The point of a dance reconstruction of this sort is to make the dance and its qualities accessible to the viewer. To this end, the reconstructor will deploy multiple camera positions, editing, close-ups, and the like in order to recreate the impression of the dance. Examples of what I have in mind include productions of the Dance in America Series, such as the reconstruction of *Western Symphony* in the 1993 production *Balanchine Celebration: Part II,* directed by Matthew Diamond.

In these cases, I suggest that the moving-picture dance reconstruction is best understood as an interpretation of an already existing dance. Perhaps an analogy will be useful here. Just as the performers of a piece of music execute what we call an interpretation of an already existing work, so the moving-picture dance reconstructor, employing her complement of visual resources, makes an interpretation of a preexisting dance or dance performance (which is itself already an interpretation).

The aim of musical performers is to make the musical work accessible to an audience; likewise, the moving-picture dance reconstructor aims at making a preexisting theatrical performance of a dance accessible to an audience by, in effect, showing them how and where to look at a preexisting dance, and how to organize the dance and its important patterns in their temporal experience. In effect, the moving-picture dance reconstruction is an interpretation of an interpretation, where the preexisting performance is itself generally an interpretation of a preexisting dance. Moreover, as there can be many acceptable performative interpretations of the same piece of music, so there can be many different, though acceptable, moving-picture dance reconstructions, each, in turn, making different aspects of the dance accessible to viewers.

In moving-picture dance reconstructions, the dance component and the motion picture component are co-equal in the sense that, though the reconstructor is constrained to be beholden to respecting the identity of the dance in question, the desired result is to render the dance accessible visually (and aurally) in a motion-picture format, thereby requiring that the dance be adjusted to the exigencies of the pertinent motion-picture mode of representation. This will often require interrupting and reorienting the movement of the dance in a battery of takes for maximal camera exposure. Moving-picture dance reconstruction requires a tender balance between the choreographer and the reconstructor, but it is not an impossible one to achieve.

Whereas the reconstructor is involved in remounting a past dance via motion pictures, the moving-picture dance constructor is aiming to produce a new work. To see what I'm getting at, it is useful to begin by recalling the modernist notion of ciné-dance. There the idea was that a ciné-dance is made for the screen, and that the way to test for success is to ask whether the dance could be realizable by theatrical means. Where it is not, that is taken as evidence that a new work has been created, one that relies essentially on the camera for its provenance. So a work like Hilary Harris's *9 Variations on a Dance Theme* (1967) is a paradigmatic ciné-dance in this tradition, since it is supposed that its penetrating geography of the body is not something obviously realizable on stage, dependent as it is on cinematic close-ups and framing.

Now, I have criticized the modernist bias of this conception, arguing that comparable theatrical realizability should not be the test of whether something counts as a moving-picture dance construction. Nevertheless, a piece of the notion of ciné-dance may still be of use to us, namely that such a construction be a new work, one brought into being and shaped by the agency of the resources of the motion picture, such as editing, camera movement, camera placement, special effects, digital processing, motion capture, computer animation, and so on. This does not mean that the moving-picture dance constructor cannot use preexisting dance material, as presumably Hilary Harris did, in the process of constructing something new by cinematic agencies; it only requires that the constructor be attempting to produce a new dance work in the process, rather than documenting or reconstructing one. Speaking of her work with Douglas Rosenberg entitled *De L'Eau* (1995), Li Chiao-Ping put this point nicely when she said that *De L'Eau* was not a translation of a work, but rather was the work.[16]

So the test of whether we have a moving-picture dance construction is whether the constructor intends to produce an autonomous work of art, using either preexisting dance material or dance material expressly composed for interacting with whatever motion picture resources the constructor has at her disposal. On this construal, it makes no difference if a comparable dance work could be realized by other means, such as theatrical ones; what makes the difference is that new work in question was in fact produced through the agency of the motion picture, for example, by cinematic or videographic means. These means, moreover, need not be unique to the relevant medium. Thus, a long-take duo by Astaire and Rogers, composed for the camera, though perhaps in some sense realizable on a stage, still counts as a moving-picture dance construction, because it is a new work, a new dance, brought into existence by the agency of motion pictures. The issue is not whether the new work could have been produced in another artform, like theater, but whether it was brought into existence by the artform of motion pictures.

Earlier I said that with respect to moving-picture dance constructions, the motion picture component is dominant. The sense of "dominance" that I had in mind is that the choreographic ingredients involved, whether designed specifically for the occasion or derived from preexisting material, are not transfigured into an integral, autonomous, original work of art until they are articulated in the idiom, whether—essential or not—of motion pictures.

But then how are we to tell the difference between moving-picture dance reconstructions and moving-picture dance constructions, in cases where the dance construction is employing preexisting dance material? Here we need to consider the artist's intention in producing the work: was she intending to create a new work or to re-interpret an already existing one? In the latter case, we have an instance of reconstruction, whereas in the former case, we are looking at a moving-picture dance construction.

Because of this reliance on authorial intention, it may be imaginable that we could have three perceptually indiscernible moving-picture dances: one a document, one a reconstruction, and one a construction comprised of preexisting dance materials. How do we say which is which? It depends on whether the author intended to make a document or a reconstruction of an existing dance, or whether she intended to make something new, something with different qualities and different significations than any preexisting dance. Is this a problem? I don't think so, since for art in general, it is the creator's intentions that fix the pertinent category of an artwork;[17] and, furthermore, where a constructor intends to create a new artwork, but produces nothing more than what—upon reflection—functions only as a document of a preexisting dance, then, unless (like Warhol with his Brillo Boxes) she is making a reflexive comment, we will say that she has failed to realize her intention to construct a new artwork, which, all things being equal, is a reason to find her moving-picture dance construction unsuccessful.

So far I have defined the genus of moving-picture dance and then further subdivided it into three species, of which the last, the moving-picture dance construction, is undoubtedly the one that we most care about, since it is the source of original artworks in this field. I claim that this is the central concept of motion-picture dance, because most of the work that one will encounter at festivals devoted to this sort of work fall into this genus and, as well, one can expect to find examples of all three of its species on the program. Though, of course, one expects to find more moving-picture dance constructions than the other sorts, nevertheless, when some documentations and reconstructions appear, one is unlikely to hear too much grumbling, since, I submit, all three species coincide roughly with our intuitions about what fits naturally into our field of interest. That is, we all understand why documentations, reconstructions, and constructions have all found their way onto the program.

However, even if my formulations suit the least controversial examples of what concerns us, they do not cover everything. As indicated previously, by invoking the requirement that motion-picture dances be comprised of dance material—however straightforward that makes our scheme of categorization—it fails to accommodate the sorts of ballet mécaniques and nonfigurative movement abstractions that are also often regarded as part of the tradition of moving-picture dance. In order to deal with cases like this, I suggest that we introduce a second, extended (rather than central) concept of moving-picture dance, thereby hypothesizing that our field is really governed by two concepts rather than only one.

That is, the central concept of moving-picture dance needs to be supplemented by the extended concept of moving-picture dance. My suggestion for this second concept is that something is a moving-picture dance in the extended sense if the image component includes a significant amount of movement presented because it is interesting for its own sake.[18] This movement may be of elements inside the frame or it may be an impression of movement generated by technical means, such as editing or special effects, such as pixilation (such as one finds in the work of Pooh Kaye). Where that movement is interesting in its own right, we have a case of moving-picture dance in the extended sense. For in these cases, we are apt to describe the movement as dance-like just because dance is the artform that specializes in the exhibition of movement for its own sake.

This is not all that dance does, of course, but when one is asked which of all the artforms specializes in the exhibition of movement for its own sake, dance seems the likeliest candidate. That is, dance is the preexisting category under which we subsume movement presented because of its intrinsic interest as movement. Consequently, when we encounter a motion picture that exhibits a significant amount of movement in a way that is interesting for its own sake, we are naturally inclined to say that it is dance-like, or, in my terminology, an instance of moving-picture dance in the extended sense.

Here I must hasten to add that a set of movements may not only be interesting for its own sake, but interesting for other reasons as well. Thus, the aerial ballets in Bruce Lee's kung-fu films, what Douglas Rosenberg calls recorporealizations, are narratively interesting at the same time that they are interesting, indeed delightful and compelling, to watch for their own sake. My requirement is simply that the movement be at least interesting for its own sake, but it need not be exclusively so. Because, as well as being interesting for its narrative content, Bruce Lee's martial ciné-choreography is also interesting for its own sake; we can call it a case of moving-picture dance in the extended sense.

Moreover, if we accept the notion of motion picture dance in the extended sense, I think we can deal with the kinds of cases the central concept of motion picture dance leaves out. Ballet mécaniques present nonhuman movements as interesting for their own sake. Abstract movement pieces—such as Doris Chase's—can also be counted as moving-picture dance constructions in the extended sense, where they picture movement that is interesting for its own sake. Even constructions comprised of ordinary movement—such as Amy Greenfield's *Tides* (1982), Elaine Summers' *Iowa Blizzard* (1973), Silvina Szperling's *Bilingual Duetto* (1994), and Ami Skanberg's warm-up *Etude* (1996)— may count as moving-picture dance movement in the extended sense, if the ordinary movement is exhibited in the context of a new artwork in a way that renders it interesting for its own sake.[19]

If we employ these two concepts of moving-picture dance—the central concept and the extended concept—I think that we can assimilate all the cases of dance-relevant motion pictures we want. Is there a problem with employing two concepts to define the field, rather than one? Perhaps some might worry that there is, because they fear that one concept, the central concept, is being implicitly privileged hierarchically over the other. But there is no reason to suppose that this must be the case. It is perfectly consistent with what I've proposed to agree that many moving-picture dances in the extended sense are superior to moving-picture dances more centrally in the category, including moving-picture dance constructions. Indeed, none of my categories are evaluative; they are all classificatory. A well-done moving-picture dance reconstruction can be aesthetically better than a lackluster or inept moving-picture dance construction.

In conclusion, I have developed a family of definitions designed to capture the range of things that I believe we feel intuitively drawn to include in the corpus of what I am now calling moving-picture dance, a label that I believe better encompasses the extension of things that concern us than do the more popular alternatives. Some readers, I know, have genuine reservations about definitional projects like mine because they fear that definitions, like Aristotle's definition of tragedy, have a tendency to turn into prescriptions—attempts by theorists to legislate what will count as art or art of a certain genre, like moving-picture dance. But I do not think that this definitional exercise has been legislative, because the framework I've offered is rather compendious, since even if the central concept limits experiments to dance movement, the extended concept opens it to any kind of movement. This allows that anything can be grist for the artist's mill, so long as it has something to do with the possibility of movement. Can any conception be more liberal? Does anyone wish to include in the category something that has nothing whatsoever to do with movement? And, in any case, my definitions are not overly exclusive from the artistic point of view, since, of course, even if someone makes a work that somehow falls outside my framework, there is no implication in what I've proposed that it cannot be art or that it cannot be of great value.

So what's the problem?

NOTES

1. For instance, to use a political example, certain definitions of what it is to be a human being have long been emancipatory instruments in struggles against racism and sexism.

2. Ed Emshwiller, "Artist's Statement," *Dance Perspectives* 30 (Summer 1967): 25.

3. This argument is developed in Noël Carroll, "Defining the Moving Image," in *Theorizing the Moving Image* (New York: Cambridge University Press, 1996).

4. Douglas Rosenberg, "Recorporealizing the Body Via Screen Dance," a lecture at the Dance for the Camera Symposium, University of Wisconsin–Madison, February 11, 2000.

5. Similar reasoning would pick out Cunningham's *Blue Studio* (1976) as a quintessential video dance, since in the chromakey segments Cunningham, through the agency of video, is able to "dance across" an impossible series of landscapes.

6. For example, the creative geography that is so important in Shirley Clarke's *Dance in the Sun* could be easily duplicated through video.

7. Roger Copeland, "The Limitations of Cine-Dance," in *Filmdance: 1890's–1983* (New York: Filmdance Festival, 1983), p. 11.

8. André Bazin was an influential French film theorist of the nineteen-forties and fifties who advocated the use of long-take, deep-focused shots—shots that allow the spectator's eye to rove across the image. Such shots approximate the conditions of seeing in real space and time, rather than breaking events apart by editing. Bazin defended this style in the name of realism. But clearly the kind of reliance on blocking in the single shot that he preferred could also be replicated in theater. See André Bazin, *What Is Cinema?* (Berkeley: University of California Press, 1971), Vol. I.

9. Jacques Tati was a French filmmaker who specialized in comedies—such as *Playtime*—of everyday life, finding humor in its mundane events. One could say that he isolated comic moments in the stream of daily living, plucking laughs out of the quotidian. He also employed Bazinian techniques to this end, encouraging viewers to discover comic interactions in scenes, much as we find Waldo in the games of the same name. Woodberry's *Invisible Dance* shares a congruent sensibility, staging bursts of dance activity amidst the rush of Wall Street lunch breaks, and inviting us to find pre-staged dance moments in the seams and on the margins of the workaday hustle and bustle.

10. N.B. Amy Greenfield made a film of *101*, though since I have unfortunately not seen it, I cannot say how still it actually is.

11. Richard Lorber, "Experiments in Videodance," *Dance Scope* 12, 1 (Fall/Winter, 1977/78): 8.

12. For further discussion of this historical approach (with respect to the issue of identifying

art in general), see Noël Carroll, *Philosophy of Art: A Contemporary Introduction* (London: Routledge, 1999), Chapter Five, pp. 249–264. Also, see the suggested readings at the end of that chapter for more references.

13. For a defense of this view of pictures, see Noël Carroll, "The Power of Movies," in *Theorizing the Moving Image,* pp. 75–93.

14. Abstractly, there is a fourth possible permutation here: where the dance element and the motion picture element have nothing at all to do with each other. But if they have literally nothing to do with each other, then we are not dealing with a case of hybridization, but, rather, with two numerically independent works. Consequently, this possibility will never be realized literally in any moving-picture dance, where dance and image are physically imprinted in one object, and, therefore, should be of no concern to us.

15. In order to avoid terminological confusion here, let me emphasize that by "reconstruction" I am talking about reconstructions of existing dances by means of moving-picture technologies; I am not referring to things like Millicent Hodson's 1987 reconstruction of *Le Sacre du printemps* for the stage.

16. Li Chiao-Ping, "The Director/Choreographer Dialectic," Dance for the Camera Symposium, University of Wisconsin–Madison, February 10, 2000.

17. Jerrold Levinson, *The Pleasures of Aesthetics* (Ithaca, N.Y.: Cornell University Press, 1996), p. 188.

18. We will say that movement is interesting for its own sake, at least if the movement itself, apart from whatever other functions it performs, is delightful, arresting, fascinating, pleasurable, compelling, or riveting to look at (as movement), or because it is stimulating to think about (as movement), perhaps for theoretical reasons. Admittedly, this does not supply us with a definition of what it is for movement to be interesting for its own sake, but it should give the reader an idea of the relevant ballpark.

19. Though the central concept of moving-picture dance is comprised of three species, I suspect that, when it comes to the extended concept, we are only dealing with the category of constructions. That is, I do not think that people are usually inclined to count documents of non-dance movements or even motion picture reconstructions thereof as moving-picture dance, even in the extended sense. The temptation only arises where the moving-picture dance work in question has some claim to being an autonomous, movement artwork. Some evidence for this is that one does not usually find such movement documents or reconstructions included in festivals for or catalogues of moving-picture dance works.

Chapter 12 The Essence of Cinema?

Gregory Currie's *Image and Mind: Film, Philosophy and Cognitive Science*[1] is a major event in the study of film. It represents the first thoroughgoing philosophy of film in the analytic tradition. Covering such topics as the essence of cinema, the nature of representation in film, the relation of film to language, the nature of the spectator's imaginative involvement in film, and problems of film narration and interpretation, the book addresses a gamut of classical questions of film theory and answers them, often in surprising ways, from a perspective richly informed by Currie's impressive grasp of the philosophy of mind and the philosophy of language. Even if one disagrees with Currie's solutions to various problems, one can only appreciate the way in which he has raised the level of analysis and argument in the area of film theory.

I stress the singular importance of this book, since this session is called *Author meets Critics.* However, though I will raise some questions about the details of *Image and Mind,* I would not want to leave anyone with the impression that my admiration for it is anything less than wholehearted.

Like any philosophical achievement, *Image and Mind* is open to dispute. What is perhaps surprising about this book is that on so many topics it seems definitive. This makes the task of an official *critic* somewhat difficult. Nevertheless, I have found one area where I can quibble with some of Currie's findings. Thus, for the remainder of this essay I will talk about Currie's characterization of the essence of cinema.

Currie begins *Image and Mind* with a discussion of the essence of cinema. By essence, Currie seems to mean common features that mark things as films rather than something else.[2] But I'm not sure that I am always following this discussion correctly, since, at times, it seems to me that Currie says he's after the essence of cinema, and at other times, he indicates that his account is stipulative.[3] Also, at still other times, Currie appears to take back parts of his account of the essence of cinema. For example, he says that cinema is an essentially pictorial medium, while agreeing that it also contains nonpictorial representations, like words. But then what are we to make of whole films composed of nothing but words or numbers?

As I understand him, Currie maintains that essentially films are representations, specifically pictorial representations, specifically moving pictures. I take it that Currie thinks that these are no more than necessary conditions, since these conditions would not differentiate film from much video or even flip books. Because of this, I'm a bit uncertain as to why Currie insists on talking about the essence of cinema, rather than that of motion pictures. Nevertheless, film is how he labels his topic.

Currie says: "Film is a representational medium" and that "film is a pictorial medium; it gives us—exactly—moving pictures."[4] Thus, I surmise that for Currie, x is a film only if it is 1) a moving 2) pictorial 3) representation. However, I question whether any of these conditions is a necessary condition for film. If one looks at some of the standard texts in film history, one can easily find counterexamples to the assertion that film is necessarily representational as well as to the claim that it is pictorial.

If we understand by a representation something that is intended to stand in for something else, then there are many films that are not representational. One entire genre of this sort is the flicker film—films that alternate clear and opaque leader (and/or colored leader) in order to present a stroboscopic effect to audiences. Two famous examples of this sort of film are Peter Kubelka's *Arnulf Rainer*—made between 1958 and 1960—and Tony Conrad's *The Flicker*, made in 1966. These films do not represent anything. Rather, they *present* visual stimulation to audiences with the intention of eliciting certain perceptual states—like afterimages—from spectators.

Created in the spirit of high modernism, these films were thought to reveal certain of the conditions of film viewing. "Flicks" or "Flickers," you'll recall, were once generic nicknames for films. So, these films were said to provide opportunities for viewers to come to understand something about the generic nature of film. And, in a less exalted vein, in the sixties, people also attempted to use flicker films to induce or to accompany hallucinogenic experiences.

The frames in a flicker film need not and most frequently do not contain representations of anything. The films are generally pure, nonreferential, visual stimulation. They do not represent. They present light at a certain pulse. When I was studying filmmaking at New York University, making flicker films was a standard exercise for mastering film rhythm. Moreover, flicker films are printed photographically for distribution and projection in the same fashion that *The English Patient* is.

In some respects, flicker films are analogous to what was called Op-Art. Both flicker films and Op-Art are predicated upon toying with the spectator's perceptual apparatus directly rather than via "mediated" representations. Furthermore, just as one would expect an analytical characterization of painting not to exclude Op-Art by definition, it seems problematic to me to exclude flicker films from the corpus of cinema in this manner. An additional problem with ignoring flicker effects is that they are sometimes incorporated in commercial films, as in the title sequence of *A Clockwork Orange,* not to mention music videos (which are frequently filmed). Similarly, the flicker genre is not the only film genre that is not representational. There are also scratch films which may be printed photographically for distribution.

A film like Tony Conrad's *The Flicker* not only raises problems for Currie's assertion that films are essentially representational, but also for the claim that they are essentially pictorial. By "picture," Currie means a visual array whose referent can be recognized simply by looking. A shot of a horse is pictorial inasmuch as I can recognize that it is a representation of a horse simply by looking, sans any subtending processes of reading, inferring or decoding. Currie says that cinema trades essentially in pictorial representations. But if this means that all films are necessarily pictorial, then Currie's characterization excludes the rich history of abstract filmmaking from the order of cinema, since such films do not possess recognizable referents.

Abstract filmmaking emerged as early as the 1920s with works like Walter Ruttman's *Lichtspiel* and Viking Eggeling's *Diagonal Symphonie.* Since the twenties, abstract films have been made by Harry Smith, Douglas Crockwell, Marie Menken, Mary Ellen Bute, Norman McClaren, John and James Whitney, Dieter Rot, Jordan Belson, Stan Brakhage, Derek Jarman, and many others. John Whitney's *Permutations* and Len Lye's 1952 *Force Radicals* are two of many examples here.

Admittedly, abstract filmmaking is not the tradition with which most people are familiar. But it is a continuous tradition, it has a position in film history books, it sometimes surfaces in the commercial tradition (e.g., the Star Gate sequence in *2001*), and it has obvious affinities with modernist art in other visual media including painting, sculpture and photography. Just as one would not discount Brancusi's *Bird in Flight* as sculpture on the grounds that it is nonpictorial (nonverisimilitudinous) and abstract, it seems equally questionable to me to frame an account of the essence of cinema that fails to include something like Brakhage's *Text of Light*. Would we accept an analysis of the essence of painting that failed to acknowledge most modern art on the grounds that it was abstract rather than pictorial?

Currie maintains that his characterization of the essence of cinema is descriptive rather than prescriptive. However, since his account excludes significant portions of avant-garde filmmaking, it seems that his view is inadvertently prescriptive or value-laden, proposing the common viewer's preference for moving *pictures* as a characterization of the essence of film.

Yet the aims of abstract filmmakers—their concern with visual rhythm and explorations of visual experience—are recognized as essential projects in media other than film. Indeed, like certain abstractionists in other media, many abstract filmmakers can be also correctly interpreted as raising questions about the essence of their medium by means of film. We don't disenfranchise such abstract/reflexive aspirations in other media. Isn't it arbitrary to rule them out of the history of film by definition?

Currie admits that films contain more than pictures. He takes note of subtitles and intertitles.[5] So he concedes that *parts* of films may be nonpictorial. However, I think that he does not appreciate where this concession will lead, since there are whole films that are comprised of nothing but words and numerals. Michael Snow's *So Is This* is a film of sentences; Takahiko Iimura's *1 in 10* is a film of addition and subtraction tables. Nor are such examples only of recent vintage; Len Lye's *A Colour Box* was made in 1935. Moreover, it is not the case that we can only find examples here in the avant-garde traditions. There are movie trailers that are all words, as well as advertisements, filmed for TV, that are made up of nothing but sentences.

Such works are created and projected by means of standard filmmaking processes. They are photographed and printed. The avant-garde examples, furthermore, are intelligible contributions to reigning filmworld discussions—about semiotics (and shifters), in the case of *So Is This,* and about structural film, in the case of *1 in 10.* In the tradition of film modernism, these films use the medium to raise questions reflexively about the nature of the medium. I see no reason to deny that they are films. What else would they be? But if films are necessarily pictorial, as Currie maintains, then these are not films.

Films like these may also raise another problem with Currie's conception of the essence of film, since these films are static. They are not moving pictures because they are not *moving* anythings, at least as far as the eye can detect. Nor are these the only examples of static films. Others include: Oshima's *Band of Ninjas* (a film of a comic strip); Michael Snow's *One Second in Montreal* (a film of photos); Hollis Frampton's *Poetic Justice* (a film of tabletop on which we see pages of a shooting script); and Godard and Gorin's infamous *Letter to Jane* (another film of photos). These are all films in the sense that they were constructed and disseminated by means of standard film apparatuses. They command a significant place in film history where the question of "What is film?" is part of an ongoing conversation internal to the filmworld—one addressed by filmmakers and theorists alike.

Moreover, these films use stasis as a stylistic choice. It is the fact that they are films that makes their stillness a pertinent, if not *the* pertinent, feature of the works in question. Had these films been slides, one would not remark upon their stillness. Movement is not a stylistic option with slides. But since these works are films, one is prompted to ask why there is no movement in them. What is the point? Any interpretation of these works has to offer an explanation of why the filmmakers under consideration have eschewed the possibility of movement. But if they were not films but something else, like photos or slides, this question simply wouldn't arise. Stillness is an integral stylistic feature of these works, one that is crucial to a correct interpretation and appreciation of them. If they are not categorized as films, but as de facto slides or photos, this property, as a significant property of the works in question, disappears. Thus, from the perspective of appreciation, it seems to me ill-advised to discount these works as films.

The point of many *still* films is reflexive—to point to aspects or elements of film that are often neglected (like narration in the case of Oshima or scripting in the case of Frampton). Subtracting movement from the visual array is a way of leading viewers—or at least certain kinds of viewers—to these reflexive observations. A concern with reflexive questions is part of what Currie elsewhere calls the "heuristic pathway" of such works. These concerns are evident in the history of filmmaking as early as the nineteen twenties. Likewise these films are produced and distributed by means of standard filmmaking processes. So, once again, I see little reason to suppose that these are not part of the history of filmmaking. Indeed, some though not I, might claim that these are examples of what was once called *essential* cinema inasmuch as they are experiments toward establishing the minimal requirements for something to count as a film.

I must concede that I may be being too hard on Currie in accusing him of making movement a necessary condition of film. In at least one place, he may be indicating that it need not be. In his stipulative characterization of films, he says "they are produced by photographic means and delivered onto a surface so as to produce or *be capable of producing,* an apparently moving image."[6] If the caveat "or be capable of producing" allows that the images may be static and that entire films can be static, then my preceding objections are misplaced. But since Currie never clarifies why he has added this talk about capabilities, I will let my objections stand until I hear otherwise.

Of course, if Currie does mean this talk of capabilities to accommodate works like *Poetic Justice,* then I have no substantive quarrel with him. This seems the right way to go—to refrain from claiming movement to be a necessary feature of film, but only to require that the relevant imagery be produced in a medium with the capacity to deliver movement.[7] Thus my only criticism of Currie here might turn out to be nothing more than a reader's request that he had been more forthcoming on this issue. On the other hand, since he doesn't raise the issue of static films, I'm not sure he takes it seriously, whereas I think he should.

I have interpreted Currie's view as maintaining that films are necessarily moving pictorial representations. However, at certain points, he indicates that his bottom line is that films are essentially visual. I am not completely certain about what this is meant to signal. But it did at least make me wonder about whether or not Currie would countenance the possibility of invisible films? There are some films that nearly approach this limit—like Brakhage's *Fire of Waters* (a night scene occasionally streaked by brief flashes of lightning[?]). And there are parts of films—such as the opening of Frampton's *Zorn's Lemma*—without any images. Likewise Guy Debord's 1952 film *Screams in Favour of de Sade* is almost completely black, save for a few bursts of white light.[8] But, even more radically, I conjecture that it might even be possible to make a completely invisible film.

Here is one scenario; there could be others. Imagine a modernist filmmaker who has been impressed by the history of solid black paintings. He makes an underexposed film that looks absolutely pitch black in a standard screening room.[9] On the soundtrack, he talks about how half the time we watch any film, the screen is literally dark. His work is meant to draw our attention to this fact. Perhaps he is a bit of an expressionist—he calls his film "The Darkness of Cinema." Or, he is Duchampian—he calls it "The Ultimate *Film Noir*." Would this be a film? My inclination is to say *yes* as long as it was made by cinematic means and it is part of an intelligible, ongoing filmworld conversation. Is this a counterexample to Currie's assertion that films are essentially visual? Maybe in his response, he will address this question.

By way of conclusion, I must confess that I realize that many readers may be of the opinion that I've been ragging Currie's account of the essence of cinema with marginal and irrelevant examples, drawn primarily from the history of the avant-garde. Perhaps some of you are tempted to say—"That stuff isn't really film." But that's the issue, and the point of my comment. Had Currie simply said that he meant to be talking about how films typically are, there would be little merit in disputing with him at such length. But he proposes to speak of the essence of cinema.

Instead, I would argue that he has only talked about certain types of cinema, albeit the most popular kinds. This belies a certain bias, frequent among film theorists, which compromises their attempts to be genuinely descriptive. With respect to the philosophy of art, we have learnt that often proposals concerning the essence of art turn out covertly to "privilege" certain kinds of art at the expense of other sorts. I worry that Currie's de facto disenfranchisement of much of the history of avant-garde film may also have this kind of untoward effect. And that would be unfortunate given the marvelous job he has done otherwise in founding an analytic philosophy of film.

APPENDIX

In response to the criticisms I made of Gregory Currie's account of the essence of cinema, Currie has argued that inasmuch as many of my counterexamples are abstract films, they should not be taken seriously, since "film, in its standard mode of production, is essentially representational; to take a film image of something is to make a representation of it."[10] That is, Currie, I presume, does not regard the history of abstract film as part of film history. For Currie, film, properly so called, is photographic film. Photography and photographically based cinematography are a distinctive form of representation, one based upon making traces of the objects before the camera. Abstract cinema putatively falls outside this category.

This is literally false, even on Currie's terms. Abstract films, such as scratch films, flicker films, or films made by inscribing images directly onto the film stock, are typically printed by a process of photographic duplication. Thus, virtually all abstract films to date involve photography, if only during the printing process. Of course, these prints do not represent the original; they are tokens of the type. Nevertheless, these prints are photographic and so should be countenanced by Currie as legitimate counterexamples to his theory.

This reply, of course, grants Currie the prerogative to gerrymander the concept of film so that it pertains to all and only photographic representations. But this is not an acceptable move. Many of the images in *Attack of the Clones* and *Spy Kids 2* are computer generated, but no one hesitates to call them film images. In the future we are likely to see entire films that have been computer generated. The recent feature film *Simone* predicts the advent of computer-generated film stars, a prospect to gladden the hearts of many a producer. I suspect that if such films look sufficiently like photographically produced films, everyone will be happy to call them movies. For movies are, first and foremost, the product of the art of using realistically looking, moving images to tell stories. How those images are derived is less germane to the relevant concept than the function they discharge.

Nor are computer-generated images the only exceptions to Currie's identification of film images with photographic representations. In films prior to CGI, there were shots that were not, strictly speaking, photographic representations in Currie's sense. In *Destination Moon,* there is a pan of the moonscape which is really of a series of painted pictures. It is not a photographic trace of any existing place. It is an image of an image, though not a representation of an image. So even in the case of more traditional films, not all film images are photographic representations in the sense of trace-representations.

Currie is very impressed by standard photographic representation because it is so distinct from other forms of pictorial representation, like painting. Typically, this sort of photographic representation is largely an affair of physical causation—the camera, suitably focused, will reproduce a trace of whatever is in front of it, once it is turned on. Paint brushes and pencils don't behave that way. And this is an interesting fact. However, I do not think that being impressed by what is unique about standard photographic representation should allow Currie to maintain that all film images are of this sort. Many are. In the past, most were. In the future, with the resources of CGI, what the proportion will be is up for grabs.

Photographic representation, though an immensely interesting phenomenon, cannot be regarded as the essence of cinema. To assert, as Currie does, that to take a film image of something is to make a representation of it is to beg the question. As film history is characteristically understood, abstract films are films, sometimes even influencing the photographically representational cinema. Thus, they would appear to be genuine counterexamples to Currie's theory.

Moreover, there is no reason to think that cinema had to take the direction it did in terms of photographic representation. One could at least imagine film evolving as a vehicle for delivering the printed word. People might never have thought to turn their cameras on people, places, things, and events, but rather might have used them to photograph words that were then projected onto billboards. After all, the idea of television was initially thought up as a way of electronically transmitting words over long distances like oceans. Film might have evolved as a form of printing with light; photographic representation was not the metaphysically necessary destiny of film technology. It is a use—undoubtedly the most popular use—of film; but there are other uses, such as abstraction, and these have an equal claim to the title of "film," even if they are the routes less traveled.[11]

Currie not only questions my invocation of abstract films as counterexamples, but also my use of films that are exclusively made up of images of words, rather than of pictures of people, places, and things. He points out that often printed or written words in films have a pictorial aspect. Think of the graphics in many Soviet Constructivist films or in Murnau's *Sunrise.* Currie is certainly right that words on film can have a pictorial dimension. But this misses the point, since there can be films composed entirely of words with no pictorial dimension, such as Michael Snow's *So Is This.* Thus, *pace* Currie, films are not necessarily pictorial.

NOTES

1. Gregory Currie, *Image and Mind: Film, Philosophy and Cognitive Science* (Cambridge: Cambridge University Press, 1996).
2. Ibid., 1.
3. Ibid., 4.
4. Ibid., 2.
5. Ibid., 7.
6. Ibid., 4 (*emphasis added*).
7. For further discussion of this issue, see Noël Carroll, "Defining the Moving Image," in my *Theorizing the Moving Image* (Cambridge: Cambridge University Press, 1996).
8. Also, the filmmaker Alain Resnais has said that he has always dreamt of making a film comprised only of a sound track.

9. Derek Jarman's film *Blue* is just that—the screen is blue, with no images, throughout its duration, accompanied by a sound track. What I am imagining is a film like Jarman's, only all black.

For an actual example of an invisible film, consider *L'Anticoncept* by Gil Wolman. This is a film of which each identical frame has a matching, transparent, perfect circle set on an opaque field of black. The film was projected at a helium balloon at midday in September of 1951 at the *Musée de l'Homme*. The clear circular image was flush with the contour of the balloon. Thus, when this film is projected as intended, it is invisible to the naked eye. This film was screened at the Queens Museum of Art, NYC 28 April–29 August 1999. For documentation, see: *Global Conceptualism: Points of Origin, 1950s–1980s* (New York: Queens Museum of Art, 1999), pp. 31, 32, 261.

10. Gregory Currie, "Reply to My Critics," *Philosophical Studies* 89 (1998), p. 356.

11. Against counting abstract cinema as part of cinema, Currie also offers the following argument. "If you want a painterly analogy with the work of an abstract filmmaker, I think it would be this: suppose someone found that by taking a canvas prepared for painting and *setting fire to it,* you could produce an artistically interesting effect. . . . While this new mode of art-production, which I shall call pyro-painting, might have its value, I am not persuaded that a student of painting proper ought so to develop his theory that it accounts for pyro-painting along side the more conventional forms. And I say the same thing about the relation between representational film and abstract film in the strict sense of the term" (Currie, "Reply to my Critics," p. 357).

But then what does Currie make of the fact that Yves Klein burnt canvases in the way he, Currie, suggests and that these works are regarded as a significant recent contribution to the history—if not of painting per se—then the history of marking surfaces, as that category, which is the pertinent one for art historians, includes media other than oil paints (i.e., the history of *painting,* as that term is typically used, is obviously broader than oil paint, since it includes many other media including tempera, pastels, etc.)?

Chapter 13 TV and Film:

A Philosophical Perspective

As film emerged as one of the dominant media of the twentieth century, critics often challenged its artistic credentials by alleging that it was nothing more than "canned theater"—not an autonomous artform, but merely surrogate theater served up in celluloid. As a result, film theorists spilled a great deal of ink trying to prove that the medium of film is *essentially* different from that of theater and that, in consequence, the possibility that film could be an artform—with equal standing as regards not only theater, but with respect, as well, to its other five sister arts—had to be acknowledged. Undoubtedly, this theoretical debate was underwritten by the fact that film and theater were economic competitors for the same audiences. But whatever its material motivation, the debate was conducted in the philosophical idiom of essential differentiae rather than in terms of more lowly considerations, such as product differentiation.

Similarly, the appearance of television (henceforth referred to as "TV") engendered comparable anxieties of influence. Theoretical spokespersons for the new medium were at pains to differentiate

TV from film—to show that TV was not just an ersatz form of cinema. TV, it was claimed, had its own unique features, features distinct from those of cinema, which, at least in principle, opened up the possibility of an autonomous art of TV. As in the debate about theater and film, this discussion was frequently cast in terms of essential or ontological distinctions. And, of course, the Film/TV debate was probably, in part, also motivated economically by the fact that the two media were in competition for roughly the same audiences. Thus, throughout its history, ontological speculation about the essential differences between film and TV has had a certain pragmatic urgency.

In this essay, I intend to review some of the leading proposals concerning the putative ontological differences between TV and film. I will then go on to attempt to undermine these alleged distinctions, generally arguing that they are based on too narrow a conception of TV (and sometimes of film). Specifically, the recurring problem is that these supposed distinctions are most frequently extrapolated by focusing on too small a sample of TV—by focusing exclusively on TV of a certain vintage (both in terms of dated technological possibilities and presentational formats) or by taking certain TV genres to stand for the whole of TV. Once one takes a broader view of the possibilities of TV, I maintain, the philosophical difference between film and TV, construed as a matter of contrasting essential characteristics, disappears. That is, I do not deny that there are differences between TV of a certain vintage and level of technological development, and comparable films, but I do deny that these historical differences amount to ontological or essential distinctions. Finally, I will conclude on a positive note, proposing that the history of film and TV is best understood as a single process, the evolution of the *moving image,* a mode of communication and expression that can be implemented cinematically, videographically, digitally, and/or in ways of which we have still to conceive.

COMMONLY CITED DIFFERENCES
BETWEEN FILM AND TV

Perhaps one of the most famous attempts to distinguish film and TV is Marshall McLuhan's suggestion that film is a hot medium whereas TV is a cool medium. A hot medium, for McLuhan, is one that is full of information and that, as a result, is relatively self-sufficient in the sense that the audience need not actively add that much to an instance of a hot medium in order to process it. A cool medium, in contrast, is more interactive; it requires audience participation to fill in or to complete particular instances. Apparently, for McLuhan

TV is a cool medium because of the low resolution of the TV image. Compared to the film image, the TV image is, informationally, less dense—standardly involving only about 480 scan lines—and this supposedly requires viewers to "complete" it. So for McLuhan at least, due to the difference in image resolution between the film image and the TV image, there is also a related difference in the nature of film spectatorship versus TV spectatorship.

Though many contemporary TV theorists part company with McLuhan's diagnosis of TV spectatorship—preferring to describe it as distracted rather than active—they continue to share McLuhan's emphasis on the low resolution of the TV image.[1] They contend that due to the greater fidelity and resolution of the film image, in addition to its larger scale, cinema elicits the rapt attention of its audiences, whereas the TV image commands less attention visually. We are not riveted to the TV image in the way that we are riveted to the film image. Some theorists attempt to mark this distinction by saying that the film image engages the *gaze* (rapt, unwavering attention), whereas the TV image elicits the *glance* (we look intermittently at the TV image, our attention often wandering distractedly from the TV set to some household event).

This distinction between the gaze and the glance is also reinforced by the fact that paradigmatically we watch films in darkened theaters where the only thing to attend to is the enormous, imposing, brightly lit screen, while we watch a diminutive TV image at home, often in a well-lit room, where all sorts of domestic affairs may divert our attention.

Those who describe TV viewing in terms of the glance implicitly analogize watching TV to one very frequent way of attending to the radio—you do it while also doing something else. Just as you fold the laundry, or do your homework while listening to the radio, one watches TV, perhaps a soap opera, looking up only intermittently (glancing), between matching your socks or eating dinner. Like radio shows of yesteryear, you can follow a TV show distractedly; it is structured to permit you to pursue distraitly other activities at the same time.

Undoubtedly, to the extent that the notion of the glance describes a frequent mode of TV viewing, this behavior can be attributed in large measure to socially contingent practices of TV viewing and not exclusively to intrinsic properties of the TV image in contradistinction to the film image. However, the contemporary TV theorist is apt to maintain that the phenomenon of the glance with respect to TV is overdetermined, since the tendency to glance rather than to gaze is significantly abetted by the low resolution of the TV image. If it were sharper (and if it were larger), it would not permit us to look away from it so easily; if the image were more commanding, it would not readily fa-

cilitate divided attention. Instead, our attention would be absorbed (as it is alleged to be with respect to the film image) rather than distracted (or dis-
tractable). Thus, the glance/gaze distinction is not merely a social artifact, but
is built into the nature of TV (versus film) at the level of image resolution.

Connected to the low resolution and small scale of the TV image versus the
film image is another difference: the scenography of film images, it is said, tend
to be highly detailed and elaborate, whereas TV imagery is minimal. TV imagery is reputed to be minimal, in turn, because it makes no sense to create
elaborate *mise-en-scènes* in TV, since, given the small scale of the screen and its
low resolution, no one could really see and appreciate much detail anyway.
Complex scenography, in other words, serves no purpose in TV, insofar as it is
effectively invisible. TV scenography does not aspire to realism because that
would be pointless. Thus, the logo in the TV newsroom is made of cardboard,
since, due to the low resolution of the TV image, there is little or no perceptible
difference between a cardboard logo versus one sculpted of stone.

Moreover, it is not only TV folk who allude to the difference in detail between the scenography of TV versus film. In the fifties, when film producers
feared competition from TV, they opted for ornate spectacles exactly because
they thought that visual cornucopias—casts of thousands and the like—were
something that film could provide but TV couldn't, given its very nature (its
low resolution and small-scale image). And, using pretty much the same reasoning, some TV theorists have maintained that the close-up is the natural shot
for TV, whereas the medium long shot suits cinema best. The Battle of the
Bulge looks better on film, framed in long shots of columns of armored battal-
ions, while the talking-head suits the small, low-resolution image of TV.

Indeed, some theorists of TV go so far as to maintain that the TV image is so
impoverished that sound, most notably talking, is the primary lever of attention in TV, whereas the image track is the primary lever of attention in film.
Talk calls the TV viewer's roving eye back to the TV screen, and incessant talk
is used to make sense of the image. A laugh track is used in TV, but not in
movies, in order to hold the audience's attention, while non-stop commentary
suffuses televised sporting events not only because the image track is not powerful enough to bind attention, but to supplement the informational inade-
quacies of the image track. So much TV is talk-TV, dominated by talking-
heads, because the image alone would soon spend the audience's interest.

Apart from the alleged differences between the cinematic and the televisual
image, another distinction is often drawn between the two media in terms of
TV's capacity to broadcast events as they occur. TV can show us a president's

denial of an extramarital affair as soon as he utters is, whereas film must show us the event after the fact, since the film strip must, at the very minimum, be developed chemically before it can be screened. TV, in contrast, at least has the capacity to show us events simultaneous with their occurrence. Of course, not all TV is a matter of simultaneous broadcast. However, some theorists contend that because of its connection with the possibility of simultaneous broadcast, TV imparts the impression (or illusion) of immediacy. That is, phenomenologically, TV strikes viewers as unfolding before them spontaneously. Film, contrariwise, strikes viewers as always a recording of a past event. TV is always, so to speak, in the present tense, while film is always in the past tense.

Further distinctions between film and TV are also charted in terms of the putatively alternative forms of narrative address of the two media. The narrative film is served up in one fully integrated, uninterrupted showing. TV narratives are shown in segments, interrupted often by advertisements. Thus, what one attends to in film is, roughly speaking, the representation of an integrated event (or a series of thematically integrated events), whereas what one watches on TV is the *flow* of disparate events—fragments of love stories interspersed with car advertisements and network coming attractions. This, of course, makes glancing to and away from the TV a very attractive strategy.

Also, it is said, the standard unit of film narration is closed (i.e., marked by closure). It presents a single story, one which poses various questions to the audience—will the lovers get married or not?—which questions are answered (decisively closed) in a single sitting. One film = one story, told from start to finish without remainder during one screening. The standard narrative unit in TV, on the other hand, is the series—the sit-com or the soap—which is an ongoing story, told in serial fashion from week to week. So whereas the film narrative is fully integrated (uninterrupted) and closed, the TV narrative is segmented and serial (open).

Like the segmented nature of TV narration, it is thought that the serial nature of TV narration also contributes to the phenomenon of flow. Different episodes of a serial, like *Sex and the City, Mad About You,* or *South Park,* flow past the viewer's attention amidst the sea of segments of disparate material without ultimate closure. Each episode ends with an implicit "to be continued" and in that sense is potentially a never-ending story. And insofar as the serial structure of TV narratives contributes to the "flow" effect, seriality reinforces the spectatorial strategy of the glance, since the viewer need not worry about missing anything irretrievably decisive. She knows that the story will just keep going on and on in roughly the same way.[2]

In summary, then, there are at least these commonly cited essential differences between TV and film: TV has an impoverished image (marked by low resolution and small scale) versus film's informationally dense imagery; the TV image is less detailed, whereas the film image is elaborate; in TV talk is dominant, while in film the image is dominant; TV elicits the glance, but film engenders the gaze; TV is in the present tense, whereas film is in the past tense; TV narration is segmented and serial, but film narration is uninterrupted and closed; and, given the previous distinction, the object of attention in TV is the flow of programming, while the object of attention in film is the individual, integrated, closed story (the freestanding feature film).[3]

Moreover, some of these alleged differences can be amalgamated in functionally interrelated ensembles: the low resolution, small scale, scenographically impoverished, talk-dominated TV image in concert with the segmented, serial forms of TV narration dispose the TV spectator to the glance as her natural viewing strategy, whereas, in bold contrast, the high-resolution, large-scale, detailed, pictorially dominated film image in concert with integrated, closed film narrative structures dispose the moviegoer to the gaze.

This is an impressive list of distinctions. We must now turn to the question of whether it is also persuasive.

DENYING THE DIFFERENCES

Though theorists are frequently concerned to find sharp distinctions between film and TV, it should be obvious that the majority of the practitioners of those media are not, in general, similarly obsessed. That in practice TV blurs into cinema should be evident, since so much of TV's product is made up of movies. Since the 1950s, movies have been a staple on TV. As a child I did most of my movie "going" via TV, on programs like *Million Dollar Movie, Movie of the Week,* and the like. Nor has this tendency in TV programming abated with time: a large proportion not only of network TV, but of cable and satellite (Direct TV) are movies. Most of the items one can purchase from pay-per-view TV are, of course, movies. That is, a striking proportion of the "software" that runs on the TV "hardware" is comprised of film.

Furthermore, this is not only the case in the United States. In Bombay, movies are the mainstay on most TV channels, where programming primarily consists not only of screening movies, but of shows devoted to previews of movies and interviews with filmmakers, especially stars. In the United States, as well, movies even supply subject matter for news programs; the *Phantom Men-*

ace became almost as much a TV event as it was a film event. Moreover, a great many TV programs themselves are shot on film and have been for some time.

If TV practitioners do not, in general, seem overly concerned with drawing a sharp distinction between movies and TV, neither do film producers. Film producers regard TV as part of the established distribution system of cinema. If in years gone by Hollywood released films in waves to first-run houses, then second-run and third-run houses, including drive-ins, today that strategy has been reconfigured so that first films appear on movie screens, then on pay-per-view TV, then on cable, then on video-cassette, then on network TV and so forth. That is, TV is accepted as an indispensable part of the distribution network for films today, and this even influences the look and structure of contemporary cinema. Where theorists think in terms of distinctions between film and TV, practitioners think in terms of what they call "synergy."

This, of course, does not show that theorists are wrong to attempt to locate essential differences between film and TV. At best, it gives us pause for thought. But in that "pause," we need to reconsider whether the considerations enumerated in the previous section are really compelling.

One frequently adduced distinction between film and TV revolves around the issue of image quality. Undeniably, in the past it has been true that the TV image has had less definition than film images. But this is an issue of technological development, not ontology. At present, the technical wherewithal for HDTV (high-definition television) is available. Instead of 480 scan lines, HDTV is likely to have 720 scan lines, and even 1,080 are technically, though perhaps not economically, feasible today. HDTV involves a digital TV transmission, and it can obtain a roughly comparable image clarity to that of a theatrical film. Some experts claim that the quality of HDTV imagery can be virtually indiscernible from film imagery.

Perhaps some theorists will balk at the qualifier "virtually" in these claims, maintaining that it allows that there may be some perceptible difference between the film image and that of HDTV. However, inasmuch as the low resolution of the TV image is said to be a condition for eliciting the glance rather than the gaze from spectators, the possibility of virtual indiscernibility is enough to warrant the conjecture that TV imagery can command audience attention with roughly the same visual authority as the film image does—that there is no reason to think that TV cannot, in principle, elicit the so-called gaze from viewers.

Admittedly, there is some dispute over whether HDTV is the wave of the future. For example, will audiences be willing to pay for it? However, insofar as our concern is with ontology, it should be clear that the issue of image resolution is a technical one, not a philosophical one. High-definition television is possible, an HDTV image is a TV image, and, therefore, image resolution does not mark an essential or necessary difference between film and TV.

Related to image resolution is the question of image scale. Traditionally the TV image has been much smaller than theatrical film images. The TV image is usually smaller than the normal viewer (discounting infants watching *Teletubbies*), whereas the standard film screen is much larger than the viewer. But this, like image resolution, is a contingent, technological matter. Larger TV screens, like Advent screens, are common (often in bars in the United States), and still larger ones are feasible which, if married to HDTV, would permit TV images as imposing and as "gaze-provoking" as typical film images.

Indeed, there is also convergence between film and TV from the cinema side of things, since plans are afoot to replace existing film projection in theaters with digitally transmitted satellite feeds, thereby reducing to nil any principled difference between future direct-HDTV and film.

Likewise, some commercially released films—such as the Danish *The Celebration* and the documentary *The Cruise*—have been shot on digital video, suggesting that in the future the distinction between film and TV could disappear altogether, it being a matter of effective indifference whether a digital image is shown in a movie theater, on TV, or on the Internet (where there is already a Digital Film Festival at www.dfilm.com).

But, in any case, it should be clear that with regard to image resolution and screen size—two variables often cited as perceptual preconditions for the unique form of TV spectatorship called "the glance"—we are not talking about essential differences in kind between TV and film, but contingent, technological differences of degree, which are narrowing dramatically even as I write.

The consequences of augmenting the TV image (in terms of resolution and scale) for the claim that the TV image must be perforce less detailed than the film image are straightforward. As the TV image approaches the film image in resolution and scale, it can sport *mise-en-scènes* as elaborate as any movie, and these will be perfectly perceptible to TV viewers. However, in fact, it is not even necessary to advert to future technological possibilities in order to refute the hypothesis that the TV image is visually impoverished with respect to detail, since it is already the case that much existing TV is aggressively pictorial.

Both *Amazing Stories* and *Beauty and the Beast* employ elaborate imagery whose expressive visual qualities audiences are meant to notice and to appreciate. Surely the shots in most episodes of the *X-Files* are more detailed than those of most B-movies (such as Ed Wood's) and comparable to many A-movies in the history of the cinema. Furthermore, not only theatrical films, but many TV miniseries and TV movies employ casts of thousands, including, for example, *Roots, Shogun, North and South, Peter the Great, Marco Polo, Jesus of Nazareth, The Winds of War, War and Remembrance,* and so on.[4] Fortunes were lavished on the sets and costumes of *Dallas, Dynasty,* and *Knots Landing.* The background shots in *Hill Street Blues* teem with activity in order to promote a realistic feel to the drama. The producers of *Lonesome Dove* were at pains to establish an "authentic" look for the series, just as the visual imagery of *Max Headroom* was one of its major drawing cards. A large part of the unnerving surrealistic effect of *Twin Peaks* had to do with its careful visual design.

In all these cases, great care and expense, in different ways, were dedicated to elaborating the visual appearance of the TV shows in question, and there can be no doubt that the look of these programs, and so many others, was and is intended to reward the audience's visual attention with visual pleasure. Moreover, immense amounts of money are frequently spent on TV advertisements, whose intricate visual designs engender perceptual curiosity even as they project diverse expressive properties.

At least since the early nineteen-eighties, perhaps beginning with *Hill Street Blues,* there has been a discernible tendency toward pronounced visual stylization in many TV programs. Not all (and probably not even most) TV programs belong to this tendency, but that there is such a tendency indicates that elaborate visual stylization is not necessarily alien to TV. Moreover, this elaborate visual stylization is clearly intended primarily to engage the eye of the audience, and there is every reason to believe that it is sometimes (and even often) successful in doing so. Moreover, this emphasis on visual interest is evident not only in TV fiction, but also in such documentaries as *The Civil War* and *American Chronicles.*

The fact that many TV programs invest such energy in promoting visual interest also undermines the claim that in TV talk necessarily dominates, while the visual dimension necessarily plays second fiddle. I would guess that it is unobjectionable to assert that image is more important than talk in *Pee-Wee's Playhouse, Mighty Morphin Power Rangers,* and *Teletubbies.* Moreover, in adult programs, there are instances of visual humor that need not rely on talk: the "wish-fulfillment" fantasies on *Ally McBeal,* the visual allusions to movies and other TV programs on *The Simpsons,* and frequently the interpolated archival footage on *Dream On.* Some TV advertisements, like a recent ad for Mountain Dew soda (accompanied by the song "Tonight"), employ no audible dialogue, while some advertisements use silence to their advantage. And, again, certain programs, like *Beauty and the Beast* and others (some cited above), bank a great deal of their expressive power on their ornate, and, in this particular case, romantic appearance, while the performances of Mr. Bean and Red Skelton before him are designed to captivate visually. Nor is talk conceivably the primary interest in *Baywatch.* Thus, though it may be true that most television has been dominated by talk, this is a contingent, albeit statistically impressive fact, and not a necessary feature of TV.

The conjecture that TV spectatorship is essentially a matter of the glance generally comes in tandem with claims about the necessarily impoverished nature of the TV image. Because of its low resolution, its small scale and its lack of visual interest, the TV image is thought to be incapable of sustaining the gaze of the spectator and instead only to elicit the spectator's glance, often by means of talk—which calls the viewer back to the TV screen and organizes the otherwise weak TV image content.

However, as we have seen, many of the alleged preconditions of the glance response need not obtain. The resolution and screen size of the TV image can be augmented so that what is called gaze response could be as probable with respect to TV as it is to theatrical film. Moreover, the idea that the TV image is impoverished or of secondary importance can already be challenged by myriad counterexamples from existing TV where TV producers rely on engaging the visual interest of viewers and often manage to hold their attention by dint of the fascination those images promote by what they show. The *X-Files, Psi-Factor,* and *Millennium* tether their audiences to the screen by what they promise to reveal *visually;* one diverts one's glance from them at one's own risk. Programs like *The Honeymooners, The Life of Riley,* and *The Tonight Show* (in Johnny Carson's day) may leave us with little to look at and be based primarily on talkative badinage, but one cannot generalize from them about all TV, since that would exclude from the order of TV not only visually ambitious shows like the *X-Files,* but also episodes—like "Invaders" and "Two"—of the *Twilight Zone* that employ minimal dialogue.

The narrative structure of TV, in contrast to the narrative structure of film, is also alleged to foster the glance response in the former case and the gaze response in the latter case. The segmented, serial structure of TV narration supposedly invites intermittent glances, while the integrated, closed structure of film narrative putatively provokes an intense gaze, as a fixed number of questions are relentlessly posed until closure leaves us nothing left to look for.

That these distinctions in narrative form between TV and film are matters of contingency rather than necessity is perhaps even more manifest than the claims about the essential differences between the TV image and the film image.

TV programs need not be serial. Many TV programs have employed the "playhouse" or "anthology" format in which a new freestanding, closed drama (or comedy), involving different characters, is presented on a week-to-week basis. Some examples include *General Electric Theater, The Hallmark Hall of Fame, Playhouse 90, Tales of Tomorrow, Zane Grey Theater, The Armstrong Circle Theater, The Philco-Goodyear Television Playhouse, One Step Beyond, The Twilight Zone, Omnibus, You Are There, The U.S. Steel Hour, Lux Video Theater, Lights Out, Alfred Hitchcock Presents, Thriller Theater, Outer Limits, Night Gallery*, and many others. Nor has the playhouse/anthology format disappeared from more recent TV, as evinced by *Tales from the Crypt, Tales from the Darkside*, and *Zalman King's Red Shoe Diaries*. Similarly, TV movies, such as *Duel, The Day After*, and *The Portrait*, and teleplays from the Golden Age of TV, such as *Marty* and *Requiem for a Heavyweight*, are closed, freestanding, non-continuing narratives which are designed to elicit the same kind of spectator attention that theatrical films do (indeed, one supposes that this must be so, since many of these teleplays were turned into movies, including not only the aforementioned, but also, among others, *The Miracle Worker, Days of Wine and Roses, Judgment at Nuremberg, No Time for Sergeants, Bang the Drum Slowly* and *The Two Worlds of Charlie Gordon*, which became the film *Charly*). And, of course, theorists who emphasize the serial form as specific to TV narration forget that much cinema also has employed a serial format—from *Les Vampires* and *Tih Minh* to *Flash Gordon Conquers the Universe*.

Consequently, if there are two modes of spectator attention—the gaze and the glance—that correlate respectively to closed narrative forms versus serial forms, then we should find them in both film and TV. Undoubtedly, the serial form predominates in TV, but it is not peculiar to TV; closed narrative forms also appear on TV, suggesting that the so-called gaze is often the mandated spectator response to the relevant TV narratives. In fact, in any event, one suspects that the gaze-response is also the mandated form of spectatorship for serials too—that is, producers intend their shows to be watched intently. And I suspect that frequently (most frequently?) this intention is fulfilled, since it is not always the case that we watch TV while doing something else. That is, much TV watching is, I conjecture, as intently focused as movie viewing, despite the serial format of its presentation.

That TV narratives need not be segmented is borne out by the fact that they can be shown without commercial interruption. This is often done in order to signal the importance of the televised event, though it is also customary on public television, some arts channels, cable TV, and satellite TV (such as Direct-TV). HBO's *The Sopranos,* for example, is shown without commercial breaks. There is, in other words, no reason to imagine that TV narration is always interrupted and, thus, that it must reinforce the glance response. And, of course, even where the program is segmented, that entails neither that the audience is thereby invited or enabled to look away from the array, nor that they do. In truth, the intervening advertisements are often so visually arresting just in order to prevent the audience's eye from wandering away from the TV screen.[5]

In short, TV narratives are not necessarily serial and/or segmented. Moreover, insofar as these are thought to be preconditions for the spectator response of the glance variety, the glance response is not invariantly enjoined by TV narration. Furthermore, it seems reasonable to conjecture that even where TV narratives are segmented and serial, that implies no necessarily divided attention on the part of the spectator; fans gaze conscientiously at episodes of *Star Trek* despite commercial interruptions. Many people are absorbed in their favorite programs without attending to other matters at the same time, even if those programs are broadcast on low-resolution, black-and-white TVs. Nor need we think that the object of the viewer's attention is always the flow of programming, since a viewer may turn on her set to see a single freestanding, closed episode on an anthology like *Hard Copy* and then turn the set off.

Finally, it is alleged that film and TV are essentially distinct, since film always delivers the impression (or illusion) of the past, while TV traffics in the impression (or illusion) of the present. The correlation between TV and the present (immediacy and spontaneity) rests on the fact that TV has the capacity for the simultaneous broadcast of ongoing events. A reporter in the foreground can tell us about an air raid on Belgrade at the same moment that bombs burst in air in the background. The association of film with pastness, on the other hand, is putatively based in the fact that movies must be processed before they are shown and are, therefore, always recordings of something that happened in the past; no movie newsreel can deliver an event to the audience as it happens. Audiences realize this basic fact about movies and, as a result, it is alleged that they always associate the film image with pastness.

It is true that TV has the capacity to broadcast events simultaneously as they unfold. However, it is also true that most TV programming is prerecorded, much of it on film. It is particularly obvious to viewers that TV shows like *Moses, Upstairs/Downstairs,* and *Brideshead Revisited* cannot be simultaneous broadcasts. And what about the adventures of Hercules and Xena not to mention programs that are clearly marked as reruns? It is absurd in these cases to think that viewers must be taken by the illusion that they are seeing spontaneous transmissions. Just imagine what unlikely beliefs about the world viewers would have to possess in order to be smitten by such an illusion. Do viewers of *Bonanza, Rawhide, Have Gun Will Travel,* and *Gunsmoke* believe that gunfighters still stalk the streets? When they see *Wagon Train* and *Dr. Quinn, Medicine Woman,* do they believe the American West remains to be settled?

Thus, I see no reason to suppose that audiences take everything they see on TV to be present. Even with more contemporary TV movies, such as *And the Band Played On,* audiences are well aware that they are not seeing an on-the-spot documentary. Likewise, since *Alien Nation, V, Earth: The Final Conflict, The Jetsons,* and *Futurama* are all explicitly set in the future, it is implausible to hypothesize that viewers are under the illusion that they are seeing events presently unfolding.[6]

Here, it might be said that it is not the case that viewers are under the illusion that TV events are present, but only that they have a certain sense of immediacy or nowness. But this seems unlikely. The producers of programs like *The Jewel and the Crown* often work very hard to give a flavor of history gone by to their dramas and, I submit, they are able to erase the aura of contemporaneity from their spectacles in such a way that viewers appreciate the historicity of the drama, not its nowness.

Again, TV does have the capacity to deliver simultaneous broadcasts, but it does not mobilize this capacity all of the time. More often it presents viewers with prerecorded material, and I, at least, have no inclination to extrapolate from TV's occasionally exploited capacity for immediate broadcast to the proposition that, in consequence, audiences either believe or have the impression that everything they see on TV is unfolding before them in the present.

Likewise, the notion that film is always in the past tense appears equally implausible. It is a known fact about film that it records past events. But this does not entail that viewers in any way take the events they see in fictions to have occurred in the past. *Star Trek Generations* is not in the past tense, nor does it imply any sense or impression of pastness. In fact, it seems virtually incoherent to suggest that a fiction such as this, signaled as occurring in the future, connotes pastness. The correlation TV/presentness::film/pastness appears, then, to be nothing more than a nonstarter.

Thus, none of the most commonly cited essential distinctions between film and TV hardly has, after close scrutiny, much to recommend them.

CONCLUSION

Construed as essential distinctions between TV and film, the most commonly cited candidates all suffer from a tendency to overgeneralize from period-specific or genre-specific properties of some TV (and some film) to claims about all TV (and all film). Claims about image resolution and scale hypostasize the present state of TV technology and ignore future technological possibilities, including some, like HDTV, that are already at hand. The notion that the TV image is visually impoverished overlooks the arresting tendency in much TV since the eighties to indulge in aggressive pictorialism. To declare that TV narration is serial is to regard certain genres—like the soap opera and the sitcom—as paradigmatic, neglecting the playhouse/anthology format which was not only of major importance in the first decade and a half of TV, but which continues to exist today. Stress on TV's connection to the present (or to immediacy), likewise, focuses on primarily one genre—a certain type of newscast—mistaking it for the whole of TV and forgetting that most TV is prerecorded and obviously so (indeed, most shows where there might be some doubt, like game shows, typically say that they are prerecorded outright).[7]

Of course, the features of TV that are often cited as its essential features, especially in contrast to film, have some basis in fact. They are features of some—frequently of a great many—TV programs. But these are programs of a certain technological vintage, or genre, or of a certain period. Observing these features, where they obtain, is informative, especially for critical purposes. It is just not informative in the way that many theorists often suppose. That is, they are not necessary or fully comprehensive features of all TV, but only contingent features of groups of historically specific TV productions. It is useful to note such contingent regularities. The problem only arises when the theorist tries to extrapolate these local regularities into the essence of TV.

The line between TV and film is not as impenetrable as many theorists have suggested. Perhaps one reason for this is that both TV and film can imitate each other and this imitation can include technological refinements like HDTV through which the TV image aspires to the clarity of the film image. This is not to deny that some TV differs from some films in the way the theorist says; the soap opera form is serial in contrast to the closed nature of most theatrical films today. Such differences are of the utmost critical importance. They need to be noticed in order to explain why the works in question are as they are. But these differences, though often critically significant, do not add up to a categorical distinction between TV and film.

In truth, my own suspicion is that as time and technology advance, TV and film will continue to converge.[8] Perhaps they will become amalgamated and combined with digital computers to the point that we no longer talk of TV or film, but more generically of moving images. From that point in the future, we will look back to the history of film and the history of TV and think of them as parts or phases of the history of the moving image, a trans-media form of expression and communication—marked by such perennial devices as point-of-view editing and metrical montage—that has sometimes been implemented by film, sometimes by TV, sometimes by digital computers, sometimes by some combination of all of these, and sometimes by that which we cannot yet imagine.

Moreover, if I am right about this, certain significant implications for educational policy would seem to follow. Instead of dividing the study of the moving image between film departments and departments of TV—between cinema studies and TV studies—it would appear to make sense to combine these generally independent branches of research into one integrated field, the study of the moving image, a trans-media phenomenon, which will also include the study of computer animation, virtual reality, and of things to come still awaiting invention. Rather than initiating classes on film in high schools, it would seem more appropriate to introduce students to the tradition of the moving image, which, as video e-mail, supplemented by sophisticated editing programs, looms ever more probable, will become an omnipresent fact of their daily lives.

NOTES

1. In the debate between McLuhan and other TV theorists about the nature of TV spectatorship—is it interactive or distracted?—McLuhan's suggestion seems by far the more unlikely. McLuhan appears to believe that the TV spectator's response is *active* because the TV viewer must fill in the low resolution TV image. But this is not what we usually have in mind when we call a viewer's response "active," since this sort of filling in occurs at the level of the viewer's automatic, involuntary perceptual responses. We don't do anything to "fill in" or to "complete" the TV image; we just look. McLuhan's conception of activity (or interactivity) here is illicitly strained.

    Later, I will also go on to raise problems with the opposing view—that TV viewing is necessarily distracted, a matter of the so-called glance.

2. There is another distinction that is sometimes drawn between film narration and TV narration, viz., that TV narration often involves direct address, but film narration is transparent (it doesn't involve direct address). I will not spend much time with this proposal, since I think that it is palpably false. There is no reason why films cannot involve direct address; for example, many shorts (like Robert Benchley's *A Night at the Movies*) and avant-garde films (like Yvonne Rainer's *Murder and murder*) have characters addressing the audience directly.

3. Another difference between TV and film is supposedly that film is an authorial medium, whereas TV is anonymous. There seems scant reason to debate this suggestion at length since: 1) it would not mark an ontological difference between TV and film, but merely a contingent social fact—there is no deep reason that TV could not be authorial; and 2) in fact, TV does often emphasize its authorship. Everyone was aware of David Lynch's creative participation in *Twin Peaks,* of Oliver Stone's in *Wild Palms,* and Steven Spielberg's in *Amazing Stories.* Rod Serling, Alfred Hitchcock, and Chris Carter all leave their signatures on their series as do Trey Parker and Matt Stone. Norman Lear and James L. Brooks are recognizable producers as is Steven Bochco. Perhaps producers are the most frequently known authors with respect to TV, whereas directors are more frequently known with respect to film, but that too is a contingent social matter and can easily change. In 1993, Universal-MCA floated the idea of a weekly series showcasing TV movies directed by noted film directors; there is no reason in principle why such a program could not appear on TV.

4. That TV can traffic in spectacle also calls into question the notion that the talking-head is the natural shot for video.

5. It should also be pointed out that in the past much movie viewing was also segmented. One went to the movie theater to see a double feature, which might be introduced and interspersed with previews, newsreels, short subjects and cartoons. Here, it might be objected that, unlike TV, the features were not interrupted with advertisements (like previews), but were shown intact. That is true, yet it is also true that moviegoers in the old days often walked in on films *in media res* and then sat through the whole "flow" of the evening's fare before seeing what they had missed before they arrived at the theater. In such cases, which were far from rare, one speculates that the film viewer's experience was not so different from the viewer's experience of the so-called segmented flow of TV programming.

6. Even with "reality TV" programs, like the *World's Wildest Police Videos,* audiences are aware that what they are watching has been prerecorded. Perhaps part of the attraction of these videos is their "immediacy," but here "immediacy" does not connote presentness, but that the material is unrehearsed and documentary.

7. This sentence is not quite right, since there are shows other than newscasts that are live; the 1997 season premiere of *ER* is an example. Nevertheless, it is still the case that most TV is prerecorded.

8. Indeed, given video cassettes and laser discs, it is probably already the case that a great many viewers see most of their movies on TV monitors, a fact that has had repercussions for film production.

Chapter 14 Kracauer's
Theory of Film

INTRODUCTION

This essay is about Siegfried Kracauer's book *Theory of Film: The Redemption of Physical Reality,* which was published in 1960.[1] It is important to stress this from the outset because, during the course of his career, Kracauer made a number of contributions to the topic of film theory, not all of which are strictly compatible with the theses of *Theory of Film.*[2] Exploring the relations and the tensions between Kracauer's earlier writings and *Theory of Film* is a worthy task for intellectual historians,[3] but, in contrast, my purpose is to examine the argument of *Theory of Film.* That book alone provides more than enough material to engage a brief introductory essay such as this one.

Perhaps the initial thing to say to someone confronting *Theory of Film* for the first time is that it is a very difficult book to read.[4] On the face of it, Kracauer's theory has a clear structure, possibly reflecting his early training as an architect.[5] Effort appears to be lavished on drawing sharp distinctions between categories, and the argument seems to progress logically. However, the deeper one goes in the text, the more the clear categories seem to muddy. As Kracauer applies his theory to examples, caveats, qualifications, extenuating circumstances, mitigating conditions, and compensating considerations multiply so that one is never sure that one could apply Kracauer's system in a way that would coincide with Kracauer's own results. Consequently, the book, as a whole, has a very ad hoc flavor to it.[6]

For example, Kracauer argues that film has a special affinity for recording and revealing "physical existence," but then he also includes under this category "special modes of reality"—"physical reality as it appears to individuals in extreme states of mind."[7] This is at least a surprising, if not inconsistent, turn in the text, since two of the cognates that Kracauer offers for "physical existence" are "material reality" and "nature," categories typically used to draw a conceptual contrast with subjective experience. Throughout the book, unexpected elaborations of the core theory, such as this one, abound, making the reader uncertain about his or her grasp of the theory.

If such slipperiness poses problems for the reader, of course, it also poses problems for an expositor of the theory such as myself. In a short essay, it is impossible to tie up all the loose ends in Kracauer's book, particularly in terms of the apparent anomalies that crop up in his applications of the theory to examples. Thus, in what follows, I only attempt to elucidate and to criticize the central arguments of the text as they are typically understood. I do not try to reconcile all the logical tensions in the book; I doubt whether I could even if I tried. Hence, this essay may be an idealization of Kracauer's text. But I see no alternative as a way of beginning a discussion of *Theory of Film*.

The Kracauer of *Theory of Film* is standardly regarded as a realist. In fact, along with André Bazin,[8] Kracauer is taken to be one of the most paradigmatic examples of this tendency in film theory. There are, of course, differences between the two theorists. Bazin, as is well known, is deeply concerned with the realist potentials of certain cinematic techniques, such as the long-take, deep-focus shot, whereas Kracauer shows no special allegiance to any particular cinematic technique, including the sequence shot. Kracauer is more concerned with the *use* of various techniques.

However, Kracauer does echo Bazin's taste for a certain level of ambiguity ("shots not yet stripped of their multiple meanings")[9] and for episodic narrative structures.[10] And, most significantly, Kracauer's and Bazin's theories converge in the shared conviction that the most important fact about film theoretically is its putative provenance in photography.

Indeed, this conviction is one of the defining features of what I call film realists in this essay. Both Kracauer and Bazin meet this criterion, since both believe that film is essentially photographic. Film realists also believe that this supposed fact about the nature of film has normative consequences—consequences about what is and is not suitable when it comes to filmmaking. Bazin's arguments and conclusions in behalf of film realism differ from Kracauer's. Our concern is with Kracauer's position.

In a nutshell, Kracauer begins with "the assumption that film is essentially an extension of photography and therefore shares with this medium a marked affinity for the visible world around us. Films come into their own when they record and reveal physical reality."[11] Furthermore, "since any medium is partial to the things it is uniquely equipped to render, the cinema is conceivably animated by a desire to picture transient material life, life at its most ephemeral."[12] And this so-called desire, in turn, gives rise to the standards of achievement that are relevant to film: "films are true to the medium to the extent that they penetrate the world before our eyes."[13] That is, films are cinematic to the extent that they realize "the desire to picture transient material life."

Kracauer calls his theory a material aesthetics because it is concerned with content, whereas, he contends, previous theories emphasized form. What content appears to mean here is something like "what is rendered." Following a theoretical persuasion popularized by people like Lessing,[14] Kracauer presumes that each medium has a certain subject matter or content that it is uniquely and best suited to represent or to render. The natural, so to speak, subject matter or content of photography, and, by extension, film comprises such things as the unstaged, the fortuitous, the indeterminate, and endlessness as these properties manifest themselves visibly in things and events. Content bereft of such properties, or things rendered in such a way that these properties are not salient, are unsuitable for film; content rendered in such a way that such properties are evident and/or emphasized are cinematic naturals. Of course, implicit in this way of thinking are certain canons of evaluation. Films are cinematic (a.k.a. good) only if they portray cinematic content and they are uncinematic (and most probably bad)[15] if they lack cinematic content or fail to foreground the relevant properties, such as indeterminacy, in the things and events they depict.

Of course, Kracauer is aware that there are more elements to film than its photographic constituents. There are, for instance, editing and set design. Kracauer refers to these other-than-photographic features of film as technical properties. And he argues that the technical properties of film should be coordinated with the photographic dimension of cinema in such a way that they support or enhance the pursuit of the natural photographic proclivities of cinema toward depicting the unstaged, the fortuitous, the indeterminate and end-lessness. That is, the technical features of film should be subservient to its essential photographic purposes. Or, photography, with its natural inclinations, leads the charge; everything else is auxiliary.

Given this conception of film, a recurring question for Kracauer is how the various technical aspects of film, such as the sound track, can be deployed to support, abet, or at least not impede the purposes of the basic photographic element and its properties. This, of course, also leads Kracauer to comment on the ways in which the technical aspects of film may conflict with or even thwart the photographic potentials of cinema. Where such conflicts occur and the technical means of the cinema are used to serve their own purposes, in contradistinction to the purposes of photographic realism, Kracauer deems such usages of the technical features of film uncinematic.

Of especial interest to Kracauer is also the question of which film genres—such as the historical film, the fantasy film, the experimental film, and so on—are suitable to the photographic commitments of cinema and which are not. Indeed, the bulk of the text is turned over to adjudicating this issue genre by genre—to assessing which ones are amenable to or compatible with the purposes of film realism and which ones are not.

Most of the core of Kracauer's theory of film is set out in the first section, entitled "General Characteristics," while most of the subsequent text is spent applying the theory to the uses of various technical features and film genres.

From a theoretical point of view, Kracauer's core theory is the first order of interest, since from the viewpoint of theory it could be the case that the theory might be solid, while Kracauer's own applications of it turn out to be problematic. If this were the case, the central theses of *Theory of Film* might be sustained at the cost of minor adjustments here and there. But the million-dollar question is whether the theory that Kracauer applies is itself compelling. Thus, I concentrate my attention on the core theory comprising the following fundamental claims: that film is essentially photographic; that the photographic nature of film has normative implications for filmmaking; that these implications include commitments to certain content or to the treatment of cinematic content in certain specifiable ways; and that failure to respect these commitments, all things being equal, results in films of dubious cinematic value.

To my way of thinking, Kracauer has two different, though related, ways of laying out and defending this theory. I call the first "the medium specificity argument" and the second "the historical/cultural argument."

THE MEDIUM SPECIFICITY ARGUMENT

Kracauer explicitly limits the domain of his theory to the black-and-white photographic film. Color films and cartoons are excluded from his purview.[16] Kracauer is frank about his reasons for these exclusions. He believes that neither color films nor cartoons are realistic. The case against cartoons is fairly obvious, though Kracauer's qualms about color films show a very period-specific prejudice. Certainly by the late sixties, the suspicion that color films were inherently unrealistic had virtually disappeared. Moreover, one might also worry whether by excluding these categories of film, for the reasons given, Kracauer doesn't beg the question in favor of his theory from the get-go by banishing obvious counterexamples to his theory by fiat.

But for heuristic purposes, maybe it is best to begin by allowing Kracauer to stipulate the domain of his theory as he sees fit. On his view, his subject is the photographic film, understood, tendentiously, as the black-and-white film. Kracauer's stated intention is to provide insight into the intrinsic nature of the photographic film.[17] From a historical point of view, one can see why Kracauer lays emphasis on the photographic film. Film can be regarded as a development of still photography—an expansion of its technological powers—and, in addition, the films known to Kracauer were standardly made by means of photography, that is, by shooting what are called pro-filmic events. Computer-generated films were beyond Kracauer's ken historically and cartoons were excluded from his theoretical domain by stipulation. However, when Kracauer calls films *photographic,* he is not merely acknowledging a historical fact. He means to make an ontological point, namely, that films are essentially photographic.

Why is this significant? As we have already noted, film has many constituents, including not only photography but editing, set design, and so on. Kracauer asks whether one of these is more essential than all the rest, since he believes that if one is more essential, then it should play an important role in the way in which we think about film. That is, he believes that if film has an essential nature, then this will provide us with a key to how it is best used. Kracauer, of course, is not shy about which constituent of film he takes to be essential. It is the photographic component.

But one wonders whether Kracauer can provide any reasons for this decision? You might think that Kracauer would answer that his conclusion is true by definition—after all, by his own stipulation, we are talking about *photographic* film. The use of photography is the feature that serves to identify mem-

bership in the class of things under discussion. But, of course, a common identifying mark need not correspond to an essential feature. Stripes serve to mark
off tigers for us, but they do not reveal the essential nature of tigers. Genetic
structure does. Perhaps because he realizes that the sort of essence he is after
cannot be verbally stipulated, Kracauer never tries this gambit.

Instead, Kracauer maintains that

> Like the embryo in the womb, the photographic film developed from distinctly sep-
> arate components. Its birth came about from a combination of instantaneous pho-
> tography, as used by Muybridge and Marey, with older devices of the magic lantern
> and the phenakistoscope. Added to this later were the contribution of other non-
> photographic elements, such as editing and sound. Nevertheless photography, espe-
> cially instantaneous photography, has a legitimate claim to top priority among these
> elements for it undeniably is and remains the decisive factor in establishing film con-
> tent. The nature of photography survives in that of film.[18]

If we read "top priority" here as signaling the essential feature or basic property
of film, then it is natural to take Kracauer to be arguing that:

1. Whatever establishes the content of a medium is its basic property.
2. Photography establishes the content of film.
3. Therefore, photography is the basic property of film.

The first premise in this argument is implicit; the second is asserted in the
penultimate sentence of the quotation. To assess either premise, we need a handle on the notion of establishing the content of a medium. One must admit
that this is a very obscure idea, both in terms of what comprises the content of
a medium and what establishes it.[19]

With regard to the first premise, one wonders whether media in general have
"established content." Part of the problem is that in many cases the content of
a medium is not established once and for all. Rather, it is open to innovation.
So, in principle, one might argue that it is impossible to fix the content of a
medium, unless Kracauer has some special sense of "establish" about which he
has not deigned to inform us.

But there is also another problem with the first premise. If we understand it
to claim that for any medium, x is its basic property if and only if x establishes
the content of the medium, then it seems false. Why? Because there are media
such as oil painting, where the basic ingredients of the medium do not establish
its content. Oil-based paint is the basic property of oil painting, but it does not
"establish" the content of the medium. You can paint anything—not only visi-

ble things but ultimate reality (remember Mondrian). So if first premise is supposed to be a thoroughly general principle for identifying the basic property of any medium, it appears questionable.

But perhaps we should understand the first premise to say: "If x establishes the content of a medium, then x is its basic property." This enables one to hold that where a medium has definable content and x establishes it, then x is its basic property. But unless we have a clear understanding of what it is to establish the content of a medium, this at least looks controversial. For at a given time a medium may be used to portray certain subject matter—say religious figures—as a result of social factors, and yet we do not conclude that these social factors, which establish the content of the medium, are the basic properties of the medium.

But, be that as it may, Kracauer might respond that it is clear what we mean by establishing content when it comes to film—it means providing what we see—and, furthermore, what we see in film is there because of photography. If there were no photography, no photographic film would have any content whatsoever. If at this point you ask, "What about animated films?" then you have begun to appreciate the force of Kracauer's exclusion of animation from the domain of his theory.

Though the supposition that photography establishes the content of film has problems that we address shortly, let us grant Kracauer this premise momentarily in order to see how he uses it. Kracauer wants to establish that photography is the basic property of cinema because he believes that if you can determine the essence of film, then that will indicate the appropriate way in which to use the medium. He believes that essence implies function. In terms of aesthetic theory, this doctrine is often elaborated in terms of the notion of medium specificity, that is, the view that each medium has an inherent nature that dictates the range of possibilities available in that medium.[20] The nature of film is essentially photographic. So the range of genuine possibility—its proper scope and limitations—is photographic.

But this pushes the question of the nature of film back a step. For in order to determine the nature of film, one must establish the nature of photography. And this is something Kracauer tackles in the introduction to his book, which is entitled "Photography." In order to plumb the nature of a medium, Kracauer suggests that we listen to the conversation concerning the nature of the medium that has arisen during the course of its history.[21] Listening to that conversation, Kracauer claims to discern two trends. There are those who favor the realist conception of photography, the view that it is the essence of photography to record reality. And there are those who favor the formative conception of photography, who see the photographer as inevitably involved in creatively shaping her or his subject matter through processes of selectivity. Proponents of the formative tendency maintain that photography does not merely record reality, but that it molds reality as well.

Kracauer agrees that both conceptions have claims to validity. But he also realizes that extreme versions of the realist and the formative conceptions tend to conflict. So, in effect, he proposes to combine the two tendencies in such a way that they turn out to be operationally compatible. The way to coordinate the two conceptions that Kracauer proposes is to say that it is the nature of photography to record and to reveal physical reality. The *recording* component of this formula evidently respects the realist conception of photography, while the *revealing* component acknowledges the claims of the formative conception, since revealing reality involves the creative activity of the photographer.[22]

What is perhaps interesting about the way that Kracauer strives to reconcile realist and formative claims is that the realist conception functions as a constraint on the formative conception. The creative activity of the photographer is endorsed so long as it is dedicated to revealing physical reality, rather than, say, to concocting reflexive abstractions or imaginary worlds. Realism is a necessary condition of photography and any exercise of the formative powers of photography must be in the service of realism rather than pure formal experimentation. The nature of photography is twofold—a matter of recording *and* revealing physical reality—with the realist half of this conjunction calling the tune.

Though one can ascertain Kracauer's grounds for isolating the two aspects of the nature of photography, I am not able to find any direct justification in the text for the proposal that the realistic tendency and the formative tendency be reconciled in the way he suggests. Why does Kracauer think that his formula is the right one? One could imagine other ways of reconciling the two tendencies. Why not suggest that the realist tendency be constrained by the formative tendency? This, in effect, is what the Soviet theorist Kuleshov advocates—proposing that editing (montage) is the central element of film and that the other elements of film should support its so-called natural effects and purposes.[23] Kracauer offers no explicit argument against this possibility. Nor does he have an argument to preclude the possibility that photography has a double nature that sometimes conflicts after the fashion of Jekyll and Hyde.[24]

However, if we extrapolate interpretively, perhaps something Kracauer says in another context has some bearing on why he believes the notion that photography records and reveals physical reality captures the nature of photography. Speaking of what justifies calling some film genres cinematic and others not, Kracauer suggests that we look to see which ones afford insight and enjoyment that are otherwise unattainable.[25] Applying a principle like this to the present case, perhaps Kracauer thinks that because the formative tendency can be realized in other media, such as painting, and is, therefore, attainable in media other than photography, his formula—out of the alternatives—zeroes in on the way of coordinating the realist and formative tendencies that is uniquely photographic.

Furthermore, since Kracauer believes that the nature of photography survives in the nature of film, he is now in a position to conclude that the nature of film is to record and to reveal physical reality. And, moreover, Kracauer maintains that photography, because of its realist nature, has natural affinities for certain content: for the unstaged (real things and events); for the fortuitous (random events); for the indeterminate (objects and events bearing the possibility of multiple significance); and for endlessness (the photograph yields the impression that what it represents is part of a larger, "endless," spatiotemporal continuum.)[26] Therefore, in so far as film inherits its nature from photography, it inherits these affinities as well. But since film adds movement to the still photograph, it also lays claim to an affinity all its own, namely, an affinity for "the continuum of life, or 'the flow of life,' which of course is identical with openended life."[27]

The basic property of film is photographic—the capacity to record and reveal physical reality.[28] This disposes film to a certain roughly definable content—the recording and revealing of the unstaged, the fortuitous, the indeterminate, spatiotemporal endlessness, and the endless flow of life. But, of course, as mentioned earlier, film has other properties besides its putative basic property, photography. Kracauer calls them "technical properties." What can one say about these? On Kracauer's view they should be subservient to the basic property of film.

They should be used in the service of recording and revealing reality. Editing, for example, ideally functions to reveal aspects of the unstaged physical world, perhaps by showing us causal processes operating across great distances—as Vertov does by cutting between city lights and the dams from whence they derive their power in his paeans to the electrification of the Soviet Union. Quite clearly, the technical properties of film stand to its basic property as the formative capacity of photography stands to its realist capacity. In both cases, the latter features constrain and direct the appropriate exercise of the capabilities of the former feature. Nor is this correlation accidental, since among the technical capacities of film are many of the major levers, like editing, for realizing formative effects upon that which is recorded.

As it is with the technical capacities of film, so it is with film genres. Film genres, especially in terms of their narrative structures, must be constrained and guided by the basic properties of film, its photographic nature and purposes. Not all the genres one finds in the historical corpus of films meet these criteria, however. Historical films, for example, employ costumes and are, as a result, apt to be stagey. So historical topics are, prima facie, unsuitable for film, unless the filmmakers can discover mitigating or compensating strategies to deal with the problem of staginess. Tragedies, Kracauer believes, present viewers with a narratively closed universe, where events transpire as the result of destiny. This is incompatible with the open-ended endlessness of the flow of life and with photography's affinity for what is accidental. Thus, tragedy is an unsuitable subject for films.

Similarly, Kracauer also maintains that detective films and films of intrigue traffic in narratively closed universes and, therefore, are, prima facie, uncinematic.[29] On the other hand, found narratives (e.g., *Nanook of the North*) and episodic narrative structures (*Paisan*) provide hospitable frameworks for showcasing the affinities toward which photography gravitates and, therefore, are presumptively cinematic.

In summary, then, Kracauer contends:

1. Photography is the basic property (element) of film. (Other properties, like editing, lens distortion, and sound, are technical properties, not basic properties.)
2. Any medium should emphasize the essential features (natural inclinations, affinities) of its basic element.
3. The essential feature of photography is its inclination for the straightforward recording and revealing of the visible world, especially in terms of the unstaged, the fortuitous, indeterminacy, and endlessness.
4. Therefore, film should emphasize the essential features of its basic element by recording and revealing the visible world, especially in terms of the unstaged, the fortuitous, indeterminacy, and endlessness (including the endless flow of life).
5. Where a medium possesses properties (elements) in addition to the basic elements, these should be deployed to emphasize the essential features (natural inclinations, affinities) of the basic element.

6. Film possesses technical properties and narrative (genre) structures in addition to its basic element.

7. Therefore, the technical properties and narrative structures of film should be deployed to emphasize the recording and revealing of the visible world, especially in terms of the unstaged, the fortuitous, indeterminacy, and endlessness (including the endless flow of life).

I call this argument the "medium specificity argument" since the second premise presupposes that media have essential (unique) features that determine what should (and, by implication, what should not) be emphasized when using the medium. The fifth premise is also a corollary to this idea. And, indeed, as we saw earlier, Kracauer's major reason for believing he has captured the essential feature of photography (in the fifth premise) may involve uniqueness claims about the medium.[30]

Let us go through this argument step by step. We have already encountered the first premise as the conclusion of a previous argument. Photography is said to be the basic element in film because it establishes the content of film. We have suggested that Kracauer might defend such a position by arguing that without photography film has no content at all, since what comprises film is the cinematography of pro-filmic events. Without photography, there is nothing to see in films and, therefore, no content.

This conclusion, however, may be precipitous. Consider the genre of avant-garde films called "flicker films," of which *Arnulf Rainer* by Peter Kubelka and *The Flicker* by Tony Conrad are perhaps the most famous. Such films can be made by alternating clear and opaque leader or black-and-white leader. No photography is necessary. Moreover, the fact that these films were made after Kracauer articulated his theory is irrelevant, since his claims are ontological, not historical.

Perhaps Kracauer would reject these counterexamples by claiming that they have no content. But this is not obvious. They are exercises in rhythm, and if rhythm is a content of music, why can't it function as content in film? Also, the films are interesting for the visual effects they engender. Why not count that as content? And, of course, critics have claimed that such films make reflexive comments about the nature of film. And that certainly sounds like content to me.

A second reply available to Kracauer might be to argue that these are really animated films and, therefore, outside the domain of his theory. But whether they are animated films is hardly self-evident; they are certainly not like paradigmatic cases of animated films. They are not cartoons. Here, Kracauer might respond: "Well, even if they aren't animated films, they are certainly not photographic films."

That's right but maybe irrelevant, since films indiscernible to these could be made photographically by taking close-shots of black walls at night and alternating them with clear leader. Would the content of these films—the rhythms, the visual effects, and the reflexive comments—be established by photography? Surely that is at least debatable. The content is not necessarily established by all and only photography because it can be fixed by the standard procedure for composing flicker films. Indeed, even with flicker films composed in the alternative way we have suggested, the content does not seem to be established by photography; rather, photography is merely a means of securing an other-than-photographic agenda.

Once again it must be emphasized that Kracauer's claims are not historical claims about films as he knew them but ontological claims about the nature of film *sub specie aeternitatis*. Admittedly, Kracauer did not envision computer-generated imagery. But it is possible to imagine computer-generated feature films of the striking verisimilitude of the stampede scene in *Jurassic Park*. Wouldn't such films be the kind of films that Kracauer intends to be talking about, since it is probably possible in principle to replicate the films he applauds by means of exclusively computer technology? And wouldn't the content of these computer-generated facsimiles have the same content as the originals? But in that case, the content of films—what we see—can be established without photography.

Here, Kracauer might say that these computer-generated facsimiles are not literally *photographic* films and, therefore, not relevant to his theory. But he calls his book a "theory of film," and it seems fair to expect the theory to encompass any technical expansion of the practice that viewers and filmmakers are willing to regard as a continuation of the same practice by other means (in the way that we are willing to consider various different technical processes photography). And certainly viewers and filmmakers are willing to count the stampede scenes in *Jurassic Park* as film. On the other hand, if Kracauer maintains that his theory only pertains, by stipulation, to the photographic technology of his own era, then we might wish to respond that then it is on its way to obsolescence, and irrelevant as a theory of film.

Of course, Kracauer might attempt to block my counterexamples by specifying what he means by "content" more narrowly than by the notion of "what we see." But one must be careful here. For if what Kracauer might have in mind as the relevant sense of content is precisely the unstaged, the fortuitous, the indeterminate, and endlessness, then his argument will beg the question in its first premise. After all, the commitment to such content is supposed to be the conclusion of his argument.

The second premise in the argument is the assertion of medium specificity: any medium should emphasize the essential feature of its basic element. This is an idea with a long history. Perhaps due to its long history, it appears obvious or even self-evident. But at the risk of sounding boorish, it seems worthwhile to ask why a medium should emphasize its essential feature. Since the principle is framed in terms of how a medium *should* be used, it must be apparent that media can be used in ways that do not emphasize their essential feature (supposing that they have one). But, despite this possibility, Kracauer contends that a medium should be used to emphasize its essential features.

What reasons can be given for this? Suppose a work of stone architecture fails to emphasize an essential feature—say weight—of its basic element or even hides it by appearing light and airy. Imagine that it leaves the impression of floating skywards toward heaven. What's the problem here, if the result is effective—if it is beautiful or thrilling?

Perhaps Kracauer and other proponents of the medium specificity principle think that such an outcome is impossible. Perhaps they believe that the medium specificity principle is a reliable predictor of what will be successful in a given medium—that there will be no successful results that do not abide by the principle. But then the medium specificity principle becomes an empirical hypothesis. And we will just have to wait and see whether or not successful films are all in accord with it.

Of course, if we simply attend to the pretheoretical record—the canon of films that are regarded as classics—then it would seem that informed viewers think that there have been successful films, like Cocteau's *Blood of a Poet,* which defy Kracauer's version of medium specificity. Moreover, if Kracauer tries to block this evidence by claiming that the informed viewers in question cannot be truly informed if they reach conclusions that deviate from his predictions, then, once again, he looks as though he is simply begging the question.

The problem here, as in so many medium specificity arguments, is that there is an ambiguity in the way that the medium specificity principle is treated. Is it supposed to be a conceptual or an empirical truth? At times, people like Kracauer seem to treat it as a conceptual truth. But it doesn't look like a conceptual truth. It's certainly not analytically true. And in fact the only putative grounds that proponents typically adduce for it seem to be empirical—that is, their claim that experience shows that all successful works of art abide by it. But in that case, it is not insulated from contestation. And with regard to every art form I know of, one can find some generally acknowledged, informed people (critics, artists, curators, publishers, and audience members) who will reasonably defend counterexamples to every reigning proposal about medium specificity.

The third premise of Kracauer's argument advances his conception of the nature of photography. It is of the essence of photography to record and reveal the visible world, especially in terms of the unstaged, the fortuitous, indeterminacy, and endlessness. As noted previously, this formulation attempts to coordinate the claims of the realist and formative conceptions of photography. But why should a friend of the formative conception agree to Kracauer's way of cutting the difference between the realist and formative conceptions? Why not suggest that the realist capacities of photography be subservient to the formative capabilities—that the realist powers of photography be devoted, for example, to the creation of imaginary beings and vistas of compelling verisimilitude?

My interpretive hypothesis is that Kracauer would answer this question by saying that the tension between these tendencies should be adjudicated in favor of effects that are uniquely attainable within the medium. Formative effects are achievable in other media, like painting, whereas photography has a unique purchase on visual reality. But this, of course, is once again just an invocation of the medium specificity principle. And, as such, its defender must explain why it makes any difference if a photographer makes a successful photograph that that success (e.g., Heartfield's "Adolf the Superman") has to be something attainable only in the medium of photography. That the photograph is successful should be all that counts.

Nor can the proponent of medium specificity block this possibility on a priori grounds. The matter of success is an empirical one. And if Kracauer attempts to invoke the medium specificity principle as an a priori truth, we may charge him with begging the question once again. That is, Kracauer can be faced with a dilemma: either the medium specificity principle can be held as an empirical truth or a conceptual truth. If it is held as an empirical generalization, it looks false; if it is held as a conceptual truth, that not only looks dubious, but it also in effect begs the question in the debate with rival views of photography.

With respect to the third premise, it is also worthwhile to comment on Kracauer's candidates for photography's natural affinities—the unstaged, the fortuitous, indeterminacy, and endlessness. Kracauer asserts that these affinities obtain; there is no demonstration, beyond citation of a few examples. I suspect that each affinity could be challenged, along with the very idea that media possess natural affinities. Moreover, what the affinities involve is very vague, which perhaps is what allows Kracauer's rather high-handed use of them when it comes to his evaluation of the various film genres.

But a more interesting feature of these so-called affinities from a logical point of view is that Kracauer never establishes that this is an exhaustive list. Thus, there may be more candidates for photography's affinities than the ones he enumerates. Thus, he has not logically precluded the possibility that there might be affinities that are more congenial to the formative persuasion and, indeed, to some of the genres and techniques that he disparages.

The fourth step in Kracauer's argument is a logically valid conclusion of the preceding premises. But, as such, it inherits all the problems that plague the medium specificity presuppositions that precede it. One can imagine a debate over Kracauer's conclusions here about how film should be used with someone like Kuleshov where Kuleshov, employing the medium specificity principle but favoring a different candidate (montage) as the basic element of film, would support a vision of film diametrically opposed to Kracauer's. How could Kracauer maneuver in such a debate? I suspect by either relying on false empirical generalizations or by begging the question by means of spurious a priori claims.[31]

The fifth premise in the argument is simply an extension or a corollary of the medium specificity principle—an application of the principle to the case where a medium has more than one element. The argument against it is of a piece with previous argumentation. Even supposing that photography is the basic element of film (something I would reject), we still need a reason why if in a given film (like *Ballet Mécanique*) emphasis on another element (say editing) is effective, though it does not emphasize photography, making that film should be illegitimate? I contend that Kracauer will not be able to advance a reason without incurring the dilemma rehearsed heretofore.

Premise 6 is true enough. Film does possess technical properties and narrative structures in addition to cinematography. But its combination with premise 5 yields a logically valid but false (or unsound) conclusion due to the problems that vex the fifth premise. Confronting the conclusion on its own terms, the problem is once again: Why should we sacrifice something like the breathtaking battle scenes in films like Visconti's *Senso,* Pontecorvo's *Burn!,* Walsh's *Captain Horatio Hornblower,* and Bondarchuk's *War and Peace* because the costumes make us aware they have been staged?

Indeed, we should also complain that Kracauer's conclusion is so vague in many of its central concepts—especially those pertaining to cinema's affinities—that it virtually guarantees the arbitrary use that Kracauer makes of them when he declares which films, genres, and deployments of techniques are uncinematic. Kracauer has not provided a firm theoretical foundation for determining what films are cinematic, and, therefore, laudable. Rather, his theory is more like quicksand.

THE HISTORICAL/CULTURAL ARGUMENT

So far we have been examining Kracauer's medium specificity argument. Kracauer develops this argument in the first section of *Theory of Film*. However, in his "Epilogue," entitled "Film in Our Time," where Kracauer discusses the importance of film, especially for contemporary society, he suggests another argument in favor of his conception of the cinematic. This argument rests on a diagnosis of culture in the age of science.

Kracauer begins by maintaining that, in large measure, we live in an era where religion and, putatively, ideology are disappearing. The result of this is that individuals experience the world as fragmented. What has brought this about is the rise of science. Science has destroyed the old gods. Moreover, science brings with it a distinct mode of thinking, one that relies on abstraction, and this penchant for abstraction further facilitates alienation, specifically alienation from the physical world and particular things. That is, science operates in terms of generalizations; the more we are engrossed in this mode of thinking, the more we are estranged from particulars.

Film, because of its supposed affinity for the physical world and for particulars, has a historic role or value in this context. Unlike past art, which transformed physical reality, film is a new art form, one that records and reveals physical reality. Thus of all the arts, film can function as an antidote to contemporary alienation from physical reality. Film, or at least cinematic film, enables us to get back in touch with particulars. Moreover, once we are back in touch with particulars, we will be in a position to evolve a new culture—not a return to religion and ideology, but a new framework that, apprised of the limits of science, will enable us to be at home in the world again. Given the awesome task that he attributes to film, it is perhaps no surprise that Kracauer falls into quasi-religious language, talking about film as the redemption of physical reality.[32]

The elements that comprise Kracauer's analysis should be familiar enough to intellectual historians. The fragmentation of modern life is a theme one finds almost everywhere, including in the works of Lukács, Simmel, Benjamin, and

Heidegger. Indeed, for Heidegger, science is once again the culprit. Also, Kracauer's emphasis on the centrality of the particular is a recurring feature of Kantian and Neo-Kantian aesthetics and even predates them in the writings of Baumgarten. In the twentieth century, theorists as diverse as Adorno, Benjamin, Bergson, and Münsterberg champion the particular in various ways. In fact, Münsterberg develops a theory of film in the context of an aesthetics of particularity which, for Münsterberg, stands in contrast to scientific generality.[33] As with all these figures, including Kracauer, the determining background influence seems to have been Kant's decisive cleavage of the faculty of pure reason from that of aesthetic judgment.

But even if Kracauer stands in a definable lineage, he develops the aesthetics of particularity in his own fashion. Moreover, it supplies him, even if he is not explicitly aware of this, with a way of laying out and defending his theory of film without relying on the troublesome notion of medium specificity. For he can argue that the function of film today is set by the needs of contemporary society. Society's greatest need, given the rise of science, is the redemption of physical reality. That is a condition that requires urgent attention. Whatever features of film can serve this purpose are the ones that deserve emphasis.

Stating the case this way, Kracauer can pick out photography as the basic element of film without invoking the notion that film has a necessary essence. What directs our attention to the photographic element of film is its capacity to fulfill a contingently, historically situated function—the task of redeeming physical reality. The approved use of film to record and reveal physical reality in terms of the unstaged, the indeterminate, the fortuitous, and endlessness does not follow here from film's putative status as essentially photographic, but from the fact that the primary role or value of film in our time is to function in a way that redeems physical reality. This value or role, albeit contingently motivated, serves in a fairly straightforward way to pick out photography as the relevant or basic element of film (for contemporary society) and to constrain and to guide the use of the articulatory processes of film (technical properties and narrative structures) at least for the duration of the current crisis of the dominance of scientific abstraction.

So, the core of the historical/cultural argument goes like this:

1. Due to the rise of science, modern society is alienated from the physical world and the experience of particularity.
2. If modern society is alienated from the physical world and the experience of particularity, then, all things being equal, any medium that can relieve that alienation should be used in a way that will enable it to do so.

3. Film can relieve the alienation from the physical world and the experience of particularity.
4. If film is to relieve the alienation from the physical world and the experience of particularity, then it must be used in such a way that its photographic element and its affinities are emphasized.
5. Therefore, film must emphasize its photographic element and its basic affinities (the unstaged, the fortuitous, the indeterminate, and endlessness).

This argument can then be continued, arguing that the technical properties and narrative structures of film should be subordinated to the purposes of the photographic element in order to fulfill the pressing social role of film—the redemption of physical reality for people lost in scientific abstraction.

We can ask at least two questions about the first premise: Is modern society alienated from physical reality and the experience of particularity? Is this the result of science? The first question is not easy to answer. How could you tell if a society is alienated from physical reality? Does driving a car put you in contact with physical reality or not? If not, why not? If it does so, since so many drive cars in first world societies (which I take it is, for Kracauer, the locus of modern society), then is alienation really so rampant? Perhaps Kracauer has something particular in mind that would discount counterexamples like this one. But then the burden of proof is on him to articulate it. Ironically, he rarely speaks in terms of abstractions less encompassing than "physical existence," "material reality," and so on.

Furthermore, even if we are amidst the crisis Kracauer adumbrates, has science brought it about? There aren't that many scientists in the population statistically and scientific knowledge does not pervade mass society. There are more people obsessed with alien abductions and satanic cults than those obsessed with quantum physics.

Moreover, pundits who believe in the crisis of abstraction have advanced other causes for it, such as bureaucracy and technology, including information technologies, a class to which film belongs. Indeed, few, I think, would endorse the end-of-ideology theme that Kracauer takes as given, and many who are sure that ideology is still alive and well might be disposed to attribute the alleged crisis of abstraction to ideology.

The question of whether science did it is especially problematic when it comes to Kracauer's third premise. For many nowadays who are disposed to agree with Kracauer that there is a crisis of abstraction would be prone to attribute it to the proliferation of information technologies, including both film and photography. We live in a mediated world, so the story goes, and you can't smell the roses if you are looking at a photograph of one.

Perhaps Kracauer would respond that the alienation from the physical world is only abetted by certain uses of film and photography, the ones that he regards as uncinematic and unphotographic. But certainly the case could be made that technological mediation in any form alienates us from the physical world, that is, if you believe that most of us are alienated from the physical world. Film, it might be said, tends, no matter how it is used, to estrange people from the flow of life, not to reimmerse them in it. (I raise this point not in order to endorse it, but only to remind the reader that if you believe that we are alienated from the physical world, particular things, and the flow of life, then you might still reject Kracauer's project of redemption because of a view of information technologies in general, which view, by the way, Kracauer has not bothered to foreclose.)[34]

Furthermore, before committing film to a crusade against abstraction, one might like to hear more from Kracauer about how film, even cinematic film, is supposed to secure this end. Why will seeing photographic pictures of particular things loosen the grip of scientific abstraction in the cases of those caught up in it? Is there some special psychological mechanism that will swing into operation here? Kracauer leaves such questions unanswered, which, in turn, leaves me skeptical.

Some aestheticians are apt to reject Kracauer's second premise—that if modern society faces a desperate situation, like the so-called crisis of alienation from the physical world, and, in addition, some artistic media can make a difference, then they should. Their grounds might be that art is and should be divorced from claims of social utility. I, however, am sympathetic to Kracauer's intuitions here. I see no genuine philosophical objection to placing art in the service of society. Nevertheless, again, I would like to have a better account of the way in which a particular art, like film, can actually alleviate the putative malaise of abstraction as well as more compelling evidence that we are, in fact, in the throes of such an epidemic.

Moreover, I should also note that Kracauer's suggestion that film serve the needs of the modern world appears inconsistent with the disparaging things that he has to say about film genres that persist because they "cater to widespread social and cultural demands."[35] For isn't this the grounds for Kracauer's historical/cultural defense of his conception of cinematic films? Here Kracauer would probably respond that he is not talking about catering, but ministering. But I suspect that his opponents will charge that this is just another case of his begging the question.

In summary, Kracauer's *Theory of Film* is an ambitious attempt to defend film realism—the doctrine that film should be realist because it is, in essence, photographic. Kracauer maintains that in order to be authentically cinematic, film should be true to its photographic nature, which brings with it an inherent commitment to realism. However, we have seen that Kracauer's defense of this conclusion frequently relies on question-begging assumptions that should be the results of his arguments rather than their premises, hidden or otherwise. In this, Kracauer's attempt corresponds to a recurring tendency in classical film theory. For the quest for the cinematic generally travels in a circle with theorists, like Kracauer, discovering this or that nature of the cinematic by presupposing it from the start.

NOTES

1. Siegfried Kracauer, *Theory of Film: The Redemption of Physical Reality* (Oxford: Oxford University Press, 1960; repr., 1973). My source is the 1973 reprint of this book. For students interested in reading more works by Kracauer, a useful guide is "Kracauer in English: A Bibliography," by Thomas Levin in *New German Critique*, no. 41 (Spring–Summer 1987).

2. For examples of some of Kracauer's earlier writings on film and mass culture, see Siegfried Kracauer, *The Mass Ornament*, trans. Thomas Levin (Cambridge: Harvard University Press, 1995).

3. It should be noted that at present there is lively interest in Kracauer's early writings on cinema among film scholars as well as a general interest in Kracauer's highly diversified writings as cultural theorist, especially in relation to his contemporaries, such as Walter Benjamin and T. W. Adorno. Some might even claim that these writings are more interesting than *Theory of Film*. Nevertheless, *Theory of Film* is an important landmark in the evolution of film theory as we now know it, and, therefore, still commands attention on its own terms. For a taste of recent writings on Kracauer as a Weimar intellectual and an émigré scholar, one place to start might be the *Special Issue on Siegfried Kracauer* presented by *New German Critique*, no. 34 (Fall 1991). Of special use for students in that issue is "The English-Language Reception of Kracauer's Work: A Bibliography" by Thomas Y. Levin. Also of interest is Dagmar Barnouw, *Critical Realism: History, Photography and the Work of Siegfried Kracauer* (Baltimore: Johns Hopkins University Press, 1994).

4. In this assessment, I differ from Dudley Andrew, who finds the book "utterly transparent." Unlike Andrew, I think that *Theory of Film* gives only the appearance of clarity. With a little probing, it turns out to be a morass. See Dudley Andrew, "Siegfried Kracauer," in his book *The Major Film Theories* (Oxford: Oxford University Press, 1976), 106.

5. For biographical information about Kracauer, see esp. Martin Jay's "The Extraterritorial Life of Siegfried Kracauer," in idem, *Permanent Exiles: Essays on the Intellectual Migration from Germany to America* (New York: Columbia University Press, 1985). Also of interest in that volume are Jay's essays: "Politics of Translation: Siegfried Kracauer and Walter Benjamin on the Buber-Rosenzweig Bible" and "Adorno and Kracauer: Notes on a Trou-

bled Friendship." For a more informal biographical account, see Leo Lowenthal, "As I Remember Friedel," *New German Critique,* no. 54 (Fall 1991).

6. Pauline Kael is very adept at demonstrating this. See Pauline Kael, "Is There a Cure for Film Criticism? Or: Some Unhappy Thoughts on Siegfried Kracauer's *Nature of Film,*" *Sight and Sound* 31, no. 2 (Spring 1962).

7. Kracauer, 58.

8. See André Bazin, *What Is Cinema?* trans. Hugh Gray (Berkeley: University of California Press, 1967), vol. 1.

9. Kracauer, 69.

10. Ibid., chapter 14.

11. Ibid., ix.

12. Ibid.

13. Ibid.

14. Gotthold Ephraim Lessing, *Laocoon* (New York: Noonday, 1969). For a brief summary of this persuasion, see Noël Carroll, *Philosophical Problems of Classical Film Theory* (Princeton: Princeton University Press, 1988).

15. The qualification "most probably" is introduced here in order to be sensitive to the fact that with particular cases Kracauer sometimes adduces compensating factors that insulate films that one might predict would be criticized on the basis of his theory from condemnation. Thus, the staginess of *The Cabinet of Dr. Caligari* is supposedly mitigated by underscoring a contrast between motion and motionless (Kracauer, 61). As I have said earlier, I find Kracauer's ingenuity in incessantly discovering such mitigating circumstances and compensatory considerations suspiciously and lamentably ad hoc. Nevertheless, since he finds so many special cases, it is safest to represent him as holding that ostensibly unsuitable cinematic content is only probable grounds for chastising a given film. One must also cinch the case at hand by assuring oneself that there are no extenuating considerations.

16. Kracauer, vii.

17. Ibid.

18. Ibid., 27.

19. Notice that although Kracauer repeatedly stresses that film finds its origins in photography, he does not use this to establish that photography is its basic element. Perhaps this is because he realizes that origin is irrelevant to essence. For example, if architecture originated in stone or wooden structures, that is nevertheless irrelevant to determining the essence of architecture, since other building materials, like steel and glass, became available to architecture after its origin.

20. For an examination of the medium specificity notion, see the first chapter of my *Philosophical Problems of Classical Film Theory.* Medium specificity theories of film appeared in Germany in the twenties, when Kracauer was a film reviewer. Indeed, one such theory that also claimed that film was realistic was propounded by Rudolf Harms, though Kracauer criticized it for other reasons. See Rudolf Harms, *Philosophie des Films: Seine aesthetischen un metaphysichen* (Zurich: Felix Meiner, 1926). For background information about early German film theory, consult Sabine Hake, *The Cinema's Third Machine: Writing on Film in Germany 1907–1933* (Lincoln: University of Nebraska Press, 1993).

21. Kracauer, 3.

22. It should be noted that the notion that film records and reveals reality may cause problems for the loose ways in which Kracauer characterizes "reality." Kracauer seems to think that talk about material reality and visible reality are interchangeable. But if we are talking about material reality, then revealing its nature (e.g., in terms of atomic structure) may be at odds with recording visible reality.

23. See Lev Kuleshov, *Kuleshov on Film,* trans. Ronald Levaco (Berkeley: University of California Press, 1975).

24. On pp. 12–13, Kracauer allows that determining the nature of certain media may be difficult, but then asserts that this is not the case for photography. Well, there's a knock-down, drag-out argument for you.

25. Kracauer, 37.

26. Ibid., 18–20.

27. Ibid., 71.

28. It is interesting to note that V. F. Perkins also develops a similar two-part approach to film that explicitly attempts to reconcile realist and formative tendencies. On his view, realism is a necessary condition for film as film and it constrains the range of formative effects. However, the range of formative effects for Perkins is not a matter of revealing reality but of making symbolic comments on it, where these comments are to be motivated by what is photographically plausible within the story world. It would be a nice question to consider how Kracauer would argue for the superiority of his theory against a competing theory as close to his own as Perkins' is. See V. F. Perkins, *Film as Film* (Baltimore: Penguin, 1972).

29. Probably Hollywood genre films, in general, tend to operate within narratively closed universes and, consequently, they would engender Kracauer's opprobrium. Perhaps this is the grounds for Heide Schlupmann's interesting suggestion that *Theory of Film* is a reaction to 1950s American films. See Heide Schlupmann's "On the Subject of Survival: On Kracauer's Theory of Film," *New German Critique,* no. 54 (Fall 1991): 121.

30. See Andrew Tudor's useful "Aesthetics of Realism: Bazin and Kracauer" for an alternative, though compatible, way of setting out Kracauer's argument in *Theories of Film* by Andrew Tudor (London: Secker and Warburg in association with the British Film Institute, 1974), 84.

31. This is not said to defend Kuleshov's view, but only to point up problems with Kracauer's. In point of fact, I reject all medium specificity arguments, including Kuleshov's. For my arguments, see Noël Carroll, *Theorizing the Moving Image* (New York: Cambridge University Press, 1996).

32. For speculation on the religious sources of Kracauer's theorizing, see Miriam Hansen, "Decentric Perspectives: Kracauer's Early Writings on Film and Mass Culture," *New German Critique,* no. 54 (Fall 1991).

33. Hugo Münsterberg, *Film: A Psychological Study* (New York: Dover, 1970).

34. For the record, I should say that I am not convinced that modern society is alienated from the physical world, since I am so unclear about what such an alienation would involve.

35. Kracauer, 38.

Chapter 15 Cinematic
Nation Building: Eisenstein's
The Old and the New

If, as Benedict Anderson has suggested, the idea of a nation is in large measure imagined retrospectively, the Soviet Union offers an interesting counterpoint—that of a nation imagined prospectively.[1] The Soviet Union literally had to be invented. As is well known, cinema was expected to play a crucial role in this process. Surely it was for such a purpose that Lenin anointed cinema the premier socialist artform. Many Soviet films of the twenties were devoted to consolidating a tradition for the new nation, commemorating its revolutionary founding in historical spectacles, like V. I. Pudovkin's *The End of St. Petersburg* and Sergei Eisenstein's *October*. But certain other films, like Dziga Vertov's *Man With a Movie Camera* and Eisenstein's *The Old and the New* (originally called *The General Line*),[2] looked primarily to the future, rather than to the past, in order to imagine what the Soviet Union could become. In this essay, we intend to look at the ways in which Eisenstein attempted in *The Old and the New* to contribute to the construction of the Soviet Union by means of what might be called "cinematic nation building."[3]

Perhaps the most important feature of the future Soviet Union that Eisenstein envisions in *The Old and the New* is that it is a nation in which agriculture and industry, the countryside and the city are coordinated—turned into a smoothly operating, reciprocally functioning system in which each side of the equation adds to the other symbiotically. Undoubtedly, part of the inspiration for this ideal picture of the Soviet Union comes from Marxist theory. In *The German Ideology*, Marx and Engels noted the tendency of the rise of capitalism to exacerbate a division, even an antagonism, between town and country.[4] But, at the same time, Marx and Engels also predicted that the antagonism between town and country would be reconciled by the advent of communism and the cooperative development of machinery.[5]

In *The Old and the New*, this theoretical blueprint becomes virtually a storyboard for illustrating the imagined community into which Eisenstein hoped the Soviet nation might evolve. In the film, a part of which is explicitly notated as a dream (a wish-fulfillment dream), Eisenstein visualizes a reverie derived straight out of the writings of Marx and Engels; he dreams of—imagines—a nation where town (industry) and country (agriculture) become as one, transcending (as the film's title suggests) the tsarist "old" in favor of the Marxist "new."[6]

If abstract Marxist theory provides part of the background of *The Old and the New*, a more proximate cause of the thinking behind the film can be found in Soviet agricultural policies of the 1920s. One of the most pressing economic (and therefore political) issues the Soviet Union faced in the mid-1920s was the need to increase agricultural production and to modernize it, where, in fact, increasing agricultural production would serve as a means toward modernization inasmuch as agricultural surpluses could then be traded for foreign currency, which could be used to purchase much-needed foreign technology.

Although some progress had been made under the New Economic Policy (following the devastation of the Civil War), there were still major problems in the mid-1920s that needed to be addressed in order to integrate agriculture into the socialist economy. These included a regular, reliable supply of agricultural raw materials for industry and of provisions for a growing urban population, as well as foodstuffs for foreign trade to earn monies for industrialization. However, as in Tsarist Russia, the relationship between the peasants and the government was volatile; although they benefited from the Bolsheviks' reallocation of land, the peasants violently resisted the state's interventions, particularly taxation and repeated emergency requisitions of food supplies.

When Eisenstein began working on *The Old and the New* in 1926, there had been a good harvest for the first time in four years and, as a result of this and the relatively free-market situation during the NEP years, an economic equilibrium obtained between industry and agriculture as well as between the peasants and the state. The "general line" of the Fourteenth Party Congress of December 1925 (for which Eisenstein's film had originally been named) called for the collectivization of farming, but it was understood then that this would be gradual. In the fall of 1927, the party endorsed a plan to double grain production within ten years. And at the Fifteenth Party Congress of December 1927, agricultural collectivization was named "the main task of the party in the countryside."[7] But this was soon followed by a massive grain crisis—due both to a lower harvest and to strong peasant resistance to state prices—and by more emergency requisitions. So by the time Eisenstein resumed work on *The Old and the New* in June 1928, there was a concentrated move by the state to speed up agriculture technologically, primarily through encouraging voluntary collectivization and large-scale, mechanized crop production (rather than small-scale subsistence farming), for which the tractor was an essential component.[8] Thus, Soviet state policy had changed from primarily treating the peasant economy as a place to obtain agricultural products to organizing and socializing it to mesh with goals of increased production in the industrial sector, a goal that would soon find concrete expression in the Five-Year Plan.

The Soviet government needed agricultural products not simply to feed the whole population but to use in the foreign trade market to raise funds for capitalization—that is, to get money to invest in industrialization. Agriculture was to be a means to develop industry, which, in turn, would reciprocally contribute to the modernization of agriculture through scientific planning, the breeding of both grains and livestock, and the introduction of machinery. In this cycle of agricultural-industrial modernization the tractor—which could replace inefficient strip cultivation of individual farms with large-scale cooperative crop production—played a central role. Erich Strauss notes that collectivization was seen as the major means to modernize Soviet agriculture; "a more effective force than the slow influence of education and example was needed. This was believed to be the mechanization of the main cropping operations . . . ; thus the tractor became the symbol of this policy [of modernization through cooperation] and the main agent of change."[9]

This theme of a nation built on the reciprocal coordination of agriculture and industry, to the mutual benefit of both—a link emblematized by the tractor—forms the basis of Eisenstein's film *The Old and the New*.[10]

RECONCILING AGRICULTURE
AND INDUSTRY VISUALLY

One of Eisenstein's abiding projects as a filmmaker was the aspiration to break out of the photographic particularity of the cinematic image in order to generalize—in order to articulate abstract ideas and concepts. In his silent films, montage provided a major mechanism for achieving this end because by inducing the spectator to infer the relation between disparate shots, Eisenstein opened up the possibility of provoking the viewer to impute linkages of greater and greater abstraction, in order to make ongoing shot chains intelligible.[11] As is well known, Eisenstein called his most ambitious attempts in this direction "intellectual montage," and in *October* he pushed this line of experimentation to the hilt in the well-known "Gods" sequence (in which he attempted to disprove the existence of God cinematically).[12] Indeed, Eisenstein even supposed that he would be able to perfect the strategies of intellectual montage to the point where he could make a film of Marx's *Capital*.[13]

Though *The Old and the New* is most frequently cited by Eisenstein as an example of what he called "overtonal montage," notably with reference to the famous religious procession, it is, as well, an experiment in intellectual montage,[14] one explicitly heralded by Eisenstein and Grigori Alexandrov as "an experiment intelligible to the millions."[15] In *The Old and the New,* Eisenstein is committed to clarifying for the plain viewer through montage an abstract social process—namely, the way in which agricultural production will make possible industrialization, which, in turn, will abet even further agricultural production. Intellectual montage, that is, is put in the service of the Soviet policy of nation building, articulating visually how enhanced agricultural output is connected to industrial modernization, which then contributes to enhanced agricultural productivity, which then . . . and so on. An underlying theme of *The Old and the New* is to make the ordinary audience conscious of an abstract causal relation—or, at least, a causal relation hopefully anticipated by Soviet planners—between agricultural productivity and industry.[16]

Intellectual montage becomes the means for cinematic nation building in *The Old and the New* by proposing to viewers a series of what might be called instances of "fantastic causation," which suggest impossible causal relations by juxtaposing shots of local agricultural activities and far-off industrialization.[17] These juxtapositions can be rendered intelligible by inferring that they pertain to an abstract causal network, one belonging to the future Soviet Union, imagined as a nation where farm and factory are part of a single, coordinated process—one where town and countryside are thoroughly reconciled.

Three examples of this editing occur in the film: in the cream separator sequence; in Marfa's dream of the state collective farm; and in the "marriage" sequence between the bull Fomka and his bride. In each of these sequences, interpolated into the edited array are shots of masses of water, pouring down the walls and over the locks of giant dams. These are, of course, hydroelectric plants, key elements in the industrialization of the Soviet Union. Their inclusion in montage sequences ostensibly depicting local argicultural activities—such as cream separating—suggests that from such humble work, great industrial power-plants will come, exactly those of which Soviet planners dreamed. That is, this imagery implies that the work of the countryside can be harnessed and coordinated (causally) to the expansion of industry.

In the cream separator sequence, the imagery of dams first occurs after the liquid gushing from the mechanism splatters all over Marfa's face. An intertitle appears: "It's thickened." And then we see three shots of mountains of water cresting the wall of a hydroelectric plant. Ensuing shots of celebratory fountains shooting water upward follow, as do shots of the laughing, happy faces of peasants. As a result of the success of the cream separator, membership in the dairy collective increases. Intertitles of the growing numbers of members, intercut with fountains spewing water, appear rapidly; "46, 48, 50"—and then we again see shots of the dam, taken from opposite directions, water cascading into the array.

The imagery of the dam water in the cream separator sequence can be interpreted in two ways. Like the celebratory fountain imagery, it can be taken as a hyperbolic cinematic simile for the liquid flowing out of the cream separator—as if the device produced oceans of milk. But it is also decipherable as part of a fantastic process of causation—from cream separators like these, mighty dams will emerge, thereby literalizing the Soviet plan to transform agriculture into the basis for industrialization.

This imagery of hydroelectric plants recurs in both Marfa's dream and Fomka's wedding. After saving the dairy collective's cash reserves, Marfa falls asleep on the money-box and dreams of acquiring a bull and, thereby, transforming the cooperative into a cattle collective. In her dream, through superimposition, a bull as large as Godzilla rises from the earth and dominates a field populated by a herd of cattle. Magically, the bull, somewhat unaccountably, seems to rain milk on the landscape. Then there are cuts to the cooling coils of

a refrigeration machine, with milk spilling over and finally coating them. Intercut with the refrigeration coils are waves of white water, sometimes represented
in reverse motion, as if the milk had gathered together in an immense torrent.[18]
But this torrent does not look as though it belongs to a natural waterway, but
more like water crossing locks. Finally, the shots of the dams from the cream
separator sequence are also interpolated in the array, their repetition underscoring the importance for Eisenstein of linking the country and industry.
Again, that is, the cutting seems to move us from agricultural production to industrialization.

As in the case of the cream separator sequence, these shots of dam water can
be read equally as metaphors of plenitude or as parts of an imaginary causal
process, one that links dairy production to industrialization. Moreover, the
theme of industry is clearly central to the cutting here, since this sequence of
milk raining down from the sky segues into a sequence in an automated milk-
bottling plant. Thus, we suggest that the best way to take the dam imagery is
both in terms of metaphors of abundance ("rivers of milk") and images of fantastic causation (more milk makes for more industrialization).

In the sequence of Fomka's wedding, the imagery of the dam appears for the
third time. As the exuberant Fomka charges, in fast motion, toward his cow
bride (so excited is he that he crosses the 180 degree line!) and as she opens her
legs, there are shots of explosions followed by dam water. The shots are undoubtedly meant to symbolize a profusion of bull sperm, but, again, they also
carry the implication of a relation between agricultural production and industry. Perhaps the explosion is doubly decipherable—not only as coitus, but as
clearing the ground for a hydroelectric plant.[19] Compressing time drastically,
what follows is a shot of Fomka's progeny, a row of at least eight calves—more
milk and meat for further capitalization.

The most obvious example of Eisenstein's use of intellectual montage to articulate the abstract plan to coordinate the farm with the factory comes in the
finale of the tractor scene. As the tractor rushes toward the camera, in some
prints an intertitle reading "Forward" appears. Then there are three shots of
fences—the fences, signaling privatization, that appeared in the beginning of
the film and that represent an impediment to agricultural productivity. Next
the tractor crashes through the fences, expressing optatively the triumph of collectivization. There ensue several shots of the tractor destroying the fences—
Eisenstein evidently relishes this spectacle and wishes the audience to do likewise.

At last, there is a shot of a tractor wheel crushing a section of wooden fencing in a furrow. Thence, Eisenstein cuts to a steel factory, where the blast from the furnace seems figuratively to be ignited by the wheel of the tractor. After three shots of smelting, two shots depict a shower of molten sparks. Next a tractor is lowered from above, presumably from an assembly line. The cutting here unmistakably implies that by opening the fields to large-scale collective agricultural production, industrial productivity results causally. Or, at least, Eisenstein's "unrealistic" juxtaposition of shots very strongly suggests such a thought.

Eisenstein continues the preceding cutting pattern several times—from shots of flaming steel to tractors swinging off the assembly line. Finally, one tractor is lowered toward the ground and, by means of a cut, it sets down "magically" on farmland, where it proceeds to churn up the earth. If at the beginning of the shot chain, agricultural developments lead to increased industrial production, by the end of the sequence, industry's contribution to agricultural production is made apparent.

From tight shots of tractors plowing the earth, Eisenstein cuts to long shots of a group of tractors plowing together in an enlarging circle—what Eisenstein refers to as the "merry-go-round."[20] If earlier shots of the film showed us multitudes of livestock, here we encounter multitudes of tractors—agricultural plenitude has been transformed into industrially produced plenitude (tractors everywhere), which, of course, will have momentous consequences for future agriculture.

The intertitle "Forward" intervenes; the circularly moving tractors are now driving off the screen in a straight line. After the intertitle "Onward," the tractors continue toward the camera, but they have just multiplied, as if by cell division, into three columns. Finally, Eisenstein pulls back for a very long shot, where we see not only columns of tractors, but other agricultural machinery. The image resembles nothing so much as a military parade—a revolutionary procession—displaying the newest agricultural hardware and celebrating the ultimate reconciliation of the farm and the city in which the countryside itself is becoming industrialized.[21]

In some prints, the parade is missing; the film cuts from the circular plowing to imposing siloes and then to enormous piles of sacks of grain. This pattern also realizes the planner's dream for the future Soviet Union, since this abundance of grain, seen in historical context, is now available for export where trade, in turn, would be a means to secure the badly needed foreign capital necessary for the further industrialization of the future Russia, the imagined modern Soviet nation-state.

Through intellectual montage, in *The Old and the New* Eisenstein visualizes existing plans for Soviet nation building. By tracing processes of fantastic causation from agricultural activities to industry, Eisenstein attempts to make abstract economic planning intelligible, by cinematic means, to the millions. Perhaps one reason why the intellectual montage in *The Old and the New* could be more intelligible to the millions than much of the editing in *October* is that it is based upon visually suggesting causal relations, albeit fantastical ones, whereas the conceptual relations required to "fill in" the "Gods" sequence in *October* rely on ordinary viewers to mobilize ideas far less familiar to them than that of causation. But, in any case, it should be manifest that by editing in a manner that strongly suggests causal relations between country and city, Eisenstein discovered a way to deploy intellectual montage for the purposes of cinematic nation building.

Along with the imagery connecting agriculture and industry, another major visual motif in the editing of *The Old and the New,* as already indicated, involves plenitude. Not only individual shots, but whole, elaborate shot series are devoted to proliferating abounding herds of cattle and other livestock, as well as, by the end, an army of tractors. This theme of multiplication takes shape, in contrast, to a darkly opening introductory sequence about divisiveness among the peasants.

As is their custom, the brothers of a rural family divide their property in half. Eisenstein depicts this bifidization process in great detail, illustrating with all sorts of cinematic devices—including not only cuts, but wipes—how the peasants take every piece of the house apart and criss-cross the land with a complicated fretwork of fences. This division between them is the source of their privation, and it is the problematic that the rest of the film promises to dispel, ultimately as the tractor smashes all the fences, unleashing the industrial and agricultural abundance described already. This movement from division to multiplication occurs in stages throughout the film, each agricultural breakthrough leading to more—more livestock, more grain, more tractors, all lovingly inventoried by Eisenstein's camera, which finds fecundity and multiplicity everywhere. The visual theme of multiplication radiates the prosperity of the imagined Soviet state through montage that not only attempts to show how agriculture and industry could be coordinated to attain this, but tries to instill enthusiasm in viewers to the point where they might be willing to participate in making this imagined abundance a reality.

Throughout *The Old and the New,* Eisenstein employs montage-in-the-single-shot, as well as editing, to make abstract Soviet economic policy visible.[22] Especially in the scenes at the state collective farm, by using a wide lens,

Eisenstein articulates the backgrounds and foregrounds of many shots in such a way that the different temporal phases of the collectivization/industrialization process are co-present simultaneously. Thus, we will see cream separators in the background of shots with cattle in the foreground, or tractors in back of, in front of, or in between cattle. The sequence—dairy collective (cream separator), cattle collective (bull-sire and/or harem), and automated collective (tractor)—is, consequently, telescoped repeatedly into a single image, visually exhibiting for and reminding the spectator of the synergies upon which Soviet agricultural planners banked their hopes for the new Russian nation.

There is also an important visual motif in the film—which is the result of neither montage in the single shot nor montage between shots—that makes the point about the relation between agriculture and industry eminently apparent. It involves the visual equation of the bull Fomka and the tractor. When young Fomka "grows up" to be a bridegroom, Eisenstein achieves this effect by quickly cutting together shots of successively larger bulls, thereby "animating" the array. Likewise, the tractor Marfa acquires from the factory is constructed through animation. Moreover, when, in superimposition, that tractor enters its shed, it appears to go through the very doors that Fomka exited to meet his bride.

Fomka and the tractor are, in other words, treated as visual equivalents. As Fomka is poisoned by envious kulaks, the collective is acquiring the tractor; and as soon as Fomka dies, the tractor arrives, ready to take his place. The visual narration suggests an exchange of Fomka for the tractor, as if the death (sacrifice?) of the bull makes way for the appearance of the tractor. And this visual theme, of course, repeats in yet another register, the recurring idea of Eisenstein's cinematic nation building. That is, from bulls come tractors, or, more prosaically, from agriculture, industry, and then back again.

MARFA'S STORY: RECONCILING AGRICULTURE
AND INDUSTRY NARRATIVELY

If through intellectual montage and related visual devices Eisenstein lays out an abstract plan for building the future Soviet nation, he also gives this scenario narrative substance, thereby literally bringing economic theorizing down to earth. That is, Eisenstein fleshes out the intended relationship between agriculture and industry—between countryside and city—that is heralded in the editing in *The Old and the New* by creating a concrete embodiment of the collectivization process in the experience of Marfa Lapkina, a case study that illustrates "what is to be done."[23]

In a departure from his practice in previous films of using mass heroes, here Eisenstein focuses on a particular hero—Marfa Lapkina, a peasant woman. Intertitles explicitly state that Marfa stands for millions of peasants. On them the success of the Soviet Union depended, and, in turn, their future was in the hands of the new state. But Marfa is also an individual—a particularly intrepid one who, though a poor peasant in straitened circumstances, shows unflagging resourcefulness and dignity.

Marfa comes to see clearly, on a personal level, that she and her neighbors will only survive through cooperation for mutual aid; yet beyond this, she realizes that the success of the community cooperative depends on the ability of the peasants to reach out from the village to link their own agricultural production with modern urban and state industry. In other words, she understands not through abstract political theorizing but directly from her own experience that the Soviet socialist model of collectivization, on the one hand, and forging a *smychka* (union) between peasant and proletarian, farming and industry, on the other, is the only way out of poverty. And the fruit of her autodidactic political consciousness is exemplary for the nation, since what Marfa makes happen on the local level—as she forms a village cooperative, which then collaborates with a group of city workers to their mutual benefit—is precisely what the Bolsheviks believed was needed in the Soviet state nationally, on a massive, nation-wide scale.

This union was also necessary at a more abstract macro-level: it was thought that agriculture in general needed to be linked to industrial mechanization and scientific planning in order for the country as a whole to survive and flourish. In the film, this desired union of agriculture and industry is finally secured allegorically in the coda, when Marfa and the male tractor-driver embrace, for the romantic ending of this story is the promise that countryside and city will live together, happily ever after—unlike the ending of Chaplin's *A Woman of Paris,* against which Eisenstein is playing here.

Although Lenin is invoked many times in *The Old and the New* and the helpful district agronomist even looks like the Bolshevik leader, crucially it is an ordinary peasant woman, a "little person," who is the representative hero of the film. This was in keeping with the tendency in Soviet art and literature at the time of the first Five-Year Plan—a period of cultural revolution as well as social construction. Inspired by Maxim Gorky, and in contrast to bourgeois writers who celebrated the actions of "great men," Soviet writers during the late twenties depicted "little men" as important actors on the world stage; however small the actions of these characters, they were still "great deeds," because they were essential to the overall functioning of society and, cumulatively, they added up.[24] Not yet the monumental heroic leader of the post-1932 Socialist Realist period, the "little person" of Soviet fiction was an ordinary industrial worker or peasant, a small cog in the social machine who nevertheless was outstanding for his contribution to socialist construction.

Marfa is exactly the kind of "little person" Gorky described, no longer to be pitied, as in so much pre-Soviet literature and art, but capable of raising herself and her neighbors to a full measure of "human dignity" and realizing her "creative" potential."[25] It is in the details of Marfa's particularized story that Eisenstein dramatizes the deplorable situation of the peasant masses and proposes a resolution. From a state of poverty, ignorance, and separation, the peasants will reach an unheard-of level of prosperity, consciousness, and cooperation by means of the union between agriculture and industry. But this does not happen magically, overnight. It is a process of economic growth and political awakening by successive stages; as Eisenstein puts it, "From a separator to a pedigreed bull, from a bull to a tractor. To two, to ten, to a hundred!"[26] It is a process of nation building through cooperation, unification, and multiplication.

At the beginning of the film, we see the general situation (the old) that needs to be rectified (the new). Individual peasant families live in squalor—what Marx called "rural idiocy."[27] This was the legacy of poverty and illiteracy, as the intertitle tells us, left to the Russian peasant (and thus to the Russian nation) by the old order. In cramped and unsanitary conditions, in chimneyless huts dimmed with smoke and puddled with rainwater, the peasants sleep indolently, right next to barnyard animals. The scene calls to mind Leo Tolstoy's play *The Power of Darkness,* a forceful and deeply disturbing outcry against the degradation and depravity of the Russian peasant in the late nineteenth century.[28] The scene raises the narrative (and political) question: can this situation be overcome?

As a farm is divided in half by two brothers, Eisenstein shows us that the peasants' problem is not only poverty and illiteracy, but the divisions between people, especially problematic in the privatization of farming. To solve their problems, to emerge from their darkness, to escape poverty, the peasants must be brought together—and Marfa will be the instrument of that movement toward cooperation. The theme of cooperation (and ultimately of collectivization) becomes as important for the narrative as the theme of the union between agriculture and industry is for the intellectual montage. Only with cooperation at every level of society will the new Soviet nation be realized.

Through editing and titling, Eisenstein narrows the focus from an undifferentiated group of peasants to "one of many"—Marfa Lapkina. A typical "poor peasant," she takes an inventory of her meager belongings.[29] Depicted as alone in her barren courtyard, she has but a wooden plow, no horse, and only one emaciated cow. It's spring. However, without the right combination of animal and equipment, Marfa can't plow. She goes to the neighboring kulaks to borrow a horse, but gets no help from them. As she fails in her attempts to use her cow to cultivate the field, and as we compare her struggle to those of her neighbors, she (and we) see the need for collaboration. Provoked by a sense of aloneness and frustration, Marfa pounds her fist against the inert plow. Eisenstein then cuts to her pounding fist at a village meeting, where now she calls for positive, constructive action—for collectivization. The ingenious matched-movement editing suggests that her indignation metamorphoses out of her frustration.

Marfa proposes that the village form a dairy cooperative—the Path of October *artel*—and she becomes its most vigorous supporter. In the face of her neighbors' skepticism, superstition, and resistance to change, she steadfastly plans for—and takes actions to build—a better future. She defends the dairy cooperative's savings. And it is Marfa who has the idea to use the profits to buy a pedigreed bull; she herself goes off to the state farm to get the bull. Thus the dairy cooperative becomes a cattle cooperative. And again, it is Marfa who drives to the city to get the tractor, and who herself becomes a tractor driver. With the tractor, the artel can become a *kolkhoz*—a collective farm that works the land cooperatively. This local transformation is a segment of the general line—the strategy of building a Soviet nation.

As she moves, often overcoming setbacks, through these three key stages of rural economic development (dairy collective, cattle collective, collective farm), Marfa simultaneously moves through levels of political consciousness as well. By organizing the dairy cooperative, she helps the villagers progress beyond individualized subsistence farming—and beyond competition and self-interest. Through the collective use of modern technology—the cream separator—the coop can produce butter, which, since it doesn't spoil as quickly as milk, can be shipped to the city for trade. And when shared profits from that trade enable the co-op to buy the pedigreed bull, at the large state farm that produced Fomka, Marfa sees the future: a marriage of agriculture and industry on a large-scale landscape, where not only is butter produced and, through genetic engineering, superior livestock are bred, but also a phalanx of tractors rolls through the fields. It is as if Marfa realizes, seeing all these things together, that from cream separators both bulls and tractors can flow and that science and industry can enrich nature.

Finally, to procure a tractor for the cooperative, Marfa teams up with city workers to cut through the bureaucratic red tape that stands in the way of forming and fully automating a collective farm for crop production.[30] Where formerly Marfa was helpless in the face of the kulaks' obstructionism, uniting with the city workers helps her overcome the equally unyielding bureaucrats (who are visually equated with the fat but stingy kulaks).[31] This collaboration, this synergistic union of country and city, of agriculture and industry, is what is ultimately needed to cultivate the land properly—to help it reach its fullest potential. The land should be worked cooperatively for the common benefit (the peasants', the proletarians', *and* the nation's). The peasants advance from individualism to collectivism; from division to multiplication; from poverty to abundance.

Moreover, the wealth created by the artel is productive, since it is communal wealth that is plowed back into development—unlike the selfish, hoarded, individualized wealth of the kulaks who refused to lend Marfa their horse and who poison Fomka. Metaphorically, we are shown through the optimistic story of Marfa and the Path of October dairy cooperative that the nation-state will flourish through collectivization, despite the antisocial acts of corrupt individuals.

In trying to reinvent culture after the Bolshevik revolution, and especially during this period in the late 1920s, when the strategy of reaching mass audiences with avant-garde artworks had emerged as problematic, artists had to decide which elements of pre-Soviet culture to discard, which to preserve, and which to rework and transform. *The Old and the New*'s fairy-tale traits are striking in this regard.

In some respects, Marfa's story resembles a traditional Russian fairy-tale. The narrative has a conventional fairy-tale structure, in which the hero embarks repeatedly on trips to fulfill a quest, undergoes various trials, has visionary dreams, solves difficult problems, and along the way encounters several magical helpers who help him attain his goal, in the form of a desired object (as well as meeting several hindrances and enemies).[32] In fact, in accordance with the typical tripartite pattern, Marfa makes three trips: the first, to the kulaks' house, where she begs for a horse; the second, to the state farm, where she buys a bull; the third, to the bureaucrats' office, where she gets permission to get a tractor on credit. Though her first trip appears unsuccessful, in fact her failure to borrow the kulaks' horse leads her to a different and ultimately far better path— literally, since the Path of October dairy collective is formed as a result of her inability to plow.

Visually, Marfa's visit both to the kulaks and then to the bureaucrats is also reminiscent of a fairy-tale, since they and the objects that surround them are huge—like fairy-tale giants—and she is minuscule. The cream separator, abundantly flowing with sustenance, recalls the various "inexhaustible" magical objects of various folktales that produce endless cornucopiae of food and drink: "the tablecloth that spreads itself," "the decanter that does the catering."[33] Similarly, the tractor that can pull an apparently endless chain of wagons seems like a feat from a wonder tale. Finally, Marfa's story has a standard fairy-tale ending, alluding not only to the happiness of the hero, but to material abundance (often in the form of food or drink, as for instance in the tale-teller's stock conclusion: "And I was there, I drank the mead and beer, it flowed over my moustache, but missed my mouth").[34] And this abundance, the film suggests, will be the bounty of the whole nation.[35]

Perhaps Eisenstein used the fairy-tale structure and imagery so familiar from oral folk culture as a deliberate strategy to make *The Old and the New* intelligible and attractive to, as he says, the millions. The use and reworking of popular folklore—the reinterpretation of fragments of tradition—is a recurring strategy of nation building.[36] Other aspects of rural folk culture—notably, the wedding ceremony, though comically displaced here from humans to cattle[37]— lace the film as well. And the celebration of the tractor's arrival meshes traditional agrarian festivals with the revolutionary civic parades associated with the Bolshevik state ever since its beginnings.[38] Thus does the sequence of the tractor's appearance in the village recapitulate the anticipated transit from the old (fertility rites) to the new (mechanization); from rural idiocy to science; from agriculture to industry.[39]

CONCLUSION

Cinema is often complicit in consolidating national traditions. So many American spectacle films, for example, restage the putative founding tenets of the republic in ancient garb—the Jews standing in as transparent cyphers for our colonial forebears, rebelliously casting off the yoke of Egyptian tyranny (*The Ten Commandments*) or struggling against Roman dominion (*Ben Hur*) in the name of freedom. In this way, a lineage is forged from the Declaration of Independence all the way back to the Bible. On the other hand, although he retools fragments of tradition in *The Old and the New,* Eisenstein is not primarily concerned with assimilating the past to the present, but rather the present to the future—he is preoccupied with imagining the Soviet Union to come and with encouraging viewers to participate in the task of nation building.

If Eisenstein has any bible guiding him in this matter, it is the writings of Marx and Engels, which promised that with the advent of communism the countryside and the city would be reconciled. Through the cooperative use of machinery, the old, it is foretold, can be remade anew—and better. Though eschewing institutionalized Christianity and its theology, Eisenstein exploits the rhythms of redemption, making the peasants the chosen people and the Soviet Union the prophetic nation. The land plentiful in milk and honey becomes a nation abundant with tractors and overflowing with grain.

To this end, Eisenstein employs a full range of cinematic effects, ranging from intellectual montage to allegory. The ambitious editing fugues of *October* are made more accessible to the ordinary viewer by being rooted in causal processes—the recurring trajectory from agricultural production to industrialization. On the narrative front, Eisenstein abandons his "formalist" commitment to the mass hero (in what might be called the plotless film),[40] and focuses the story on a single figure, Marfa, who emblematizes the ideal citizen of the future, collectivized Soviet state. Like the modifications in intellectual montage, this too is a gesture predicated upon making the film intelligible to the millions.

But by particularizing the narrative center of his film, Eisenstein has not forsaken the project of deploying the photographic resources of cinema for the purpose of making generalizations, since Marfa is an anagogical figure representing an entire class of future Russian citizens. In this manner, she prepares the way for subsequent Eisensteinian characters, notably Alexander Nevsky and Ivan the Terrible, who will also stand for all Russia, albeit in different ways.[41]

NOTES

1. Benedict Anderson makes this argument in his classic *Imagined Communities: Reflections on the Origin and Spread of Nationalism* (London: Verso, 1983).
2. See Vance Kepley, "The Evolution of Eisenstein's *Old and New*," *Cinema Journal* vol. 14, no. 1 (Fall 1974): 34–50.
3. It might appear strange to speak of nation building with respect to a communist state like the U.S.S.R., since insofar as it is Marxist, the Soviet Union should be committed to internationalism, not nationalism. However, as early as December 1924, Stalin had articulated the principle of "Socialism in One Country," which, of course, entailed a policy of nation building, especially (as this essay emphasizes) in terms of economic development. (See Robert Service, *A History of Twentieth-Century Russia* [Cambridge, Mass.: Harvard University Press, 1998], pp. 156–57.)

   A second caveat: throughout this essay, the authors should not be taken to be in sympathy with the policies they describe; these policies are discussed in order to clarify and to explicate Eisenstein's intentions and decision-making with respect to *The Old and the New*. We come not to praise, or even to criticize, but to explain.

4. See, for example, the section entitled "The Real Basis of Ideology" in Karl Marx and Frederick Engels, *The German Ideology* (Moscow: Progress Publishers, 1968).

5. See, for example, Marx and Engels, *The German Ideology*, pp. 40–41. Eisenstein makes this concern explicit in both the intertitles of the film—for instance, the intertitle that reads "And so the divisions between city and countryside are being erased"—and in his co-authored article "An Experiment Intelligible to the Millions," where he speaks of the "profound collaboration: the town and the countryside." (S. M. Eizhenshtein, G. V. Aleksandrov, "Eksperiment, ponyatnyi millionam," *Sovetskii ekran*, 5 February 1929, reprinted as Sergei Eisenstein and Grigori Alexandrov, "An Experiment Intelligible to the Millions" in *The Film Factory: Russian and Soviet Cinema in Documents 1896–1939*, ed. Richard Taylor and Ian Christie, trans. Richard Taylor [Cambridge, Mass.: Harvard University Press, 1988], p. 257).

6. James Goodwin points to Lenin's suggestive use of the need for dreaming in his *What Is To Be Done?* There Lenin exclaims "We should dream!" Maybe it is not too farfetched to speculate that Eisenstein is taking Lenin seriously in *The Old and the New*. Moreover, since Eisenstein was familiar with Freud's theories, it is not surprising that his "dream," like Marfa's in the film, should turn out to be a wish-fulfillment dream. (See James Goodwin, *Eisenstein, Cinema, and History* [Urbana: University of Illinois Press, 1993], pp. 98–99. The relevance of dreaming to *The Old and the New* is also discussed by Jacques Aumont in his *Montage Eisenstein*, trans. Lee Holdreth, Constance Penley, and Andrew Ross [Bloomington: Indiana University Press, 1987], pp. 73–107.) For our purposes in this essay, the relation between "dream" and "imagine"—as in *imagined* community—is especially pregnant.

7. Quoted in R. W. Davies, *The Industrialisation of Soviet Russia 1: The Socialist Offensive: The Collectivisation of Soviet Agriculture, 1929–1930* (Cambridge, Mass.: Harvard University Press, 1980), p. 38.

8. Since the party's "general line" regarding agriculture was in flux, the film was retitled *The Old and the New*.

9. Erich Strauss, *Soviet Agriculture in Perspective* (New York: Praeger, 1969), p. 50. Strauss points out that this approach did not originate with Lenin, but with Marx, who wrote in 1881 that "[the Russian peasants'] familiarity with the *artel* [handicraft cooperative] would greatly facilitate the transition from agriculture by individual plot to collective agriculture; that the physical configuration of the Russian soil demands combined mechanical cultivation on a large scale" (qtd. in Strauss, p. 51).

10. Eisenstein's film should not be understood as a brief in favor of Stalin's forced collectivization of the countryside and the violent liquidation of the kulaks, which began in 1929. The film was conceived and completed before the killing began. Though the film is critical of the kulaks, it never—even remotely—recommends their individual destruction. Undoubtedly, *The Old and the New* celebrates collectivization, but not the sort of forced collectivization that led to the deaths of millions. In our exposition of *The Old and the New*, we have reconstructed Eisenstein's celebratory intentions, not because we endorse Soviet agricultural policy of the twenties uncritically (we don't), but because our aims in this essay are interpretive.

11. Noël Carroll, "For God and Country," *Artforum* vol. 11, no. 5 (January 1973): 56–60,

reprinted in Noël Carroll, *Interpreting the Moving Image* (Cambridge: Cambridge University Press, 1998), pp. 80–91. For the best general overview of Eisenstein's theory of montage, see David Bordwell, *The Cinema of Eisenstein* (Cambridge, Mass.: Harvard University Press, 1993).

12. Carroll, "For God and Country." For an alternative interpretation of this sequence, see Bordwell, *The Cinema of Eisenstein*, p. 92. Also see Sergei Eisenstein, "The Dramaturgy of Film Form (The Dialectical Approach to Film Form)," in S. M. Eisenstein, *Selected Works, Volume I: Writings 1922–34*, ed. and trans. Richard Taylor (London: BFI Publishing; Bloomington, Ind.: Indiana University Press, 1988), pp. 161–80.

13. See Annette Michelson, "Reading Eisenstein Reading *Capital*," *October* no. 2 (Summer 1976): 27–38. Also, see Annette Michelson, "Reading Eisenstein Reading *Ulysses:* Montage and the Claims of Subjectivity," *Art & Text* no. 34 (Spring 1989): 64–78.

14. On overtonal montage, see S. M. Eisenstein, "The Fourth Dimension in Cinema," in Eisenstein, *Selected Works, Vol. I*, pp. 181–94.

15. Eisenstein and Alexandrov, "An Experiment," pp. 254–57. Interestingly, there is a potential ambiguity in this essay as to whether the authors are referring to agricultural collectivization as the experiment to be made intelligible to the millions or to the film itself, which is intended to depict/explain collectivization. We think the authors mean both. (The term "intelligible to the millions" did not originate with Eisenstein and Alexandrov in this article. The resolution passed by the December 1928 Conference of Sovkino Workers stated, in part: "an essential part of any experimental work [should] be *artistic expression that is intelligible to the millions*" [emphasis in original]. Quoted in L. Trauberg, "Eksperiment, ponyatnyi millionam," *Zhizn' Iskusstva*, 1 January 1929, p. 14, translated as Leonid Trauberg, "An Experiment Intelligible to the Millions" in Taylor and Christie, *Film Factory*, pp. 250–51.)

16. One might mistakenly suspect that the relation of agriculture and industry would, perforce, be a theme in any film about collectivization, and, in consequence, that we are making too much of Eisenstein's attention to this theme. It just comes with the territory, it might be said. But this is wrong. For example, in Dovzhenko's *Earth*, also a film about collectivization, there is scarcely a moment devoted to the relation between town and countryside. Thus, it seems fair to assume that the emphasis on this theme in *The Old and the New* represents Eisenstein's special theoretical spin on the process of collectivization.

17. See Noël Carroll, "Causation, the Ampliation of Movement and Avant-Garde Film," *Millennium Film Journal* nos. 10/11 (Fall/Winter 1981–82): 61–82, reprinted in Noël Carroll, *Theorizing the Moving Image* (Cambridge: Cambridge University Press, 1996), pp. 169–86.

18. Call this a socialist "wet dream."

19. This interpretation was first suggested in Carroll, "Causation," p. 185 n. 20.

20. Eisenstein and Alexandrov, "An Experiment," p. 255.

21. Processions and parades were an integral part of the public iconography of the new Soviet state. (See James von Geldern, *Bolshevik Festivals 1917–1920* [Berkeley: University of California Press, 1993].) Thus it is striking, in terms of the theme of nation building that we explore here, that the finale of *The Old and the New* is a parade—moreover, a parade

in an agragrian setting, in the fields themselves, which supplies another link between country and city (where most revolutionary parades and processions took place).

22. David Bordwell discusses montage-in-the-single-shot (*mise en cadre*) in *The Cinema of Eisenstein,* pp. 150–55.

23. In "For a Workers' Hit," written in 1928 (when he resumed work on *The Old and the New*), Eisenstein does not specifically mention the film, but shows that he was interested in "how to elevate a particular case into a social epic" (Eisenstein, *Selected Works, Vol. I,* p. 110).

24. Maxim Gorkii, "On little men and their great work," in his *O literature* (Moscow, 1955), quoted in Katerina Clark, "Little Heroes and Big Deeds," in *Cultural Revolution in Russia, 1928–1931,* ed. Sheila Fitzpatrick (Bloomington, Ind.: Indiana University Press, 1978), p. 191.

25. Eisenstein's Marfa is a more successful character, aesthetically speaking, than many of the "little men" who populate the novels of the period. Katerina Clark notes the many problems with much of the literature of this period and concludes that the bulk of the industrial and construction novels "represent a nadir in Soviet literature" (p. 202).

It should be noted that when Marfa visits the kulaks, Eisenstein literalizes the idea that she is a "little person," so tiny is she in the background of many of the shots.

26. Sergei Eisenstein and Grigori Alexandrov, "Vostorzhennye budni [Enthusiastic Workdays]," *Rabochaia Moskva,* 22 February 1929, section II, p. 22, reprinted in Sergei Eisenstein, *Izbrannyie proizvedeniia v shesti tomakh,* vol. 1 (Moscow: Iskusstvo, 1964), p. 143. Translation by Sally Banes.

27. Karl Marx and Friedrich Engels, *The Communist Manifesto,* ed. Joseph Katz, trans. Samuel Moore (New York: Washington Square Press, 1964), p. 65.

28. Adaptations of classics for contemporary times (*peredelki*) were rife on the early Soviet stage—partly due to a shortage of new plays and partly as a way of renovating elements of the old culture that were deemed worth keeping. Proletkult, the organization for revolutionary proletarian culture (for which Eisenstein had worked as a theatre director from 1921–24), was especially active in producing theatrical peredelki; Eisenstein's 1923 Proletkult production *The Wiseman,* based on Alexander Ostrovsky's *Enough Simplicity in Every Wise Man,* was a notorious example. The "circusization" both Vsevolod Meyerhold and Eisenstein used in their theatrical directing, especially in their peredelki, was employed first in Yuri Annenkov's 1919 Petrograd production of Leo Tolstoy's anti-alcoholism play *The First Distiller,* and several theatres staged Tolstoy's *Power of Darkness.* Perhaps *The Old and the New* can be seen as a cinematic peredelka of *The Power of Darkness* for Soviet times. (See von Geldern, pp. 115–16; Robert Leach, *Revolutionary Theatre* [London: Routledge, 1994], pp. 52–54; and Konstantin Rudnitsky, *Russian and Soviet Theater, 1905–1932,* ed. Lesley Milne, trans. Roxane Permar [New York: Abrams, 1988], pp. 48–49.)

29. The Soviet government classified peasants into three categories: *kulak* (wealthy peasant), *serednyak* (middle peasant), and *bednyak* (poor peasant). See Davies, *Industrialisation,* p. 23. In *The Old and the New,* when the district agronomist first appears at the meeting where Marfa proposes forming the dairy cooperative, he specifically addresses the villagers (in an intertitle) as "comrade poor and middle peasants."

30. Earlier, in a reversal of the scene where two brothers divided up a farm, the city workers come to the country to help the cooperative build a cow shed.
31. Eisenstein depicts both the kulaks and the bureaucrats in terms of giganticism. In the early scene of Marfa's visit to the kulak compound, the wealthy peasants and their animals—often dominating the foregrounds of shots—dwarf Marfa like giants out of a fairytale. Similarly, Eisenstein also uses close shots, wide-angle lenses, and montage-in-the-single-shot to exaggerate the bureaucrats' "instruments"—typewriters, pencil-sharpeners, official stamps, and such—until they, and some of the bureaucrats who use them, appear oppressively immense. By making the kulaks and the bureaucratic "machinery" *large,* Eisenstein literalizes the rebus that they are *big* obstacles on the "Path of October" to socialism.

    Also, whereas the indolence of the kulak is indicated by his lazily imbibing *kvass,* the bureaucrats' decadence is marked by their ridiculously ostentatious, excessive smoking. The kulaks and bureaucrats are a fraternity of vice.

    Eisenstein singles out kulaks and bureaucrats as leading impediments to the building of the new Soviet state. In this, bureaucrats are especially dangerous because bureaucracy would appear to be an ineliminable part of any modern state. Thus, in *The Old and the New* Eisenstein emphasizes the need for the peasants and proletarians to work together against bureaucratization, and he even comically alludes to the real campaign against this problem in the shot where a pen, an ashtray, and two (bureaucratic) cigarettes rest on an obviously forgotten pamphlet entitled "Fight Bureaucracy."
32. See Vladimir Propp, *Morphology of the Folktale* (1928), trans. Laurence Scott. 2d ed. (Austin: University of Texas Press, 1968).
33. See Yuryi Mateevich Sokolov, *Russian Folklore* (1938), trans. Catherine Ruth Smith (Hatboro, Penn.: Folklore Associates, 1966), p. 425.
34. Sokolov, *Russian Folklore,* p. 431. Other conventional endings include: "They lived happily ever after, in the enjoyment of their property," or "Now they live there and eat their bread."
35. Yet, in other ways, *The Old and the New* is a counter-fairytale, for unlike the standard female characters in fairytales, Marfa is never seen doing women's chores—such as cooking, spinning, weaving, or tending the oven (a symbol of female fertility)—within the household (though women did participate in farm chores in the tales as well). (See Joanna Hubbs, *Mother Russia: The Feminine Myth in Russian Culture* [Bloomington, Ind.: Indiana University Press, 1988], pp. 48–49.) It is true that she finds a love interest at the end of the film, but for the bulk of the film Marfa is concerned with agricultural production and with community organizing. This aspect of Marfa as hero of the film contrasts with the conservative, superstitious peasant women in the village who resist change and also makes her an important role model for women spectators, whose political liberation was an integral part of the Soviet project, and an exemplar of the new Soviet woman for male spectators as well.
36. See Eric Hobsbawm, "Introduction: Inventing Traditions," in *The Invention of Tradition,* ed. Eric Hobsbawm and Terence Ranger (Cambridge: Cambridge University Press, 1983), pp. 1–14.
37. There is a connection in Russian folklore between human weddings and cattle. Accord-

ing to Sokolov, "the bed for the newly married couple was often made in the cattle shed, or not far away from the cattle shed, in the belief that the first sexual act of the young woman would exert a magical influence on the fertility of the cattle" (p. 206).

38. See von Geldern, *Bolshevik Festivals.*

39. There are other aspects of folk culture—those having to do with superstition and religion—that the film criticizes, in line with the aggressively anti-religious policy of the Soviet Union at the time. The ecstatic religious procession in search of rain compares the celebrants to sheep but also recalls pre-Christian spells for rainmaking. When Fomka is poisoned by the kulaks, the women of the village revert to magic spells, carrying out a ritual exorcism against cattle plague that dates back to pagan times (and perhaps casting spells against local sorcerers who "spoil" cattle as well). (On rainmaking rituals, see Hubbs, p. 255 n. 8, and on cattle disease exorcisms, see Hubbs, p. 46. On "spoiling" livestock, see Linda J. Ivanits, *Russian Folk Belief* [Armonk, N.Y.: M. E. Sharpe, 1989], p. 109.)

But both these incidents are framed as parts of a misguided belief system that contributes to the ignorance, poverty, and degradation of the peasant and that hinders progress and cooperation. The cream separator, represented as a shining new icon of a scientific, modern faith, replaces the old Orthodox icons. (When the cream separator is first unveiled, it glows like a sacerdotal object, recalling a giant chalice.) Technology and scientific planning deliver the goods, where religion and superstition only delude and deceive. (Eisenstein writes that the scientific breeding of better livestock will put "an end to secret sorcery," and he envisions "a hundred experimental guinea pigs" murmuring, "We'll climb up to the heavens; we'll drive away all the gods" [Eisenstein and Alexandrov, "Enthusiastic Workdays," p. 143].) The new Soviet state was intended to be a rational prodigy; its campaign against religion in the late 1920s derived not only from the classical Marxist idea that religion is the opiate of the people and keeps peasants in a state of degradation, but from the recent rise of religious observance and conversion among peasant youth that posed a threat to socialist nation building. (According to Sheila Fitzpatrick, in 1928 the Baptist "Bapsomols" and Mennonite "Mensomols" were said to outnumber the Komsomols, or communist youth ["Cultural Revolution as Class War," in Fitzpatrick, ed., *Cultural Revolution,* p. 20].)

40. Eisenstein links films with a mass hero (i.e., the absence of an individual hero) to the absence of a plot in "The Problem of the Materialist Approach to Form," in Eisenstein, *Selected Writings, Vol. I,* pp. 59–64.

41. Our descriptions and analysis of *The Old and the New* are based on our viewings of two different prints: one, released in video by Castle/Hendring, is held by the British Film Institute; the other is the London Film Society version.

Chapter 16 The Professional Western: South of the Border

INTRODUCTION

The topic of this essay is a series of four thematically related American Westerns: *Vera Cruz* (1954), *The Magnificent Seven* (1960), *The Professionals* (1966), and *The Wild Bunch* (1969). In each, a group of American mercenaries finds itself south of the border and becomes involved in what may be described as various Mexican revolutions. Because these Westerns involve a paramilitary group of expert warriors, they are apt to be categorised as members of the sub-genre called the professional Western. The professional Western, in turn, has been theorised as a celebration of expertise that reflects the ethos of an emerging social class in America which has been alternatively referred to as the managerial class, the technocracy, the professional managerial class or, more recently, the overclass. However, this interpretation of these particular Westerns does not strike me as adequate, especially because it pays scant attention to the recurring theme of indigenous revolution that runs through the films in this cycle.[1] The purpose of this essay is to develop an interpretation that takes account of the significance of the appearance of Mexican revolutions in these Westerns.

The notion of the professional Western is explored in depth in an ambitious book by Will Wright entitled *Six Guns and Society: A Structural Study of the Western.*[2] According to Wright, the American Western (from 1931 to 1972) can be divided into four major types: the classical plot, the vengeance variation, the transition theme and the professional plot. These groups are not exhaustive, nor are they necessarily exclusive. The typology was derived from the study of best-selling Westerns, defined as those that were among the highest grossing films of the year in which they appeared.

Wright's analyses are aimed not only at identifying the plot structures of these Westerns, but also at correlating these Westerns with developments in American society. In addition, Wright notices a change in the incidence of Westerns of different sorts. Whereas from the 30s to the late 50s the classical plot is preponderant, from the 60s onwards the professional plot becomes the dominant form.

Of the films that interest me here, *The Professionals* and *The Wild Bunch* are identified by Wright as examples of the professional plot and are discussed at length by him. He does not address *The Magnificent Seven,* since, presumably, it did not meet the criterion of being one of the highest grossing films of 1960. Nevertheless, I think that it is pretty uncontroversially what he calls a professional Western. On the other hand, he categorises *Vera Cruz* as an exemplar of the classical plot, but, for reasons to be discussed, I think that at best it is a mixture of classical and professional elements, if not a professional Western outright.

In characterising the professional plot, Wright says:

> All these films are about a group of heroes working for money. They are not wandering adventurers who decide to fight for a lost cause because it is right, or for the love of a girl. They are professionals, men doing a job. They are specialists who possess the unique skills used in their profession. No longer is the fighting ability of the hero the lucky attribute of a man who happens to be in the right place at the right time [a mark of the classical Western plot, exemplified by a film such as *Shane*]. Now it is a profitable skill that the heroes utilise professionally, and this profitable skill *explains* why they are in that particular place at that particular time.[3]

In the classical plot, the hero, often a lone gunfighter like Shane, is an outsider. He comes upon a situation where positive social forces are in conflict with a group of antagonists, noteworthy for their superior talent for violence. Initially, the hero avoids involvement in the conflict, but eventually enters it on the side of society, defeating assorted villains, to the advantage of whatever the film regards as positive social forces. The hero is marked by special abilities, especially martial ones. And, persuaded by reasons of justice, he comes to pit his virtually mythic prowess against the forces of oppression. Often, but not always, he then becomes incorporated in society and thus is no longer an outsider.

In contrast, the professional plot presents viewers with a group of heroes, each remarkable for his special abilities. Furthermore, this group is co-ordinated; they function as a unit. Specifically, the imagery is of a military unit. The actions they undertake against this or that villain are putatively not motivated by reasons of justice, but rather by the promise of money. They are mercenaries, or soldiers of fortune. But if at times they seem willing to take risks unjustifiable solely in terms of dollar value, it is because of their professionalism—which is not only a matter of their guild-like fidelity to abiding by their contracts, but also involves the pride and emotional satisfaction that they derive from exercising their special skills as warriors.

The professionals in these films have their own code of conduct. This code distinguishes them from the members of ordinary society. Unlike the hero in the classical Western, in Wright's view, the professional hero is not motivated by claims of justice, but by the code of the professional. Wright argues:

> In many ways, the professional plot is similar to the classical plot: the hero is a gun-fighter, outside of society, whose main task is to fight the villains who are threatening parts of society. But the relations between the different characters of the story have changed significantly. The heroes are now professional fighters, men willing to defend society only as a job they accept for pay or love of fighting, not from commitment to ideas of law and justice. As in the classical plot, society is portrayed as weak, but it is no longer seen as particularly good or desirable. The members of society are not unfair and cruel, as in the transition theme; in the professional plot they are simply irrelevant. The social value of love, marriage, family, peace, and business are things to be avoided, not goals to be won. As a result, the relations of the heroes, or of the villains with society are minimal. Society exists as a ground for the conflict, an excuse for fighting, rather than as a serious option as a way of life. The focus of the professional plot is on the conflict between the heroes and the villains. Typically, both are professionals and their fight becomes a contest of ability for its own sake. A concern with a fight between equal men of special ability is an aspect of all Westerns, yet only in this particular version of the myth does the fight itself, divorced from all its social and ethical implications, become of such central importance. The final gunfight that climaxes such films as *Shane* or *Stagecoach* has become a battle extending throughout the film with skirmishes, strategies, and commanders. How the fight is fought is now the crucial issue, since the fight itself generates the values that replace the values of society in the myth.[4]

The disappearance of society from the value nexus of the narrative and its substitution by the professional ethos of martial skill provides a central element in Wright's characterisation of the ideological work that the professional Western performs. According to Wright, among others, the recent development of capitalist economies has placed more and more emphasis on, to use Habermas's terminology, 'sets of leaders of administrative personnel', or as Wright glosses that, a 'technical elite'.[5] Perhaps this group is also what others have called the 'professional-managerial class', or the 'overclass'. Of this class, Wright remarks:

> Membership in the technostructure provides great social satisfaction for the individual. He works closely with a group that depends on him and on whom he depends; he is close to a source of power and receives social prestige accordingly. He is a professional; he identifies with the group and the corporation, and they in turn recognise and reward his contribution.[6]

Moreover, 'The individual in the technostructure identifies his goals with those of the corporation, and these goals become social goals. Though the individual seems to be working for the newly defined social goals, he is in fact working to maintain his group'.[7] In Wright's view, decision by the technostructure is replacing democratic decision-making with management in terms of expertise. Society is allegedly being run by experts—by professionals—for whom 'the social group [i.e. the professional cadre] satisfies every requirement for meaningful social relationships, except commitment to social values'.[8]

This characterisation of the technocrat, furthermore, is reflected in the heroes of the professional Western.[9] These figures reflect the ethos of the managerial élite. The professional Western, in this regard, is a celebration of the ideology of the managerial élite. And, in addition, it addresses not only fellow celebrants in the managerial élite but the rest of society as well, promoting a view of the professional ethos as heroic. Through the iconography of the Western, professionalism is represented as a worthy ideal. Its anti-democratic bias is obscured by the colourful apotheosis of perfectionism. In short, the professional Western performs a suspect legitimating function for managerialism.

Whether this interpretation is successful for the professional Western in general is a question too large for this paper. Instead, I want to focus on what I take to be a subset of the professional Western, namely those that take place south of the border. In these cases, I think that the relationships of the professional heroes to representatives of the Mexican people force us to reconsider the ideological themes that are in play in films like *Vera Cruz, The Magnificent Seven, The Professionals,* and *The Wild Bunch.*

In Wright's theory of the professional Western, the professional group becomes the centre of value, and ordinary society becomes, as Wright says, 'simply irrelevant'. It more or less disappears, or functions only as the backdrop against which professional competitions are staged. However, this is not the case in the professional Westerns set in Mexico. For though *American* society may recede from view in these films, *Mexican* society, generally in the form of some sort of indigenous revolution, does not. Nor is the relation of the professional heroes to the representatives of what we might call the Mexican resistance either incidental or merely instrumental (i.e., merely financial). The professional heroes become emotionally and/or existentially involved with these resistance movements and they are willing to stake their very lives on their outcome.

Wright, of course, is interested in a general theory of the professional Western. Thus, it is perhaps no surprise that he ignores certain details that only recur in a small number of the films that he considers. However, I think that, by overlooking the role of Mexican society in the professional Westerns set south of the border, he misses the ideological wish that these films sustain. But before elucidating the ideological operation of these films, we need to analyse them each in turn.

VERA CRUZ

Vera Cruz is set in Mexico during the reign of Maximilian in the aftermath of the American Civil War. A rolling title informs us that it is a time when the Mexican people were struggling for their freedom. A lone horseman, Ben Trane (played by Gary Cooper), dismounts his limping horse. Later, we learn that the horse has a broken leg. Ben walks to a churchyard, where he meets Joe Erin (played by Burt Lancaster) who sells him another horse for the exorbitant price of $100. As they ride off, they are attacked by a group of Maximilian's imperial lancers. Joe explains to Ben that the horse that he is riding is stolen. There is a rousing chase in which they evade the lancers. Ben then tricks Joe, riding off on Joe's horse and leaving him with the stolen one.

Several important themes are established in the opening scene. There is the three-way conflict between Ben, Joe and the imperial government that continues both above and below ground throughout the film. And there is the somewhat complex relationship between Ben and Joe. Joe admires Ben's skill and gumption even as Ben outdoes him. They are competitors, but they also respect each other's martial skill—a mark of the professional Western, according to Wright.

The opening scenes also establish that Ben has a strict sense of justice and what Joe calls a 'soft spot', exemplified by the care he shows for his injured horse, which will come to mark the central difference between Ben and Joe throughout the story.

Ben rides into town and when members of Joe's gang realise that he has Joe's horse, they prepare to slice him to pieces with a broken bottle. However, Joe arrives, saves Ben from his gang and invites him to join up. Presumably Joe admires the way that Ben handles himself. Ben is a refugee from the Civil War. He suggests at times that he may have done something that caused him to flee the States. He says that the war cost him everything but the shirt on his back and he implies that he is in Mexico for the sole purpose of getting money.

Joe's gang, along with Ben, travels to another village in order to find an employer. After an episode in which Ben, showing his ethical uprightness, rescues a woman named Nina from some slavering gringos, an agent of Maximilian's, the marquis (played by Cesar Romero), shows up with an offer of work. But the proceedings are interrupted by General Ramirez and his peasant army of freedom fighters who attempt to take both the imperial troops and the Americans prisoner. Ben, showing his 'soft spot' once again, points out that there are children in the line of fire, an insight Joe exploits by taking them hostage. The freedom fighters retreat, and the marquis is pleased by the performance of his newly acquired mercenaries. This scene is especially important because it introduces another important force—the Mexican revolutionaries—into the narrative equation.

Ben consistently talks the part of the mercenary cynic but, given his concern for his injured horse, Nina and the children, the audience suspects that his cynicism is ultimately a pose. Joe, on the other hand, is a rascal, one whose big smile may make him appear loveable, but who, as the film progresses, is revealed to be an irredeemable egoist and sadist.

Ben, Joe and the gang, along with the marquis and his lancers, arrive at Maximilian's palace in Mexico City in the midst of a ball. Energy is spent contrasting the barbarism of the Americans with the behaviour of the French (and the Austrians?). It is the old opposition of the uncouth but vital Americans against the artificial, false pretensions of Europe. When Maximilian arrives, the Americans display their skills in a round of bravura sharpshooting, and Maximilian offers them fifty thousand dollars to accompany the carriage of a countess to Vera Cruz.

In this scene, we learn more about Ben; it is suggested that he has come to Mexico to earn money in order to rebuild his plantation, especially in terms of securing the welfare of its former inhabitants (the film is not explicit about who these people are, but one assumes it is probably his family and perhaps his former slaves). To Joe, this is more evidence of Ben's soft spot. The scene is also an occasion for Ben and Joe to display their awesome professional skill with weaponry—semi-competitively and with mutual admiration. Joe also admires, as he will later in the film as well, Ben's bargaining ability, as Ben raises Maximilian's bid from $25,000 to $50,000.

The entourage sets out. Ben and Joe come to realise that the countess's carriage has a false bottom that contains $3 million in gold, which is supposed to go to Paris in order to buy more troops for Maximilian. They also learn that the countess has made plans to abscond with the money. The three of them form a compact, though each of the thieves distrusts the others. Joe and the countess are outright, merciless cutthroats; the audience is less certain about Ben. One has the feeling that he would like to trust Joe, even if in some sense he knows that that is inadvisable.

The caravan is subject to guerrilla warfare. At one point, it is ambushed by Ramirez's troops and nearly captured. Nina, the woman Ben had rescued earlier, leaps on one of the wagons and drives it to safety. Though she appears to be on the side of the caravan, in reality she is a freedom fighter, as we eventually learn. At the same time, the marquis is aware of the countess's machinations and he plans to remove the gold before Joe, Ben and the countess can steal it. So, there evolves an intricate five-way fabric of deception between Ben, Joe, the countess, the marquis and Nina, each with his or her own agenda. In such a context, it is not surprising that the theme of trust emerges with Joe as the ideologue of the 'you can't trust anyone' point of view, and Ben talking about money but acting with palpable care and concern for others, including Joe.

Ben falls in love with Nina, a figure perhaps for his final 'seduction' to the cause of the freedom fighters. But the marquis successfully spirits the gold to Vera Cruz. The professionals set out after the carriage, but the carriage, now empty, is a diversionary tactic. The empty coach and the professionals are surrounded by Ramirez's army. Ben strikes a deal with Ramirez, and the freedom fighters, along with the professionals, lay siege to Vera Cruz.

It is a brutal battle. Ben remarks that if the freedom fighters get the gold they will have deserved it; Joe says he wouldn't give them the sweat off his brow. Ben, we divine, has been won over to the revolution, his Confederate idealism (in terms of the point of view of the film) rekindled by the rebel sacrifices (along with prodding from Nina). Joe remains the selfish egoist. The wagon laden with gold falls into Joe's hands. But Ben steps in and the two men shoot it out.

Ben wins, but his face in victory is etched with frustration and disappointment. One feels that he liked Joe and that he had hoped that Joe's egoism would melt away when the chips were down. But in the end, he had to destroy the only person equal to him in ability in the world of the film.

Despite his harsh talk of mercenary interests and the suggestion that he may be wanted by the law stateside, Ben's actions consistently point to his decency. He shows ethical concern for animals, children, women, the displaced folks back on his plantations, and, ultimately, for the Mexican revolutionaries. He is trustworthy and clean. Joe is his *doppelgänger*—vicious to one and all, untrustworthy as a matter of principle, and cursed with a virtually perpetually dirty face throughout the film (perhaps the better to show off Burt Lancaster's glowing ivories). Joe's gang, for the most part, is made up of the dregs of humanity. The French are equally untrustworthy (marked by being insincere and over-civilised), as well as being tyrannical bullies. A score of lancers tortures a captured freedom fighter like cats playing with a mouse.

In this matrix the only other locus of decency, apart from Ben, are the Mexican revolutionaries, represented primarily by Ramirez and Nina. Like Ben, the Mexicans are clean, as opposed to the French who are too clean, and Joe and his gang who are too dirty. Ramirez speaks in a deliberate, judicious manner about freedom—indeed, he has the diction often reserved for saints in Hollywood films—and Nina fiercely speaks in favour of justice. The trajectory of the plot pulses towards bringing the forces of decency together.

There is also a subplot of racial tolerance. One of the members of the professional gang is an African-American named Ballard. Like Ben, he too appears to have a 'soft spot' and a sense of justice. Like Ben, he saves Nina from potential rapists. Thus, unsurprisingly perhaps, he is Ben's one genuine ally in the gang. Decency bonds across racial differences—white, black and mestizo. Moreover, Ben's ultimate support of the Mexican revolutionaries is not represented as a corollary of his love for Nina. He is converted, against his cynical wariness, to their cause. In a world of deception, as represented by Joe, the countess and the rest of the French, he has found something to believe in again.

Perhaps because of the theme of Ben's reintegration into society, Wright felt justified in categorising *Vera Cruz* as an example of the classical plot. But it also accords with his characterisation of the professional Western, especially in terms of the relationship between Ben and Joe, who themselves are contrasted to the professional French soldiery. Joe is in it for the money unequivocally and Ben equivocally. Both are fantastically skilled, and they form a mutual admiration society on that basis. The rest of the gang is not highly individuated in terms of their abilities, but they are very effective in their business (indeed, they are more effective than the French), which business is killing. However, *Vera Cruz* is not marked by the absence of society as an active force of positive value, once one realises that the relevant society is Mexican society as represented by the revolutionaries.

If Wright responds that it is for this very reason that *Vera Cruz* should not be considered as an example of the professional Western, I would begin to suspect, given the elements I've cited, that he may be begging the question. Moreover, this same oversight shows up in cases where the status of the films as professional Westerns is uncontroversial.[10]

THE MAGNIFICENT SEVEN

In *The Magnificent Seven,* which was adapted from *The Seven Samurai,* the presence of Mexican society is more pronounced than it is in *Vera Cruz.* Set somewhere vaguely in the late 19th century, the film begins as thirty or forty bandits, led by Calvera (Eli Wallach), ride into a Mexican farming village to exact tribute. Calvera speaks civilly, as if he were a good friend of the villagers, but this makes their situation all the more humiliating. One of the villagers resists, and is shot down. When the bandits leave, the farmers discuss their plight, and, following the advice of an old wise man, they head for the border to buy guns in order to fight back when the bandits return. What is perhaps most notable here is that the decision-making is roughly democratic, in the sense that the men of the town (though not the women) evolve their plan communally.

Across the border, the farmers witness a display of nerve, verve and firepower when Chris (played by Yul Brynner) and Vin (played by Steve McQueen) escort a hearse, carrying a dead Native American, to the graveyard. This introduces the theme of racial tolerance, since the local townspeople have denied the Indian burial rights because he is not white. Called 'Injun Lovers', Chris and Vin blast their way to Boot Hill. The scene also establishes their martial expertise, coolheadedness under fire, and mutual admiration for one another's skill.

The Mexicans approach Chris to help them buy guns. But he says that nowadays men are cheaper than guns and suggests that they commission some hired gunmen. They offer him the job, and after he delivers a speech about how hard such a war would be (in order to test their commitment), he agrees. Next ensues a series of scenes in which the rest of the Magnificent Seven are enlisted.

Vin is first. Though the pay is a measly $25, plus room and board, he agrees because his only alternative is to work in a grocery store. The mere prospect of an opportunity to exercise his warrior skills outweighs the option of productive citizenship. A man called Reilly (played by Charles Bronson) is next. Chris and Vin appeal to him by flattery, talking about his legendary exploits in Travis County and Salina (which also informs the audience of his professional prowess). He is down on his luck, and also agrees to join. Next they approach Reb (played by James Coburn), who displays his special ability, knife-throwing, in a show-down with a cowboy. Having heard of the venture, Harry (played by Brad Dexter) and Lee (played by Robert Vaughn) approach Chris, and the professionals are ready to head south.

Along the way, they are followed by Chico (played by Horst Buchholz), a journeyman gunman, who has appeared in earlier scenes, but who had been rejected by Chris for being unseasoned. His persistence wins them over, and now the professionals number seven. They ride into the Mexican village and, auspiciously enough, their first full day there is on the occasion of the anniversary of the founding of the town. It is hard not to read this as an Independence Day celebration, replete with native dancing and fireworks. It is a way of analogising the resistance of this Mexican village to the American Revolution.

The professionals prepare the town's defences, training the farmers in a montage of rudimentary boot camp exercises and rigging all manner of traps—walls, moats and so on. In all this, the growing confidence of the farmers is a major theme, since, to a great extent, the autonomy of the villagers is what this film is about. When the bandits return, there is an extended shoot-out; not only the professionals, but the farmers fight splendidly, and the bandits beat a disorderly retreat. However, they have not left the field entirely. They head for the hills to regroup and to launch their next attack.

The interlude between battles provides breathing space for a number of important developments. Bernardo Reilly's interactions with some of the children of the village lead him to rediscover, as they say, his Mexican roots. Gradually his commitment to the farmers is transformed from mercenary to emotional. He tells the children that they should honour their fathers for their everyday courage. Chris and some of the other gunmen philosophise about the lonely life of the professional, their tone signalling that it contrasts unfavourably with the life of ordinary folks who have people and a place that means something to them and to which they mean something. A love interest blossoms between Chico and one of the young women of the village. Love, here, stands as another of the values that mundane society proffers in contrast to professionalism. Thus, though this film fits the professional formula, its underlying argument is that social life in a community, as represented by the Mexicans, is superior to the professional alternative. Professionalism for its own sake is not celebrated, but rather it is justified in the service of defending the ordinary social values evinced by the farmers.

Moreover, it turns out that both Bernardo Reilly and Chico are of Mexican heritage. This establishes a commonality between the professionals and the community. When each, in turn, acknowledges this, the argument for society is advanced. Of all the professionals, only Harry appears to remain completely mercenary in his relation to the village, and even this may be ambiguous. The rest of the professionals, it seems, become committed to the village because of the social value it represents.

While the town awaits the next attack, dissension begins to erupt among the villagers. They fear that they have got more than they bargained for. While the professionals attempt to deliver a surprise attack on the bandit camp, some of the villagers turn the town over to the marauders. When the professionals return home they are surrounded and forced to abandon the village. Rather than returning north, however, they stage a counterattack, in which they are woefully outnumbered, until the farmers, their courage regained, join the battle and the bandits are decisively vanquished.

Of the professionals left standing, Chico decides to remain in the village with his newfound love, a choice that rhetorically stands for the superiority of the social life over the professional life. An old man suggests that Chris and Vin also stay, but it is conceded that the villagers really won't care one way or the other. The village is something permanent—the farmers are the land and the gunmen merely the wind that blows over it. Chris and Vin leave, looking back at the village wistfully, with a tangible sense of loss. 'Only the farmers won. We lost. We always lose.'

The overt theme of the film is that the gunslinger's life is inferior to that of ordinary society. With its professional motif, it is rather like *The Gunfighter* writ large. Martial prowess is celebrated, but ultimately it must be integrated with society, as it is when the farmers are turned into warriors. Society must acquire the military capacity to defend Itself if it is to remain autonomous. Skill at arms is not valuable for its own sake, but only as an instrument in the service of autonomy. The film is about resisting tyranny in defence of the values of ordinary society.

One might say that even if that is the major narrative theme, it is not the major visual theme. The major visual theme is violence and martial prowess. But however much truth there is in that observation (and there is a great deal), it is important to remember that the final defeat of the bandits is achieved by the farmers wielding chairs, machetes and hoes and not by the gunfighters. The triumphal feelings that the battle engenders in the audience have as their objects the Mexican farmers fighting for their own freedom.

Wright does not consider *The Magnificent Seven* in his book. However, I would contend that it is clearly a professional Western. In some regards, it may even be a prototype. But it does not accord with the notion that society recedes in this type of film. For in this film, social values, in the shape of Mexican resistance to tyranny, are not just the pretext of the film, but its emotional fulcrum as well.

THE PROFESSIONALS

The Professionals is one of Wright's paradigms of the sub-genre that, in fact, takes its name from the title and the language of this film (wherein terms like 'professional code' and 'specialists' appear). For my own part, I think this film shows the influence of *The Magnificent Seven*. Under the titles, we see the professional team assembled in vignettes that recall the enlistment of several of the Magnificent Seven. Rico Fardan (played by Lee Marvin) is shown demonstrating a .30 calibre Browning water-cooled machine-gun; Ehrengard (played by Robert Ryan) is involved in horse training; Jake (played by Woody Strode) is delivering a fugitive from justice to the law. Each of these vignettes gives us a sense of the professional's special abilities. Bill Dolworth (played by Burt Lancaster) is discovered in an adulterous tryst, which associates him with the erotic life, a characteristic which will ultimately figure in the major plot reversal of the film.

Set somewhere in the early teens, the film shows how the professionals are assembled by Mr Grant (played by Ralph Bellamy). As he introduces them to each other, he elaborates on their extraordinary skills, thus giving the audience a glimpse of their professional prowess. Rico, wearing clothes that are highly suggestive of military attire, is a tactician. Ehrengard is an expert horse trainer. Jake is a scout and an archer. The theme of racial tolerance is made explicit when Grant asks Rico and Ehrengard if they object to working with a Negro (Jake). Rico looks at him as if the question were beneath contempt. For professionals, at least, skill is the criterion, not skin pigmentation.

Grant explains that he has brought them together to rescue his wife Maria (played by Claudia Cardinale) who has been kidnapped by Raza (played by Jack Palance). Rico, who, along with Dolworth, has ridden with Pancho Villa and Raza, talks of the impossibility of such a rescue operation. He argues that

Dolworth, a demolitions expert, must be added to the group as an 'equaliser'. Grant agrees, Dolworth is enlisted, and the professionals are briefed. They are ready to head south.

The journey provides the opportunity for Rico and Dolworth to extol Raza's martial prowess. They are perplexed that Raza would stoop to kidnapping. It does not correspond to the Raza they knew. The professionals ride on, and they are attacked twice, which enables them to display their own skills to great advantage. There is some dissension in the ranks. Ehrengard, introduced to us under the credits as a horse lover, resents what he takes to be Dolworth's cold-heartedness, although every time that he opposes what he thinks is Dolworth's ruthlessness, his judgements (about not killing the horses, and about the goat herder) turn out to be wrong.

The professionals enter Raza's territory and they witness Raza and his troops attack a federal army train. Raza and his men execute the federal troops, which leads Ehrengard to express his disgust. Dolworth tells him to shut up and then explains that the troops in question are guilty of numerous atrocities against the Mexican people, including the savage murder of Rico's Mexican wife whom they stripped and ran into a cactus. This reduces Ehrengard to asking, somewhat dismissively, why Americans would be involved in the Mexican revolution anyway, to which Dolworth replies, 'Maybe there's only been one revolution since the beginning. The good guys against the bad guys. The question is who are the good guys.'

This exchange introduces a hint of something upon which the plot will ultimately hinge. Who are the good guys and the bad guys here? Is Raza really the bad guy? It also endorses revolutionary activity in the abstract. Combined with the previous question, it suggests the possibility that Raza is a genuine revolutionary. After all, consider his name; 'la raza' means 'the people'.

Reaching Raza's domain, the professionals reconnoitre, plan their attack against outlandish odds and begin their assault at dawn, exploiting Dolworth's expertise with dynamite to simulate the effect of an artillery barrage. The deployment for the attack and the battle itself are veritable miracles of split-second timing and applied technique—a fantasy of military professionalism. Rico and Dolworth sneak into Mrs Grant's dwelling in order to carry her off, but a complication develops. Raza arrives apparently to rape her, but she responds more in the manner of a consort than a captive. Rico and Dolworth conk Raza on the head and abduct Mrs Grant. But they know that something is not quite right about their assignment.

Raza and his men take off in hot pursuit of the professionals, who now possess Mrs Grant. Several ingenious action scenes ensue. As the escape continues, the professionals learn that Mrs Grant was not kidnapped. She has always been Raza's lover. Her father had unconscionably forced her to marry Mr Grant. But her love for Raza and the Mexican revolution has never flagged. She conspired with Raza to send Mr Grant the ransom note in order to buy guns and bullets for the revolution. In effect, it is the professionals who are the kidnappers, and Mrs Grant is not a compliant damsel in distress.

Mrs Grant tries to rekindle Rico's commitment to the revolution. The theme of the superiority of fighting for what one believes in over fighting for money is repeated several times. Furthermore, Dolworth admires Mrs Grant and tells Rico that her spiritedness reminds him of Rico's dead wife. This intimates that Dolworth's sympathies may be shifting and, sensing this, Rico says, implicitly invoking the professional credo, that he'll deliver Mrs Grant to her husband if he has to do it himself.

Raza and his men are fast on the heels of the professionals. In order to slow the Mexicans down, Dolworth stays behind to ambush them in a ravine. Dolworth's performance is spectacular. He kills all of Raza's men and severely wounds Raza himself. Lastly, he kills Lieutenant Chiquita, a former lover of his from his days with Villa. While kissing her lips as she dies, Dolworth recognises, as he puts it, that he's a sucker for love.

Meanwhile, the professionals arrive for their rendezvous with Mr Grant. In short order Dolworth arrives with Raza in tow, followed by Grant and his men. Will the professionals turn Mrs Grant over or not? Rico reverses the situation, noting that they were hired to rescue a kidnapped woman and that, in fact, Mr Grant is the kidnapper. So they turn a willing Mrs Grant over to Raza. Raza and Mrs Grant head south in a buckboard and the professionals ride off, leaving an enraged Mr Grant empty-handed. Perhaps the viewer recalls Dolworth's speech about knowing who the good guys are. We thought Mr Grant represented righteousness, but all along Raza was the good guy, and therefore, in the terms of Dolworth's argument, the genuine revolutionary article.

The Professionals does not present us with ordinary society in the manner of *The Magnificent Seven*. Indeed, if one thinks that Mr Grant represents (American) society, then it surely seems fallen. However, that is the wrong place to look for society in *The Professionals*. The Mexican revolution, represented by Raza and his men, stand for the values of society against the tyrannical federal troops. As is often the case, love here (the relation between Raza and Mrs Grant) symbolises social value but, as in *Vera Cruz* and *The Magnificent Seven*, love is also associated with resistance to tyranny.

Society figures in *The Professionals* as social revolution. And as in *Vera Cruz* and *The Magnificent Seven,* the professionals commit themselves to the cause of justice, rather than to their code. Indeed, Rico sophistically interprets their contract so that it works out in terms of the authentic lovers and the cause they represent. Once again, professionalism appears justified in the service of society. It is not divorced from society, construed as a Mexican revolution.

THE WILD BUNCH

From the point of film history, *The Wild Bunch* is probably the most important film in the group under discussion. Along with *Bonnie and Clyde* it initiated a new style of cinematic violence, employing accelerated montage and slow motion. Made during the Vietnam War, its massacres were compared at the time to firefights on the Mekong Delta. Set in roughly the same period as *The Professionals,* it begins as a group of bandits, the Wild Bunch, led by Pike (played by William Holden) and Dutch (played by Ernest Borgnine) ride into town disguised as horse soldiers. Their arrival is intercut with a group of sadistic children torturing scorpions by pushing them into hordes of furious red ants. One supposes that the scorpions stand for the professionals.

As the gang enters the railway office that they intend to rob, we learn that it is a trap. Bounty hunters led by Thornton (played by Robert Ryan), who was formerly Pike's partner, have them surrounded. To complicate matters, a crackbrained temperance parade is marching into the line of fire. This doesn't deter the bounty hunters. They open fire on the robbers, who shoot their way out of town, sustaining heavy losses, though in all it seems that the town has taken more casualties than either the bounty hunters or the gang. As the robbers ride past the children, the kids burn up the scorpions, a gesture that seems to refer symbolically to the conflagration we have just witnessed as well as to the ultimate fate of the Wild Bunch.

The depiction of the town in terms of sadistic children and evangelical temperance nuts gives a poor picture of settled society but, as in other films in this cycle, American society is not the relevant locus of social value here: Mexican society is. The Wild Bunch head for the border, intending to recuperate in the village of their Mexican member, Angel. A posse led by Thornton and composed, it seems, of mental defectives is hot on their trail.

After the raid, the Wild Bunch learn that they have been duped. The money bags they stole contain nothing but worthless metal washers. This disappointment is occasioned by several of them saying that they had hoped this would be their last job. Pike, for example, emphasises the theme that they are getting too old for this business. They know that their way of life is on the way out. There are several conflicts in the group. At one point, Tector Gorch (played by Ben Johnson) seems ready to kill Old Sykes (played by Edmond O'Brien). This prompts Pike to make a speech: 'We're gonna stick together just like it used to be. When you side with a man you stay with him. And if you can't do that you're like some animal. You're finished. We're finished. *All* of us.' This conception of commitment becomes especially important at the end of the film.

Arriving at Angel's village provides a kind of idyll amid all the violence and depravity in the film. We learn that in Angel's absence, federal troops led by General Mapache raped the village and killed Angel's father. Angel's girlfriend left the village to become Mapache's mistress. Angel wants revenge. His anguish is contrasted with the festivities and warm social life in the village. It seems to reduce Tector and Lyle Gotch (played by Warren Oates), the most degenerate members of the Wild Bunch, to engaging in chaste playfulness. There is a celebratory dance, and goodwill is shared all around. When the Wild Bunch finally leave the village, they parade out to lilting guitar music and singing. Swathed in a mist, they ride past the townspeople who regard them lovingly, bestowing gifts and flowers on them. One senses that they bond with this community and that their experiences dispose them against Mapache and towards the Mexican people and the guerrilla resistance, since it is this special moment that closes the film by means of a flashback.

The Wild Bunch approach Mapache in the hope of selling him their extra horses. When Pike suggests that Mapache is a bandit just like they are, Dutch objects: 'We ain't nothing like him. We don't hang nobody. I hope these people here kick him and the rest of the scum like him into their graves.' Angel responds, 'We will if it takes for ever.'

When Angel sees his former girlfriend in Mapache's arms, he shoots her. But Mapache doesn't kill the Wild Bunch. Instead he offers them a job—to rob a US Army train and seize the guns and ammunition on it. The Wild Bunch agree; one of their conditions is that Angel be released. Angel, on the other hand, refuses to work for Mapache and against his own people until Pike and Dutch promise to give him some of the guns for the Mexican guerrillas. The highjacking of the train is a breathtaking exercise in timing. But unbeknownst to the Wild Bunch, Thornton has anticipated their attack and no sooner are the Wild Bunch on their way than Thornton and his band of subhumans are after them. The Wild Bunch elude them by blowing a bridge out from under the bounty hunters. But when the gang settle down for the night, they are surrounded by the guerrillas who have come for the guns Angel has promised them. Perhaps surprisingly, most of the Wild Bunch hardly resent this. Instead, they express their admiration for the guerrillas. Dutch says, 'I'd say those fellas know how to handle themselves.' Pike adds, 'If they ever get armed, with good leaders, this country will go up in smoke.' 'That it will, son, that it will,' Old Sykes concludes.

After a series of pretty dicey negotiations with Mapache and his men, the Wild Bunch begin a complicated transfer of the arms to the federal troops who have just been dealt a defeat by Pancho Villa. However, as the last transaction is under way, Mapache seizes Angel who he has learnt has given rifles and ammunition to the guerrillas.

As the Wild Bunch discuss what to do about this, they realise that Thornton's posse is still after them. They decide to go to Mapache's stronghold, since that is one place where Thornton will not follow them. Arriving there, they see Angel being tortured—he is being dragged by a Model T while children burn him with flares, rather as the scorpions were torched in the opening of the film. They try to buy Angel from Mapache, but they fail. Mapache's troops, roughly two hundred men, drink themselves into a stupor, and members of the Wild Bunch spend the night with whores.

The next morning, Pike approaches Lyle and Tector Gorch and says, 'Let's go.' 'Why not?' Lyle agrees. Nothing about what they intend to do is stated, but the men all seem to understand each other. Dutch just has to look at a fellow professional and he knows. They get their rifles and go to Mapache to demand Angel's release. Mapache feigns compliance, but instead slits Angel's throat. Pike shoots Mapache and there is a pause, as if no one knows what to do. Then the Wild Bunch start shooting Mapache's staff and a battle royal is joined. As is well known, it is quite a sustained gunfight for its period in film history, and by the end Pike, Dutch and the Gorch brothers are dead, but not before they have seemingly wiped out Mapache's entire army.

When Thornton's posse arrives, almost everyone is dead. Then the posse, *sans* Thornton, ride offscreen where they are killed by the guerrillas, led by Old Sykes. The guerrillas return to the killing field to strip Mapache's men of their guns and their ammunition. The Wild Bunch's last stand is a *de facto* victory for the revolution, supplying the rebels with a large store of arms while also decimating the federal army. Old Sykes invites Thornton to join the guerrillas. Thus, in effect, what is left of the Wild Bunch—recall that Thornton was once Pike's partner—becomes part of the Mexican revolution. And then the whole story is rounded off with flashbacks of the members of the Wild Bunch celebrating their camaraderie, and culminating, significantly enough, in their best moment, their bonding with the people in Angel's village.

Since the members of the Wild Bunch never say why they decide to confront Mapache, one cannot be certain of their motives. But the film does make clear that the significance of their last battle is to be understood in terms of advancing the cause of the revolution towards which they had expressed their sympathies. Part of the reason for their showdown with Mapache surely has to do with Pike's earlier speech about commitment to one's partners. The Wild Bunch had to rescue Angel as part of the code of the professional. But Angel is also the leading representative of the Mexican revolution, and in standing by him they also advanced the revolution and the cause of the people they admired.

The Wild Bunch presents a cankered vision of an American society made up of religious temperance fanatics, nasty children, lunatic lawmen, unscrupulous, vicious railroad representatives, and an incompetent army. But the Mexican people, represented by Angel's village, are portrayed in an affirmative light and their revolution (the head of Angel's village is one of the guerrillas) is endorsed throughout the film. Whether or not it is the express intention of the Wild Bunch to forward the revolution (and there is some evidence in this direction) as a matter of fact (in the world of the fiction), they die fighting for it.

CONCLUSION

In my descriptions of these four films, I have tried to show that, *pace* Will Wright, the professional Westerns situated south of the border do not accord, in significant respects, with his model. Most importantly, I have wanted to emphasise that society is not irrelevant in these films, once one realises that the society in question is Mexican society, which, in turn, is closely associated with various Mexican resistance movements. I do not think that Wright failed to note this because he was ethnically blinkered, but because he aspired to create a general model of the professional Western, and Mexican society only figures in a subset of them. However, I do think that, in ignoring this feature of films like *The Professionals* and *The Wild Bunch,* he missed a key dimension of their ideological operation.

Wright's story about the ideological operation of the professional Western in general is that it is an expression and/or celebration of the technocratic ethos. Thus, from his viewpoint, the professional Western reflects and reinforces attitudes that we might say are significant internally to contemporary American society. However, the professional Westerns that travel south of the border cross national boundaries, and therefore it is natural to suppose that they have something to do with prevailing ideological attitudes concerning international affairs.[11]

As I hope I have established, a major recurring motif in these films is that of professionals who devote their energies in support of certain social values, namely, freedom and resistance to tyranny. Although certain of the professional attitudes that Wright describes appear in these films, they coexist with and are often outweighed by sympathy for the struggles of the Mexican people. The professionals in these films are hardly as oblivious of society as Wright contends. In each of these films, the heroes, professionals though they be, wind up on the side of social revolutions for the sake of justice, not money. They may fight for their love of battle and because of their fidelity to the group. But, equally, they are motivated by a hatred of tyranny, an attraction to the social value of freedom, and/or an admiration for the Mexican people.

Quite clearly, from a political point of view these films are about an opposition to oppression and the support of social liberation. Underlying these films is the presupposition of a principle that the justification of professional prowess rests in its service for freedom and against tyranny. At the same time, there is a pretty clear-cut association of the professionals in these films with the military. They either have military backgrounds (Ben Trane, Rico Fardan, Bill Dolworth), or they wear military regalia (Rico Fardan, the Wild Bunch), or they exhibit military behaviour (the Magnificent Seven training the peasants). Putting this together with the previous principle, we see that these films rest on the view that the justification of the military is its promotion of freedom.

Moreover, if these professionals represent the military, they are the American military operating outside their national boundaries. Thus, we may hypothesise that what these films are about is what Americans want to believe, namely, that American military operations abroad are undertaken in the defence of freedom.

I am not saying that these films accurately represent American intervention abroad. They express a wish; they show how a great many Americans wished to conceive American foreign policy throughout the period of the *Pax Americana*. Like the professionals in these films, America may appear mercenary, driven by commercial interest, but finally it turns out that they are freedom fighters allied to indigenous, authentic social revolutions. These films express that ideological conviction at the same time that they reinforce it. That is the central ideological function of the south-of-the-border, professional Western.

To some readers, it may seem strange that the professional Western takes such a favourable view of the Mexican revolution, on the one hand, and the Mexican people on the other. Surely, there is a history of American antipathy and prejudice regarding both. However, it is important to remember that from the Second World War onwards, in part due to the war (and the need for a reliable ally to the south), American attitudes towards both the revolution and its vicissitudes, and towards Mexicans, became increasingly more positive than they had been.[12] This is perhaps reflected somewhat in the themes of racial tolerance and acceptance that run through all of these films, which, of course, also correlate with an important phase of the American civil rights movement.

Given the way in which American society appears to be represented in these films—the suggested injustice of the Union in *Vera Cruz,* the prejudiced town in *The Magnificent Seven,* Mr Grant in *The Professionals,* and the pervasive degeneracy in *The Wild Bunch*—a superficial reading of these films might propose that they are involved in social criticism. However, this overlooks the fact that it is the professionals who mobilise the audience's allegiance and that those professionals cater to an American self-conception of itself as a nation committed to freedom. This self-conception, abetted in part by these professional Westerns, had important ideological work to do in the throes of the Cold War.

The Western genre, along with the crime film, addresses American politics in a particularly straightforward way. They are forums for the expression of political anxieties, beliefs, desires, sentiments, and convictions. Films like *Posse* and *Bad Girls* attempt to serve as vehicles for contemporary identity politics. The south-of-the-border professional Western presupposed, as a condition of narrative intelligibility, audiences that would easily accept the plausibility of these paramilitary, American professionals risking everything for the cause of freedom. Since this was a sentiment, albeit idealised, that Americans already embraced about themselves as a nation, these films activated it reliably and, in the process of activating it, reinforced it.[13] Nor, as the Gulf War indicates, is this sentiment merely an artefact of the past.

The films I have been discussing span a period of fifteen years, years in which public attitudes towards American intervention abroad changed, often momentously. Some of those changes are reflected in these films. However, in this essay I have been less concerned with year-to-year fluctuations in opinions about American foreign policy than with what I contend is an underlying, unvarying conviction, shared by American conservatives and radicals alike, regarding intervention, namely, that it is justified in the name of abetting freedom. Virtually everyone in the debate avails themselves of this rhetoric no matter what the situation. Thus, what I have found to be of note in these professional Westerns is not that they reflect contemporary American opinions about specific foreign policy issues, but that they reveal something about the enduring framework in which Americans regard such issues. Americans want to believe that intervention is justified in support of social justice. They are predisposed emotionally to respond favourably to situations depicted in this light. This is one of the reasons that the professional Westerns we have examined are successful. And it is also a perennial disposition that can be readily exploited for ideological purposes.

NOTES

1. There are other films in this cycle. I have focused on these four because I think that they are the best known. *A Fistful of Dynamite* (1972) is also an important example, but I shall not dwell on it because it is an Italian production and, for reasons that will become obvious when I discuss the ideological operation of these films, I am concerned with American productions.

   I call this series of films a cycle for a number of reasons. Not only do they share settings, themes and plot motifs. They also share actors, a number of whom appear in two of the films under discussion. And, more importantly, the earlier films in this series seem to have influenced the later films in a multiplicity of ways from dramatic development to costumes to props. For two examples, consider the ways in which the professionals are introduced in *The Magnificent Seven* and *The Professionals,* and the similar weaponry in *The Professionals* and *The Wild Bunch.* Moreover, I am not the first person to note the importance of Mexican revolutions to these films. Richard Slotkin regards *Vera Cruz* and *The Magnificent Seven,* among other films, as part of a series concerned with Mexican revolutions which he calls 'the counterinsurgency scenario'. See Richard Slotkin, *Gunfighter Nation: The Myth of the Frontier in Twentieth-Century America* (New York: Atheneum, 1992), pp. 435–40.

2. Will Wright, *Six Guns and Society: A Structural Study of the Western* (Berkeley: University of California Press, 1975).

3. Wright, p. 97 (bracketed remarks added).

4. Wright, pp. 85–6.

5. Wright, p. 177.

6. Wright, p. 178.

7. Wright, p. 179.

8. Wright, p. 179 (bracketed remarks added).

9. Of course, the theme of the professional is not restricted to the Western. It is often important in caper films. War films, such as *The Guns of Navarone,* also celebrate the theme. Parenthetically, it is interesting to note that several of these sorts of films have numbers in their titles—not only *The Magnificent Seven,* but *Ocean's Eleven* and *The Dirty Dozen.* The integer usually refers to the number of professional heroes in the film.

10. On p. 41 of *Six Guns and Society,* Wright categorises *Vera Cruz* as a classical Western on

the grounds that the hero (Ben Trane) is accepted by the arbiters of respectable society after he saved it from destruction. This is not exactly accurate descriptively, since he has
not saved the Mexican revolutionaries from destruction, but rather aided them. However, it is true that Wright does somewhat abstractly acknowledge the importance of a society, which happens to be Mexican, in this film. Nevertheless, he surprisingly fails to
discuss the degree to which the film also coincides with his characterisation of the professional Western. So,despite what he says, I think that on his own terms he should consider it at least a mixed case. Moreover, this has repercussions for his accounts of other
professional Westerns, since, as I hope to show, in both *The Professionals* and *The Wild
Bunch,* the gunfighters manifest a sympathy for Mexican revolutionaries rather like Ben
Trane's. Thus, his distinction between the classical Western and the professional Western
is unstable throughout his theory. Moreover, with respect to *Vera Cruz,* I think that the
film shares more elements with Wright's characterisation of the professional Western
than it does with the classical Western and, therefore, merits the criticism advanced
above. But, apart from questions of categorisation, I also think that Wright ignores the
importance of the *Mexican* people in the film and this is ultimately the crux of my criticism.

11. Indeed, Richard Slotkin regards them as thought experiments concerning counterinsurgency. See Slotkin, pp. 439–40.

12. For information on attitudes towards the Mexican Revolution, see John A. Brittan, *Revolution and Ideology: Images of the Mexican Revolution in the United States* (Lexington:
University of Kentucky Press, 1995). For information on changing American attitudes
towards Mexicans, especially along the border, see David Montejano, *Anglos and Mexicans in the Making of Texas, 1836–1986* (Austin: University of Texas Press, 1987) and
Arnoldo De Leon, *They Called Them Greasers* (Austin: University of Texas Press, 1983).

13. For a more general account of the operation of ideology in narrative film, see Noël Carroll, 'Film, Rhetoric and Ideology', in Salim Kemal and Ivan Gaskell (eds) *Explanation
and Value in the Arts* (Cambridge: Cambridge University Press, 1993).

Chapter 17 Moving and Moving: From Minimalism to *Lives of Performers*

In retrospect, *Lives of Performers* strikes one as an allegory of its time—of Yvonne Rainer's (and the avant-garde filmworld's) movement from minimalism to something else. The film begins with rehearsal footage of the dance *Walk, She Said,* which gives every appearance of being a minimalist exercise devoted to the exploration of movement as such.[1] Though a rehearsal (and, therefore, by definition something that looks toward the future), this dance, oddly enough, points back to the past—to minimalism with its commitment to a modernist aesthetic of austerity. In a narrow sense, the dance rehearsal points backwards to Rainer's own distinguished career as a choreographer—a career which she was, with *Lives of Performers,* preparing to exchange for a career in filmmaking. From another, wider, angle, one can also gloss the rehearsal material from *Walk, She Said* as a synecdoche for the aesthetic milieu of the time, where not only the dance world, but the worlds of fine arts and film were all dominated by minimalism, the filmworld variant of which was structural film.

Sandwiched in between the shoots of the rehearsal is the "real" content of the film. Sally Banes has called *Lives of Performers* a backstage musical—that is, we get a view of the fictional *lives of the performers,* ostensibly in between their rehearsals of the minimalist *Walk, She Said.* Thus, what is excluded by minimalist mandate from *Walk, She Said*—emotion and narrative— becomes the focus of the film we see. What is backstage comes on stage, while what should be on stage, by minimalist standards, is actually backstage, since it is only a rehearsal.[2]

Walk, She Said is an eminently minimalist-sounding title. "Walk" signals the commitment to ordinary movement on the part of minimalist choreographers, especially those associated with Judson Church and now called "postmodern." "Walk," of course, could aptly describe a work like Steve Paxton's *Satisfyin' Lover* where forty-two performers pace across the stage at their everyday cadence. Minimalist works like this were committed to discovering the essential conditions of dance as well as the minimal conditions of dance perception.[3]

Similarly, in the entire phrase—"Walk, She Said"—the verb "walk" appears in the imperative mood, revealing the essential nature of choreography as a matter of instruction, of the type that Rainer herself exemplifies in the rehearsal footage in *Lives.* In this way, the expression "Walk, She Said," is nothing short of a score for the most stripped-down, essential piece of minimalist choreography imaginable. Thus, the rehearsal footage in *Lives* represents art at its most abstract and pared down, setting up a contrast to what sits between its appearances—the seemingly messy, complicated lives of the performers, no longer depicted in their universal aspect as mere walkers—mere bodies in movement, neatly and sharply deployed in space—but fictional lovers with shifting psychological states, occupying an unstable inner space.[4]

If *Walk, She Said* stands as a specimen for the type of choreography that obsessed ambitious dancers and choreographers of the early seventies, it also corresponds to the aesthetic inclinations of the filmmakers who dominated that moment in American avant-garde cinema called "structural film," which was represented, perhaps most illustriously, by Michael Snow, Hollis Frampton, and Ernie Gehr. Structural filmmakers—like the minimalist postmodern choreographers—attempted to pare down whatever seemed extraneous in their work in order to discover the nature of film. They sought to shrink their repertoire of devices to just those that would foreground the essential elements of the medium. If a film like *Wavelength*—a zoom shot, sometimes interrupted, of a loft—contained anecdotal or narrative material, it was only there in order to be parodied and, ultimately, to be bypassed in favor of the real star of the show: cinema as personified by the play of pure cinematic devices, such as the zoom shot, which itself was predicated upon engaging the audience in a rarefied act of apperception regarding the conditions of the cinematic experience.[5]

Moreover, if a structural film contained language, it was not there so much for what is said, but as another specimen for minimalist interrogation, dissection, and analysis. Just as the minimalist choreographer attempted to peel dance down to its core, so structuralist filmmakers used austere design to explore what made film, film; narrative, narrative; and language, language. Thus, the placement of *Walk, She Said* at the opening of *Lives* symbolizes the kind of aesthetic venture, the kind of film, that Rainer "should" have been making, given the taste of the time, thereby setting up a studied contrast to the film to come—not only literally the film to come in the next seventy minutes or so, but "the film-to-come" in the larger sense of the kind of avant-garde film that would eventually displace structural filmmaking from the center of attention to a position nearer the periphery.

If, as the Russian formalists argued, art history is an affair of shifting dominants, then the movement from *Walk, She Said* to the lives of performers in this film prophesizes a shift from the dominance of structural film, with its commitment to minimalist aesthetics, to a re-engagement with life—the lives of performers—which, perforce, involves a return to narrative and emotion, subjects excluded from the minimalist program in favor of pure artistic, formal, and perceptual research.

Nevertheless, though *Lives of Performers* returns to the very human and impure topic of the passions—returning to well-known scenarios of courtship, fear of rejection, jealousy, betrayal, insensitivity, anger, reconciliation, and ambivalence—the film does not take up these issues oblivious to the ambitions of modernism.[6] For while aspiring to tell stories about the *loves* of performers, Rainer also, at the same time, wants to comment analytically on the nature of narrative—or, at least, certain aspects thereof—in this film.

One way to appreciate this is to recall how generic the narratives in the film are—or, rather, how they are made to appear generic. For example, there is for the viewer the recurring question of whom the narrative is about, due to the frequent, uncertain, underdetermined juxtaposition of word and image. Is the text about this person or that person; this couple or that couple? Because of the ambiguity of the spoken and written references in the film, these questions force themselves on the viewer again and again. Moreover, the ambiguity of the spoken and written references in the film—vis-à-vis the ongoing narrative— serves to generalize the scenario: to suggest that this is the story of many people *or* that stories themselves are (very often) generic. That is, we lay them on the experiences of many different people—on many different characters—monotonously.[7]

In this way, generic narratives might be thought of as clichés, and, of course, we have been alerted to the importance of cliché to Rainer's conception of *Lives* by the opening quotation from Leo Bersani: "Cliché is, in a sense, the purest art of intelligibility; it tempts us with the possibility of enclosing life within beautifully inalterable formulas, of obscuring the arbitrary nature of imagination with an appearance of necessity." Through Bersani's quotation, that is, Rainer heralds her sense of the nature, function and appeal of the generic narratives she is about to explore.[8]

Here it is also interesting to consider the use of the psychoanalyst Carl Jung in *Lives*. In a number of her films, Rainer employs what might be thought of as psychoanalytic reference points. In *Journeys from Berlin,* Lacan plays this role; in *Murder and murder,* Rivière. In *Lives,* the psychoanalytic reference point is Jung, whom Rainer mentions four times and quotes approvingly in the film, notably in the section in which still photographs of *Grand Union Dreams* are shown. But what is the relevance of Jung to *Lives?* I think it is this: Jung believed in the psychic existence of archetypal or stereotypical characters and narratives, templates according to which we make sense of life.

For Jung, epic narratives of the gods, such as those alluded to in the photographic montage of *Grand Union Dreams* in the early portion of *Lives,* are archetypal narratives of this sort. Thus, Rainer might be interpreted as using this "Jungian narrative" to register the point that many (most?) narratives, such as those to follow, have a stereotypical cast. That is, the voice-over narration of events in the personal lives of the performers, when juxtaposed against the mythic material from *Grand Union Dreams,* suggests that these personal tales are instances of mythic narratives.[9]

Though deployed to limn the experience of individuals, these myths are nevertheless generic. Thus, by sounding this refrain, Rainer remains enough of a committed modernist so that if she is going to tell stories, her modernist conscience also requires her to tell us something about the nature of such stories.

Perhaps the clearest example of generic narration in *Lives* is the trio among Shirley Soffer, John Erdman, and Valda Setterfield. Executed in a medium shot with the dancers facing the camera, it is accompanied by off-screen commentary, read by Setterfield, which begins: "You might describe it that way. It's also a story about a man who loves a woman and can't leave her when he falls in love with another woman." As Setterfield recounts the various affective permutations circulating this virtually archetypal love triangle, the three dancers reorient themselves toward and away from one another—sometimes lying down, sometimes hugging, sometimes somersaulting, but mostly just changing facings. Each change of facing is unavoidably read as a shift in affection, given the commentary.

Ironically, without the voice-over commentary, this dance would appear as a quintessential minimal dance, a piece of moving geometry, bereft of emotional qualities. But the accompanying narrative overlays a charge of passion. As the man turns away from one woman to the other, in the context of the voice-over, it is natural to interpret this as signaling an alienation of affection. However, the voice-over narrative makes it difficult to correlate precisely the women in the dance with the women in the text.

They are called No. 1 and No. 2, and if this isn't abstract enough, it is hard to keep track of which one is which relative to the story. The spectator, especially on an initial viewing, cannot be sure that she's consistently mapped the spoken narrative onto the visuals. Which one of the dancers is No. 1 and which one is No. 2 is tauntingly ambiguous for the normal viewer.[10] Yet this, I submit, is not a mistake on Rainer's part, but a way to manipulate the viewer's experience of the dance in order to motivate the theme that this perennial tale of the love triangle is a generic narrative, one that might fit the plight of either of the women, and, by extension, others. It is, of course, a story that we have all told about ourselves or others—more than once—in our own lives.

One part of Rainer's reflexive investigation in *Lives,* then, emphasizes, as I've already indicated, the generic aspect of narratives. Another phenomenon that Rainer takes up for examination is the paradoxical effect of narrative, and perhaps particularly visual narrative, to possess an aura of finality—the "appearance of necessity," as Bersani says—despite the fact that narratives are made up of a contingent ensemble of events and reversible choices.

Thus, in *Lives of Performers,* characters are often played by different actors,[11] and scenes are putatively rehearsed and played in alternative ways, though each instantiation of the written text appears absolutely authoritative visually. At one point, for instance, Setterfield seems to think aloud about how she should play a scene—one involving an entrance into a room already occupied by John Erdman and Shirley Soffer.[12] Then what follows is nothing less than an elaborate inventory (including as many as ten variations) of how she might enter (or even not at all enter) the room.

This is an exercise in the subjunctive mood, an exploration of alternative, possible narrative worlds, pointedly reminding us that, though the modal status of narratives—perhaps particularly visual ones—feels like some kind of necessity, it is really, with respect to fictional constructs, nothing more than a matter of possibilities carefully staged and advanced from a repertoire of contingent choices.

Throughout *Lives,* we see emerging in Rainer's film work a preoccupation with theory, which will become one of her signatures as a cineaste. But even in its earliest appearance, we note that she is not a doctrinaire theorist, but rather one who tries to motivate and to make available to audiences theoretical insights through their experience of the film. The insights she has to offer about the nature of narrative in *Lives of Performers* are not dictated at the audience as they might have been in so many New Talkies, but rather they emerge from one's experience of the film.[13]

For instance, Rainer's insight into the generic nature of narratives, despite the appearance of particularity that dominates individual narratives, emerges from the simultaneous ambiguity and tempting applicability of the narratives with which the viewer is confronted while trying to match the spoken text with the visuals. And this, in conjunction with the allusions to Jung, should encourage the informed viewer, maieutically, to an appreciation of the putatively archetypal dimension of narrative structure.

Similarly, the play of necessity and possibility—of the indicative and the subjunctive—in the deep structure of the film is something that Rainer makes available to the audience through demonstration rather than protestation, committed as she has been not just to advancing theoretical points, but to making theorists—that is, to engendering the participation of audiences willing to reflect thoughtfully on the stories, images, and their reciprocal configuration as they encounter them in *Lives.* If Rainer succeeds in disclosing the apparent necessity of narratives as, in part, a function of their generic structures, she also deconstructs that appearance by underscoring that such narratives are really composed from a network of contingent possibilities, alternative artistic choices of the sort she exhibits.

With Rainer's concern with narrative comes an interest in the emotions, since the emotions are the most common engine for the production of action in our fondest stories of human affairs. That is, the emotions are the springs that make action happen, which, in turn, becomes the stuff of stories.

As is well known, Rainer has said that she moved from dance to film in order to pursue her interests in the emotions. But though this is a cliché of Yvonniana, Sally Banes has asked the good question of why Rainer had to embrace film in order to approach the emotions, since the dance of her immediate predecessors—the moderns, including, most notably, Martha Graham—made the emotions their privileged domain.[14] But as Banes points out, that sort of approach to the emotions—the modern-dance approach—was not available to Rainer, and not simply because of her avowed minimalism.

The modern dance approach involved exhibiting, expressing or projecting emotion—making it visible on the surface of the body in a way often predicated upon arousing emotions in the audience. Modern dancers sought to provoke emotion as they showed it forth bodily. Emotion from one body was designed to infect other bodies, igniting feeling in spectators.

Yet this approach was antithetical to Rainer's concern with emotion, which, paralleling her interests in narrative, focused on reflecting on the nature and structure of the emotions—on their stereotypical or archetypal scenarios—rather than on being caught up in their rhythms, swamped by affect and, in the worst case, wallowing in it. This is why, I hypothesize, Rainer moved from choreography to film, since film allowed her the opportunity to reflect on the emotions dispassionately. Whereas existing dance vocabularies tended to absorb audiences rather than to afford a space for reflection—indeed, since the presence of any emotional body in dance is apt to infect the audience affectively—Rainer moved from dance to film in order to secure a space for reflection, to distantiate the audience from emotive engulfment, setting emotion at a remove where spectators could observe the emotional states of characters as if under a microscope.[15]

It may sound strange to speak of film as a means for "anesthetizing" emotions for the purpose of observation. So many genre films—from action and suspense films to horror and melodrama—are about activating emotions, not about scrutinizing them. But what Rainer saw as a filmic possibility was the option of dissecting emotional states, of dissolving them into their parts in a way that not only undercut their potential infectiousness, but dismantled them for one to view their parts dispassionately and contemplatively.

What Rainer realized was the possibility of separating the parts of the emotion—of prying apart the inside and the outside—and redistributing said parts across the various visual and linguistic channels of cinematic articulation—intertitles, voice-over, and visual enactment, both photographic and cinematic. We often speak of channeling our emotions. In *Lives,* Rainer re-channels and redistributes the emotions of her characters across several informational tracks, separating the behavioral and the propositional dimensions of emotions so that one can reflect on each dimension cooly, without being caught up in the holistic emotional undertow.[16]

The characters are often literally frozen, or, at least, frequently deadpan as we hear or read of their inner turmoil. Their demeanor is not only a sort of realistic acknowledgment of the suppression of affect amongst modern middle-class professionals, but also a device to keep the audience on the outside looking in—rather like anatomists of affect.

Just as Brechtian acting techniques, including the third-person deliveries of lines, alienate the actors from their characters, so the disembodied verbal affect distantiates the viewer, so that one can chart the repetitions, stereotypes, and generic structures in the emotional lives of the characters, including romantic syndromes of approach and avoidance, patterns of reconciliation, envy, betrayal, and anger.[17] Moreover, additional distantiating devices, including the low-key acting style, the ever-so-discreet frontal medium shots, and the foreswearing of emotionally aggressive close-ups,[18] decouple affect from gesture, thereby short-circuiting the likelihood of the bodily emotional infectiousness that is the hallmark of much modern dance and most popular film.

Nevertheless, if most of the film brackets or de-emphasizes the bodily expression of emotion, concentrating on the mental or propositional content of the emotive states portrayed, the bodily realm is not forgotten. The film reinstates it, so to speak, in the coda, an enactment of a series of stills from the published scenario of G. W. Pabst's *Pandora's Box,* which sequence is nothing so much as a catalogue of a range of stereotypical bodily manifestations of emotional states. By means of this protracted montage of photographic recreations (each pose is held for twenty seconds before it is relaxed), Rainer is able to set forth for reflection readily recognizable, recurring forms of emotive appearances, thereby continuing her meditation on the generic structure of the emotions at the same time that the film reunites emotive thinking with its natural habitat in the body.

Most of this coda is silent, and the *stillness* of the sequence—both in terms of movement and sound—along with the narrative decontextualization of the images invites the viewer to scrutinize these highly legible, in some cases conventionalized, expressions of emotion almost diagnostically. That is, appropriately defamiliarized, these poses become opportunities to contemplate the generic face of emotion.

At the same time, the relevance of this coda to the rest of the film is reflective, reminding us of the emotive upheaval that underlies the putative lives and loves of the performers who have engaged us for most of the film so far. At one point, a snatch of the Rolling Stones song "No Expectations" intervenes, about which B. Ruby Rich comments: "In a stagy replica of the 1928 melodrama, the four characters get to exhibit extremes of emotion never displayed in the preceding footage. Lest the viewer, however, thereby assume that the emotions themselves were not in evidence (albeit devoid of a matching acting style), Rainer slyly matches the last three minutes of the 'stills' to the Rolling Stones song . . . of yet another affair of the heart gone wrong."[19]

However, even if in the "Lulu" section Rainer finally grants the emotions some measure of bodily visibility (and audibility), both the "heat" of the acting style and the music are buffered by the configuration of cinematic strategies, so that the audience, instead of being affectively inflamed, stays at a meditative distance, clinically taking note of the generic emotive forms of fright, abandon, passion, amusement, and derangement. Thus, it is as if in the coda, Rainer returns to the home territory of modern dance—to the topic of the embodiment of emotion—but with a difference. For by presenting the intense expression of emotion, as abstracted from a silent expressionist film, in the medium of effectively still images, she has arrested their contagious powers, calling forth contemplation rather than empathy, kinetic or otherwise. Thus, in turning to film, Rainer discovered a way to acknowledge and address the life of the emotions, without being overwhelmed by it.[20]

NOTES

1. *Walk, She Said* was performed at the Whitney Museum on April 12, 1972, as part of a larger piece by Rainer entitled *Performance.* Several other sections of *Lives of Performers* were also recycled from this material, including the "Lulu" coda.

2. Sally Banes, "Dance, Emotion, Film: The Case of Yvonne Rainer," a talk at the symposium on the work of Yvonne Rainer sponsored by the Humanities Institute of New York University in April 1999.

3. Annette Michelson refers to this tendency as "autoanalytical" in her pioneering article "Yvonne Rainer, Part I: The Dancer and The Dance," in *Artforum,* vol. 12, no. 5 (January 1974), p. 58.

4. In her famous "NO manifesto," when Rainer said "no to moving and being moved," this referred, as Sally Banes has shown, to being moved affectively and to moving the audience emotionally. Thus, in *Lives,* Rainer is taking up the issue of emotion in dance that had been generally exiled during her more minimalist moments. See: Sally Banes, *Dancing Women: Female Bodies on Stage* (London: Routledge, 1998), p. 223.

5. In personal correspondence, Yvonne Rainer has objected to my analogy between Snow's zoom shot and the Judson use of ordinary movement, like walking. She points out that whereas the zoom might be a unique feature of motion picture images, walking is not a unique feature of dance. We all walk even when we are not dancing. This disanalogy is well observed. It leads me to think that when we speak of minimalist essentialism, we need to keep in mind that there are at least two types. One type seeks after the basic features of an artform which are unique to it. The other looks to fundamental features—building blocks, if you will, of the artform—whether or not they are unique to it. Snow's

essentialism with respect to the zoom shot is an example of uniqueness essentialism; the Judson use of walking is more a matter of building-block essentialism—it strips the choreography down to its most minimal or basic elements, but not in a way that marks it off as distinguishable from ordinary walking. It is a matter of getting down to essences, but not categorically distinct essences.

6. It may seem strange that I keep calling Rainer's project in the late sixties and early seventies "modernist," since she is associated with postmodern dance. However, postmodern dance was not postmodern*ist*. It was a revolt against the modern dance and, in that sense, postmodern, but it essayed that revolt in the name of a reflexive interrogation of movement as such. Thus, though postmodern, it was also modernist in its ambitions, as was minimalism, despite Michael Fried's deprecations. Postmodern dance was minimalist dance and, for that reason, not postmodernist as that concept was to evolve in the late seventies (as a foil to minimalism). Admittedly these labels can be confusing, especially if one tries to use them as they were used in the relevant historical context. For further terminological clarification, see Sally Banes, *Terpsichore in Sneakers* (2nd edition) (Middletown, Conn.: Wesleyan University Press, 1987), pp. xiv–xv.

7. As Peggy Phelan points out, *Lives* is concerned with "the most ubiquitous narrative of all, the love story." Peggy Phelan, "Yvonne Rainer: From Dance to Film," *A Woman Who . . . Essays, Interviews, Scripts,* edited by Yvonne Rainer (Baltimore: Johns Hopkins University Press, 1999), p. 13.

8. In her essay, "A Likely Story," Rainer asks "Can the presentation of sexual conflict or the presentation of love and jealousy be revitalized through a studied placement or dislocation of *clichés* borrowed from soap opera or melodrama?" Since *Lives* is subtitled "a melodrama," it is hard to resist reading this as a rhetorical question stating her intentions with respect to that film. See: Yvonne Rainer, "A Likely Story," in *A Woman Who . . . Essays, Interviews, Scripts,* p. 139 (emphasis added).

9. Phelan notes: "Rainer's attraction to emotional narrative also led her to conceive of her own life as a sort of 'mythic' source. Phelan, p. 11.

10. In personal correspondence, Yvonne Rainer has pointed out to me that the ambiguity of the enactment of this triangle is heightened in what immediately follows it. After the dance, there is a close-up of Shirley Soffer asking, "Which woman is the director most sympathetic to?" Then, also in a close-up, Valda Setterfield replies: "I think No. 1, maybe simply because she appears first." But this doesn't clarify anything, since neither woman appeared first in the image; the indeterminacy about which one is which, therefore, doggedly remains, perhaps even more uncomfortably than before. See pp. 67–68 of the script of *Lives of Performers* in Yvonne Rainer, *The Films of Yvonne Rainer* (Bloomington, Indiana: Indiana University Press, 1989).

11. On the soundtrack, for example, Rainer says: ". . . did I mention that I'm going to be taking some of John's parts?" See *Lives of Performers* in *The Films of Yvonne Rainer,* by Yvonne Rainer (Bloomington: Indiana University Press, 1989), p. 68.

12. This occurs on pp. 72–73 of the script of *Lives of Performers.*

13. Though I have elsewhere argued that avant-garde artworks, including films, can rarely produce theories in any full-blooded sense of the terms, I nevertheless do refer to Rainer's interests in *Lives* as theoretical. I do so not only because filmmakers, as a matter of his-

torical fact, often think of themselves as involved in theorizing, but also because I do not deny that filmmakers can illustrate (as opposed to proving) theoretical insights. In this way, they may be thought of as tutoring audiences—frequently, as in Rainer's case, maieutically. And though tutoring theory is very different than making theory, there is no compelling reason to refuse the label "theoretical" to the former—so long as we are aware of what we're doing. Moreover, it is in this sense that I would call *Lives* theoretical. For further discussion of this issue, see: Noël Carroll, "Avant-Garde Film and Film Theory," in *Theorizing the Moving Image* (New York: Cambridge University Press, 1996); and Noël Carroll, "Avant-Garde Art and the Problem of Theory," in *The Journal of Aesthetic Education* (Fall 1995).

Judith Mayne makes the interesting point that Rainer's filmmaking can also be considered theoretical in the sense that it constantly undermines or, at least questions, reigning filmworld theories dialectically. This is especially true, I think, of *Journeys from Berlin/1971* and *The Man Who Envied Women,* but less pertinent, I believe, to *Lives.* See: Judith Mayne, "Theory Speak(s)," in *A Woman Who . . .* For a similar conception of *Journeys from Berlin/1971,* see Noël Carroll, "Interview with a Woman Who," also in *A Woman Who . . . .*

14. Banes, "Dance, Emotion, Film."
15. It is true that Rainer explored emotional material in live pieces such as *Grand Union Dreams, Performance,* and later the staged version of *Story about a Woman Who.* But, I speculate, even treating emotional material on stage in her own distantiating idiom, was not, from her point of view, as effective as rendering it on film. For as long as the human body remains present to the spectator, the potential for emotional response is highly likely. Film, on the other hand, can be used in such a way that the medium itself becomes an alienation technique in its own right (by decorporealizing, disembodying, and, thereby, distancing the human presence of the performers from the audience).
16. For an account of the different components of emotional states, see Noël Carroll, *The Philosophy of Horror* (New York: Routledge, 1990), Chapter One.
17. Rainer makes clear her interest in the generic structures of the emotions in a letter to Nan Piene following a screening of *Lives of Performers.* She writes: "the more I get into it the more I see how such things as rage, terror, desire, conflict, et al., are not unique to my experience the way my body and its functioning are." Yvonne Rainer, *Work 1961–73* (Halifax: The Press of the Nova Scotia College of Art and Design, 1974), p. 238.
18. There are, of course, close-ups in *Lives.* But two things need to be said about them. Where there are close-ups of persons' faces, they are not emotionally arresting, because, with the exception of the "Lulu coda," the performers' faces are generally impassive and, in addition, sometimes almost still. This makes it very hard to read their emotional significance. Thus, though close-ups of faces, they are not emotionally infectious ones. One of the only deviations from this norm that I remember occurs when Valda, slyly smiling in a medium close-up, turns away from Fernando after their discussion about her solo.

As well as close-ups of faces, the film also contains a wealth of close-ups of "detached," sometimes decontextualized, body parts—feet, midsections, and the like. Frequently this occurs while emotionally significant material is being read on the soundtrack. But these close-ups tend to decouple the affect of the words from the images. By fragmenting the human body in this way, Rainer depersonalizes it, rendering it anonymous and de-nuding it of its expressive powers.

When we see shots of the legs or shoulders of characters, these do not visually narrate the situation in a way that stimulates an affective response, even if such a response might be appropriate, given the accompanying text. Though these shots in some sense illustrate the story, not only do they fail to engage the viewer emotionally, they even block such re-actions, disposing us toward calmly heeding the flatly delivered propositional content of the emotional states, rather than being revved up by their bodily manifestation.

19. B. Ruby Rich, "Yvonne Rainer: An Introduction," in *The Films of Yvonne Rainer,* p. 6.
20. A version of this article was presented as a talk at the conference on the work of Yvonne Rainer, sponsored by the Humanities Institute of New York University, April 1999. The author wishes to express his gratitude to Yvonne Rainer and Sally Banes for their comments on an earlier version of this essay.

Chapter 18 Prospects for Film
Theory: A Personal Assessment

INTRODUCTION: THE THEORY
IS DEAD, LONG LIVE THEORY

The rapid expansion of the film studies institution over the last two decades in the United States was undoubtedly abetted, in one way or another, by something called film theory, or, as its acolytes are apt to say, simply Theory—a classy continental number, centrally composed of elements of Louis Althusser, Jacques Lacan, and Roland Barthes, often with optional features derived, often incongruously, from Michel Foucault, Julia Kristeva, Pierre Bourdieu, Gilles Deleuze, and (*maybe* sometimes) Jacques Derrida, along with contributions from French cinéphiles like Christian Metz, Raymond Bellour, and Jean-Louis Baudry, although generally filtered, albeit with a difference, through exegetes like Stephen Heath, Kaja Silverman, and Teresa de Lauretis.

Universities regarded film studies programs as an economic boon, likely to spur demand and, in this context, Theory, so called, played an economic role in legitimating the formation of film programs. For what went by the name of Theory was surely abstruse enough to convince an uninformed administrator or a hesitant trustee that film studies was at least as complex intellectually as string theory, DNA, or hypotheses about massive parallel processing.

Whether it was necessary to enfranchise film studies in this way is an open question. Perhaps (as I tend to think) market forces alone would have sufficed to establish the institution. But, in any case, Theory appears to have played the ideological-institutional role of enfranchiser, even if the role was ultimately an epiphenomenal one. Furthermore, the expectation of gold in "them thar hills" also encouraged too many university presses to invest in film publications, especially when the arcane peregrinations of Theory facilitated their rationalization of their relaxation of their traditional role as academic gatekeepers. Hence film studies has been flooded with repetitive decoctions of the Theory in search of the same market in much the same way that consumers are confronted with so many marginally differentiated shampoos.

Interestingly, now that film studies seems ensconced in American universities—with TV studies and cultural studies queuing up behind it for legitimation—Theory looks to be on the wane. Certainly people like myself would like to imagine that this is a result of the recognition that the Theory has been soundly refuted, though even I would have to concede that more accurate explanations may be that Theory has outlived its academic utility or that it has merely run out of gas (that is, exhausted itself). But, in any case, however the demise of Theory came about, as it continues to petrify, it becomes appropriate to speculate about whether theorizing—in a small "t," not-a-proper-name sort of way—is possible. For even if Theory is dead, one wonders whether theorizing about film has a future.

Given these circumstances, it is the aim of this essay to explore the prospects for film theory. In order to approach this subject, I shall begin by sketching, in the longest part of this essay, what I take to be major obstacles to film theorizing at present, many of which are legacies of the Theory alluded to above. It is my conviction that as long as these obstacles continue to grip the imaginations of scholars, fruitful theorizing about film will be unlikely.

I will also attempt, in a more abbreviated way, to provide a minimal characterization of what I take to be the most useful framework that we might employ for film theorizing today. Lastly, I will look at the consequences of adopting that framework for assessing one of the leading debates (or, maybe, one of the *only* debates) among contemporary film theorists, namely: the rivalry between psychoanalytic film theory and cognitive theory (a tendency represented by some of the essays in this volume).

IMPEDIMENTS TO FILM THEORIZING

1. Monolithic conceptions of film theory. The history of film theorizing, it seems to me, has been dominated by a conception of what a film theory should be in terms of the model of a unified body of ideas with certain core propositions from which conclusions about concrete cases follow in various ways, once certain empirical possibilities are considered. Metaphorically, we might call such a construal of film theory foundationalist. It is my contention that such monolithic conceptions of film theory stand in the way of productive theorizing about film, which theorizing might be best construed in terms of producing film theories rather than Film Theory.

Film theor*y*, as most frequently practiced heretofore, has been singular; a film theory was generally conceived to be a rather comprehensive instrument that was supposed to answer virtually every legitimate question you might have about film. This view naturally contrasts with a view of our arena of inquiry as plural, that is, a view that commends thinking in terms of film theor*ies* rather than in terms of film theor*y*. That is, rather than theorizing about every element of film style in light of a set of limited theoretical presuppositions—for example, about the purported commitment of the medium to realism or about its inevitable ideological destiny to suture—one might proceed by constructing local theories—for example, of film suspense, of film metaphor, of camera movement, or narrative comprehension, and even of the rhetoric of ideology—without expecting that these small-scale theories can be collected and unified under an overarching set of presuppositions about either the nature or function of cinema.

Nor is there any reason to think that film theorizing must be restricted to the stylistic features of film. Let us call hypotheses about the operation of international markets on corporate decision making film theory, so long as the hypotheses involve general conjectures about patterns or regularities in the practices of filmmaking, which practices include distribution and its influences as well as cinematic construction and reception. That is, let anything count as film theorizing, so long as it involves the production of generalizations or general explanations or general taxonomies and concepts about film practice.

This view of film theorizing conflicts sharply with certain of the most traditional preconceptions of film theory. What is often called classical film theory not only conceptualizes the activity as Film Theor*y*, but as *Film* Theory—that is, as committed to medium specificity in such a way that whatever counts as theorizing about film must be connected to features of the medium that are thought to be uniquely or essentially cinematic. Film theory must pertain to what is distinctly cinematic, otherwise it shall not count as film theory but as something else, like narrative theory.

Admittedly, narrow, essentialist views of film theory of this sort are infrequently voiced nowadays. However, where they remain influential, as they do in the work of the psychoanalytic film theorist Christian Metz and in the conception of photography of Roland Barthes and his cinematic followers, they are impediments to film theory and need to be dismantled dialectically.

Of course, the greatest problem with essentialist film theory is that it gives every indication of being false. But at the very least, another problem with essentialist film theory is that it blinkers the theoretical imagination by limiting what questions are the correct ones to ask about cinema. Yet, especially since cinematic essentialism seems philosophically dispensable, there appears to be scant reason to abide its restrictions.

Instead of thinking of film theory as a unified, single theory, it might be better to think of it as a field of activity, perhaps like sociological theory, where many different projects—theories of homelessness in America, of generic social cohesion, of class conflict in India, of the resurgence of religious fundamentalism worldwide—of different levels of generality and abstraction coexist without being subsumed under a single general theory. Similarly, film theorizing today should proceed at varying levels of generality and abstraction.

Even if some day, film theorizing might be organized into a general theory (which seems unlikely to me), nevertheless we are hardly in a position to frame such a theory now, since we know so little at this time. And, in any event, the only way that we shall come to know more is by developing small-scale theories about virtually every imaginable aspect of film.

Film theorizing, as I have argued elsewhere, should be piecemeal. But it should also be diversified. Insofar as theorists approach film from many different angles, from different levels of abstraction and generality, they will have to avail themselves of multidisciplinary frameworks. Some questions about film may send the researcher toward economics, while others require a look into perceptual psychology. In other instances, sociology, political science, anthropology, communications theory, linguistics, artificial intelligence, biology, or narrative theory may provide the initial research tools which the film theorist requires in order to begin to evolve theories of this or that aspect of film.

In opposition to the essentialist theorist who might disparage explorations in other disciplines as fatally alloyed, it is my claim that anxieties about theoretical purity are impediments to theoretical discovery. Film theorizing should be interdisciplinary. It should be pursued without the expectation of discovering a unified theory, cinematic or otherwise. That is, it should be catholic about the methodological frameworks it explores.

Perhaps at this historical juncture is seems strange to urge that film theory be multidisciplinary, since it might be asserted that the Theory—that assemblage of Althusser, Lacan, Barthes, et al.—is patently interdisciplinary, given that Althusser was a philosopher, Lacan a psychoanalyst, and Barthes a literary critic. And yet, I wonder about the interdisciplinary pretensions of Theory since Theory, as it is practiced in film departments—and neighboring literature departments—is really a body of canonical texts or authors, which body of authors serves rather like the paradigm of a *single discipline* in the making. It hardly encourages multidisciplinary exploration. It always endorses, when it comes to pictorial perception, for example, another look at the enigmatic sayings of Foucault on *Las Meninas,* rather than reading any recent experimental psychology on the topic of vision.

Indeed, in the mid-1970s, a leading French film Theorist was introduced to an audience which was reassured that, in addition to his expertise in cinema, the speaker was also a master of anthropology, philosophy, art history, semiotics, psychoanalysis, literary studies, linguistics, and so on; to which one wag replied: "Of course, in Paris, it's all the same thing anyway." Whether or not this remark did justice to Parisian intellectual life, at this point in time it provides a fair characterization of Theory (U.S. style) which, far from being multidisciplinary, is rather the approved reading list of assorted departments of textual analysis (both literary and cinematic).

Ironically, film studies in the United States was probably more interdisciplinary in the early seventies, before its apotheosis or, at least, "professionalization" under the auspices of Theory. But that period of experimentation with alternative frameworks—from anthropology and kinesics to phenomenology—was stamped out by the juggernaut of Theory.

It hardly pays to be too nostalgic about the theoretical excursions of the early seventies since, in almost every case, it was dilettantish rather than rigorous, a tendency unfortunately continued under the dispensation of Theory, since its practitioners are almost always getting their philosophy or anthropology from a second- or thirdhand source (rather than generating it themselves). Ideally, film theorists in the future will be genuinely interdisciplinary in the sense that they will have at their command the genuine expertise of a practitioner in more than one discipline, rather than being epigones of a school of thought, united by an approved reading list, with designs for cross-disciplinary imperialism.

Like classic essentialist theory, Theory is an obstacle to authentic theorizing, because it is presented as a unified or totalizing system. Under its aegis, the film theorist sets out to subsume every aspect of cinematic phenomena under the putative laws and categories of his or her minimally customized version of the reigning orthodoxy. Theorizing becomes the routine application of some larger, unified theory to questions of cinema, which procedure unsurprisingly churns out roughly the same answers, or remarkably similar answers, in every case. The net result, in short, is theoretical impoverishment.

The antidote to this impoverishment, I think, is to resist the temptation of totalizing film theory and to follow the lead of piecemeal theorizing wherever it takes us. We should countenance as film theory any line of inquiry dedicated to producing generalizations pertaining to, or general explanations of, filmic phenomena, or devoted to isolating, tracking, and/or accounting for any mechanisms, devices, patterns, and regularities in the field of cinema. As already remarked, this inquiry may transpire at many different levels of generality and abstraction and may take as its objects things as different as cutting practices and industrial contexts.

What makes something film theory is that it is a general answer to a general question that we have about some phenomenon which we think, pretheoretically, falls into the bailiwick of film. Such inquiry is theoretical because it is general, and it is film theory because it pertains to filmic practice. Furthermore, since we can ask so many different kinds of general questions about film, there is no common feature that all of our answers should be expected to share. Some theoretical questions about film—for example, about cinematic perception—may have answers that primarily advert to cinematic forms and structures, whereas other different answers to different questions might refer to economic forces. That is, some theories may be formal, while others may be social. Our collection of film theories may very well comprise a mixed bag. There simply is no reason to think that every film theory will have something to tell us about the same subject—such as the way in which each and every aspect of film figures in the oppression or emancipation of the film viewer.

2. The conflation of film theory with film interpretation. Perhaps the major impediment to film theory in the present moment is the confusion of film theory with film interpretation. Many film scholars imagine that they are producing film theory when they are actually merely contriving interpretations of individual films, albeit in arcane, "theoretically" derived jargon. Unquestionably, it seems to me, one reason we have reached this impasse is that film scholars generally have little, if any, background in the actual practices of theory building, since most of them have exclusively hermeneutical training, as opposed to education in theoretical disciplines such as the natural or social sciences, or philosophy. Consequently, most film scholars do not really understand the difference between theory and interpretation, an obvious liability if film theory is to prosper.

As has been pointed out by David Bordwell in *Making Meaning,* film theory is generally integrated into film studies as a template from which film scholars strike interpretations of individual films. Film theory supplies major premises from which interpretive conclusions can be deduced, once the film has been described (or misdescribed) in such a way as to yield pliable (a.k.a. equivocating) minor premises; or film theory provides the so-called semantic fields against which the exegete does something which looks very much like free association. Moreover, this expropriation of theory for the sake of interpretation is exacerbated by the typical condition of film education, which puts such a high premium on the construction of interpretations of individual films, since standardly film education is mired in the one class/one film format (a format reflected in a great many professional articles on film).

One could, of course, imagine the production of a theory of film interpretation. However, the interpretation of individual films is not theory, no matter how technical the language of the interpretation appears. For theory involves evolving categories and hypothesizing the existence of general patterns; but finding that those categories and hypotheses are instantiated in a particular case is not a matter of theory. It's the difference between discovering the existence of a viral syndrome and finding that Henry has it.

In addition, not all, but a great deal of theorizing involves causal reasoning, which is different from the interpretation of meaning. What is so strange about the spectacle of "film theory" over the last two decades is that so often film exegetes proceed by reading the Theory into a film, as if the presence of subject positioning—putatively a causal process—could be confirmed by hermeneutically alleging to find the allegory of the Imaginary retold in a selected film. Given enough latitude, you can probably allegorize anything to say whatever you wish, but that won't establish causal connections where there are none. Where film theory provides interpreters with allegories to read into whatever they wish, the prospects for causal research are bleak.

There are no grounds for thinking that film theory must have anything to do with film interpretation in every case. Indeed, in many cases, one would anticipate that the two activities would have to part company. Film theory speaks of the general case, whereas film interpretation deals with problematic or puzzling cases, or with the highly distinctive cases of cinematic masterworks. Film theory tracks the regularity and the norm, while film interpretation finds its natural calling in dealing with the deviation, with what violates the norm or with what exceeds it or what re-imagines it.

Perhaps, at times, film theory provides a background that enables a critic to locate what is interesting about some divergence from the general pattern or function of a device or a cinematic figure. Even allowing this possibility, two other thoughts should be kept in mind. First, that one doesn't require a theory in order to spot a divergence, since an intuitively constructed comparison class will turn the trick. Second, that not every theory can function in this way. Certain economic theories of industrial formation may be irrelevant to interpretation, due to their level of generality, while certain physiological theories of film perception may be equally irrelevant, because they are exceptionless. And, of course, it is also the case that the theory of some standard filmic device, like point-of-view editing, may remark upon some phenomena so mundane that it turns out to be never germane to interpretation.

Nor, in fact, would a general theory be a panacea for interpretation. For showing that a film is an instance of a general theory would imply that the film is, in certain respects, routine, that is, pretty much like everything else in the same theoretical domain, and, therefore, not really worthy of special interpretation.

Over the last two decades, what has been called Interpretation Inc. has proceeded, oblivious to the preceding objection, applying the Theory, or fragments of the Theory, like a philosopher's stone, transforming every film in sight into a glittering interpretation. But not only does this seem in tension conceptually with the idiographic (as opposed to the nomothetic) direction of interpretation; it also becomes deadly monotonous as every film comes out of the standard-issue sausage machine, looking and smelling the same.

Not only do contemporary film scholars pretend to find technique after technique and film after film that exemplify this or that general pattern—such as imaginary identification or subject positioning—film scholars also claim to find films that *express* the theories in question, that is, films, including B pictures, that share themes with such figures as Freud, Lévi-Strauss, and Lacan. Probably anything can be made to say anything else once interpretive protocols get as loose as they are in criticism departments nowadays, but the problem I wish to point to is not the obvious anachronism of so many of these interpretations, but to the fact that counterfeiting such interpretations does not constitute theory building. If indeed it could be plausibly shown that the film *Every Man For Himself and God Against All* independently discovered the Lacanian scenario of the child's entry into language, then it would be Herzog and not his exegete who would count as a theorist.

Moreover, where the purposes of interpretation drive theory choice, the prospects for film theory are slim. For the theories that are most serviceable for exegetes will be those whose central terms are maximally vague, ambiguous, or unconstrained in terms of criteria of application. For such theories can be applied to the widest number of cases, if only by equivocation and fanciful association. Interpretive productivity would seem to vary inversely with the precision of a theory. Theories with the greatest "weasel factor" are more attractive to scholars concerned primarily with producing interpretations, because such theories will be applicable almost everywhere and in more ways than one. They will be, as the saying goes, "productive." And yet, where clarity and precision are altogether ignored, theory might as well be skywriting.

Not only has theory been confused with interpretation in recent film scholarship; it also becomes conflated with film criticism, where Post-Structuralism gets identified with modernist, or, if you prefer, postmodernist film practice. Thus, Laura Mulvey discovers that classical filmmaking is nothing short of psychosexually regressive, while the difficulty of her own counter-cinema promises evolution to the Symbolic, as if avant-garde, modernist film practice went hand in hand with maturity. Indeed, far too often over the last two decades has so-called Theory been enlisted to serve in the partisan cause of various film movements.

It might be argued that the preceding characterization of the conflation of interpretation and theory fits the eighties better than it does the present. For today, it might be said, there is much less faith in the Theory than there was yesteryear. Fragments of the Theory remain in the vocabulary of film scholars; they talk of subject positioning, for instance. But this is done without commitment to the full Theory from which such fragmentary phrases derive. However, if this is true, it provides an even greater obstacle to future theorizing, since the persistence of archaic Theory-talk accentuates the illusion that people are doing theory. Thus, whereas in the past the prospects for theory were impeded by the conflation of interpretation with theory, now it seems that what can be said about Interpretation Inc. is that interpretation is being conflated with the illusion of theory.

3. Political correctness. As has been repeated endlessly in narratives of the cinema studies establishment, its Theory was perceived to have been erected on the barricades as part of the cultural upheavals of the late sixties and early seventies. May 1968 is the date fashionably bruited about, though this is more a matter of symbolical than historical significance, as far as the literal institutionalization of film studies is concerned. Nevertheless, it is true that the by-now middle-aged film establishment underwent its rite of passage through the New Left, and, though presently well over thirty, the survivors still trust themselves as keepers of the light.

Certainly, one would not want to demean what was humane and just in the political claims of the student movement of the Vietnam years, nor to deny that a great deal of that agenda was and still is worthy of endorsement. However, it is not clear that those ideals are served in any respectable way by allegiance to the Theory.

Proponents of the Theory let on that the Theory grew out of the student movement and out of a resistance to oppression everywhere. Consequently, from their point of view, criticism of the Theory virtually represents a clear and present danger to the very Revolution itself. Anyone who opposes the Theory, for whatever reason, is politically suspect—probably a ruling class, neoconservative, homophobic misogynist. Criticisms of the dubious psychoanalytic premises of the Theory are denounced as reactionary—in a political sense!—as if a belief in the equality of the races requires assent to Lacan and the rest of the pet paraphernalia of the Theory. Wrapping themselves in virtue, as others might wrap themselves in a flag, Theorists frequently resemble nothing so much as radical versions of those scoundrels whose last resort is said to be patriotism.

Though the issue of political correctness on American college campuses is generally ballyhooed by the right wing through horror stories about student suspensions and the theft of newspapers and artworks, it seems to me that the real threat of political correctness is far more subtle. Namely, it protects bad scholarship. Fear that one will be denounced as politically incorrect—as racist, sexist, classist, homophobic, etc.—intimidates generally liberal scholars in such a way that they refrain from speaking out honestly about the extremely poor quality of much of what passes for argument and research in the humanities today. Instead they complain in hushed tones among themselves. Academic cowardice promotes self-censorship both inside and outside film studies, restraining frank criticism of often shoddy thinking and slapdash scholarship on the part of many who fear being publicly labeled politically suspect, even in cases where the actual voting records and the actual political positions—on gay rights, the ERA, affirmative action, and so on—of many of those who hawk Theory and those who oppose it would be indistinguishable.

The Theory has been effectively insulated from sustained logical and empirical analysis by a cloak of political correctness. Speaking from personal experience, I can recall more than one occasion when, as a result of my criticism of the Theory, people told me that they were surprised by my conversion to neoconservatism, despite no discernible changes in my real-world political views (which amount to a version of democratic socialism).

Skepticism about the theoretical usefulness of concepts like the male gaze, or, to be more timely, about the glance, invites accusations of reactionary backlash. It is as if Lacanian psychoanalysis and civil rights advocacy (for persons of color, for women, for gays) were so indissolubly linked logically that one could not affirm one without the other. This is not only patently ridiculous; it is also an immensely self-serving idea for proponents of the Theory to encourage. And, it almost goes without saying, such an atmosphere is inimical to a context in which genuine theorizing might flourish, since theoretical discourse requires open channels of critical communication, not repression.

In film studies, rival theories to the Theory are rejected out of hand as politically pernicious. One very popular gambit, which I will discuss, is to argue that competing views are "formalist." These "arguments" are little more than ad hominem attacks. Furthermore, inasmuch as the very practice of theorizing requires maximally free and open debate, the veil of political correctness that envelops film studies compromises the very discursive structure that makes film theory possible.

Contemporary film Theorists, along with many of their colleagues in literature departments, are very confident of their ability to detect the ideological perspective of rival theories. Rather than debate the explicit, cognitive claims of competitors, they seek to unmask the putatively underlying politics of critical views of the Theory. In this, they appear to ape the Marx and Engels of *The German Ideology.* However, I wonder whether these exercises in "ideology critique" are really fundamentally sound.

A great many film theories come without political badges affixed to them. And in such cases, it is surely a mistake to think that the theory strictly entails any specific political view on concrete issues, such as gay civil rights, the thirty-five-hour work week, abortion, or ecology, or even broad political stances, such as Leninism. I have evolved theories of movie music and point-of-view editing, but they do not, in any sense that could be called logical, imply my political position about anything from gun control, to sexual harassment, to communal ownership of the means of production. For these theories, like so many others, underdetermine whatever political allegiances a given individual might believe in addition to believing them. Many film theories, including ones which their proponents (like Eisenstein) may think have explicit political implications, may in fact be compatible with an extremely wide range of political alignments, including even nonconverging and conflicting political commitments.

If with respect to a given specific film theory, an ideologue can tell a story about how it goes with reactionary politics, it is generally the case that, logically speaking, one can tell just as good a story about how it might go with emancipatory politics. For example, one might say that the New Criticism in post–World War II literary studies was reactionary because it bracketed political considerations, but, equally, the case might be made that it was democratic, since it freed the reader from the supposed tyranny of The Author. Moreover, this sort of egalitarianism, even if it is ultimately misplaced, is certainly as discernible in the writings of Monroe Beardsley as it is in those of Roland Barthes.

Insofar as aesthetic theories, such as film theories, generally underdetermine the political viewpoints with which they are compatible, there is generally no real point in diagnosing them for their political allegiances. Of course, in a concrete case, a film theorist may actually link a theory with a political agenda, and that linkage is certainly worth comment, especially in terms of whether the linkage really has the logical substance its proponents aver. For example, the claimed linkage may be exaggerated. Think of how many avant-garde pretensions to Marxism come to look strained in retrospect. However, the likelihood that many explicitly unallied theories actually entail political positions is too low to warrant the wholesale, unrestrained witch-hunt for unacknowledged ideological taintedness abroad in the humanities today.

I would not want to preclude the possibility that someone might hold a certain theory due to ideological bias. And such bias, where it can be shown to exist, deserves criticism. Nevertheless, one has to establish the bias *independently of the theory held.* For as we've seen already, a theory that makes no explicit political reference rarely wears any political affiliation on its sleeve. Furthermore, even when a given theorist has been shown to be politically biased, one still must ask whether the theory might be held by others for reasons that are unbiased.

Film Theorists, like their colleagues in literature departments, appear to accept something like a holistic account of theoretical commitments, by which I mean they believe that every aspect of a theorist's belief system has repercussions for every other aspect. It is something like the doctrine of internal relations applied to the belief systems of theorists. This is why when it was discovered that people like Paul de Man and Martin Heidegger had Nazi sympathies, the hermeneutical establishment in this country was thrown into apoplexy. For since it was presumed that theory entails politics and vice-versa, the personal Nazism of the theorists in question raised worries about the latent fascism of the theories.

But, if I am right, and the relation between theory and politics in most cases is logically indeterminate, then there was in reality little reason for the comic efforts at damage control that were staged in the name of deconstruction. One might have observed that, for example, Heidegger's Nazism was a personal inclination logically detachable from the more abstract formulations of existential phenomenology. Ironically enough, deconstructionists were unable to avail themselves of such sober detachment because their Hegelian proclivities predisposed them to a residue of unacknowledged holism.

Generally, literary theories and film theories underdetermine political commitments. Rarely does a theory follow in any strict sense from one's politics, or vice-versa. Given theories may be espoused by either the forces of light or the forces of darkness. If only for this reason, one should be chary of assessing film theories solely in terms of ideology-critique. Moreover, in order to establish that a theory is ideologically tainted, one needs to show that it is false *and* that one could only come to embrace the theory for politically unsavory reasons (involving some motive of political domination). But in order to show even this requires a discursive theoretical context free from and unconstrained by preemptory, ad hominem charges of political incorrectness.

4. Charges of formalism. This impediment is really a corollary of the problem of political correctness. For it seems a fair conjecture that charges of political incorrectness are most often leveled at rivals to the Theory in the language of formalism. To call an alternative theory formalist is, in other words, a way of saying that the alternative theory is politically incorrect.

Like most bullying epithets, "formalism," as used in contemporary film studies, is rather ill-defined. In general, it seems counterposed to the "political." Sometimes, of course, it is also opposed to the "historical," but usually by persons who presume, strangely enough, that a historical approach is coeval with a politically sensitive one. Calling a theorist a formalist may signal that the theorist is concerned with form rather than content, with structures rather than their political consequences, or with cinematic forms, irrespective of the political content that is thought to be inherent in those forms.

In the current context of theoretical debate, charges of formalism are most frequently leveled at positions that are often labeled cognitivist. Cognitivism itself is not a unified theory. Instead, it is a stance toward film research, one that advocates the exploration of hypotheses about film reception in terms of the cognitive and perceptual processes of spectators, rather than in terms of the unconscious processes and syndromes favored by the Theory.

Proponents of the Theory usually endorse psychoanalysis because they believe that ideology works through unconscious processes. Insofar as they are confident that they can link the interaction of cinematic structures and unconscious processes to ideology, they think that their program is not formalist. But inasmuch as cognitivists proceed as if they can analyze some forms of cinematic perception without connecting them with political consequences, cognitivists are said to be formalist. Indeed, it is generally assumed, though never demonstrated, that cognitivism cannot, in principle, deliver insight about the political consequences of cinematic design for audience reception.

But, in at least one respect, the charge of formalism against cognitivists is bogus. For there is no reason to think that putative connections between cinematic form and political consequences can only be forged by psychoanalysis, and not by cognitivism. The cognitivist need not be a formalist in the sense of asserting—like some latter-day Clive Bell—that film has nothing to do with politics, or that cinematic structures never have political consequences. That would be absurd.

Film has political and ideological dimensions. Cognitivists have never rejected that fact, and they have even attempted to analyze such phenomena where it has seemed pertinent. For example, though I am frequently called a formalist, I have tried to provide theoretical frameworks for discussing the image of women in film and the relation of film, rhetoric, and ideology, and in doing this I surely acknowledge that cinematic structures can have political consequences. David Bordwell, reputedly the epitome of arch-formalism, has examined the institutional bases of film technology and the political significance of Ozu's films.

Cognitivists can readily acknowledge that film has a political dimension, and they can and have studied it. Though, of course, insofar as they are cognitivists, they will attempt to discover the role that *cognitive* processes play in the dissemination of ideology. Nothing, in principle, implies that it is impossible for cognitivists to illuminate the relation between film and politics, and, in point of fact, some cognitivist research in this direction has already been attempted. Surely there can be nothing politically or theoretically suspicious about hypothesizing that ideology might engage cognitive processes. After all, if one studies the action of ideology on cognitive processes, one must acknowl-edge the relevance of politics. Moreover, why should anyone antecedently as-sume that hypotheses about cognitive processes in the formation of ideology are any less germane than psychoanalytic ones?

But this concession, of course, would indicate that cognitivism is a rival to the established Theory, a rival that proposes alternative ways of dealing with many of the same phenomena that interests proponents of the Theory. And if this is the case, shouldn't one refrain from prejudging which hypotheses are su-perior, until the debate has been fully joined?

Unfortunately, the frequent ad hominem charges that cognitivism is naught but formalism attempt to block meaningful debate before it begins. Propo-nents of the Theory muddy the waters by crudely insinuating that cognitivists cannot even play in the same political ballpark that the Theory does. Such alle-gations attempt to shout cognitivism off the playing field. In this regard, charges of formalism are an evasion and in that sense an impediment to gen-uine theoretical debate.

Film scholars, in my experience, seem so anxious about the issue of formalism because of their convictions that we find ourselves in a moment of political crisis, in which an understanding of the operation of ideology is paramount. In such circumstances, a concern with forms and structures strikes them as being as friv-olous as Nero fiddling while Rome burned. But this obsession with crisis, again, should not, in principle, set them against cognitivism, since cognitive hypothe-ses about the operation of ideology in film and TV may be as useful as tools, or even more useful than those available from the Theory. Thus, if political under-standing is really what they care about, rather than preempting the debate be-tween cognitivism and the Theory, shouldn't film scholars want it to proceed?

There is, of course, one noteworthy difference between cognitivists and pro-ponents of the Theory. Cognitivists, unlike proponents of the Theory, tend to believe that there are aspects of cinematic reception that can be studied inde-pendently of questions of political or ideological consequences. Thus, one will find cognitivists offering theories about cinematic perception or about narra-tive comprehension, without talking about the political or ideological conse-quences of these processes. Cognitivists like myself would even contend that, in certain relevant respects, some of these processes may be politically or ideolog-ically neutral.

But this does not make me a formalist *tout court,* since I also agree that there may be—indeed, I think there *are*—other processes crucial to film research where the consideration of political and ideological consequences is pertinent. I think, for example, that one can theoretically isolate certain mechanisms that are responsible for the propagation of racism through film. Thus, though I think that theories about point-of-view editing might be framed, pace Daniel Dayan, without a discussion of some putatively invariant, ideological effect, I am not a formalist in the sense that I think it is never intelligible to examine the relation of film and ideology.

Proponents of the Theory are likely to respond to this as proof that cognitivists like me are formalists. For they believe that *every* level of cinematic reception is fraught with political and ideological repercussions. Yet this, it seems to me, must be an empirical conjecture. And as such, it seems highly dubious.

For example, if we are studying horror films, it strikes me as incontrovertible that filmmakers often play upon what psychologists call the "startle response," an innate human tendency to "jump" at loud noises and to recoil at fast movements. This tendency is, as they say, impenetrable to belief; that is, our beliefs won't change the response. It is hardwired and involuntary. Awareness of this response enables theorists like me to explain the presence of certain audiovisual patterns and effects in horror films, without reference to politics and ideology. Indeed, insofar as the startle response is impenetrable to belief, it could be said to be, in certain respects, beyond politics and ideology. Moreover, such examples indicate that there is a stratum of theoretical investigation at the level of cognitive architecture that can proceed while bracketing questions of ideology.

I would not, of course, deny that a film critic might want to analyze the use of the startle response in a given horror film in terms of the political agenda of the film in question. But as I argued earlier, this is a matter of film interpretation, not film theory. The fact that cognitivist theoretical insights at the level of generic structures might enable political interpretation in no way indicates that cognitive research cannot advance without bracketing political questions in certain cases.

It is my contention that certain questions that theorists of cinema address are, in relevant respects, nonpolitical, and that the answers theorists provide to them are also nonpolitical. Theories about the perception of cinematic movement and about the recognition of cinematic images are obvious candidates here. Theories in this domain may indeed concentrate on what might be thought of as forms and structures. But, again, this stance is not formalism *tout court,* since the cognitivist may, in addition, freely acknowledge that other cinematic phenomena, such as the reinforcement of sexual stereotypes, will involve considerations of both content and the mechanisms by which that content is conveyed.

But proponents of the Theory, on the other hand, presuppose that every aspect of cinema is implicated in ideology and that the cognitivist attempt to conceptualize some aspects of cinema as detachable from ideology is nothing but rank formalism. As I have already argued, this claim seems empirically insupportable. Nor is it conceivable that all cinematic phenomena are by definition political. Surely, the perception of cinematic movement, the recognition of the cinematic image, and the comprehension of narrative will have the same biological, psychological, and cognitive foundations in any humanly imaginable, nonrepressive, classless, egalitarian utopia that those perceptual and cognitive processes have in present-day Los Angeles. To stamp one's feet and to insist that every dimension of film must have an ideological dimension (by dint of cinematic ontology?) is simply dogmatic.

But perhaps the proponent of the Theory will defend her or his political perspective by saying that it is simply a *heuristic* hypothesis. In other words, it might be advocated that it is empirically productive to begin with the supposition that, when approaching any cinematic phenomena, it is most fruitful to think about it in terms of ideology. That is, in every case, first ask yourself how the phenomenon at hand contributes to ideology. This is always a revelatory question. This is a powerful research program, and it will yield compelling results.

Maybe.

And yet, if this is how the Theory is to be defended, I would argue that we have already seen its results and they are underwhelming. For the last two decades, under the pressure of this heuristic hypothesis, we have witnessed an array of hypotheses that stretch credulity. They have been either vacuous or strained to the breaking point by "explanations" that turn out to be little more than puns. This is not the place to enumerate, once again, the well-known flaws of the Theory, but only to point out that as a heuristic, the record shows that it has little to recommend it.

The underlying presupposition of the Theory, on the basis of which it dismisses its competitors as formalist, is that every aspect of cinematic reception is ideological. But if the preceding discussion is accurate, then this presupposition is unwarranted and the charges that have been issued on its account are overdrawn. This, of course, does not mean that no aspect of cinematic reception involves ideology. And, indeed, a theoretical position that embraced that assumption might, in fact (depending on its details), be formalist, and, in any case, false, at least to my way of thinking. However, competitors to the Theory, like cognitivism, do not presuppose that questions about ideology are necessarily foreign to theoretical research, and cognitivists have attempted to model some cognitive mechanisms that might be important to understanding the operation of ideology in film.

Whether cognitivism provides the best inroad to studying the role of ideology in film remains to be seen. However, there may be one insight of the cognitivist approach that commends itself for future film theorizing. The cognitivist regards the phenomena to be explored as multidimensional. Some dimensions may invite ideological analysis, others may not. Theorizing must be adjusted appropriately. Some theoretical questions may be best answered in what might be called formal or structural terms, others may be best answered with an eye toward political consequences. Sometimes the theoretical answers to questions about one dimension of analysis may be sequed with answers from another level of analysis; sometimes not. Future theorizing depends on openness to a variety of research projects of different levels of abstraction in the theoretical field.

On the other hand, to suppose, as the regnant Theory does, that all theorizing must be political is, as I have been proposing, a dogmatic obstacle to future theorizing. It is an inexcusable contraction of the field. Moreover, indiscriminate charges of formalism, as they are currently bandied about, are an instrument of that dogmatism; we can hope for little progress in film theorizing until there is a moratorium on such name-calling. To continue otherwise, at this point in time, is nothing less than an evasion of the intellectual responsibilities of film theorizing.

5. Biases against truth. Oddly enough, though the last two decades of film studies are generally heralded in terms of the importance of Theory, there is often a reluctance among film scholars to say that they believe that theoretical hypotheses (including, presumably, their own) are true. Indeed, often objections to the Theory are discounted on the grounds that critics like me hold onto the naïve, benighted belief that theories might be true or false, whereas your sophisticated, postmodernist film Theorist realizes such thinking is a merely residual Enlightenment fantasy.

I have actually attended a film conference where one of these sophisticated, postmodernist film Theorists announced that he and his confreres were skeptical about ideas of truth and falsity. He said that they doubt the idea of truth. But, I (probably naïvely) must confess that I couldn't make any sense of this paradoxical pronouncement, since it seemed to say that he and his friends believe that the idea of truth—or the proposition that "some statements are true"—is not true, or, perhaps, that it is false. But such judgments unquestionably presuppose some conception of truth in order to be intelligible.

Of course, if we jettison notions of truth and falsity, it is hard to imagine the way in which film theorizing will proceed. Perhaps it will be suggested that this is simply my own failure of imagination, since we might talk about film theories in terms of plausibility and implausibility, rather than in terms of truth and falsity. But then again, it is hard to get a handle on the concept of plausibility without a notion of truth, since to be plausible is to give the appearance of truth, or to be worthy of acceptance as true, or to be likely to be true.

On the other hand, maybe some notion of political efficacy is supposed to substitute for the role that truth and falsity play for the likes of me in evaluating theories. But how can one gauge what is politically efficacious—that is, truly politically efficacious—without some background notions of truth and falsity, or plausibility or implausibility? Indeed, what could political efficacy come to if it were determined altogether independently of what is or is not the case, or, at least, what is likely or unlikely to be the case? And, furthermore, who could care about a conception of political efficacy totally divorced from what is or might be the case?

Film scholars are not alone in abjuring truth. It is open season on truth throughout the humanities. But why, one wonders, are scholars across the humanities so cavalier about their commitment to the idea of truth? Especially where the scholars in question are politicized, one would predict that they should be concerned with the truth, since most frequently in the real-world political debates that they care about, they are more likely to have the truth than they are likely to have the ballots on their side.

But that is not the way it is. Throughout the humanities, those who cleave to standards of truth and falsity are regarded as at best a confused remnant and at worst the academic equivalent of racist skinheads. How did truth come to get such a bad name?

It seems to me to rest on a fallacious argument that has many variations in different arenas of humanistic discourse. I call it the refutation of absolute truth argument, or the argument from absolute truth, for short. Before sketching the general form of this argument, however, it is useful to consider some of its most familiar variations. The first one goes like this.

Consider the interpretation of a text, filmic or otherwise. Most texts (indeed, it is frequently said, *all* texts) have more than one legitimate interpretation. Therefore, it is surmised, there is no true interpretation of a text. Now clearly this argument is stupendously unconvincing. For a text may have more than one, true interpretation. It is true that *Animal Farm* is about totalitarianism *and* it is true that it is about Stalinism. Thus, it does not follow that if a text has more than one interpretation, that there are not true interpretations of the text. For, obviously, there may be more than one *true* interpretation of a text.

But why do people think that the no-true-interpretation argument is acceptable? Because they seem to believe that if an interpretation is true, then that means that it is exhaustive—that it says everything that there is to say about a text. In other words, they assume that truth is a matter of what we might more accurately call Absolute Truth, where the Absolute Truth about a text gives you everything that there is to know about it. If an interpretation is absolutely true, then there is nothing left over to add.

But there is generally something else to say; there is generally room for further interpretation. So, no interpretation is absolutely true, or, at least, the prospects for an absolutely true interpretation are very, very, very slight (pertaining perhaps to some minimal texts that are virtually completely and determinately explicit, if there are any such texts).

So far, so good. But the fatal error in the refutation of absolute truth argument is to move from a denial that there are *absolutely* true interpretations to a denial that there are *true* interpretations—that is, true interpretations in the garden-variety sense of truth that applies to propositions like "George Washington was the first president of the United States."

Similarly, it is often argued with respect to narratives that no narrative can be true. Why? Because with respect to a given event or state of affairs, it can always be emplotted as an element in another story. But again, that the assassination of Lincoln can figure in the history of the Reconstruction *or* in the history of nineteenth-century acting does not show that both stories cannot be true. It only shows that neither history is absolutely true, or, to say it differently, it only shows that there are no Absolute Stories (perhaps of the sort to which Hegel aspired).

But the plausibility of the conjecture that there are no (or, perhaps, very, very few) Absolute Truths of the variety suggested above does not show that there are not true stories or true interpretations. Nor does the implausibility of there being any Absolute Truths—that is, completely exhaustive, comprehensive, final statements—about my furniture undermine the truth of the time-indexed proposition that "My computer is now on my red table."

What does this excursus into Absolute Truth have to do with the vaunted suspicion of truth amongst film scholars? Simply this: Just as film scholars suppose that there is no absolutely true film interpretation, they suppose that there is no absolutely true film theory—one that is completely comprehensive, that says everything there is to say about film from every perspective, and that is final, unrevisable in principle, and closed *sub specie aeternitatis*.

Well, that's (dare I say it?) true. But, even if this admission begins to make some sense of our colleagues' professed skepticism about truth, it certainly doesn't justify that skepticism. For there might be some limited theoretical conjecture—about the perceptual process of recognizing a cinematic image of Gregory Peck to be the image of a man—which is true, but which does not pretend to be an exhaustive analysis, theoretical or otherwise, of any given image from *Behold a Pale Horse*. That is, one may recant the dream that film theories are "true," in the sense of exhaustive, final-word, unrevisable, Absolute Truth, while still employing what high school teachers, perhaps not so jejunely, sometimes call the concept of "small-t" *truth*.

When one questions film scholars and their colleagues in literary criticism about their oxymoronic "doubt of the concept of truth," the argument from absolute truth is what I have generally been offered in return. But clearly the argument is directed at a straw man (straw person?).

Put schematically, it maintains that, for any imaginable topic, there is always something more that can be said about it than can be summarized in a single pronouncement, assertion, theory, story, interpretation, and so on; therefore, there is no true pronouncement, assertion, theory, story, interpretation, and so on. But this conclusion makes logical sense only if we take it to indicate that there is no *single,* final true assertion, theory, story, or interpretation about the subject. And this is compatible with there being more than one true assertion, story, interpretation, theory, and so on. Thus, the argument poses no objection to the discourse of garden-variety truth and falsity when it comes to constructing and evaluating aesthetic theories.

A major ramification of this for film theory is that proponents of the Theory cannot resort to the argument from absolute truth in order to silence their critics. For in the pertinent context of debate, the argument is made of straw. It wrongly presupposes that critics of the Theory, like me, are possessed by some childish faith in Absolute Truth, the silliness of which can be quickly exorcised with a splash of postmodernism. But this putative refutation is painfully irrelevant. When I claim to evaluate tenets of the Theory in light of ordinary standards of truth and falsity, I have nothing so arcane as Absolute Truth in mind, and, in consequence, my objections, and objections like them, cannot be dismissed as Enlightenment extravagances.

Contemporary Theorists not only suspect truth for the roughly pop-philosophical reasons just rehearsed, but also because they believe experience has taught them that horrible things have been done in the name of the truth. Racial discrimination and sexual oppression have been justified in virtue of theories that were said to be true. Claims about truth have been used to deny certain people opportunities on the grounds that it was supposedly *known* that the people in question were unsuited for education, for intellectual labor, or even civilized treatment. Thus, it is concluded, it always pays to distrust or to be wary of truth claims, since they may be as useful, if not more useful, a lever for social domination as a cudgel. Hence, skepticism about truth.

But, of course, before reaching this conclusion, one must consider whether there is *anything* that cannot ever be used in the service of social oppression. For it should be clear that we cannot refrain from every practice and every concept that might be manipulated or distorted to advance social oppression. Instead, one must be careful and vigilant, rather than ataractic in the ancient skeptical sense. It is one thing to greet truth claims with healthy distrust, as any scientist would, and another thing to deny the relevance of criteria of truth and falsity altogether. That is throwing the baby out with the bath water. Moreover, disregarding the baby in question is particularly reckless when one recalls that the most effective weapon against ideological rationalizations advanced in the name of truth is the possibility of revealing them to be false.

Perhaps one of the strangest results—at least from the viewpoint of emancipatory politics—of the inveterate skepticism of film scholars toward truth was the response of many members of the Society for Cinema Studies to the tape of the Rodney King beating. Insofar as many SCS members are skeptics about truth, they also appear to doubt the evidentiary value of film and video. Consequently, their theory parted company with their politics in the King case. Politically they wanted to be as outraged as everyone else, whereas theoretically they "had proven" antecedently that film and video could never convey truths, but only fictions.

In order to negotiate this embarrassment, some members of the SCS declared the doctrine of "strategic realism." This seems to be the notion that if it suits your politics, then you can talk with the vulgar and act as if film images and videotape can be evidentiary, even though you know that, theoretically, this is a pipe dream. However, strategic realism can hardly be a satisfactory solution. Not only does it strike members of the vulgar crowd, like myself, to be opportunistic and, indeed, a form of lying (one that is so transparent that it seems laughable); but strategic realism does not stave off the necessity for acknowledging standards of truth and falsity for long, since notions of truth and falsity will surely come into play in determining what does and does not suit one's political purposes in a given context.

As long as standards of truth and falsity are thought to be altogether eminently dispensable, Neanderthal throwbacks, film theory will flounder. It will be difficult to understand the way in which we should take theoretical "assertions," including those of the Theory, as well as how we are to assess them. At the same time, without notions of truth and falsity, along with derivative concepts, like plausibility and implausibility, it is unclear how we shall criticize theoretical hypotheses. But if we are unable to criticize theoretical hypotheses, there are no prospects for film theory.

A FRAMEWORK FOR FILM THEORIZING

I have just indicated my conviction that criticism is integral to film theory. In this, I am not claiming film theory is distinctive, but that, like most other forms of theoretical inquiry, it proceeds dialectically. Theories are framed in specific historical contexts of research for the purpose of answering certain questions, and the relative strengths of theories are assayed by comparing the answers they afford to the answers proposed by alternative theories. This conception of theory evaluation is pragmatic because: (1) it compares actual, existing rival answers to the questions at hand (rather than every logically conceivable answer); and (2) because it focuses on solutions to contextually motivated theoretical problems (rather than searching for answers to any conceivable question one might have about cinema).

I suspect that if one were to scan the history of film theory, one would see that the dialectical element is generally present in one way or another in most film theories. Film theorists have always been involved in debates in which they advance the superiority of their findings over competing views. This is to be expected since dialectical criticism has been a basic route for theoretical inquiry at least since Plato. Defending one's own theory by demonstrating that it succeeds where alternative theories falter is a natural direction of argument, as well as of spirited conversation. Even proponents of the Theory begin by criticizing alternative approaches as a primary means for arguing for the advantages of their own hypotheses over others. Thus, in maintaining that the fundamental framework for film theory is dialectical, I am not saying anything very contentious. Few today, I suppose, will want to maintain explicitly that film theories typically derive from first principles or axioms.

However, although a conception of film theorizing as dialectical is unexceptionable, I suspect that the importance of this feature for the practice of film theory has been frequently underappreciated. For sustained, detailed, intertheoretical debate and criticism are rare in the history of film theory. There are, of course, exceptions. Christian Metz's writings are particularly noteworthy for their careful, extended consideration of previous research and its shortcomings; and the deft way in which V. F. Perkins (in *Film as Film*) introduces his own theory by first clarifying the dialectical context in which its intervention is to make a difference is exemplary.

Nevertheless, in the normal course of events in film theory, the dialectical moment is hasty. Nowadays this tendency is particularly pronounced in discussions of cognitivism, which view is swiftly dismissed by castigating buzz-words like "formalism" or maybe "idealism," uttered just before the author goes on to repeat at length, yet again, the received wisdom of Theory.

Speaking as a self-appointed reformer, I wish to emphasize the need for film theorizing to become more conscious of its dialectical responsibilities. Where film theory blurs into film criticism, there is the ever-present danger that theoretical premises will be taken as given—as effectively inoculated from criticism—and, once so assumed, then used to generate "interesting" interpretations. My concern is that more attention be focused on these premises, that they be subjected to intense theoretical criticism, and that alternative answers to the questions these theories address be developed and analyzed through dialectical comparison with each other.

In the spirit of such reform, many of the essays in this volume are critical, especially of the established theories, and many introduce criticism of the flaws in extant theory as part of a process of dialectical argumentation by which new theories are advanced, constructed, and defended. Indeed, generally one of the most effective ways in which to argue in behalf of a theory and to defend it is to show that it does a better job answering the questions posed by competing views, or by showing that there is a better way to pose the questions that animate existing views. That is why criticism is so integral to film theory, as well as other areas of inquiry.

Theory building builds on previous histories of theorizing as well as upon data (which may be theory-laden). Present theories are formulated in the context of past theories. Apprised of the shortcomings in past theories, through processes of continued scrutiny and criticism, present theories try to find more satisfactory answers to the questions that drive theoretical activity. Sometimes advances involve incremental improvements within existing paradigms; sometimes new paradigms are required to accommodate the lacunae made evident by the anomalies that beset previous theorizing. Sometimes the driving theoretical questions need to be redefined; sometimes they need to be broken down into more manageable questions; sometimes these questions need to be recast radically. And all this requires a free and open discursive context, one in which criticism is not the exception, but the rule.

Methodologically, as I have already indicated, I believe that in the present context piecemeal theorizing is the way to go. In many cases, this means breaking down some of the presiding questions of the Theory into more manageable questions, for example, about the comprehension of point-of-view editing, instead of global questions about something vaguely called suture. As compelling answers are developed to small-scale, delimited questions, we may be in a position to think about whether these answers can be unified in a more comprehensive theoretical framework.

The considerations here on behalf of piecemeal theorizing are practical, not philosophical. For it is my hunch that we do not yet know enough to begin to evolve a unified theory, or even the questions that might lead to a unified theory. So, for the duration, let us concentrate on more manageable, small-scale theorizing. Perhaps one day we will be in a position to frame a unified or comprehensive theory of film. I have no argument to show that this is not possible. But whether our theories are large-scale or piecemeal, the process of theorizing will always have a dialectical component.

By emphasizing the dialectical dimension of theorizing, one concedes that it is historical. For debates will be relative to the disputants involved and the situated questions that perplex them. Thus, film theorizing under the auspices of the dialectical model does not pretend to the discovery of Absolute Truth. The theoretical answers it advances are shaped in response to the existing questions it answers and refines and to the perspectives and theoretical interests that are inscribed in those questions. Moreover, insofar as a dialectical conception of film theorizing admits that theorizing evolves over time, the dialectical film theorist must be aware that his or her theories may be open to revision as the debate matures. A dialectical conception of the film theory is not a form of absolutism since it neither supposes total comprehensiveness nor unrevisability. Rather, it is pragmatic.

Nevertheless, in conceding the historicity and revisability of theories, I have not given up truth as a regulative ideal for film theorizing. For the fact that theorizing has a history does not compromise the possibility of discovering what is the case, since that history may involve, among other things, the successive elimination of error. Furthermore, the fact that we are constantly revising our theories in the light of continued criticism and new evidence does not preclude the possibility that our theories are getting closer and closer to the truth. In the physical sciences, we may refer to some of our theories as approximately true, acknowledging that they may be revised, augmented, and refined, but that they are on the right track. Moreover, there is no persuasive reason to concede that we cannot also craft film theories in the here and now that are approximately true.

The dialectical conception of film theory that I am advocating is consistent with trends in the postpositivist philosophy of science. It respects the Kuhnian, antipositivist emphasis on the importance of historical and social contexts for inquiry. It is also not positivist in that it conceives of the process of theoretical argumentation as situated as a debate between existing rivals, rather than as a debate between every conceivable theory, before a court of fully rational participants, endowed with full information.

On the other hand, I do not think that we are compelled, on the basis of Kuhn's insights, to become social constructivists, a tendency exemplified by the Edinburgh Strong Program and widely shared in the humanities. We may argue that the history in question may represent the process of a society (for example, the community of chemists) whose social practices have evolved to provide a better and better purchase on what is approximately true.

I am presuming that what can be claimed for science may be claimed eventually for film theory. This does not mean that I think that film theory is a science, or that it can be or should be transformed into one, though I do think that there may be certain questions of film theory—perhaps concerning perception—that may be pursued scientifically. Rather, I invoke discussions about scientific methodology in proselytizing for a dialectical conception of film theory, not because I believe film theory is a natural science, but only because the philosophy of science provides us with some of our best models for understanding theoretical inquiry.

Undoubtedly, some will dismiss my suggestions on the grounds that I am confusing film theory with natural science. Let me say now that this is a misinterpretation. What I am saying is: let us take advantage of the insights derived from reflection on the scientific enterprise in order to think about what the structure of our own practice might be. We should not attempt to slavishly imitate any of the natural sciences. We need to be alert to the special features of our own field of inquiry, and to modify our methods appropriately. And yet we may still derive some useful hints about the process of inquiry by listening to sophisticated discussions about science.

Even this moderate proposal is apt to be met with revulsion by the film studies establishment, since they, like their cohorts in literary criticism, are as skeptical about science as they are about truth—perhaps not accidentally, since it is common to think of the scientific enterprise as truth-tracking. However, the arguments for suspecting science are as feckless as those for suspecting truth.

Sometimes science is decried because it is noted that certain scientific programs in the past, like eugenics, have served the forces of oppression. Right. But so have the law, humanism, poetry, music, and even putatively emancipatory politics. And anyway, the dubitable science in question, where we are not talking about its technological implementations, has, through dialectical criticism, been unmasked by the continued, self-correcting application of scientific practice. We need to be very careful about accepting scientific theories as incontrovertible, especially where they have political implications. But that sort of wariness is no rebuke to scientific thinking; it is a testament to it.

Nowadays, humanists, including film scholars, express misgivings about science because they claim that it parades its findings as if they were infallible. This is merely a variation on the argument from absolute truth, and it is no more conclusive than the other specimens of that gambit that we've seen so far. The argument begins by noting, as I have, that scientific theories are historically situated and revisable. Hence, again for reasons I have already produced, scientific theories cannot pretend to absolute truth. Therefore, they are arbitrary. In effect, we are presented with a disjunctive syllogism: either scientific theories are absolutely true or they are arbitrary. They are not absolutely true; so they are arbitrary. And if they are arbitrary, why should they or the methodologies that yield them be privileged?

But as is always the case with such arguments, the conclusion depends on canvassing all the viable alternatives. And in this instance, it is easy to see that there are overlooked options. One is what is called *fallibilism,* which I would contend provides a much better framework for comprehending scientific practice than the allegation that it aspires to infallibility.

The fallibilist agrees that he or she may have to revise his or her theories in light of future evidence or in response to the implications of later theoretical developments, because the fallibilist realizes that theories are at best well-justified and that a well-justified theory may turn out to be false. There is no claim to absolute truth here. But that does not entail that the theories in question are arbitrary. For we are not open to revising our theories in any which way, but only in virtue of the best available, transcultural standards of justification, that is, ones that have a reliable track record.

The fallibilist does not believe that we can revise all our theories and methods at once. He or she accepts the possibility that any subset thereof might be revised in the appropriate circumstances, and even that all our theories might be revised, but only ad seriatim. Theories and methods are revisable. They do not yield absolute truth. But they are not arbitrary either. For they are only revisable in accordance with practices that, though themselves incrementally revisable, have a reliable record for tracking the truth. The truth, here, where we do secure it, is approximate truth, in the garden-variety sense of the term, not Absolute Truth. But if we can conceive of science in such a way that detaches it from pretensions to Absolute Truth, then taking note of its failure to deliver Absolute Truth should not dispose us to dismiss it as arbitrary.

Humanists in general and film scholars in particular reject science because they endorse a strong social constructivist conception of science. Science, on this view, is historical not simply in the sense that there is a history of scientific practice, but in the sense that that practice is embedded in a sociohistorical context, which it reflects. Under this view, the history of a scientific movement often makes the movement sound like an allegory of the social concerns of the period in question. And where this variant of social constructivism takes a Marxist turn, scientific discoveries are frequently characterized as answering to pressing economic forces.

But the social constructivist view scarcely fits the facts. If scientific theories were as historically and culturally relative as the social constructivist declares, how could one explain that scientists operating in different historical and cultural contexts can concur on the same theories? How can one account for convergence between Maoist and American physicists? Moreover, is it plausible to hypothesize that Newton's explanation of Kepler's celestial ellipses by means of the inverse square law answered the pressing economic needs of seventeenth-century merchants and seamen? They would have preferred better chronometers.

Social constructivists and their followers in film studies, and elsewhere, like to say that science *constitutes* reality, putatively in ways that facilitate prevailing cultural agendas. But such talk of constituting reality is barely intelligible. If science constitutes reality, then how are we to explain the fact that scientific theories are constantly confronted by contrary data and anomalies? That is, where did they come from, if the scientific theory constitutes reality?

In any case, social constructivism seems to totter on the brink of self-refutation. It claims to have *discovered* that all theories are culturally relative, but that discovery itself is a theory, one that appears to request transcultural assent. But why should we grant such immunity to social constructivism? That sounds really arbitrary!

I have spent so much time sparring with contemporary academic skepticism about science for two reasons: first, because in the current context of debate, any proposal, like mine, that a framework for aesthetic theorizing might profit from thinking about scientific theorizing is apt to elicit an intemperate rejoinder on the basis of one or more of the considerations I have just attempted to undercut; and second, because it is frequently alleged that cognitivism, a stance often defended in this volume, is an attempt to turn film theory into science, and, therefore, cognitivism can be "refuted" handily by the preceding skeptical arguments about the integrity of science. But I contend that these arguments refute nothing, except possibly social constructivism itself.

Many of these arguments begin, as I do, with an acknowledgment of the insights of postpositivist philosophy of science. However, where many humanists and film scholars often take those insights to imply the arbitrariness of science, I try to exploit them in favor of a view of science as a dialectical, incremental process for securing approximate truths through practices of, among other things, error elimination and criticism. Furthermore, this very broad conception of inquiry may be fruitful to our thinking about film theory. In order to test its usefulness and to descend from the preceding perhaps unduly rarefied stratosphere of abstraction, I shall apply this conception of the dialectical framework for film theory to a contemporary question, namely, the issue of cognitivism.

COGNITIVISM VERSUS PSYCHOANALYSIS

Psychoanalysis, conjoined with Marxism and later blended with various other radical, political perspectives, has dominated film theorizing for two decades. In the eighties, an approach to film theorizing, labeled cognitivism, began to take shape as an alternative to psychoanalysis. Cognitivism is not a unified theory. Its name derives from its tendency to look for alternative answers to many of the questions addressed by or raised by psychoanalytic film theories, especially with respect to film reception, in terms of cognitive and rational processes rather than irrational or unconscious ones. This might involve explicit reference to cognitive and perceptual psychology or to Anglo-American–style linguistics rather than to psychoanalysis. Or the hypotheses might be more homemade.

Some so-called cognitivists may offer armchair speculations about audience reasoning, practical and otherwise, while others advert to established theories of cognitive processing or even experimentation. Some cognitivists try out conjectures employing suppositions about natural selection where others fear to tread.

Cognitivism is not a unified theory, not only because the theoretical domains cognitivists explore differ, but because cognitivist film theorists, like cognitive psychologists, may disagree about which proposals—of the competing cognitivist proposals—best suit the data. So, once cognitivists stop arguing with psychoanalysts, they will have to argue with each other. And this is why it is a mistake to imagine that cognitivism is a single, unified theory. It is a stance.

However, it is a stance that has increasingly come to define itself as an alternative to psychoanalysis in film studies. It advances its hypotheses, as diverse and as discordant as they may be, by claiming to characterize or to explain phenomena better than extant psychoanalytic theories. Cognitivists have increasingly come to conceptualize their project dialectically. Cognitivists take their task to be a matter of answering certain questions about film, especially about film reception and comprehension, most of which questions have already been asked or at least acknowledged by psychoanalytic film theorists. But cognitivists claim that they do a better job answering those questions than psychoanalytic film theorists have.

Some film scholars have responded to cognitivism with high dudgeon. I have already suggested a number of their reactions. However, as befits the pluralistic zeitgeist, others are insouciant. "What's the big deal?" they want to know. You can have cognitivism, if you want it; the others can have psychoanalysis. The more the merrier. Why not have them all? It's good to have lots of theories.

And, of course, anyone who believes that the dialectical conception of film theory is the most productive one should readily concur, because, it would appear, the more theories that are in play, the more opportunity there is for heightened theoretical refinement. Doesn't theoretical pluralism seem like it should go hand in glove with a dialectical conception of film theory?

Here it pays to distinguish between two versions of theoretical pluralism, one which suits the dialectical conception of film theory, and the other, which doesn't. One kind of theoretical pluralism might be called peaceful coexistence pluralism. Coexistence pluralism is very laid back. Everyone has his own theory; if you want to conjoin theories, well, that's a matter of personal taste. You can accept some cognitivist hypotheses, but if you also like some aspects of psychoanalysis (at this point, it is usually said, "I find it useful"), you can have that too.

On the other hand, there is also methodologically robust pluralism. On this view, it is good to have lots of theories around as well. But it is good to have these theories around so that they can be put in competition with each other.

From the point of view of the robust methodological pluralist, it is good to have a number of theories in the field at the beginning of the day, but by the end of the day, one hopes that some will be eliminated through processes of criticism and comparison in light of certain questions and the relevant evidence. Some ostensibly competing theories may, upon examination and debate, turn out to be complementary or supplementary. But many are also likely to fall by the wayside.

Obviously, from my manner of describing these alternative pluralisms, I believe that the type of pluralism that is presupposed by a dialectical conception of film theory is robust methodological pluralism. It presumes that lots of theories are a methodologically good thing just because they provide grist for robust criticism. Undoubtedly, some readers will chide my competitive metaphors for being too agonistic or macho. But, on the one hand, we are talking about eliminating theories, not people; and, on the other hand, feminist theories are standardly advanced on the grounds that they provide better explanations than their patriarchal competitors. It is hard to resist the intuition that theory selection involves some competition.

Perhaps the coexistence pluralist will demand to know why we need to eliminate any theories at all. But the answer is simple: some theories are provisionally superior than others and they exclude a number of alternative theories. This is not to say that the alternatives cannot, so to speak, make a comeback. But that presupposes a forum where debate, rather than coexistence, is the norm. Theories compel assent, at least provisionally, by demonstrating that they provide certain explanatory advantages and solutions to certain anomalies lacking in their opposing number.

This view of theory should not surprise psychoanalytic film theorists. For they should recall the way in which Freud argues for his own theory of dreams. Prior to Freud, dream research regarded dreams as purely somatic phenomena, the reaction of a mental organ veritably sunk in the state of sleep in response to environmental stimuli which partially activate it. By examining the content of certain dreams, Freud showed that this theory was not comprehensive—it did not cover a great many facts presented by the data—and that it was unable to provide any functional-biological account of why we dream. (N.B.: Psychoanalytic critics who chastise cognitivists for dabbling in biological hypotheses should remember that Freud was not averse to speaking about biological functions.)

Freud's own theory not only supplied the wherewithal to account for the anomalies ignored by previous dream research but was also able to identify a candidate for the function of dream, namely, that it was the guardian of sleep. It has been the burden of subsequent researchers to see how well Freud's theory squares with the data and to develop alternative hypotheses to accommodate the anomalies in the data that erupt from the collision between the evidence and Freud's famous generalizations, such as the hypothesis of wish fulfillment.

Staging the debate between psychoanalytic film theory is too elaborate a task even for a longish essay like this. One reason for this is that, since cognitivism often proposes piecemeal theories, a thorough confrontation would require facing off each cognitivist theory—of narrative comprehension, of cinematic perception, of the horror film, of melodrama, of film music, and so on—with its psychoanalytic counterparts, where there are counterparts. Nevertheless, it is still possible to offer some overarching comments about the rivalry between cognitivism and psychoanalysis in what remains of this chapter.

I have urged that we think of theories in terms of dialectical competition. However, due to certain conceptual features of psychoanalysis, the debate between cognitivism and psychoanalysis is peculiar in a way that said competition redounds to the advantage of cognitivism. What is special about psychoanalysis and what makes the debate between cognitivism and psychoanalysis somewhat different from most other theoretical debates is the fact that psychoanalysis is a theory whose object is the irrational. Or, to put the matter differently, the realm of psychoanalysis is the irrational, which domain has as its criterion of identification that it be phenomena that cannot be adequately accounted for in terms of rational, cognitive, or organic explanations. It is analytical to the very conception of psychoanalytic explanation that its appropriate field of activity is defined by what is not rationally, cognitively, or organically explicable.

Psychoanalysis, in other words, kicks in where there is an apparent breakdown in the normal functioning of our cognitive-perceptual processing, our capacities for rational calculation and decision making, our conative and emotional behavior, our motor capabilities, and so on, which breakdowns cannot be explained either organically or in virtue of the structural features of the processes in question.

If I cannot walk because I have lost my legs in a car accident, there is no call for psychoanalysis. But if I am biologically sound, and no rational motive can be supplied for my inaction, psychoanalysis is appropriate. If I am angry when I am mugged, ceteris paribus, that is a rational response, where psychoanalysis is out of place. But if I consistently explode whenever a teacher asks me a question, we think about psychoanalysis. Similarly, errors in adding long strings of large numbers can be readily explained by the way in which such input might overload the processing system. But if I consistently answer "three" to the question "how much is two plus two," then a visit to a therapist may be in order. In short, there is a conceptual constraint on psychoanalysis; it is restricted to dealing with phenomena that cannot be explained by other means.

Moreover, this has interesting consequences for the debate between cognitivist and psychoanalytic film theories. Namely, wherever a plausible cognitivist theory can be secured, the burden of proof is shifted to the psychoanalytic theorist. For a plausible cognitivist theory precludes the necessity for psychoanalysis. The mere plausibility of a cognitivist theory gives it a special advantage over psychoanalytic theories of the same phenomenon.

It is not generally the case that the mere plausibility of one scientific theory excludes a respectable, competing theory from the field. But insofar as psychoanalysis is defined as just what explains what otherwise has no *plausible* rational explanation, psychoanalytic explanation starts with a disadvantage where plausible cognitivist theories are available.

Contemporary film theorists, like Judith Mayne in her recent book *Cinema and Spectatorship,* tag cognitivist theorists with the complaint that they simply bracket the psychoanalytic approach, as if willfully. What such criticism fails to comprehend is that where we have a convincing cognitivist account, there is no point whatsoever in looking any further for a psychoanalytic account. It is not the case that psychoanalysis is being unfairly or inexplicably bracketed. It is being *retired,* unless and until good reasons can be advanced to suppose otherwise.

Psychoanalytic theories face a special burden of proof when confronting cognitivist theories. For a psychoanalytic theory to reenter the debate, it must be demonstrated that there is something about the data of which given cognitivist (or organic) explanations can give no adequate account, and which, as well, cannot be explained by some other cognitive theory, which remainder is susceptible to psychoanalytic theory *alone.* I have no argument to prove conclusively that no psychoanalytic theory will ever be able to cross this hurdle. But, at the same time, I think it is also fair to say that psychoanalytic film theorists behave as though they are unaware of this obstacle and, in any event, they have failed to meet it *even once* in their skirmishes with cognitivists.

Because of this special burden of proof, the possibility of pluralistic coexistence between cognitivism and psychoanalysis is never a foregone conclusion. Confronted by cognitivist hypotheses about the perception of the cinematic image, the psychoanalytic critic must show that there is something about the phenomena that is alien to cognitivist theorizing. That is why it is not enough for psychoanalytic theorists, like Richard Wollheim and Richard Allen, to merely tell a coherent, psychoanalytic story about pictorial perception; they must also establish that there is something about the data that cognitivists are unable to countenance before they, like psychoanalysts, postulate the operation of *unconscious* psychic mechanisms like projection. For if their cognitivist competitors can frame a coherent, comprehensive account of the data without resorting to unconscious mechanisms, postulating unconscious ones is a nonstarter.

Dialectical arguments are primarily matters of shifting the burden of proof between rival theories that are grappling with roughly the same questions. Quite frequently (most frequently?) it is difficult to find a completely decisive refutation of rival theories. That is one reason why we must fall back on the laborious processes of removing the burden of proof from ourselves and redistributing it amongst our competitors. The preceding argument has not shown that psychoanalytic theories of film will never be admissible. At best, what it may show is that the burden of proof is now with the psychoanalysts. Perhaps they will rise to the occasion.

However, if I am correct in maintaining that psychoanalytic film theorists have not yet even recognized that they have this burden of proof, then that indicates that, at present, the ball belongs to the cognitivists. Psychoanalytic film theory may succeed in countering this argument dialectically, but unless it does, the continued elaboration of the psychoanalytic paradigm, conducted in isolation from cognitivist challenges, represents an evasion of film theory, not a contribution to it.

Furthermore, there is another general problem with psychoanalytic film theory that deserves mention. Putting aside the admittedly pressing question of whether psychoanalysis as a general theory is acceptable, something disputed by many psychologists, philosophers, and psychiatrists, it is nevertheless the case that we can say that psychoanalysis is an empirical discipline. It may not be generally concerned with testing, but it typically has an empirical basis, namely, the practice of therapy. Psychoanalysts from Freud (Sigmund and Anna), to D. W. Winnicott, Melanie Klein, Karen Horney, Heinz Kohut, Erik Erikson, and Otto Kernberg base their concepts and their postulation of psychic forces with their attending regularities, as well as their criticisms of other psychoanalytic theorists, on their therapeutic observations. Without a therapeutic practice, psychoanalysts would have no grounds for introducing, adjusting, modifying, refining, and even, at times, abandoning their concepts and theories.

However, when we turn to psychoanalytic film theorists, we note immediately that most, if not all, of the leading theorists have no therapeutic practice. They modify previous psychoanalytic theories and they even introduce new concepts, concoct novel theories, and project patterns, but on what basis? One would think that such theory building should be keyed to some group of analysands—to their experiences and associations, and the analysis thereof. But psychoanalytic film theorists do not have therapeutic practices. They are confecting theories, but with no empirical constraints. How can they pretend to implement an empirically based inquiry like psychoanalysis without any data? Perhaps that question can be answered theoretically. But until it is, the rest of us, on legitimate *psychoanalytic* grounds, will want to know how contemporary psychoanalytic film theory is possible.

Concerns about empirical evidence are generally ridiculed by film theorists. For, as Judith Mayne recounts, empirical research is seen by proponents of the Theory as part and parcel of the philosophical position of empiricism. But such reservations about empirical research rest on little more than an equivocation. It is certainly the case that there are few philosophical positions as beleaguered as empiricism. However, it is equally true that there is no necessary connection between the philosophical doctrine of empiric*ism* and an empiri*cal* research program.

Obviously, gestalt psychologists advanced their theory on the basis of empirical evidence. But their theory of perception was forged in the teeth of an empiricist philosophy of perception. And one can certainly construct macroeconomic theories without any commitment to an empiricist theory of the mind and its related epistemological doctrine of phenomenalism. Chomsky relies on empirical data—elicited linguistic intuitions—but his arguments in favor of innateness are stridently unLockean. And so on. It is just a howler to respond to requests for empirical evidence on the grounds that since the philosophy of empiricism has been discredited, evidence is tacky or out of style. For even *if* empiricism were down for the count, empirical research would still be independently creditable.

I have just outlined two of the many challenges that cognitivism has evolved for psychoanalytic film theory. Inasmuch as film theory is a dialectical procedure, it now falls to psychoanalytic film theorists to show how they can negotiate the special burden of proof with which cognitivists confront them and to account for how psychoanalytic film theory is possible in the absence of the sort of empirical base that psychoanalytic theory, outside the environs of film and literature departments, requires. So far, psychoanalytic film theorists have evaded these charges. If they continue to evade them, then the prospects for intellectually exciting theorizing in film studies, as it is presently constituted, are meager.

CONCLUDING REMARKS

Throughout this chapter, and elsewhere, my criticisms of the prevailing Theory have been stern. I predict that this approach will be rebuked, especially by peaceful coexistence pluralists. They will want to know how I can hope to sway proponents of the Theory if my tone is so relentless.

But, I must admit that I have little or no expectation about changing the hearts and minds of advocates of the Theory. There are sound sociological reasons for believing that scholars who are already deeply invested in a paradigm are unlikely to surrender it. Careers, tenures, promotions, publications, and reputations have been and continue to be built by espousing the Theory. There is too much social investment already at stake in propounding the Theory to anticipate that many of its adherents will be moved, in a disinterested spirit, by rational argumentation. The Theory has too much institutional weight behind it to permit conversion. And, in any case, most academics remain locked in the paradigm they learned in graduate school. It is too late for most of them to change their spots.

So I do not write for defenders of the Theory. I have no illusions about the possibility of converting them; thus I make no concessions in portraying how dreadful their Theory is. There is no point in pulling one's punches. If anything, that might worsen the situation by implying that things in film studies are not as bad as they are.

But if I am not writing the Theorists, who is my intended audience? The uncommitted: those in film studies and those (historians, sociologists, psychologists, philosophers, and so on) in related disciplines that study film who are interested in evolving frameworks for comprehending cinema but who are doctrinally unaligned. Let them decide between the claims of psychoanalysis and the claims of cognitivism. Let them weigh the different voices in the discussion. It is for this audience that I and other cognitivists have staged the debate.

Perhaps the most important sector of this uncommitted audience is made up of dedicated film students, both advanced undergraduates and graduate students. Neither their minds nor their careers are at present so set in stone that they are unable to respond to the claims of alternative voices. And, anyway, they are the ones who will inevitably reconstruct film studies or whatever, in the wake of technological innovation, the field becomes.

Of course, it may be that my pessimism about the adherents of the Theory is too extreme. Maybe some of them, along with the unaligned, will take a serious interest in the debate that cognitivists have initiated. But, in that case, the rigor with which I have propounded my arguments will serve their purposes, insofar as it will supply them with strong, clear objections to attempt to refute. For it will be more convenient for them to confront robust positions than it would be for them to confront ones that are politely hedged or that are overly qualified and conciliatory.

The prospects for film theory hinge on critical debate. In the best of circumstances, the participants of that discussion will include cognitivists, psychoanalysts, and unaligned scholars. In my view, over the last two decades, film studies has squandered what may turn out to have been a once-in-a-lifetime opportunity by effectively stifling debate between Theory and alternative paradigms. Whether film theory has a genuine future depends on its becoming truly dialectical.

APPENDIX

Since the publication of "Prospects for Film Theory: A Personal Assessment," this article has been subjected to criticism. In this brief appendix, I will try to address some of the objections.

One recurring criticism is that I misconstrue film theory as a form of natural science.[1] But, although I do believe that natural science is relevant to certain questions that are traditionally addressed in film theory, such as the physiology of the perception of movement, I do not imagine that we are in a position now to reduce film theory to natural science. Moreover, I grant that many questions of film theory are not the sort to be treated as one does natural processes. But I do maintain that film theory is a form of rational inquiry and that, as such, it is useful for film theorists to take advantage of the insights of contemporary philosophy of science, since the philosophy of science provides us with some of the most fully developed, positive accounts concerning the conduct of rational inquiry that we have. I am not advocating that film theorists adopt the procedures of natural scientists across the board nor that they imitate them slavishly. Film theorists need to be alert to the special features of their own field of inquiry. And yet, we may still derive useful hints about the process of rational inquiry by attending to sophisticated discussions of science.

One aspect of scientific inquiry, called to our attention by Kuhn and others, is that scientific inquiry is dialectical. That is, theories are framed in specific historical contexts of research for the purpose of answering certain questions, and the relative strengths of the relevant theories are assessed by comparing the answers a given theory affords to the answers advanced by alternative theories. Such a position is postpositivist or antipositivist because it regards theory evaluation as a matter of the critical comparison of actual, existing answers to the questions at hand, rather than, in a positivistic spirit, regarding theory evaluation as the comparison of a given theoretical answer to every logically conceivable, rival answer. The dialectical conception of science is historical, as opposed to the positivist conception. And it is this sort of essentially dialectical approach that I, taking the hint from philosophers of science, am recommending to film theorists.

This does not entail a reduction of film theory to natural science. I merely propose that film theorists, like natural scientists, proceed dialectically by critically comparing competing answers (competing theories) regarding the historically presiding and emerging questions of their field of inquiry.

Nor is this a revisionist perspective on film theory. If one were to scan the history of film theory, one will find that the dialectical element is generally present in one way or another in most film theories. Film theorists, like Bazin, have always been involved in debates in which they advance the superiority of their findings over competing views. That is to be expected, since dialectical criticism has been a basic route for theoretical inquiry at least since Plato and Aristotle.[2] Defending one's own theory by demonstrating that it succeeds where alternative theories falter is a natural direction of argument. Even proponents of contemporary film theory begin by criticizing alternative approaches as a primary means for advancing their own hypotheses over others. Thus, in maintaining that the fundamental framework for film theory be dialectical, I am not saying anything very controversial, and certainly not that film theory become natural science.

On the dialectical conception of theorizing, the rivalry between theories is primarily a matter of shifting the burden of proof from one's own theory to those of one's competitors. Of course, since there is always the logical possibility that one's competitors may find a way in which to shift the burden of proof back to you, theories produced under the dialectical conception are generally acknowledged to be provisional, or, as I prefer to say, fallible. That is, the dialectical method is an historically continuing process; a burden of proof can always, in principle, be returned with interest.

At present, there is a debate among film theorists between what has been called cognitivism and psychoanalysis. Cognitivists and psychoanalytic film theorists

have fielded a number of hypotheses in order to explain a wide gamut of cinematic phenomena, including, at least, narrative comprehension, point-of-view
editing, the operation of ideology (including sexism) in film, the perception of
the single shot, and so on. This debate will proceed as proponents of each side
compare these hypotheses one by one, assaying their relative strengths and
weaknesses. However, I maintain that there is also a systematic feature of the
debate between cognitivism and psychoanalysis that places psychoanalytic film
theorists in a difficult position in terms of the issue of the burden of proof.

For psychoanalysis and cognitivism are not just any old competing theories.
Due to certain conceptual features of psychoanalysis, namely that cognitivism
turns out to be a defeasibility condition for psychoanalysis, the dialectical encounter between cognitivism and psychoanalysis puts special constraints on
the way in which psychoanalytic theorists must negotiate the burdens of proof
that cognitivists manage to shift to them. That is, psychoanalysis has a special
relation to cognitive explanations—specifically that psychoanalytic explanations are otiose wherever plausible cognitive explanations are available—and
this entails that the psychoanalytic film theorist confronts a special burden of
proof when debating cognitivists. This an an obscure point; let me clarify it.

The object of psychoanalysis is the irrational. Moreover, this domain has as
its criterion of identification that it is concerned with phenomena that cannot
be accommodated—that cannot be explained—in terms of rational, cognitive,
or somatic processes. It is analytical to the concept of psychoanalytic explanation that its appropriate field of activity is defined—conceptually—by what is
not rationally, cognitively, or organically explicable. Psychoanalysis, in other
words, kicks in where there is an apparent breakdown in the normal functioning of our cognitive-perceptual capacities for rational calculation and decision
making, or in our conative and emotional behaviors such that these breakdowns
cannot be explained either organically or in virtue of structural and/or functional features of our cognitive, perceptual, conative, or somatic apparatuses.

If I cannot speak because I have lost my vocal cords, there is no call for psychoanalysis to explain my silence. But if I am biologically sound and no rational explanation can be supplied for my speechlessness, psychoanalysis may be
appropriate. If I am angered by racism or by the treatment of gays in the military, those are rational responses and do not warrant psychoanalysis. But if I
explode very time I see a red car, you might suggest that I think about a shrink.
Likewise, the fact that I cannot correctly compute large strings of numbers
rapidly—for example, that I cannot find the sum of the serial numbers on the
cars of a passing train—does not show that I should be psychoanalyzed, since

my incapacity can be explained in terms of the limits of normal cognitive processing. On the other hand, if I consistently answer the question "how much is two plus two?" with the number 3, while exhibiting no other innumeracy, then we might contemplate psychoanalysis. In short, there is a conceptual constraint on psychoanalysis. It is restricted, by its very nature, to dealing with phenomena that cannot be explained by other means—notably by reference to the rationality of the agent, or by reference to the structure and limits of our cognitive architecture, or somatically.

This constraint is not something that I have made up. Practicing psychoanalysts respect it. There are many phenomena that they refer to other kinds of clinicians. Some examples include facial tics, somnambulism, and extreme cases of the Tourette syndrome, among others. These are cases where there is reason to believe that the afflictions arise somatically and should be treated medically. But there are also cortical functioning disorders, like dyslexia, where the patient will be referred to a psychologist rather than to a psychoanalyst. Psychoanalysts refer these cases to other specialists because they realize that the cases do not fall into their bailiwick which is defined as that which cannot be explained by rational, cognitive, or organic means.[3] Where such explanations are available, other specialists are apposite.

Moreover, the preceding has interesting consequences for the debate between cognitivist and psychoanalytic film theorists—namely, that whenever a plausible cognitive theory of some phenomenon can be secured, the burden of proof is automatically shifted to the psychoanalytic theorist. For a plausible cognitivist theory methodologically precludes the necessity of psychoanalysis. The mere plausibility of a cognitive theory gives it special logical authority over psychoanalytic theories of the same phenomenon. It defeats competing psychoanalytic theories unless and until the psychoanalytic theorist shows that there is something about the phenomenon that cannot be explained rationally, cognitively, or somatically, and that justifies the use of the special explanatory apparatus of psychoanalysis (which apparatus is designed expressly to handle the irrational).

Psychoanalytic theories then face a special burden of proof when confronting cognitivist theories. For a psychoanalytic theory to re-enter the debate after a plausible cognitive theory has been fielded and defended, it must be demonstrated that there is something about the data of which cognitive (or somatic) explanations can give no adequate account, and which, as well, cannot be explained by some other cognitive theory, which remainder is susceptible to psychoanalytic theory *alone*. I have no brief to prove conclusively that no psychoanalytic theory will ever be able to cross this hurdle. But, at the same time, I believe that it is fair to say that psychoanalytic film theorists behave as though they are unaware of this methodological desideratum, and, in any event, they have not engaged this issue in their exchanges with cognitivists so far.

At present, with respect to film theory, the cognitivists, such as myself, have served up a volley; now it is up to the psychoanalytic film theorists to attempt to return it, constrained by the special burden of proof that I have been discussing. Because psychoanalysis is the science of the irrational, the defense of a psychoanalytic theory involves demonstrating not only that it does a better job with the data than competitors, but that there is no plausible, existing cognitive or biological theory that can manage the data. That is, a special burden of proof besets the psychoanalytic theorist. To meet it, she must remove the pertinent cognitive theories from the running.

The structure of the debate which I have been adumbrating is in evidence in some of the most interesting disagreements between psychoanalytic theorists and others. For example, in *The Freudian Slip,* the marxist philologist Sebastiano Timpanaro argues that there is no need for Freud to deploy psychoanalysis in his analysis of the *aliquis* parapraxis, since it can be explained perfectly in terms of what philologists, who know a great deal about errors in recalling classical texts, dub "the tendency to banalize a highly irregular syntactic structure."[4] That is, the error can be explained thoroughly in virtue of the way in which the cognitive system is known to be apt to malfunction in cases of highly irregular syntactic structures.

Likewise, Timpanaro explains the inversion of *ex nostris ossibus* (instead of *nostris ex ossibus*) by Freud's interlocutor in terms of the young man's Austrian training in reciting Latin hexameters, according to which he attended to rhythmic stresses, rather than to the grammatical accents on individual words. Thus, the inversion can be explained and historically motivated in light of the young man's attempt to conform with a historically situated, cognitively established norm. Timpanaro's cognitivist hypotheses make Freud's exegesis—however delightful as literature—beside the point from a theoretical perspective. Similarly, cognitivist hypotheses in film theory have rendered many competing psychoanalytic theories extraneous.

Upon hearing my argument that cognitivist explanations preclude psychoanalytic ones, several proponents of psychoanalysis have responded that I've overlooked the possibility that the phenomena in question are overdetermined; they may have more than one cause, and while one may be cognitive, the other may originate in psychopathology.

Certainly events can be overdetermined. For example, if Mary injects me with enough poison so that I will die at 7:45 pm and at exactly 7:45 pm Michael shoots me, then my death is overdetermined. It had two causes, each of which was sufficient to kill me at 7:45 pm. If at 7:45, Michael missed his shot, the poison would have done me in; if at 7:45 pm I was given an antidote to the poison, the bullet would have killed me. Two separate lines of causation determined or guaranteed my death at 7:45 pm. When an event would have been brought about by either of two or more events—all of which obtained—the event is overdetermined.

But is this idea of overdetermination relevant to the debate between cognitive and psychoanalytic film theorists? I don't think so. For example, the cognitive film theorist says that pictorial recognition is the result of certain hardwired perceptual capacities. The psychoanalytic film theorists says that it is due to regression to the mirror stage. Why not say that the phenomenon is due to both processes—that pictorial recognition is overdetermined? But that would be to claim that either process would be sufficient to bring about the pictorial recognition. That is, display a cinematic image while somehow blocking the relevant cognitive-perceptual processing and mirror stage regression alone will result in pictorial recognition (or suppress mirror stage regression, and the cognitive processes alone will get the job done). That is what would be required for the situation to be overdetermined. However, even supposing that there is such a process as mirror stage identification, isn't it absurd to think that pictorial recognition will occur if we somehow suspend the operation of the cognitive-perceptual system? Mirror stage identification, even if it exists, sans cognitive-perceptual processing, will never result in pictorial recognition. On the other hand, there is no problem conjecturing that cognitive-perceptual processes on their own will yield pictorial recognition. But if these conjectures are correct, then we don't really have a case of genuine overdetermination here.

This is not a case of overdetermination because only one of the processes on its own could conceivably bring about pictorial recognition. Mirror stage regression is not a cause on a par with cognitive-perceptual processing. Mirror stage regression, if there is such a thing, could not conceivably bring off pictorial recognition by itself and so it does not co-determine this effect. At best, it is an explanatory embellishment tacked on to the real engine of change in this case—the cognitive-perceptual processing. Mirror stage regression does no explanatory work and, for that reason, it is dispensable.

Moreover, I would add that a similar pattern of argument can be applied to the rest of the current debates between cognitivists and psychoanalysts. There is no question of overdetermination. Cognitive explanations of the relevant phenomena are perfectly adequate. And where the cognitive explanations suffice, there is no reason to resort to psychoanalysis.

In concluding, let me briefly mention another objection that has been voiced against my discussion of the debate between psychoanalysis and cognitivism in film theory. I began with a nod toward Kuhn and his philosophy of science. But some commentators have remarked in conversation that I am not really true to Kuhn. For Kuhn says that competing scientific paradigms are incommensurable. Thus, the question arises about how dialectical competition between theories in general, and between cognitivist and psychoanalytic film theories in particular is possible. That is, the framework I've recommended calls for theory comparison, but isn't theory comparison impossible if the theories in question are incommensurable? In short, psychoanalysis and cognitivism cannot be compared, if we are following Kuhn's account.

The answer to this objection is straightforward. I do not accept Kuhn's account in its entirety. Specifically, I reject strong claims of incommensurability. Kuhn's own theory of scientific revolution requires that there be competing paradigms. On Kuhn's own account, these paradigms joust over the solution of certain anomalies *shared by all the rival theories in question*. So if we accept what Kuhn says about scientific revolutions, there is commensurability between competing theories, at least in terms of the relevant anomalies. Kuhn's position is inconsistent otherwise. Thus, Kuhn must abandon either his strong claims about incommensurability or his historical theory of scientific revolutions. I believe that it is fairly obvious that the strong incommensurability claims should be abandoned. And, in any case, to return the discussion to film theory, I think that it is clear that cognitivism and psychoanalysis are not utterly incommensurable. For example, everyone in film theory agrees on the meaning of the term "point of view shot"; indeed, Daniel Dayan and I will exhibit an amazingly high degree of convergence in picking them out.

NOTES

1. See Bryan Vescio, "Reading in the Dark: Cognitivism, Film Theory, and Radical Interpretation," *Style,* vol. 35, no. 4 (Winter 2001), pp. 572–89; and Malcolm Turvey, "Can Science Help Film Theory?" in the online *Cinema Journal* (*www.uca.edu/orgccsmi/journal*). A similar charge was leveled at my earlier work in Karen Hanson, "Provocations and Justifications of Film," in *Philosophy and Film,* edited by Cynthia Freeland and Thomas Wartenberg (New York: Routledge, 1995), pp. 33–48.

2. Slavoj Zizek maintains that my position is not truly dialectical because it is not Hegelian. But an unbiased examination of the history of philosophy will show, I believe, that Hegel

has no patent on dialectics. Zizek also contends that cognitivists like me do not acknowledge our "very position of enunciation." Specifically, we are guilty of false mod-
esty, claiming that our theories are provisional and of limited scope while immodestly ex-
empting ourselves as objects of scrutiny. I find this charge difficult to square with the
lengths to which I have gone in order to clarify my methodological presuppositions. Indeed, someone might accuse me of too much self-scrutiny. For Zizek's criticisms, see:
Slavoj Zizek, *The Fright of Real Tears: Krzsztof Kieslowski between Theory and Post-Theory*
(London: BFI Publishing, 2001), pp. 14–16.

3. By the way, it is not an objection to this point that psychoanalysts sometimes ignore
these considerations. Such transgressions do not show that psychoanalysis is not committed to these limitations, but only that sometimes psychoanalysts over-reach themselves. I would regard some of Freud's psychoanalyzing of otherwise rationally explicable
cultural phenomena as examples of this over-reaching tendency.

4. Sebastiano Timpanaro, *The Freudian Slip: Psychoanalysis and Textual Criticism* (Atlantic
Highlands, N.J.: Humanities Press, 1976), p. 39.

Credits

The original places and dates of publication of the articles in this volume are as follows: "Forget the Medium," in *Screen-Based Art,* ed. Annette Balkema and Henk Slager (Amsterdam: Lieren Boog, 2000), pp. 55–62; "Film, Attention, and Communication: A Naturalistic Account," in *Great Ideas Today: 1996* (Chicago: Encyclopedia Britannica, 1996), pp. 2–49; "Film, Emotion, and Genre," *Passionate Views,* ed. Carl Plantinga and Gregg Smith (Baltimore: Johns Hopkins University Press, 1999), pp. 21–47; "Ethnicity, Race, and Monstrosity: The Rhetorics of Horror and Humor," *Beauty Matters,* ed. Peg Brand (Bloomington: Indiana University Press, 2000), pp. 37–56; "Is the Medium a (Moral) Message?" *Media Ethics,* ed. Matthew Kieran (London: Routledge, 1998), pp. 135–51; "Film Form: An Argument for a Functional Theory of Style in the Individual Film," *Style* vol. 32, no. 3 (Fall 1998), pp. 385–401; "Introducing Film Evaluation," *Reinventing Film Studies,* ed. Linda Williams and Christine Gledhill (London: Edward Arnold, 2000), pp. 265–78; "Nonfiction Film and Postmodernist Skepticism," *Post-Theory: Reconstructing Film Studies,* ed. David Bordwell and Noël Carroll (Madison: University of Wisconsin Press, 1996), pp. 283–306; "Fiction, Non-fiction, and the Film of Presumptive Assertion: A Conceptual Analysis," *Film Theory and Philosophy,* ed. Richard Allen and Murray Smith (Oxford: Oxford University Press, 1997), pp. 173–202; "Photographic Traces and Documentary Films," *Journal of Aesthetics and Art Criticism* vol. 58, no. 3 (Summer 2000), pp. 303–6; "Toward a Definition of Moving-Picture Dance," *Dance Research Journal* vol. 33, no. 1 (Summer 2001), pp. 46–61; "The Essence of Cinema?" *Philosophical Studies* no. 89 (1998), pp. 323–30; "TV and Film: A Philosophical Perspective," *Journal of Aesthetic Education* vol. 35, no. 1 (Summer 2001), pp. 15–29; "Kracauer's *Theory of Film,*" *Defining Cinema,* ed. Peter Lehman (New Brunswick: Rutgers University Press, 1997), pp. 111–31; co-authored with Sally Banes, "Cinematic Nation-Building: Eisenstein's *The Old and the New,*" *Cinema and Nation,* ed. Mette Hjort and Scott MacKenzie (London: Routledge, 2000), pp. 121–38; "The Professional Western: South of the Border," *Back in the Saddle Again: Essays on the Western,* ed. Edward Buscombe and Roberta Pearson (London: British Film Institute, 1998), pp. 46–62; "Moving and Moving: From Minimalism to *Lives of Performers,*" *Millennium Film Journal* no. 35/36 (Fall 2000), pp. 81–88; "Prospects for Film Theory: A Personal Assessment," *Post-Theory: Reconstructing Film Studies,* ed. David Bordwell and Noël Carroll (Madison: University of Wisconsin Press, 1996), pp. 37–68.

Index

Absolute Truth, film theory and, 376–85

abstract film and images, 24–25, 257–58, 261–63, 264n.11

action films, 12–13, 32, 55n.2

actualité film, 181; photographic traces in, 231; presumptive trace films and, 210–12; terminology concerning, 194

adolescents, attention spans in, 31

"Adolf the Superman," 294

Adorno, T. W., 33–34, 297, 300n.3

advertisements (television), stylization of, 273–74

aesthetic judgment, and film theory, 150, 163n.1, 297–300

Affair to Remember, An, 74–77, 81

affect, film and, 59–61

affinities of photography, 294–96

African Americans. *See also* race: functional account of film and, 144–45; stereotyping of, in horror and humor, 96–103, 105n.28, 106n.29

Alexander, Robert, 247

Alexandrov, Grigori, 306, 319n.15

Alfred Hitchcock Presents, 275

alienation, Kracauer's discussion of, 297–300, 302n.34

Alien Autopsy, 196

Alien Nation, 277

"A Likely Story," 354n.8

Allen, Richard, 223n.24, 390

All That Heaven Allows, 197

Ally McBeal, 273

Alpha web site, 100

Althusser, Louis, 357, 361

alto flute, as art medium, 8

Amazing Stories, 272–73, 280n.3

Amberg, George, 2

America Is Waiting, 229

American Chronicles, 273

American culture, internationalization of, 12–13, 55n.2

Amos and Andy, 115

Anderson, Benedict, 303

Andrew, Dudley, 300n.4

And the Band Played On, 277

And Then There Were None, x

403